W9-AMR-713

▶ Second Edition

Career Counseling

Process, Issues, and Techniques

Norman C. Gysbers
University of Missouri

Mary J. Heppner
University of Missouri

Joseph A. Johnston
University of Missouri

Boston • New York • San Francisco
Mexico City • Montreal • Toronto • London • Madrid • Munich • Paris
Hong Kong • Singapore • Tokyo • Cape Town • Sydney

Editor-in-Chief: Paul Smith
Executive Editor: Virginia Lanigan
Editorial Assistant: Robert Champagne
Marketing Manager: Taryn Wahlquist
Production Editor: Christine Tridente
Editorial Production Service: Chestnut Hill Enterprises, Inc.
Manufacturing Buyer: Chris Marson
Cover Administrator: Kristina Mose-Libon

For related titles and support materials, visit our online catalog at
www.ablongman.com

Between the time Website information is gathered and published, some sites may
have closed. Also, the transcription of URLs can result in typographical errors. The
publisher would appreciate notification where these occur so that they may be
corrected in subsequent editions.

Library of Congress Cataloging-in-Publication Data

Gysbers, Norman C.
    Career counseling : process, issues, and techniques / Norman C. Gysbers, Mary J.
Heppner, Joseph A. Johnston.-- 2nd ed.
        p. cm.
    Includes bibliographical references and index.
    ISBN 0-205-34055-5 (alk. paper)
        1. Vocational guidance--Study and teaching. I. Heppner, Mary J. II. Johnston, Joseph
A. III. Title
    HF5381 .G95 2002
    158.7--dc21
                                                                2002066544

Printed in the United States of America

10 9 8 7 6 5 4 3 2 1   06 05 04 03 02

*To all our graduate
students and colleagues
worldwide who have
suppported and
encouraged the
development and writing
of this book*

Contents

Preface

Vast and far-reaching changes are taking place in the nature and structure of the social and economic systems in which people live and the industrial and occupational structures in which they work. The values and beliefs individuals hold about themselves, about others, and about the world are changing. More and more people are seeking meaning and coherence in their lives. Our society also is becoming multiracial, multilingual, and multicultural. Women are entering the labor force in record numbers and men are questioning traditionally held beliefs about their roles.

Far from being a standard or rote procedure, career counseling now, more than at any other time in our history, must be a dynamic, creative, and highly individualized process. Because of this, you may wish to update your knowledge about the ever changing contexts and conditions in which people will live and work in the twenty-first century. You may wish to revisit and revitalize how you conceptualize and structure the career counseling you do with clients. You may be looking for specific interventions to help you gather information about clients, understand that information, and interpret it so that interventions can be chosen to assist your clients to reach their goals or resolve their concerns.

PURPOSE OF THE BOOK

The purpose of this book is to help you expand and extend your vision of career counseling and the skills and techniques in your career counseling repertoire. Specifically, this book is designed to assist you to update and add to the skills and techniques that will help you to understand and interpret information gathered and behavior observed during career counseling. It is designed to help you understand and interpret information and behavior in terms of themes, or the ideas, beliefs, attitudes, and values clients hold about themselves, others, and the world in which they live. It will enable you to assist clients of all ages and circumstances to relate such information and behavior in their quest to achieve their career goals or resolve their career problems.

This book is our attempt to incorporate the strongest parts of our traditional knowledge base in career counseling with the ever changing demands of the 21st century. In addition to incorporating new challenges into solid traditional practice, there is also the need to create and synthesize new knowledge. Specifically, we believe that the *process* of career counseling has been long overlooked, as if this particular brand of counseling was devoid of process. We propose a process for career counseling and focus particular attention on how this process can be helpful in expanding options and empowering the authentic life choices of women, men, racial and ethnic minorities, nonethnic minorities such as gay, lesbian, and bisexual clients, and individuals with disabilities. Although we are keenly aware that these do not cover all forms of diversity in human life, we choose to highlight these and hope that much of what we express is transferable to the issues of other diverse groups as well.

To help you gain these specific skills, this book brings together selected concepts and techniques from counseling and career psychology. It is a book for individuals looking to enhance their theoretical knowledge and expand their practice skills through the in-depth examination of specifically selected career counseling interventions. It is a book for individuals who want to update and expand their ability to gain insights into client behavior, to develop hypotheses about such behavior, and to apply this knowledge to the selection of effective career counseling techniques.

OVERVIEW OF THE CONTENTS

Part I, "Career Counseling in the 21st Century: Evolving Contexts, Challenges, and Concepts," provides you with foundation knowledge and perspectives concerning our changing world in the 21st century. Chapter 1 focuses on the career counseling process and the phases that are involved in working with clients. It describes the career counseling process from a life career development perspective. Chapter 2 presents seven theories and approaches to understanding career development with emphasis on the use of theoretical constructs in the practice of career counseling. Chapter 3 highlights for you the implications of increasing diversity for career counseling. Chapters 4 and 5 describe women's and men's issues as they affect career counseling. Finally, Chapter 6 focuses on empowering the life choices of people with disabilities. While Chapter 7 examines the changes that have been occuring and will continue to occur in the worlds of work and family.

Part II, "Opening and Gathering Information Phases of the Career Counseling Process: Selected Techniques and Instruments," provides in-depth discussions of issues and selected techniques and instruments, all tied to the first phase of the career counseling process that was detailed in Chapter 1. Chapter 8 examines the opening phase of career counseling. Chapters 9, 10, and 11 feature qualitative techniques—a structured interview, the genogram, an occupational card sort—to gather information about clients in the gathering information phase of career counseling. Then, Chapter 12 presents an in-depth discussion of how selected standardized tests and inventories provide information about clients' interests and personality. Finally, Chapter 13 discusses career transition issues in general and then features the Career Transition Inventory as a way to work with clients who may be involved in making transitions.

Part III, "Understanding and Interpreting Client Information and Developing Hypotheses Phases of the Career Counseling Process," focuses on how we take the information gathered during the first phase of the career counseling process and use it to select interventions to assist clients to reach their goals and resolve their problems. Chapter 14 examines the concept of life career themes and how these themes assist in the development of hypotheses concerning client goals or problems. Chapter 15 deals with resistant clients, the kinds of resistance they may exhibit, and ways to respond to clients who are resistant.

Part IV, "Taking Action, Using Information, Career Planning, and Closing Phases of the Career Counseling Process," emphasizes career counseling strategies to assist clients in reading their goals or resolving their problems. Chapter 16 pays particular attention to the use of information in the career counseling process, while Chapter 17 presents the details of how clients can set goals and develop career plans based on the outcomes clients and counselors have arrived at through their work in career counseling. Chapter 18, the final chapter, examines closure in career counseling. How to bring closure to the career counseling process and the issues that are involved in closing the working alliance between client and counselor are featured.

WHO SHOULD READ THIS BOOK?

This book is designed for several groups of readers. First, practicing counselors in many different work settings who do career counseling will find this book to be an excellent in-depth update of contemporary career issues and techniques. But it is more than just an update for practitioners. With its four carefully crafted and connected parts, all organized around a holistic perspective of the career counseling process, this book is a source of renewal for practitioners. Second, this book is also for counselors-in-training in counseling psychology and counselor education programs because it provides them with the prerequisite knowledge and skills to do career counseling. It features the career counseling process based on a life career perspective with particular attention to diversity, disability, and gender issues. The book takes counselors-in-training through the phases of the career counseling process providing in-depth presentations of selected techniques and assessment procedures. It offers a framework for integrating qualitative and quantitative techniques and information into the career counseling process directly and naturally, something that many counselors-in-training have difficulty doing.

New to This Edition

Because interest in career counseling continues to increase and because the literature on career counseling trends, issues, and practices has expanded substantially, it was clear that *Career Counseling* was in need of revision. In this, the second edition, we thoroughly updated our chapters with current literature and research concerning the many contextual variables that influence our work as career counselors as well as the theory and practice of career counseling. Our goal was to enhance the theoretical foundations and contextual underpinnings of our field, while at the same time maintaining our emphasis on the practical. Some of the most significant revisions and additions include:

- A new chapter presenting selected career theories and approaches and their applications to the practice of career counseling
- Greater infusion of social class as an important variable in career counseling
- A more thorough review of literature concerning the unique career issues faced by lesbian, gay, bisexual, and transgendered individuals
- Updates of current literature concerning career counseling with individuals with disabilities

Acknowledgments

This book was written with the support, encouragement, and tangible contributions of many colleagues. We particularly acknowledge the contributions of Helen Neville and John Koscuilek; Helen for her substantial contributions to Chapter 3, "Empowering Life Choices: Career Counseling in Cultural Contexts," and John for his writing of Chapter 6, "An Empowerment Approach to Career Counseling with People with Disabilities." Thank you, Helen and John!

We also wish to thank the following individuals who read various drafts of book chapters: Craig Anderson, Bret Fuller, Carolyn Cox, Patrick Feehan, Marie Hammond, Carolyn Humphrey, Glenn Good, Jennifer Jordan, Noboru Komiya, Felissa Lee, Roderick Lilly, Mary Beth Llorens, Amy Linderer, Pat Wright Tatum, Russ Thye, and Sherri Turner. For the second edition we want to especially thank Holly Savoy. We appreciate too, the insightful and useful suggestions of the manuscript reviewers: Alan Burkard, Marquette University; Thomas J. Hernandez, SUNY Brockport; and Jill C. Jurgens, Old Dominion University.

Finally, this book could not have been completed without the very effective and efficient work of our administrative associate, Linda Coats, and our secretaries, Elizabeth Knoblauch and Jacy Perrin. Thanks.

▶ 1

Career Counseling: A Life Career Perspective

Work gets done. Time passes. Careers—sequences of work experiences over time—unfold. A career depicts the person, the elementary unit in work arrangements. Careers invoke relationships within and among firms. Careers spell economic and social outcomes. Put simply, everyone who works has a career. And everyone's life outside work is connected to the career. As lives are lived, a focus on careers, rather than on jobs, insists that we account for time and its implications.
—CAREERS MATTER!(ARTHUR & ROUSSEAU, 1996, P 3).

The theory and research base of counseling psychology has expanded substantially over the past thirty years. Growth in the theory and research base of career psychology during the same period has been equally dramatic, resulting in a convergence of ideas from counseling and career psychology concerning career development and the interventions to facilitate it (Savickas & Lent, 1994). This convergence of ideas has stimulated a reexamination of the nature and structure of career counseling. This reexamination has also stimulated new ways of gathering client information as career counseling unfolds. As important, it has given us new ways to think about and develop hypotheses concerning client information and behavior. It has also opened up new ways to apply these hypotheses to the selection of interventions used to assist clients in resolving their problems and achieving their goals.

To set the stage for the rest of the book, the first part of Chapter 1 examines the impact of the convergence of ideas from counseling psychology and career psychology on the nature and structure of career counseling. This discussion is presented to provide a perspective and an organizer for the career counseling interventions that are described in the chapters that follow. Then, in the second part of Chapter 1, a holistic view of career development, called *life career development*, is described to provide a conceptual foundation and point of departure for work with clients in career counseling.

CAREER COUNSELING

What is career counseling? Is it different from other forms of counseling? Is it the same? Is there overlap? These questions are being asked with increasing frequency today as attempts are being made to clarify this form of counseling (Anderson & Niles, 1995; Blustein & Spengler, 1995; Hackett, 1993; Rak & O'Dell, 1994; Schultheiss, 2000, Sharf, 2002; Swanson, 1995; Walsh & Srsic, 1995; Zunker, 2002). Central to the ongoing discussion about career counseling are two issues. First is the issue of the nature of career counseling. What are its intrinsic characteristics and qualities? Are psychological processes involved? Second is the issue of structure. Does career counseling have structure? If so, what is the configuration, sequence, and interrelationships of the phases and subphases involved?

The Nature of Career Counseling

"Historically, career and vocational counseling have served as the cornerstones upon which the counseling profession was built" (Dorn, 1992, p. 176). Unfortunately, along the path of history, it became stereotyped. In many peoples' minds it became time-limited, it was devoid of psychological processes, and it focused on outcomes and methods (Osipow, 1982). Swanson (1995), paraphrasing the work of Manuele-Adkins (1992), underscored this point:

> *Manuele-Adkins (1992) described elements of a stereotypic view of career counseling that discredit its psychological component and affect the quality and delivery of career counseling services. In this stereotypic view, career counseling is a rational process, with an emphasis on information-giving, testing, and computer-based systems; it is short-term, thus limiting the range of possible intervention strategies and obscuring psychological processes such as indecision; and it is different from personal counseling, thus*

lowering the perceived value of career counseling and increasing a false sep-aration between work and nonwork (p. 222).

Counselors who do career counseling are seen by some as active and directive because they use qualitative and quantitative assessments and infor-mation. Counselors who do personal–emotional counseling, on the other hand, are seen by others as facilitative and exploratory because they focus on psychological processes, that is, on client–counselor interactions (Imbimdo, 1994). This dichotomy of views led to the classic stereotype of career counsel-ing as "three interviews and a cloud of dust" (Crites, 1981, pp. 49–52). It is not surprising, therefore, that career counseling does not fare well in the eyes of practitioners when compared to personal–emotional counseling, given the classic stereotype.

Contrary to the classic stereotype, we believe that career counseling belongs in the general class of counseling because it has the same intrinsic characteristics and qualities that all forms of counseling possess. It differs from the rest of the class, however, because presenting problems often focus on work and career issues, and quantitative and qualitative assessment pro-cedures and information are used more frequently. Swanson (1995) sug-gested this characterization of career counseling when she defined it as "...an ongoing, face-to-face interaction between counselor and client, with the pri-mary focus on work- or career-related issues; the interaction is psychological in nature, with the relationship between counselor and client serving an important function" (p. 245).

As those of you who are practicing counselors know, client presenting problems often are only a beginning point, and that as counseling unfolds, other problems emerge. Career issues frequently become personal–emotional issues and family issues, and then career issues again. Psychological distress is often present (Multon, Heppner, Gysbers, Zook, & Ellis-Kalton, 2001). Thoughts, emotions, and feelings are all involved.

Emotions are the genie in the bottle of career development, the winds whip-ping around inside a client, while s/he wears the polite mask of reasonable-ness. For career counselors to be fully effective, they must unbottle the emotions that often accompany clients' struggles toward career goals (Figler, 1989, p. 1).

The stereotyped division of counseling into the separate classes of per-sonal–emotional and career is artificial and cannot stand in practice because many clients are dealing with multiple personal–emotional and career prob-lems simultaneously, many of them all connected together (Phillips, Christo-pher-Sisk, & Gravino, 2001; Sharf, 2002). As Amundson (1998) pointed out, "most people come to counseling with life problems that do not fall neatly into the categories of career or personal: life just does not define itself that neatly" (p. 16).

If career counseling belongs to the same class as other forms of counseling, then why do we use the term career counseling at all? We advocate the use of the term partly because of history. As stated earlier, the use of the word *vocational*, now *career*, is part of our heritage.

History alone, however, is not a sufficient reason to continue to use the term career counseling. There is another reason—the need to focus attention on client problems dealing with work and career issues that require theoretical conceptions and interventions originating from career development theory, research, and practice. These needed theoretical conceptions and interventions are not usually found in the literature that surrounds other forms of counseling. At the same time, theoretical conceptions and interventions that emerge from and undergird personal–emotional counseling perspectives are not usually found in the literature that surrounds career counseling. According to Collin and Watts, "... the conceptual power of 'career' derives from its capacity to link the private world of the individual to the social and economic structure" (Collin & Watts, 1996, p. 343).

In the worlds of today and tomorrow, theoretical conceptions and practical interventions from both the career and personal–emotional arenas are needed to work effectively with many clients. Our starting point should be our clients, not predetermined distinctions of counseling. Zunker (2002) made this same point when he stated that "we are not just career counselors, we counsel individuals" (p. 7). The emphasis on client problems to guide and work with clients was suggested by Blustein and Spengler (1995) in their domain-sensitive approach.

> *In effect, a domain-sensitive approach is characterized by the counselor's concerted interest in and awareness of all possible ramifications of a client's psychological experience and its behavioral expression. In this approach, the counselor clearly values the client's experiences in both the career and non-career domains. The counselor bases a decision about where to intervene on informed judgments about where the problem originated and where it is most accessible for intervention (p. 317).*

In the domain-sensitive approach, the career problems clients have are not automatically converted to personal–emotional problems. Nor are personal–emotional problems automatically converted to career problems. "The underlying asset of a domain-sensitive approach is that interventions are not based on discrete or arbitrary distinctions between treatment modalities but are determined by the unique attributes of each client's history and presenting problem" (Blustein & Spengler, 1995, p. 318). The terms career counseling and personal–emotional counseling should remain as ways to organize theory and research, but not as ways to restrict our view of clients and limit our work with them. Hackett (1993) suggested this same point when she stated that, "I see our most pressing tasks as determining how to more effectively integrate or coordinate career counseling and therapy without losing sight of vocational issues and concerns" (p. 112).

The Structure of Career Counseling

Based on our discussion of the nature of career counseling, the next task is to consider a way to organize the work of clients and counselors in career counseling. Can the work of clients and counselors in career counseling be organized into phases and subphases? If so, how are the phases and subphases arranged and sequenced? Are the phases and subphases interrelated?

Beginning with the work of Parsons (1909), many writers have described possible ways to structure career counseling (Brooks, 1984; Crites, 1981; Isaacson & Brown, 1997; Kinnier & Krumboltz, 1984; Krumboltz, 1983; McDaniels & Gysbers, 1992; Seligman, 1994; Super, 1983, 1984; Walsh & Osipow, 1990; Williamson, 1939, 1965). For purposes of this book, the structure of career counseling we suggest has two major phases and a number of subphases. An outline of these phases and subphrases appears in Table 1–1.

In addition, because we agree with Swanson's (1995) statement that the relationship between counselor and client serves an important function in career counseling, Table 1–1 also pictures how we envision the counselor client relationship or working alliance with the phases and subphases of career coundeling. We see the working alliance evolving during career counseling moving from forming the working alliance, to strengthening it, to fulfilling it, to finally closing it upon competition of career counseling. (A full discussion of the working alliance including setting goals, establishing tasks to be completed, and creating the bond between counselor and client appears in Chapter 8.

Keep in mind that all of the phases and subphases of career counseling may take place during one session, but more likely, will unfold over a number of sessions with most clients. In some agencies and institutions policies dictate the number of sessions possible. In this case, it is important that clients and counselors understand these time constraints and make decisions about what can be accomplished in the time available. In these situations there may be agreed-upon unfinished business when the relationship is closed.

Also keep in mind that, while these suggested phases and subphases logically follow one another on paper, in actual practice they may not. There often is a back-and-forth flow to career counseling in that it may be necessary to backtrack to earlier phases or subphases before moving on again. Sometimes the *taking action* subphase is reached only to realize that other interven-

TABLE 1.1   The Structure of Career Counseling

Phases and Subphases	Working Alliance

Client Goal or Problem Identification, Clarification, and Specification Opening—
• Identifying initial client presenting goals or problems
• Listening for internal thoughts and feelings and underlying dynamics
• Defining and clarifying client–counselor relationships and responsibilities
 	
*Gathering client information—*using counselor leads, quantitative instruments, and qualitative procedures to clarify and specify presenting goals or problems for the purposes of:
• Exploring clients' views of themselves, others, and their worlds (world views)
  • Language clients use to represent their views
  • Racial/gender identity status
• Exploring clients' ways of making sense out of their life roles, settings, and events; past, present, and future
• Review possible personal and environmental barriers or constraints
• Identify clients' decision styles
 	
*Understanding and hypothesizing client behavior—*applying the language and constructs from career, counseling, and personality theories as well as multicultural and gender literature to understand and interpret client information and behavior in light of clients' presenting (and possible subsequent) goals or problems by:
• Forming hypotheses based on theory/literature concerning client goals or problems to guide intervention selection
• Focusing on cultural/gender specific variables that may influence client behavior
• Listening for and responding to possible client resistance
 	
Client Goal or Problem Resolution
*Taking action—*using theory-research-based interventions, including counseling techniques, quantitative and qualitative assessments, and information to assist clients to achieve their goals or respond to their problems in the context of the working alliance.
 	
*Developing career goals and plans of action—*developing with clients' career goals and plans of action to achieve goals and resolve problems and overcome environmental and bias barriers when and where present
 	
*Evaluating results and closing the relationship—*closing relationship when clients' goals are achieved or problems are resolved
	Forming the working alliance
	• Identifying initial goals to be addressed
	• Specifying beginning tasks to be undertaken
	• Creating the bond between counselor and client
	
	Strengthening the working alliance
	• Pursuing and/or modifying mutual goals and tasks, adding new goals and tasks, dropping goals and tasks no longer applicable
	• Enhancing the bond between counselor and client
	
	Fulfilling the work alliance
	• Achieving clients' goals through tasks and completion; setting aside some goals as unfinished business
	• Completing the bond between counselor and client
	
	Closing the working alliance

tions, not anticipated, may be needed, necessitating a return to the *gathering client information* subphase. To picture this point, you can see that the phases and subphases of career counseling just presented in linear outline form in Table 1–1 are now placed in a circular format in Figure 1–1. Note how the working alliance evolves and interacts with the phases and subphases and how central it is to the structure of career counseling.

Finally, keep in mind that not everyone who seeks help wants to or needs to go through the full process of career counseling. Some may want or need only limited assistance. Other clients, however, may need to be involved in the full process over time but may be resistant to do so. Dealing with resistance may be a first priority in the *opening* subphase as the working alliance is beginning to be formed. Even if resistance seemingly is handled then, be aware that it may reoccur again and again, perhaps later in career counseling as some clients struggle with their problems. Remember, for these clients, dealing with reoccurring resistance is part of the psychological processes involved in career counseling. (See Chapter 15 for a detailed discussion of resistance in career counseling.)

LIFE CAREER DEVELOPMENT: A HOLISTIC PERSPECTIVE

As we have seen, a major task in career counseling is gathering information concerning the presenting and subsequent goals and problems clients bring

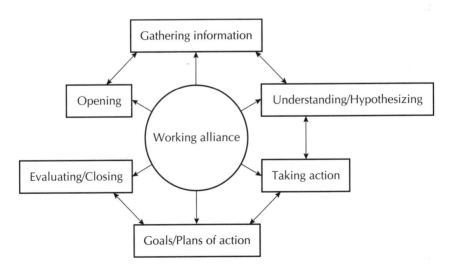

FIGURE 1–1   The Structure of Career Counseling

to career counseling. Equally important are the tasks of understanding client goals and problems, developing hypotheses about them, and selecting appropriate interventions to empower clients to reach their goals and resolve their problems. To aid you and your clients to work through these career counseling tasks, we advocate a broad holistic perspective of career development called *life career development*. "What is needed in career theory and practice is a more holistic view of the individual, one that encompasses all spheres of activity and all corresponding facets of personal identity" (Hall, 1996, p. 7).

What Is Life Career Development?

The Initial Definition

First proposed in 1973 by Gysbers and Moore, life career development was defined as self-development over the life span through the interaction and integration of the roles, settings, and events of a person's life. The word *life* in the term life career development meant that the focus was on the total person—the human career. The word *career* identified and related the roles in which individuals were involved (worker, participant in leisure, learner, family member, and citizen), the settings where they found themselves (home, school, community, and workplace), and the events, planned and unplanned, that occurred over their lifetimes (entry job, marriage, more advanced positions, divorce, and retirement). Finally, the expression life career development brought these separate meanings together, but at the same time a greater meaning emerged. Life career development described people with a diversity of lifestyles.

An Expanded Definition

Can the original concept of life career development first described in 1973 be made more relevant for today and tomorrow? The answer is yes. While the basic configuration of life roles, life settings, and life events interacting and unfolding over a lifetime is still of value, it is clear that there are other important factors at work that influence the life career development of all individuals that need to be added. McDaniels and Gysbers (1992) responded to this concern by adding the factors of gender, ethnic origin, religion, and race to the original conception of life career development. These were added to underscore the importance they have on shaping the life roles, life settings, and life events of individuals of all ages and circumstances. In addition, they were added to provide individuals with greater explanatory power to understand the dynamics of their life career development.

Figure 1–2 depicts this broader definition of career development in life career development terms. Note the headings *life roles, life settings,* and *life events* at the top of Figure 1–2. The words circled underneath are examples of various life roles (parent, spouse, and so on), life settings (such as home, school, and work), and life events (marriage, retirement, entry job, divorce). They are interspersed throughout Figure 1–2 to indicate the dynamic interaction that occurs among them over the life span. Near the bottom of the figure, the words *gender, ethnic origin,* and *race* remain from the first edition. We changed the word *religion* to *spirituality* and the words *socioeconomic status* to *social class.* These changes were made to reflect current thinking in our discipline. In addition, we have added a new factor, *sexual orientation.* These changes were made and the new factor was added to provide even greater explanatory power to the concept of life career development.

Providing individuals with the ability to more fully explain and understand the what, why, and how of their overall life career development, the career goals they may have, or the career problems they may face, is important, particularly in today's complex society. We live in a nation that is a part of a world economy. This nation is increasingly diverse racially, spiritually, and ethnically, and yet it has common themes that connect us all. This nation continues to change its views on what it means to be female or male educa-

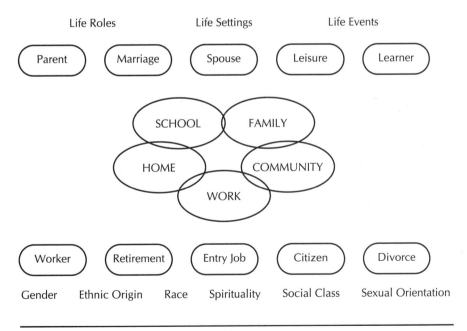

FIGURE 1–2   Life Career Development
Adapted from McDaniels, C., & Gysbers, N.C. (1992). *Counseling for career development.* San Francisco: Jossey-Bass. Used with permission.

tionally and occupationally. Social class and sexual orientation continue to play an important role in shaping an individual's socialization, and current and future status. Spirituality is also an important part of many individuals' lives (Gunther, 2001; Stanard, Sandher, & Painter, 2000).

> *To the extent we can set aside simplistic notions that self-actualization is the pinnacle of human motivation, this makes room to consider how family feeling, community membership, and spirituality are transcendent aims of human development (Mirvis & Hall, 1996, p. 252).*

Thus, the influences of these factors on the life career development of individuals need to be understood more completely and reckoned with more directly if they are to achieve their goals or resolve their problems.

Creating Career Consciousness

A major goal of having individuals use life career development as a lens to identify, describe, and understand the dynamics of their career development past, present, and future is to create within them career consciousness—the ability to visualize and plan their life careers. "Included within the idea of consciousness is a person's background, education, politics, insight, values, emotions, and philosophy" (Reich, 1971, p. 15). But consciousness, according to Reich, is more than this. It is the whole person. It is their way of creating their own life. Thus the challenge is to assist individuals to become career conscious. The challenge is to assist them to project themselves into future possible life roles, life settings, and life events, realizing the importance of gender, ethnic origin, spirituality, race, social class, and sexual orientation on their development, and then relate their projections to their present situations for consideration and incorporation into their plans to achieve their goals or resolve their problems. "Even when we dream, in the sense of a daydream, we often dream of things that are yet to be as though they already were" (Hendricks, 2001, p. 38).

Contained in the concept of career consciousness is the notion of possible selves described by Markus and Nurius (1986). What are possible selves? "Possible selves represent individuals' ideas of what they might become, what they would like to become, and what they are afraid of becoming, and thus provide a conceptual link between cognition and motivation" (Markus & Nurius, 1986, p. 954). Why are possible selves important? "Possible selves are important, first, because they function as incentives for future behavior (i.e., they are selves to be approached or avoided) and second, because they provide an evaluative and interpretive context for the current view of self" (Markus & Nurius, 1986, p. 954).

Using Life Career Development in Career Counseling

Life career development serves as a wide-angle lens that can bring into view a broad picture of an individual's career development. It provides individuals with a realistic, graphic representation of major life possibilities and responsibilities as well as a language to describe them—their possible selves. It is difficult to consider possible selves, however, if the lens being used by individuals to view the future is too small to capture the full scope of their life career development, and the screen on which it is being projected is not large enough to portray its many dimensions, dynamics, and relationships. Things not seen cannot be a part of individuals' possible selves. "Information that is not known is beyond consideration and cannot form a part of the data necessary for establishing a possible self" (Cornford, 1995, p. 41).

The life career development view of human development and behavior also provides ways to analyze and understand individuals' development and behavior in career terms; to expand their vision of career, from a work-only focus, to a broader view involving life roles, life settings, and life events that include work, all interacting over the life span. This allows them to focus on a specific life role while, at the same time, connecting that life role to other life roles (Gouws, 1995); to appreciate the influence various life settings may have on life roles; and to anticipate the possible impact that planned and unplanned events or nonevents may have on career planning and decision making. By adding the six factors of gender, ethnic origin, spirituality, race, social class, and sexual orientation and their potential influences to the original life career development perspective, a broadened real-life frame is available on which individuals can display, organize, and understand the impact these factors may have on their socialization and on their current and possible selves (Hill & Spokane, 1995; Markus & Nurius, 1986; Meara, Day, Chalk, & Phelps, 1995), in essence, their life career development.

To illustrate the potential of this conceptualization, consider individuals who are struggling with work and family issues and concerns. It is sometimes difficult for them to identify, sort out, and understand the dynamics involved. What is required is an orientation to conceptualize these dynamics and to have a structure on which to display them. Often the issues and concerns involved pertain to more than work and family. They also may involve other life roles, settings, and events. Hence the orientation used needs to be broad enough and sensitive enough to identify and respond to these related problems. Bachiochi (1993), paraphrasing the work of Brief and Nord (1990), stressed this point by stating "that to understand the connections among work and other life domains, we must adopt an orientation to the total collection of roles a person plays" (p. 136).

Life career development is such an orientation, and thus is a lens through which individuals can view and understand work and family concerns. Add the factors of gender, ethnic origin, race, spirituality, social class, and sexual orientation and the lens becomes even more powerful. Now individuals have a way of bringing their personal histories and the histories of their reference groups into focus. Now they can see how these factors have directly or indirectly influenced them, their views of themselves, others, and the world in which they live. Now they have six additional factors to use to understand and respond to their struggles with work and family issues and concerns.

IMPLICATIONS FOR CAREER COUNSELING

The broadened understanding of career development in life terms makes it clear that we must respond to the developmental needs of people as well as to their crisis needs. Obviously, crises in individuals' lives must be dealt with, but crises are not the only emphasis in career counseling. Such thinking has a number of implications. Here are two.

Prediction and Development

The first implication revolves around the words *prediction* and *development*. Traditional career counseling practices emphasize the assessment of individuals' abilities, aptitudes, personality, values, and interests to aid in the selection of appropriate educational programs or making occupational choices. This emphasis, while important, is not sufficient. What is needed, in addition, is attention to individuals' life career development so that goal achievement and problem resolution can be based on the broadest and most well-informed perspective possible. As Tennyson (1970) stated:

> *By concentrating upon assessment of abilities presumed to be related to choice outcomes, counselors have neglected to concern themselves with the development of abilities and aptitudes. While it is generally recognized that what a person is able to do depends to a considerable extent upon what he (sic) has learned or practiced, guidance personnel have been inclined to capitalize upon aptitudes already developed rather than cultivating new talents (p. 262).*

Deficits, Skills, and Competencies

The second implication focuses on the words *deficits*, *skills*, and *competencies*. A major focus of career counseling is on helping individuals deal effectively with problems. Personal crises, a lack of information about training opportunities and the job market, and ineffective relationships with spouse, children, fellow employees, or supervisors are examples of problems to which counselors frequently are asked to respond. This focus must continue, and better ways of helping individuals with their problems must be found. In addition, a preventive focus is needed to help individuals develop and use their talents and competencies to create a better world for themselves and for society.

The preventive focus is not new. It has been a part of the counseling language and literature since the turn of the century. What is new is a sense of urgency about the importance of helping people develop and focus on their competencies rather than only on their deficits. Bolles (1981) developed an assessment technique to identify what he called functional/transferable skills. Although some people do not think of themselves as having skills, everyone possesses a substantial number of skills, and their identification is an important part of positive growth and development.

Tyler (1978) suggested that our perceptions of people will change if they can develop as many competencies as possible.

Competencies represent a completely different way of structuring our perceptions of others. The more competencies other people have the better for each of us, and it is essential for the functioning of a complex society that individuals develop different repertoires of competencies. The absolute limits of each person's living time make all-around competence for one individual impossible. We need one another (pp. 104–105).

Ensuring Counselor Competence

The broadened understanding of career development in life terms requires that counselors who work from this holistic perspective must have appropriate competencies to work with clients of all ages and circumstances. They must also have the self-confidence to use these competencies. What competencies are required? O'Brien and Heppner (1995) identified 25 competencies they thought counselors who do career counseling should possess. The 25 competencies form the items for an instrument they developed titled the Career Counseling Self-Efficacy Scale (CCSES). It assesses the level of confidence that counselors have in their ability to perform the task involved in each competency. The CCSES with its 25 competencies is found in Table 1–2.

The CCSES evidenced moderate to high internal consistency and strong test–retest reliability over a two-week period (O'Brien, Heppner, Flores, & Bikos, 1997). Convergent validity was supported by correlations with years of career counseling experience and several scales of an emotional-social counseling self-efficacy measure. Discriminant validity was evidenced through an absence of relations between the CCSES total score and years of an emotional-social counseling self-efficacy measure. Discriminant validity also was evidenced through an absence of relations between the CCSES total score and years of emotional-social counseling experience, emotional-social counseling

TABLE 1–2 Career Counseling Self-Efficacy Scale

Below is a list of activities regarding counseling. Indicate <u>YOUR CONFIDENCE IN YOUR CURRENT ABILITY TO PERFORM EACH ACTIVITY</u> by circling the appropriate answer next to each question according to the scale defined below. Please answer each item based on how you feel now, not on your anticipated (or previous) ability.

0	1	2	3	4
Not Confident		Moderately Confident		Highly Confident

1. Select an instrument to clarify a career client's abilities.   0 1 2 3 4
2. Provide support for a client's implementation of her/his career goals.   0 1 2 3 4
3. Assist a client in understanding how his/her non-work ife (e.g., family, leisure, interests, etc.) affects career decisions.   0 1 2 3 4
4. Understand special issues related to gender <u>in career decision-making.</u>   0 1 2 3 4
5. Develop a therapeutic relationship with a career client.   0 1 2 3 4
6. Select an instrument to clarify aspects of a career client's personality which may influence career planning.   0 1 2 3 4
7. Explain assessment results to a career client   0 1 2 3 4
8. Terminate counseling with a career client in an effective manner.   0 1 2 3 4
9. Understand special issues related to ethnicity in the workplace.   0 1 2 3 4
10. Understand special issues that lesbian, gay and bisexual clients may have <u>in career decision-making.</u>   0 1 2 3 4
11. Provide knowledge of local and national job market information and trends.   0 1 2 3 4
12. Choose assessment inventories for a career client which are appropriate for the client's gender, age, education, and cultural background.   0 1 2 3 4
13. Assist the career client in modulating feelings about the career decision-making process.   0 1 2 3 4
14. Apply knowledge about current ethical and legal issues which may affect the career counseling process.   0 1 2 3 4
15. Understand special issues present for lesbian, gay and bisexual clients <u>in the workplace.</u>   0 1 2 3 4
16. Communicate unconditional acceptance to a career client.   0 1 2 3 4
17. Select an instrument to assess a career client's interests.   0 1 2 3 4
18. Select an instrument to clarify a career client's values.   0 1 2 3 4
19. Understand special issues related to gender <u>in the workplace.</u>   0 1 2 3 4
20. Understand special issues related to ethnicity in <u>career decision-making.</u>   0 1 2 3 4
21. Listen carefully to concerns presented by a career client.   0 1 2 3 4
22. Synthesize information about self and career so that a career client's problems seem understandable.   0 1 2 3 4
23. Help a career client identify internal and external barriers that might interfere with reaching her/his career goals.   0 1 2 3 4
24. Use current research findings to intervene effectively with a career client.   0 1 2 3 4
25. Be empathic toward a career client when the client refuses to accept responsibility for making decisions about his/her career.   0 1 2 3 4

---

self-efficacy, and research self-efficacy. In addition to the above, construct validity was evidenced by increases on the CCSES after a career course, and varying levels of efficacy commensurate with status in the field (i.e., practicing psychologists held higher self-efficacy beliefs than graduate students). Finally four factors emerged with accounted for 73 percent of the variance. The above findings and the use of this instrument for training and evaluating therapists who provide career counseling is discussed in the O'Brien et al. (1997) article.

Both total and scale scores can be calculated for this instrument. The total score is calculated by summing all of the items. Scores on each of the four factors are obtained by summing the items comprising each factor. Higher scores indicate considerable confidence in one's ability to perform career counseling.

The first factor is labeled "Therapeutic Process and Alliance Skills" (TPAS) and is comprised of ten items with factor loadings ranging from .88 to .65. This factor assesses the counselor's confidence in developing a therapeutic relationship, providing support, synthesizing information, identifying barriers, and terminating the career counseling relationship in an effective manner. The following items load on this factor: 2, 3, 5, 8, 13, 16, 21, 22, 23, and 25.

The second factor, consisting of six items, is titled "Vocational Assessment and Interpretation Skills" (VAIS) and has factor loadings from .97 to .69. This factor assesses confidence in one's ability to select appropriate instruments to assess interests values, personality and to explain assessment results to career clients. Items, 1, 6, 7, 12, 17, and 18 comprise this factor.

The third factor is titled "Multicultural Competency Skills" (MCS), and consists of six items with factor loadings from .92 to .56. This factor addresses the importance of multicultural counseling competencies in interventions with career clients. Specifically, this factor assesses confidence in understanding the special issues related to ethnicity, gender, and sexual orientation in both the workplace and career decision-making. Included on this scale are items 4, 9, 10, 15, 19, and 20.

The final factor is labeled "Current Trends in the World of Work, Ethics, and Career Research" (TWER), and consists of three items with factor loadings from .80 to .77. This factor assesses knowledge of current research findings, ethical and legal issues, as well as local and national job market trends. Items 11, 14, and 24 comprise this scale.

CLOSING THOUGHTS

Wolfe and Kolb (1980) summed up the dynamic life-centered view of career that has evolved over the past decades when they described career development as involving one's entire life:

Career development involves one's whole life, not just occupation. As such, it concerns the whole person, needs and wants, capacities and potentials, excitements and anxieties, insights and blind spots, warts and all. More than that, it concerns him/her in the ever-changing contexts of his/her life. The environmental pressures and constraints, the bonds that tie him/her to significant others, responsibilities to children and aging parents, the total structure of one's circumstances are also factors that must be understood and reckoned with. In these terms, career development and personal development converge. Self and circumstances—evolving, changing, unfolding in mutual interaction—constitute the focus and the drama of career development (pp. 1–2).

Note that Wolfe and Kolb closed their definition of career development with the words "the drama of career development." We call this drama, "the drama of the ordinary" because it is unfolding and evolving every day. And because it is ordinary, it is not often seen or appreciated by individuals. It is veiled by ordinariness. As a result, clients may fail to understand its dynamic nature and the substantial impact it has throughout their lives. By using the broader concept of life career development as an orientation to understand human growth and development—the human career—we propose to make the drama of career development, the drama of the extraordinary.

REFERENCES

Amundson, N. E. (1998). *Active engagement: Enhancing the career counseling process.* Richmond, BC: Ergon Communications.

Anderson, W. P., & Niles, S. G. (1995). Career and personal concerns expressed by career counseling clients. *The Career Development Quarterly, 43* (3), 240–245.

Arthur, M. B., & Rousseau, D. M. (1996). Introduction: The boundaryless career as a new employment principle. In M.B. Arthur & D. M. Rousseau (Eds.), *The boundaryless career* (pp. 3–20). New York: Oxford University Press.

Bachiochi, P. D. (1993). Effects of work and leisure-role salience on career development. In J. Demick & P. M. Miller (Eds.), *Development in the workplace* (pp. 129–138). Hillsdale, NJ: Erlbaum.

Blustein, D. L. & Spengler, P. M. (1995). Personal adjustment: Career counseling and psychotherapy. In W. B. Walsh & S. H. Osipow (Eds.), *Handbook of vocational psychology: Theory, research, and practice* (pp. 295–329). Hillsdale, NJ: Erlbaum.

Bolles, R. (1981). *The three boxes of life.* Berkeley, CA: Ten Speed Press.

Brief, A. P., & Nord, W. R. (1990). Work and non-work connections. In A. P. Brief & W. R. Nord (Eds.), *Meanings of occupational work: A collection of essays* (pp. 171–199). Lexington, MA: Lexington Books.

Brooks, L. (1984). Career counseling methods and practice. In D. Brown, L. Brooks, & Associates (Eds.), *Career choice and development.* San Francisco: Jossey-Bass.

Collin, A., & Watts, A. G. (1996). The death and transfiguration of career—and career guidance. *British Journal of Guidance & Counselling, 24* (3), 385–398.

Cornford, I. (1995). Career counseling, possible selves and changing occupational skill requirements. *Australian Journal of Career Development, 4* (2), 40–42.

Crites, J. O. (1981). *Career counseling: Models, methods, and materials.* New York: McGraw-Hill.

Dorn, F. J. (1992). Occupational wellness: The integration of career identity and personal identity. *Journal of Counseling & Development, 71,* 176–178.

Figler, H. (1989). The emotional dimension of career counseling. *Career Waves, 2* (2), 1–11.

Gouws, D. J. (1995). The role concept in career development. In D. E. Super & B. Sverko (Eds.), *Life roles, values, and career: International findings of the work importance study.* San Francisco: Jossey-Bass.

Gunther, M. (2001, July 9). God & business: The surprising quest for spiritual renewal in the American workplace. *Fortune, 144,* 581–80.

Chapter 2

Gysbers, N. C., & Moore, E. J. (1973). *Life career development: A model.* Columbia, MO: University of Missouri.

Hackett, G. (1993). Career counseling and psychotherapy: False dichotomies and recommended remedies. *Journal of Career Assessment, 1* (2), 105–117.

Hall, D. T. (1996). Long live the career. In D. T. Hall and Associates (Eds.), *The career is dead—long live the career.* San Francisco: Jossey-Bass.

Hendricks, J. (2001). *It's about time.* In S. H. McFadden & R. C. Atchley (Eds.), *Aging and the meaning of time: A multidisciplinary exploration.* New York: Springer Publishing Company.

Hill, A. L., & Spokane, A. R. (1995). Career counseling and possible selves: A case study. *The Career Development Quarterly, 43* (3), 221–232.

Imbimbo, P. V. (1994). Integrating personal and career counseling: A challenge for counselors. *Journal of Employment Counseling, 31,* 50–59.

Isaacson, L. E., & Brown, D. (1997). *Career information, career counseling, and career development* (6th ed.). Boston: Allyn and Bacon.

Kinnier, R. T., & Krumboltz, J. D. (1984). Procedures for successful counseling. In N. C. Gysbers & Associates (Eds.), *Designing careers: Counseling to enhance education, work, and leisure* (pp. 307–335). San Francisco: Jossey-Bass.

Krumboltz. J. D. (1983). *Private rules in career decision making.* Columbus, OH: National Center for Research in Vocational Education.

Manuele-Adkins, C. (1992). Career counseling is personal counseling. *Career Development Quarterly, 40,* 313–323.

Markus, H., & Nurius, P. (1986). Possible selves. *American Psychologist, 41* (9), 954–969.

McDaniels, C., & Gysbers, N. C. (1992). *Counseling for career development: Theories, resources, and practice.* San Francisco: Jossey-Bass.

Meara, M. W., Day, J. D., Chalk, L. M., & Phelps, R. E. (1995). Possible selves: Applications for career counseling. *Journal of Career Assessment, 3* (3), 259–277.

Mirvis, P. H., & Hall, D. T. (1996). Psychological success and the boundaryless career. In M. B. Arthur & D. M. Rousseau (Eds.), *The boundaryless career: A new employment principle for a new organizational era* (pp. 237–267). New York: Oxford University Press.

Multon, K. D., Heppner, M. J., Gysbers, N. C., Zook, C., & Ellis-Kalton, C. A. (2001). Client psychological distress: An important factor in career counseling. *The Career Development Quarterly, 49,* 324–335.

O'Brien, K. M., Heggner, M. J., Flores, L. Y., & Bilsos, L. H. (1997) The career counseling self-efficacy scale: Instrument of development and training applications. *Journal of Counseling Psychology, 44,* 20–31.

O'Brien, K. M., & Heppner, M.J. (1995). *The Career Counseling Self-Efficacy Scale.* (Available from K.M. O'Brien, Psychology Department, University of Maryland, College Park, MD 20742).

Osipow, S. H. (1982). Research in career counseling: An analysis of issues and problems. *The Counseling Psychologist, 10,* 27–34.

Parsons, F. (1909). *Choosing a vocation.* Boston: Houghton Mifflin.

Phillips, S. D., Christopher-Sisk, E.K., & Gravino, K. L. (2001). Making career decisions in a relational context. *The Counseling Psychologist, 29,* 193–213.

Rak, C. F., & O'Dell, F. L. (1994). Career treatment strategy model: A blend of career and traditional counseling approaches. *Journal of Career Development, 20* (3), 227–238.

Reich, C. A. (1971). *The greening of America.* New York: Bantam Books.

Savickas, M. L., & Lent, R. W. (Eds.). (1994). *Convergence in career development theories.* Palo Alto, CA: Consulting Psychologists Press.

Schultheisis, D. P. (2000). Emotional-social issues in the provision of career counseling. In D. A. Juzzo (Ed.), *Career counseling of college students* (pp. 43–62). Washington, D.C.:American Psychological Association.

Seligman, L. (1994). *Developmental career counseling and assessment* (2nd ed.). Thousand Oaks, CA: Sage.

Sharf, R. S. (2002). *Applying career development theory to counseling* (3rd ed.). Pacific Grove, CA: Brooks/Cole.

Stanard, R. P., Sandhu, D. S., & Painter, L. C. (2000). Assessment of spirituality in counseling. *Journal of Counseling and Development, 78,* 204-210.

Super, D. E. (1983). Assessment in career guidance: Towards truly developmental counseling. *The Personnel and Guidance Journal, 61,* 555–562.

Super, D. E. (1984). Career and life development. In D. Brown, L. Brooks, & Associates, (Eds.), *Career choice and development* (pp. 192–234). San Francisco: Jossey-Bass.

Swanson, J. L. (1995). The process and outcome of career counseling. In W. B. Walsh & S. H. Osipow (Eds.), *Handbook of vocational psychology: Theory, research, and practice* (pp. 217–259). Hillsdale, NJ: Erlbaum.

Tennyson, W. (1970). Comment. *Vocational Guidance Quarterly, 18,* 261–263.

Tyler, L. (1978). *Individuality, human possibilities and personal choice in the psychological development of men and women.* San Francisco: Jossey-Bass.

Walsh, W. B., & Osipow, S. H. (1990). *Career Counseling.* Hillsdale, NJ: Erlbaum.

Walsh, W. B., & Srsic, C. (1995). Annual reviews: Vocational behavior and career development—1994. *The Career Development Quarterly, 44* (2), 98–145.

Williamson, E. G. (1939). *How to counsel students.* New York: McGraw-Hill.

Williamson, E. G. (1965). *Vocational counseling.* New York: McGraw-Hill.

Wolfe, D. M., & Kolb, D. A. (1980). Career development, personal growth, and experimental learning. In J. W. Springer (Ed.), *Issues in career and human resource development.* Madison, WI: *American Society for Training and Development.*

Zunker, V. G. (2002). *Career counseling: Applied concepts of life planning.* Pacific Grove, CA: Brooks/Cole.

2

Ways of Understanding Career Behavior

Selected Theories and Approaches

"Why study theory?" "What does theory have to do with practice?" "Most of the courses I took in my training to become a counselor were too theoretical!" "Theory gets in my way when I am trying to listen to and respond to my clients!" These and similar questions and comments are heard frequently when counselors get together and discuss their current work and previous training. Why do they express these attitudes? Partly because there is, in fact, a gap between theory and practice. Many books and articles describe theory. Fewer books and articles explain how theoretical language is used in counseling.

Theory has been defined as a statement of general principles supported by data and offered as an explanation of a phenomenon (Shertzer & Stone, 1980). Swanson & Fouad (1999) stated that "a theory is a series of connected hypothetical statements designed to explain a particular behavior or set of behaviors" (p. 3). For us, a useful theory summarizes and generalizes a body of information. It facilitates our understanding of and provides an explanation for the phenomena described by that body of information. It acts as a predictor of future developments, and it also stimulates further research.

Thus theories provide the foundation knowledge from which you draw useful concepts to explain client behavior. Theories offer a framework within which client behavior can be examined and hypotheses formed about the possible meanings of that behavior. In turn, this knowledge helps you identify, understand, and respond to clients' goals or problems.

How do clients, the counseling process, and theory interact? Keeping the graphic representation of this interaction as presented in Figure 2–1 in mind, let us look more closely at how theory informs practice.

Clients often become involved in career counseling because they are in transition, either by their own choice or because of conditions over which they have only limited control or no control at all. Internal thoughts and feelings concerning these transitions abound often without shape or form. They may appear jumbled and confused, at least on the surface. What should I do? Which direction should I go in? How should I respond to and resolve my problem or achieve my goal? These are the kinds of questions clients may be

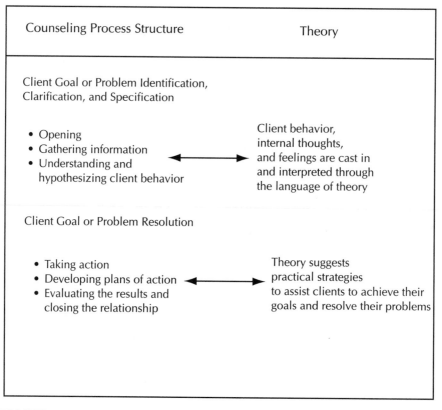

**FIGURE 2–1   The Interaction of the Career Counseling
Process and Theory**

struggling with. Sometimes the questions, let alone any possible answers, are not clearly formed in clients' minds.

So, how does theory inform practice to help you and your clients deal with these issues? Theory helps us identify and interpret client behavior and information. It provides us with ways to give meaning to the internal thoughts and feelings of clients. That meaning can then be connected to practical strategies for assisting clients in pursuing career goals or resolving problems.

While career theories help us understand and respond to clients' problems and goals, they also provide us with insights into the possible outcomes of counseling for career development. Super (1990) made this point as follows:

> *Career development theory makes clear what is to be fostered—occupational self-concept clarification and implementation and handling of the developmental tasks. It is growth in autonomy, time perspective, and self-esteem; exploration in breadth and then in depth for the crystallization, specification, and implementation of occupational self-concepts, interests, and a vocational preference; establishment with trial, stabilization, consolidation, and perhaps advancement; maintenance with adaptability, which means at least holding but better still keeping up, innovating, and in some cases transferring; and decline, or disengagement, and the shift of role emphases (p. 254).*

This chapter presents brief descriptions of selected career theories and approaches that explain the nature, structure, and process of career development. We did not intend to offer descriptions of every career theory or approach because there are a number of excellent books that do that. Rather, our intent was to describe several theories and approaches to illustrate how the constructs from these theories and approaches can facilitate our understanding of client behavior as well as facilitate clients' understanding of their own behavior. The theories we have chosen are: (1) Super's life-span, life-space approach to career development; (2) Holland's theory of vocational personalities and work environments; (3) Schlossberg's adult career development transition model; and (4) Lent, Brown, and Hackett's social cognitive career theory. In addition, we present several approaches to understanding career development that we feel offer helpful ways of thinking about and understanding client behavior. These approaches are not fully developed theories, but offer many practical ideas for your work as career counselors. Thus, we include: (1) Krumboltz's model of planned happenstance; (2) Cook, Heppner and O'Brien's ecological model; and (3) Holland's theory of career intervention and change.

The presentation of each theory and approach begins with a brief description of its basic tenets. Then we identify their implications for clients, counselors, and the counseling process. Emphasis is placed on how the constructs of these theories and approaches help us understand client behavior and information more fully and select practical strategies to assist clients achieve their goals and resolve their problems.

THEORIES OF CAREER DEVELOPMENT

Super's Life-Span, Life-Space Theory of Career Development

Super (1990) described his theory as "a segmental theory. . . . a loosely unified set of theories dealing with specific aspects of career development, taken from developmental, differential, social, personality, and phenomenological psychology and held together by self-concept and learning theory" (p. 199). His initial ideas for his theory began forming in the late 1930's. According to Super, Savickas, and Super (1996) these ideas originated in his interest in work and occupations, the developmental studies of Buehler (1933), and the studies of occupational mobility by Davidson and Anderson (1937). These beginning ideas were brought together in Super's book *The Dynamics of Vocational Adjustment* (1942) in which he presented a developmental view of career choice. The point that career choice was a process not an event was "Super's single most important idea" (Super, Savickas, & Super, 1996, p. 122).

In the early 1950's Super (1953) introduced the first outline of his theory in his presidential address to the Division of Counseling and Guidance (now the Division of Counseling Psychology) of the American Psychological Association, in part in response to a challenge by Ginzberg, Ginsburg, Axelrod, and Herma (1951) that vocational counselors lacked a theory to guide their work. In his address he identified the elements that he thought made up an adequate theory of vocational development. These elements, described in more detail by Super (1953), included individual differences; multipotentiality; occupational ability patterns; identification and the role of models; continuity of adjustment; life stages; career patterns; development can be guided; development the result of interaction; the dynamics of career patterns; job satisfaction, individual differences, status, and role; and work as a way of life. He then presented a series of ten propositions that organized these elements into what he called "a summary statement of a comprehensive theory" (Super, 1953, p. 189). Later, two more propositions were added and still later two more were added making a total of fourteen (Super, 1990).

In developing his final fourteen propositions, Super (1990) drew upon four diverse domains, namely, differential psychology, developmental psychology, occupational sociology, and personality theory. Differential psychology provided a knowledge base about the various traits individuals possess and the variety of occupational requirements. Developmental psychology contributed insights into how individuals develop abilities and interests and the concepts of life stages and developmental tasks. Occupational sociology offered new ideas about occupational mobility and the impact of environmental influences. Finally, personality theory contributed the concepts of self-concept and person-contract theory.

The first three propositions emphasize that people have different abilities, interests, and values, and because they have, they may be qualified for various occupations. No person fits only one occupation; there are a variety of occupations available for an individual and occupations accommodate a wide variety of individuals. The next six propositions focus on the self-concept and its implementation in career choices, on life stages with their mini and maxicycles, and on the concepts of career patterns and career maturity. The next five propositions deal with the synthesis and compromise between individual and social factors and work and life satisfactions. Finally, the last proposition looks at work and occupation as the focus for personality organization as well as the interplay of such life roles as worker, student, leisurite, homemaker, and citizen.

In 1951, a major research program called the Career Pattern Study (CPS) was undertaken in Middletown, New York, to test some of the hypotheses of Super and his colleagues. The CPS began following the lives of 138 eighth-grade boys and 142 ninth-grade boys. Super and his colleagues theorized that the movement of individuals through life stages was a typical process that could be loosely tracked according to an age-referenced time line (See proposition 5). The participants were followed up briefly at age twenty-one, more intensively at age twenty-five, and then again at about age thirty-six. The findings from the CPS have been made available periodically in a series of monographs (Jordaan and Heyde, 1979; Super and Overstreet, 1960), in an article by Super (1985), and in a dissertation by Fisher (1989).

Super's (Super, Savickas, & Super, 1996) life-span, life-space approach to career development organizes the concepts of life roles and life stages into an interactive system. This system is represented pictorially as the Life Career Rainbow (Figure 2–2). The five life stages shown in relationship to age appear on the outside rim. He called them maxicycles, and, while they are linear, not everyone goes through these stages in the same way or at the same age. Transitions from one stage to the next often involve minicycles or going back through various stages before moving on. Within each of the stages developmental tasks are to be mastered before movement to the next stage occurs. "Success in adopting to each developmental task results in effective functioning as a student, worker, or retiree [for example] and lays the groundwork for mastering the next task along the developmental continuum" (Super, Savickas, & Super, 1996, p. 131).

An important concept in Super's formulation of career development is that of career maturity. While there are differences of opinion about the definition of *career maturity*, there is general agreement that this term denotes a

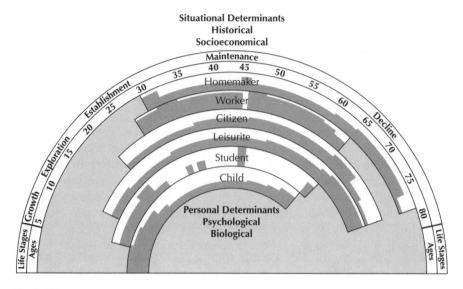

FIGURE 2–2   The Life-Career Rainbow: Six Life Roles in Schematic Life Space.

From D. Brown: *Career Choice and Development,* 2/e. Copyright © 1990 by Jossey-Bass. This material is used by permission of John Wiley & Sons, Inc.

readiness to engage in the developmental tasks appropriate to the age and level at which one finds oneself. Maturity, however, is not something that is ever reached, but instead is the goal relative to where one is at any given time. This formulation of the concept helps to promote a life-span notion rather than a static, irreversible pattern of career development. Later Super refined his notion of career maturity. He suggested that the term for adults should be *career adaptability.* Included in his formulation of career maturity (adaptability) are the constructs of planfulness (including autonomy, self-esteem, and reliance on a time perspective), exploration, information, decision making, and reality orientation.

In addition to life stages, the Life-Career Rainbow found in Figure 2–2 also features life roles located in the space and time of life stages (life-space). Super identified six life roles that individuals participate in over the life span including homemaker, worker, citizen, leisurite, student, and child. Individuals often participate in multiple roles at the same time; the amount of time and effort varies by life stage and age. Note how the life roles fluctuate depending on age and other circumstances across the life span. Super depicted this idea by the amount of shading that occurs in each of the roles of the life span.

While Super's work on theory building was substantial and continuous over a long period of time, he also saw the need to concentrate on the use of his theory in practice. He was particularly interested in applying his theoretical concepts to career counseling. To that end he, along with a number of colleagues, developed the career development assessment and counseling (C-DAC) model (Niles 2001; Super, Osborne, Walsh, Brown, and Niles, 1992).

According to Super, Savickas, and Super (1996), the C-DAC begins with a session that focuses on the client's concerns and a review of data about the client. Then four phases of assessment are undertaken with the first phase being the assessment of the importance of the work role in relationship to other life roles. Then in the next phase, attention is given to determining the career stage and career concerns of the client followed by the identification of resources for making and implementing choices as well as assessing resources for adapting to the work world. Next, interests, abilities, and values are assessed following trait and factor methodology. The last phase focuses on the assessment of the client's self-concept and life themes using qualitative assessment procedures.

The final step in the C-DAC is the integration of assessment and interview data into a meaningful whole.

A final step integrates the interview material and the assessment data into a narrative that realistically and sensitively portrays the client's vocational identity, occupational self-concept, and coping resources and then locates the individual in the context of multiple roles with their developmental tasks. Comparing this narrative to the client's career concerns begin the process of formulating, in collaboration with the client, a counseling plan designed to foster the client's career development (Super, Savickas, & Super, 1996, p. 151).

Super (1990) summarized the status of his theory as follows:

During the past decade, this career development model has been refined and extended. Differential psychology has made technical, but not substantive, advances. Operational definitions of career maturity have been modified, and the model has been modified with them. Our understanding of recycling through stages in a minicycle has been refined, but the basic construct is essentially the same as when it was first formulated, years ago. Ideas about how to assess self-concepts have evolved as research has thrown light on their measurement, and knowledge of how applicable self-concept theory is to various subpopulations has been extended, but this segment of the model has not greatly changed. Life-stage theory has been refined but mostly confirmed by several major studies during the past decade. The role of learning theory has been highlighted by the work on social learning, but to the neglect of other kinds of interactive learning. The career model is perhaps now in the maintenance stage, but health maintenance does not mean stasis but rather updating and innovating as midcareer changes are better recognized and studied.

*The concept of life stages has been modified in recent years, from envi-
sioning mainly a maxicycle to involving minicycles of growth, exploration,
establishment, maintenance, and decline, linked in a series within the maxicycle. Reexploration and reestablishment have thus attracted a great deal of
attention, and the term* transition *has come to denote these processes. . . .
Important, too, is the greater emphasis on the fact that the typical impetus
for any specific transition is not necessarily age itself, for the timing of transition (stage) is a function of the individual's personality and abilities, as
well as of his or her situation (pp. 236–237).*

Implications of Super's Life-Span, Life-Space Theory for the Practice of Career Counseling

1. Because individuals' life career development involves more than the choice of occupation and the adaptation to it (work role), career counseling should focus attention on how work roles interact with other life roles.
2. Because occupational decisions are related to other life decisions and often continue to be made throughout the life span, career counseling needs to be provided to individuals of all ages and circumstances.
3. Because career development can be described as a stage process with developmental tasks at each stage and since the nature of these stages is not linear but cyclical, earlier stages of development, counselors need to help clients understand that they are not venturing outside of normalcy when they do.
4. Because people who are at different stages of development may need to be counseled in different ways, and since people at similar stages but with different levels of career maturity also need to be counseled in different ways, it is important to learn how to use life stages and tasks to make diagnoses and select appropriate intervention strategies.

Holland's Typology of Vocational Personalities and Work Environments

Holland has a gift for making us think theory in practical terms. He opens his most recent book (Holland, 1997) stating that his theory is designed to provide some explanations for three common and fundamental questions:

1. What personal and environmental characteristics lead to satisfying career decisions, involvement, and achievement, and what characteristics lead to indecision, dissatisfying decisions, or lack of accomplishment?
2. What personal and environmental characteristics lead to stability of change in the kind and level of work a person performs over a lifetime?
3. What are the most effective methods for providing assistance to people with career problems? (p. 1).

From the beginning to the end of this book, he emphasizes the practical application of the theory. He, in fact, summarizes the theory in a few pages, leaving the rest of the book to an elaboration of practical ways to apply the theory. We will follow his lead here. The theory in its simplest terms suggests that at first people can be characterized in terms of their resemblance to each of six personality types: Realistic, Investigative, Artistic, Social, Enterprising, and Conventional (hence the reference to it as a RIASEC model). The closer they resemble a type, the more they exhibit the traits and behaviors of that type. Second, environments can be characterized as well in terms of their resemblance and support of the types. As Holland goes on to state: "...the pairing of persons and environments leads to outcomes that we can predict and understand from our knowledge of the personality types and the environmental models" (Holland, 1997, p. 2).

It should then be obvious that it is important to know all we can about how to describe the personality types and the corresponding environments. Research supports his contention that there are six distinct personality types and these types differ in terms of their interests, vocational and avocational preferences, goals, beliefs, values, and skills. Table 2–1 outlines what we know about the types and you can read elsewhere in this book about the various instruments that can be used to assess one's resemblance to the types.

To apply the theory you need to know the distinguishing features of the personality types and understand a few key principles. Table 2-1 provides a comprehensive description and an overview of the salient characteristics of the types. The table comes directly from *The Self-Directed Search Professional User's Guide* (Holland, Powell, & Fritzsche, 1994), an assessment instrument commonly used to determine one's resemblance to the types. You would do well to read this guide thoroughly if you use the instrument. You can go to the technical manual (Holland, Fritzsche & Powell, 1994b) for an even more complete description of the characteristics associated with the types.

Beyond understanding the six types and the corresponding environments, there are a number of other key principles that help one make appropriate use of the theory. These include: knowing the relationship of one type to another *(calculus)* or understanding the hexagon in Figure 2–3 (Holland, 1997, p. 6), appreciating *consistency* of the types as well as the environments, *congruence* of types with environments, *differentiation* of types, and *vocational identity*.

Calculus—Visualizing the Relationship within and between Types and Environments.

First, and probably most important, is to understand the calculus or relationship of one type to another. This is best seen visually by placing each type at a particular point and in a particular order on the hexagon (Figure 2-3). You start with Realistic, next is Investigative, Artistic, Social, Enterprising, and finally Conventional. Placed in this order (RIASEC) you can visualize the

TABLE 2–1 Personality Types and Salient Characteristics

	Realistic	Investigative	Artistic	Social	Enterprising	Conventional
Traits	Hardheaded Unassuming Practical Dogmatic Natural Uninsightful	Intellectual Curious Scholarly Open Broad Interests	Open Nonconforming Imaginative Intuitive Sensitive Creative	Agreeable Friendly Understanding Sociable Persuasive Extroverted	Extroverted Dominant Adventurous Enthusiastic Power-seeking Energetic	Conservative Unimaginative Inhibited Practical-minded Methodical
Life goals	Inventing apparatus or equipment Becoming outstanding athlete	Inventing valuable product Theoretical contribution to science	Becoming famous in performing arts Publishing stories Original painting Musical composition	Helping others Making sacrifices for others Competent teacher or therapist	Being community leader expert in finance and commerce. Being well liked and well dressed	Expert in finance and commerce Producing a lot of work
Values	Freedom Intellectual Ambitious Self-controlled Docility	Intellectual Logical Ambitious Wisdom	Equality Imaginative Courageous World of beauty	Equality Self-respect Helpful Forgiving	Freedom Ambitious (-) Forgiving (-) Helpful	(-) Imaginative (-) Forgiving
Identifications	Thomas Edison Admiral Byrd	Madame Curie Charles Darwin	T. S. Eliot Pablo Picasso	Jane Addams Albert Schweitzer	Henry Ford Andre Carnegie	Bernard Baruch John D. Rockefeller
Aptitudes and competencies	Technical	Scientific	Arts	Social and educational Leadership and sales Interpersonal	Leadership and sales Social and educational Business and clerical Interpersonal	Business and clerical
Self-ratings	Mechanical ability	Math ability Research ability	Artistic ability	——	——	Clerical ability
Most competent in	Mechanics	Science	Arts	Human relations	Leadership	Business

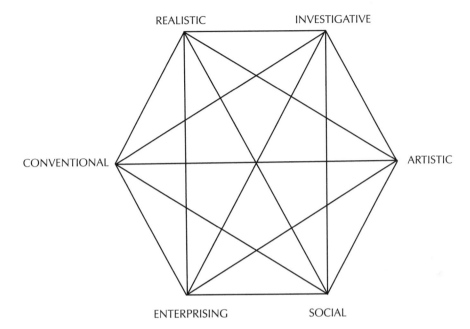

FIGURE 2–3   A Hexagonal Model for Defining the Psychological Resemblances among Personality Types and Environments and their Interactions. (Reproduced by special permission of the publisher, Psychological Assessment Resources, Inc., from *Making Vocational Choices*, copyright 1973, 1985, 1992 by Psychological Assessment Resources, Inc. All rights reserved."

resemblance of one to the other. The closer one type is to another type on the hexagon, the more it resembles the other. R and I are next to one another, for example, and these two types are close in terms of how they are described and how they can work together while R is furthest away from the Social which is a type most unlike the Realistic. A person's resemblance to the various types, ones that may be close or far away from one another, predict the ease or difficulty with finding environments that will support their particular pattern of traits.

Consistency—Defining the Relatedness between Types and Environments.

Once you understand this principle you begin to see how the theory predicts the ease or difficulty of one's making a career choice. If people identify with types that are close to one another on the hexagon, Holland defines that as being consistent. Their career exploration proceeds much easier than would be the case for those with inconsistent identifications. That would be the case for one who expresses preferences for working in environments that are across from one another on the hexagon. That concept is used in describing both the personality types and the work environments.

Congruence—Defining the Fit between Types and Environments.

It would be a logical expectation that the theory provide additional help in predicting how one will find satisfaction or dissatisfaction with a choice. For that, Holland introduces the principle of congruence, that is, thinking about the agreement between a person's personality type and the environment; i.e. the more the agreement or congruence, the more the satisfaction with the choice. When an R type finds an R environment or an I type finds an I work environment, then we are dealing with congruence; when an R type is in a social work environment or an I type is in an E or enterprising environment, then we describe it as incongruent. Predictions about the ease or difficulty of making a career choice or finding satisfaction with that choice flow in a fairly logical way from this and some other concepts still to be discussed.

Of course, this would appear to be an oversimplification of matching personalities with work environments. But when you realize all people have some identification with all six personality types, more so with some than with others, you realize that describing this theory as a matching process hardly does it justice. The same applies to the concept of work environments. All environments, while they may be described as being mainly comprised of people with particular personality patterns, we never find pure environments. Nor are people represented equally in any environment, so the matching becomes more complex both in terms of our description of it and in its practical application. Holland introduces a principle of differentiation, for example, to further refine the process.

Differentiation—Defining How Well a Person or Environment Can Be Described.

Differentiation helps one refine or modify predictions of vocational behaviors. While we all relate in some way to each of the personality types and the six environments as well, some bear much stronger resemblance to one type than to another. A highly differentiated type, for example, might strongly identify with one type and bear little or no identification with another type. A less differentiated type might bear strong resemblance with all types or no types. But employing the principle of differentiation is another way to help us make practical use of the theory.

Identity—Describing the Carity or Stability of One's Goals, Interests, and Talents.

The personality types, the work environments, principles of consistency, congruence, and differentiation, all help us think creatively in applying the theory. There is still another idea that emerged from Holland's efforts in refining the theory. That concept is vocational identity. It is establishing how clear a picture one has of his/her current career plans or simply who or where one is in a vocational sense. He developed the instrument, My Vocational Situation (Holland, Daiger, & Power, 1980; Holland et al., 1994), to measure the state of one's identity and it is described in Chapter 12. One can be assessed as having a clear or an unclear picture of career goals and of the tasks needed to become clear. The vocational identity concept, and the instrument to measure it, has proven to be another way of making practical what is offered by the theory. The theory makes clear that career decisions are easy for some and difficult for others. Offering help with decision-making, career explorations, and the like can be aided if one has a sense of the vocational identity of those requesting help. The concept can also be used to describe work environments; they too can be defined as clear or unclear in terms of goals, tasks, and rewards provided.

Vocational identity then is one more way we can add to our ability to answer the three basic questions posed by Holland. Along with the other principles discussed, we have some basis for talking about how and why people make the career decisions they do; why some are satisfied and others are not; why some persist with their career choices and others do not; and finally, why some interventions are better than others in providing career assistance.

Implications of Holland's Typology of Vocational Personalities and Work Environments for the Practice of Career Counseling

1. We can help clients *assess* their personalities and work environments and then help them see the relationships between the two. Either the Vocational Preference Inventory (VPI) or the Self-Directed Search (SDS) can help with the process. Given limited time, the Party Exercise (Bolles, 2001, p. 289) popularized in *What Color is Your Parachute? 2001* may prove effective.

2. Consider using an occupational card sort with clients that classifies all the occupational titles according to the Holland codes. Use the Occupational Dreams Inventory (ODI) to stimulate discussion of client aspirations and then assign Holland codes to the dreams (this and the SDS are described elsewhere in the text).

3. Work with clients to help them see how their traits, life goals, values, aptitudes and competencies, involvements and achievements can be associated with the match of personality with work environments.

4. Use the My Vocational Identity (MVI) to quickly establish client needs for help.
5. Consider using the Career Attitudes and Strategies Inventory (CASI) developed by Holland and Gottfredson (1994) to help employed people assess their current work environments.
6. Organize and reference your career and occupational information according to the Holland codes. Use the Holland et al. (1982) Dictionary of Occupational Titles that classifies all occupations according to the codes as a guide.

Schlossberg's Adult Career Development Transition Model

The transition model provides a systematic framework for counselors, psychologists, social workers, and others as they listen to the many stories—each one unique—of colleagues, friends, and clients. The transitions differ, the individuals differ, but the structure for understanding individuals in transition is stable (Schlossberg, Waters, & Goodman, 1995, p. 26).

The Adult Career Development Transition Model has three major parts according to Schlossberg, Waters, and Goodman (1995). The first part focuses on approaching the transition including transition identification and process. The second part deals with identifying coping resources while the third part emphasizes strategies that can be used to take charge of the transition.

Approaching Transitions

To understand transitions it is important to identify the type. Schlossberg, Waters, and Goodman (1995) identified three types. The first type is the anticipated transition. This transition is caused by expected events that occur as a part of one's life cycle. The second type is the unanticipated transition that occurs caused by life events that are not predictable. It is not planned for. The last type is called the non-event transition. This type of transition is caused by events anticipated and planned for but which did not happen.

In understanding transitions it also is important to appreciate that what is anticipated by one individual may not be by another. The context of the events that shape transitions is another important consideration. Does the event occur to the individual or to another person? Is it personal or interpersonal? Finally, the impact of the transition on the individual is important to consider. Sometimes too, transitions come in bunches; while an individual is experiencing one transition, other transitions occur at the same time.

The Transition Process

"Although the onset of a transition may be linked to one identifiable event or non-event, transitions are really a process over time" (Schlossberg, Waters, & Goodman, 1995, p. 35). While in transitions, clients pass through a series of identifiable phases. At first transitions are pervasive. There is often total preoccupation with the transitions and the complete disruption in clients' lives. There is a disbelief ("This can't be happening"), then a sense of betrayal ("I worked for this organization for thirty years"), confusion ("What do I do now?"), anger (I'll sue somebody!"), and finally, after a period of time, resolution ("I have many skills and I can get another job!").

It is tempting to oversimplify these phases and what is involved in them. Schlossberg, Waters, and Goodman (1995), stressed that transitions often contain many complex dynamics and that their satisfactory resolution depends on the characteristics of the clients and the nature of the contexts in which the transitions take place. Sometimes, for some clients, transitions end in deterioration. There is no satisfactory resolution.

How do counselors assess where clients are in the transition process? Schlossberg advised starting with clients' perceptions, because some clients view where they are in transitions differently from other clients who are involved in the same transitions. Another means of appraisal is to assess how preoccupied clients are with their transitions. Schlossberg (1984, p. 56) suggested that the continuum counselors are assessing begins with "pervasiveness," (transitions completely permeate clients' attitudes and behaviors) and ends with "boundedness" (transitions are contained and integrated into clients' self-concepts). Finally, measures of life satisfaction can be used to assess where clients are in their transitions, the assumption being that clients will express more satisfaction with their lives as they move toward transition resolution.

Factors that Influence Transitions

Schlossberg, Waters, and Goodman (1995) pointed out that there are four major factors that influence how individuals handle transitions. They are the situation, the self, support, and strategies. These are shown graphically in Figure 2–4.

The Situation   What are the variables characterizing the transition that counselors need to understand? Some of these variables are: the trigger (what triggered the transition?), timing (does the transition relate to the social clock?), the source (where does control lie?), role change (does the transition involve role change?), duration (permanent or temporary?), previous experience with similar transitions, and concurrent stress.

The Self   To understand the coping resources clients have available, it also is necessary to identify their personal situation, and psychological resources. Personal and demographic variables that need to be considered include socioeconomic status, culture/race/ethnicity, gender role, age and stage of life, and state of health. Psychological resources encompass variables related to ego development, personality, outlook, and commitment and values.

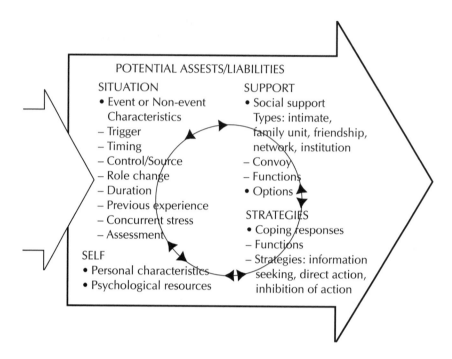

FIGURE 2–4   Coping Resources—The 4 S's

According to Schlossberg, Waters, and Goodman (1995), the following questions can be used to assess clients self:

- Are they able to deal with the world in an autonomous way? Can they tolerate ambiguity?
- Are they optimists? Do they see the glass as half-full or half-empty?
- Do they blame themselves for what happens?
- Do they feel in control of their response to the transition?
- Do they believe that their efforts will affect the outcomes of a particular course of action? (p. 67)

Support   The last category of variables to be considered are those that focus on clients' environments. As counselors work with clients in transitions, it is important to consider the social support clients have (intimate relationships, family, friendship network, and institutions), functions of the support available to them (affect, affirmation, aid, and feedback), and their options—actual, perceived, used, and created.

The following questions can be used to assess support:

- *Is this client getting what he/she needs for the transition in terms of affect? Affirmation? Aid?*

- *Does the client have the range of support—spouse or partner, other close family or friends, co-workers/colleagues/neighbors, organizations, strangers, and institutions?*
- *Has the client's support system . . . been interrupted by this transition?*
- *Does the client feel the support system for this transition is a low or high resource? (Schlossberg, Waters, & Goodman, 1995, p. 70).*

Strategies   Coping responses can be subdivided into functions (controlling the situation, its meaning, and the associated stress) and strategies (information seeking, direct action, and the inhibition of action). The following questions can help assess ways of coping:

- *Does the client use a range of strategies?*   *Yes   No*
- *Does the client sometimes take action to change*   *Yes   No*
  the transition?
- *Does the client sometimes try to change the*   *Yes   No*
  meaning of the transition?
- *Does the client try to take stress in stride?*   *Yes   No*
- *Does the client know when to do nothing?*   *Yes   No*
- *Does the client feel that he/she can flexibly*   *Yes   No*
  choose different strategies depending on the
  challenge at hand?
- *Taking all the above into account, does the*
  client rate his/her

  Strategies as:

  A high resource   *Yes   No*
  A low resource   *Yes   No*
  A mixed bag   *Yes   No*
  Okay   *Yes   No*
  (Schlossberg, Waters, & Goodman, 1995, p. 76)

Implications of Schlossberg's Adult Career Development Transition Model for the Practice of Career Counseling

1. Because more individuals are changing occupations at later stages of their career development, counselors should be open to clients who want to change and should understand and empathize with the frustration, pain, and joy involved in the transition process.
2. Because clients who are going through transitions are often experiencing anxiety and emotional upheaval, it is essential to provide a safe environment—a counseling relationship that focuses on the use of listening and responding skills, and attending and focusing skills.
3. Because clients involved in transitions often have difficulty reframing and refocusing their situations, counselors need to provide new perspec-

tives to them through interpretation, theme identification, and the presentation of internal and external information.

4. Because clients involved in transitions usually need assistance in moving on, it is important to help them develop problem-solving, decision-making, and coping skills.

5. Because social support is a key to successfully coping with transitions, counselors should provide clients with skills that aid them in developing social support systems and networks.

Lent, Brown, and Hackett's Social Cognitive Career Theory (SCCT)

Social cognitive career theory (SCCT; Lent, Brown, & Hackett, 1994) is a relatively new theory in comparison to the foundational theories of Super and Holland. It is unique from the other theories in its "focus on the personal constructions that people place on events related to career decision making." (Swanson & Fouad, 1999, p. 125). It has also been noted for its utility in explaining the vocational behaviors of racial and ethnic groups and for its greater attention to contextual factors that influence career development. Indeed, since this theory was proposed, it has spawned several research studies with racially diverse samples (e.g., Flores & O'Brien, in press; Fouad & Smith, 1996; Gainor & Lent, 1998; Morrow, Gore & Campbell, 1996; Tang, Fouad, & Smith, 1999).

Lent and his colleagues (1994) developed this comprehensive theory to explain three intricately linked aspects of career development (a) the development of interests, (b) the choice of educational and career options, and (c) performance and persistence in educational and vocational realms. Lent et al. (1994) extended Bandura's (1986) Social Cognitive Theory and Hackett and Betz's (1981) career self-efficacy theory to develop this theory of career development that hypothesized the influence of individual and contextual factors on the sociocognitive mechanisms of self-efficacy, outcome expectations, and goals, and their influence on interests, actions, and performance. In this chapter, we will briefly describe the three components of the model but refer the reader to the original monograph which describes each component in a great deal more depth (Lent et al., 1994).

Figure 2–5 depicts the theorized sociocognitive determinants of interests. Thus, the theory hypothesizes that self-efficacy beliefs and outcome expectancies both predict academic and career interests. Self-efficacy beliefs are defined as "people's judgments of their capabilities to organize and execute courses of action required to attain designated types of performance" (Bandura, 1986, p. 391). Outcome expectancies are defined as "personal beliefs about probable response outcomes" (Lent et al., 1994, p. 83). Thus, beliefs about their abilities in particular areas and their beliefs about probable

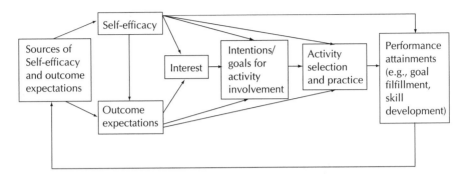

FIGURE 2–5   Model of How Basic Career Interests Develop Over Time. This Model Highlights Cognitive and Behavioral Influences During Childhood and Adolescence

outcomes both lead to the development of interests. These interests (together with self-efficacy beliefs and outcome expectancies) predict goals which in turn lead to the selection of activities and the practice of activities. This in turn leads to performance attainment (e.g., goal fulfillment and attainment), trying out various activities and feeling successful at them. Thus, our perceptions of self-efficacy and outcome likelihood are hypothesized to figure prominently into the development of our career interests.

Figure 2–6 depicts a model of career choice. This part of the theory proposes that "person inputs" which refer to variables of individual differences, including genetic or inherited characteristics (predisposition, gender, race/ethnicity, disability/health status) and background and contextual factors together influence learning experiences which influence both self-efficacy beliefs and outcome expectancies. These, as described in the previous section, then influence interests, goals, choice actions, and performance attainment.

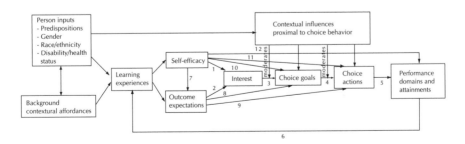

FIGURE 2–6   Model of Person, Contextual, and Experimental Factors Affecting Career-Related Choice Behavior.

Figure 2–7 depicts the portion of the theory that predicts performance level. Different from the first two segments of the model which involve the content of career choice, this last segment predicts the level of performance toward which one would aspire in any given career field. Thus, this segment predicts that ability and past performance lead to both self-efficacy beliefs and outcome expectations. These in turn lead to the performance of subgoals, and to performance attainment.

Implications of Lent, Brown, and Hackett's Social Cognitive Career Theory for the Practice of Career Counseling

1. Counselors should help clients examine the importance of the learning process and the specific learning experiences that they have had that have helped to shape their current career path.
2. Specifically, it would suggest an investigation of how previous learning has helped to shape both clients confidence or self-efficacy about their career plans, but also how these experiences may have shaped their outcome expectations, and eventual career interests.
3. It may be very useful to examine how career related self-efficacy beliefs developed and what barriers the clients experienced in the development of their confidence around various career-related experiences.
4. The theory would emphasize the need to carefully examine person inputs such as gender, race, sexual orientation, level of ability or disability, and social class, in the formation of self-efficacy beliefs.

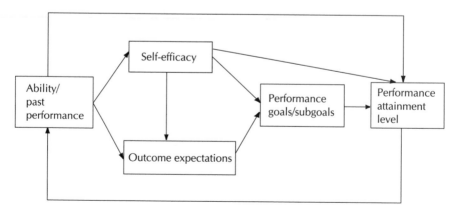

FIGURE 2–7   Model of Task Performance, Highlighting the Roles of Ability, Self-Efficacy, Outcome, Expectations, and Performance Goals.

5. It may also be helpful to examine past performance attainment and the client's perceptions of future performance goals. Specifically, examining both the clients' self-efficacy beliefs and their outcome expectancies with regard to their future performance level would be useful.

6. In this theory, an important role for counselors is in helping the client examine positive and realistic expectations for themselves and helping them develop specific goals to meet these expectations.

APPROACHES TO CAREER DEVELOPMENT

Planned Happenstance

One of the earliest approaches (Parsons, 1909) emphasized applying logic or "sound reasoning" to the process of career planning. We find such thinking useful and clients respond well to logical explanations as to how they should proceed with their career planning. We encourage clients not to leave things to chance, but rather to carefully plan their careers. Talking decisions through with us will help them make better choices; and we believe we have skills that can aid them with the process. However, we also recognize that in our own planning, as well as in what we hear from others, chance or happenstance often assumes a significant role. We just do not know how to talk about it or whether we should pay much attention to it.

The Role of Chance in Career Planning

Krumboltz (1998) argues, in our efforts to be as rational as possible, whether using a social learning theory or any other theory, we may have overlooked the importance of happenstance. But we encounter it so often we cannot ignore it, even though we think we cannot plan for it. Krumboltz is not the only one who has advanced this idea. He cites others who acknowledge the place of happenstance in their theories (Bandura, 1982; Betsworth & Hansen, 1996; Cabral & Salomone, 1990), but he contends they are not explicit about incorporating it. Planned happenstance interventions, he claims, should be designed to "assist clients to generate, recognize, and incorporate chance events into their career development" (Mitchell, Levin and Krumboltz, 1999).

Acknowledging Chance in Our Own Career Planning

Krumboltz suggests that we examine how chance may have played a role in own our planning. Being someplace at the right time, meeting a certain person by chance, casually being introduced to an opportunity or a job, being laid off and then finding an opportunity in an entirely new field, are all examples of happenstance assuming a role in our lives. What may be important is learning how to recognize and use such opportunities in our career planning.

Reexamining Our Role As Career Counselors

Incorporating happenstance may mean we need to encourage clients to be open-minded. When one comes to us for help in career planning we often assume our role is to resolve ambiguity, reduce anxiety, find quick solutions, administer interests tests, or deliver a barrage of career information. But an alternative might be to help clients become comfortable with their present situation so they can remain open to opportunities that constantly present themselves; opportunities that will not be recognized while they are under such stress. Uncertainty too often narrows our perspective and thinking and happenstance is then not seen for what it could be.

Uncertainty Has Its Merits

Gelatt (1989) proposed that being uncertain about career goals might be what will lead one to discover new ideas or opportunities. Once decided, we tend to focus only on affirming our choice. We may not be as open to seeing chance events as new opportunities. Helping one tolerate the ambiguity of not knowing, then may emerge as an appropriate task for career counselors.

Skills Needed to Promote Planned Happenstance

Planned happenstance, according to Mitchell, Levin, and Krumboltz, (1999) includes two concepts: "(a) exploration generates chance opportunities ..., and (b) skills enable people to seize opportunities" (p. 118). The necessary skills to promote opportunities are five in number: curiosity, persistence, flexibility, optimism and risk-taking. It should not surprise us that Krumboltz and his colleagues would suggest our role is to help clients learn new skills. That is a major theme in his social learning theory (Krumboltz, 1979); it also is a theme in planned happenstance. Again, he is not alone in arguing that learning is an important part of our role as career counselors. We lean heavily on seeing our role as educators and thus we need to help clients learn how to incorporate happenstance into their career planning.

Implications of Planned Happenstance for the Practice of Career Counseling

If you accept that happenstance should be considered a major factor in determining what one does or becomes, then obviously we need to consider ways to make it happen. That is, we need to consider how to plan for it. That may suggest we change our thinking so as not to minimize its importance but rather to recognize and find ways to increase its importance in the career counseling process.

To incorporate happenstance into our work, we challenge commonly held wisdom about the way we do career planning. Can we be seen as advocating that "indecision," for example, should not be stigmatized as undesirable, but rather as a desirable stance? Can we be seen as advocates for open-mindedness as a stance that may most help one find direction? Why not! We do not see that as radical, nor if presented properly, do we see it as a point of view that will not gain acceptance. We may be slow in documenting the illusive role of happenstance, but we can be quick to cite convincing examples of its importance. Like any new idea that challenges the traditional way of thinking, we should expect resistance. Studies documenting its importance are beginning to appear (Williams et al., 1998), and we expect you will see more attention to this point of view in the next few years.

Mitchell, Levin, and Krumboltz, (1999) after giving countless examples of happenstance in career planning, offers what they say may be somewhat radical advice for career counselors. Here are their five suggestions:

1. *Acknowledge that it is normal, inevitable, and desirable for unplanned events to influence careers.*
2. *Think of indecision not as a problem to be remedied, but as a state of planful open-mindedness that will enable clients to capitalize on unforeseen future events.*
3. *Teach clients to take advantage of unplanned events as opportunities to try new activities, develop new interests, challenge old beliefs, and continue lifelong learning.*
4. *Teach clients to initiate actions to increase the likelihood of beneficial unplanned events in the future.*
5. *Follow through with clients to provide continuing support for their learning throughout their careers (p. 123).*

Race/Gender Ecological Model of Career Development

Another even newer model that may be useful in understanding contextual factors in the vocational development of individuals was developed by Cook, Heppner, and O'Brien (2001). They used an ecological model to develop what they title a Race/Gender Ecological approach to career development. The ecological model states that human behavior results from the ongoing, dynamic interaction between the person and the environment. Behavior is the result of a multiplicity of factors at the individual, interpersonal, and broader sociocultural levels. Vocational behavior can then be understood as an "act-in-context" (Landrine, 1995, p. 5) where the context is essential to the naming and meaningfulness of the individual's behavior.

Bronfenbrenner (1977) developed the most widely cited ecological model and it is the one Cook and her colleagues use as their guiding theoretical framework. Bronfenbrenner (1977) identified four major subsystems influencing human behavior: (a) the microsystem which includes the interpersonal interactions within a given environment such as home, school or work setting; (b) the mesosystem which constitutes interaction between two or more microsystems such as the relation between an individual's school and her work environment; (c) the exosystem which consists of linkages between subsystems that indirectly influences the individual, such as one's neighborhood or the media; and the (d) macrosystem which are the ideological components of a given society including norms and values.

The Race/Gender Ecological Model of career development, as depicted in Figure 2–8, recognizes that by their very nature, humans live interactionally in a social environment. The model recognizes that every person has both a gender and a race and that these factors decisively shape the individual's career throughout life, as she or he encounters opportunities or obstacles because of race or gender. It reminds us that career behavior does not occur in a vacuum, but rather emerges from a lifelong dynamic interaction between the person and her or his environment.

In addition, career behavior is thought to be determined by the interrelationships between the subsystems in a larger ecosystem (Bronfenbrenner, 1977). Implicit in the model is the knowledge that interrelationships occur simultaneously on multiple levels, so that a focus on any one level of interaction is by definition a limited picture of the dynamics shaping career behavior at any one time. The model also recognizes that although individuals of the same biological sex or race may encounter similar circumstances because of their demographics, each career path is unique because of individual circumstances, and the unique interactions of their subsystems. Clients bring their ecosystems into counseling primarily by conveying how they understand and react to it. For example, perceptions of opportunities or the lack of opportunities, positive or negative comparisons of self to desired models, optimistic or pessimistic conceptions of the future, or internalization of stereotypes as per-

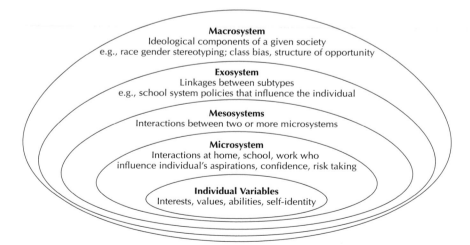

FIGURE 2–8   Race/Gender Ecological Model. (From Cook, Heppner, & O'Brien, 2001. Reprinted with permission.)

sonally salient or irrelevant. Individuals are also thought to shape the environment around them in complex ways as they overtly reward or punish the career behaviors of others.

In applying the Race/Gender Ecological Model, an example might be helpful. The larger culture operating as a macrosystem perpetuates career myths and stereotypes related to race and gender and, in fact, institutionalize forms of race/gender discrimination. This macrosystem embodies values such as white male privilege, Eurocentric world views, race/gender appropriate ideologies or race/gender typing of occupational choices. Macrosystem values may be internalized by the individual (e.g., internalized oppression), and on the microsystem level influence how others treat a people because of their gender or race.

Implications of the Race/Gender Ecological Model for the Practice of Career Counseling

1. The model reminds the career counselor that we can change the person–environment interaction in numerous ways for any given client. Examples include changing the environment through counselor or client initiatives, helping the client identify and practice skills to cope with the environment more effectively, and addressing the client's cognitive processes which shape their transactions with the environment.
2. In addition to more traditional career counseling interventions that help the individual alter perceptions about desirable and appropriate career alternatives, this model calls on counselors to serve as client advocates working toward environmental and societal changes that may facilitate the development of present and future clients.
3. Careful assessment of the client's ecosystem determines how and where career counseling interventions can be most effectively implemented for an individual.
4. The counselor serves as a liaison, working as a partner with the client to effect more successful and satisfying interactions with the world of work.
5. The counselor uses diverse methodologies and emphasizes that clients are best served when a diverse range of conceptualizations and interventions are considered.
6. The model requires a range of skills not typically required in intrapsychically oriented interventions, but respects the complexity of influences shaping an individual's life over time.

Career Intervention and Change Approach

Much has been written to suggest that the career theories and models just described are not adequate in explaining how people of various cultures do their career planning. As our society becomes more multicultural and counselors from diverse cultures find themselves working with clients from a host of diverse backgrounds, we must cautiously apply our trusted but not necessarily true theories for others. Our professional journals report numerous studies that test established theories on culturally diverse samples; some document similarities but others report real differences. It will take a long time before we know and understand all the ways our theories apply and differ in diverse samples.

There is another way to recognize and work effectively with these differences whatever they are. It may be a way that will prove safer and more productive for practice at least in the short run. We can proceed as if everyone has his or her own personal career theory (PCT). To do so would be to adopt the goal of first uncovering that personal "theory" and then helping clients assess its effectiveness rather than applying pre-existing theory. It would change our role as a career counselor. However, it might give us opportunity to be of help in ways we can at first only dimly perceive. Throughout the process, we would not risk misunderstanding our client, and we would learn more about cultural and individual differences firsthand. We will describe personal career theory within a context that Holland (1997) describes as a "Theory of Career Intervention and Change" (p. 205). The content and structure can be thought of in much the same way as we did the hexagonal or RIASEC model advanced by Holland. We will conclude with some ways to make use of it and suggest how it could have profound impact on the way you see yourself as a career counselor.

In presenting this as the last model or approach in this chapter, we recognize it as a new way of looking at career theory. We see obvious implications and we hope you will too. It is not clear how much it will lead to revisions and refinements in other theories, but we can be certain that it will help counselors of diverse backgrounds transition to serving a much more diverse population.

Defining the Career Intervention and Change Approach
Holland (1997) offers three basic assumptions for this approach: (a) Everyone has a theory about careers, i.e., everyone has a "personal career theory" (PCT, p. 205); (b) When that theory does not seem to work they seek help of some sort, sometimes from professionals like us; (c) When asked, we can provide interventions that will help one implement, revise, or refine that theory. It follows that a first step for us in working with a client is to do what we can to understand their PCT. Holland offers that we apply a diagnostic scheme as we listen. We can listen for evidence of how we should best describe the theory. He suggests that we think of the PCT in terms of three dimensions: its validity, its complexity, and its comprehensiveness. When a client comes for help, we define interventions based on what we have come to know as most effective given these particulars of the theory. We cannot stress how important it becomes then to listen for all the clues as to how both to describe the

theory and also to come to know what works best to help one implement, refine, or revise the theory.

To provide a framework for using this approach, we suggest one start with the three continua suggested by Holland (1997, pp. 205–206) and listen for what clients provide until you can judge where it belongs along each of the three dimensions offered below (Gottfredson & Cook, 1984; Prochaska, Norcross, & DiClemente, 1994):

Assessing One's Personal Career Theory
1. invalid . . . . valid
2. primitive . . . . complex
3. incomplete . . . . comprehensive

You can then let your experience guide you with what works best if you need to help with implementation of an only somewhat valid theory or a refinement of a primitive theory, or maybe the revision of an incomplete theory. Clearly we will begin to see particular interventions as being more effective with one versus another kind of PCT.

Holland (1997), always at the forefront with suggestions for implementing ideas, offers, for example, a "four-level diagnostic and treatment plan" (p. 207):

> *Level 1 for people with valid [complex and comprehensive] personal theories . . .*
>
> *Level 2 for people whose theories have an occupational knowledge section that requires extension, revision, or adaptation to an unusual work or unemployment situation;*
>
> *Level 3 for people whose theories have a weak translation unit or lack a reliable formula for relating personal characteristics to occupations, special occupational roles, or specialization, or for managing job changes;*
>
> *Level 4 for people whose personal theory has pervasive weaknesses. . . . (pp. 207–208) "*

Level 1 describes people who need little help as they have a well-developed PCT while Level 2 people need some help with at least some part of their theory—a minor extension, revision, or adaptation may suffice. Level 3 people have difficulties in seeing themselves in particular occupations or making changes in their jobs. They need substantial help, probably one-on-one career counseling focused on resolving a particular weakness in their thinking. Level 4, however, needs extensive help as there are major flaws or weaknesses in their PCT.

While not the last word or not as fully developed a diagnostic system as will be forthcoming in time, it does help us begin to think of clients as truly unique in terms of what they bring to us. It suggests that our experience is important in helping us develop and provide appropriate career services for each and everyone. While we may have something for everyone, it should not be the same for everyone.

Implications of the Career Intervention and Change Approach to the Practice of Career Counseling

1. As counselors we need to recognize that every person has a personal career theory that informs his or her life decisions. Our role is to help them articulate and refine that theory.
2. We can encourage clients to describe how they understand their PCT and while they are talking, we can be thinking about its validity, complexity, and comprehensiveness.
3. If the client has developed a personal career theory that seems valid, complex, and comprehensive, perhaps what is needed most is career information and reassurance that he/she seems on the right track.
4. If parts of the PCT seem to lack validity (e.g. conclusions built on faulty reasoning, irrational beliefs) or are overly simplified understandings or incomplete in important ways, the counselor can then help "flesh out" the theory to help clients better describe their life circumstances.
5. All of the other theories and models presented in this chapter can be used in helping individuals "flesh out" a personal career theory. For example, one might help them understand where they are in their developmental progression (Super); how their choices reflect person-environment fit (Holland); how their self-efficacy and outcome expectations may be influencing their interests, choices or goal attainment (Lent, Brown, & Hackett); how being in a transition is influencing their life course (Scholssberg); how macro, exo, meso, and micro forces are shaping and reshaping their choices (Cook, Heppner, & O'Brien) and how chance events have shaped and will continue to shape their life course (Krumboltz).

Thus, in some ways TCIC can be seen as recognizing individual differences and how various aspects of career theory can be applied to help clients describe their own unique career paths. Ultimately our theories must "ring true" to the people they are designed to help. They must be seen as useful in actually explaining career behavior. By encouraging our clients to design their own personal career theories we capitalize on their own wealth of self-understanding, which may ultimately lead to the most valid, complex, and comprehensive theories for them to use in guiding their own life pattern.

CLOSING THOUGHTS

Career theories should ultimately help our clients understand the story of their lives and the role that work and other important life roles have in that story. The theories and approaches in this chapter are meant to provide a starting point for counselors as they work with clients in understanding these unique life stories. Although some counselors work from a "unitheoretical" stance (Savickas, 1996, p. 193) in which they see all client behavior through one theoretical lens, most effective counselors find "theoretical eclecticism" (p. 193) as a more useful stance. They seek to help clients understand their career behavior by flexibly using a repertoire of different theories and approaches depending on the circumstances and life context of the individual client.

From our own experience, we have found theory to be an invaluable guide in our work with clients. The more knowledgeable we are about various theories and approaches the more flexibly we can use them and the more helpful we ultimately are in working with clients. This flexibility does not come quickly or easily, but rather out of many years of study, reflection, and practice. It comes from reading these theories in their original form, rather than relying solely on the brief summaries provided in texts like ours. It comes from thinking deeply about the strengths and shortcomings of each theory for various populations, and it comes from years of work with individual clients, seeing firsthand what works best for what clients under what circumstances.

The ultimate test of any theory is in its ability to provide clarity and insight to clients about their life journey. We hope that the theories and approaches briefly provided here will help you in working with your clients as they try to explore, expand, and understand their own fascinating life stories.

REFERENCES

Bandura, A. (1982). The psychology of chance encounters and life paths. *American Psychologist, 37*, 747–755.

Bandura, A. (1986). *Social foundations of thought and action: A social cognitive theory.* Englewood Cliffs, NJ: Prentice Hall.

Betsworth, D. G., & Hansen, J-I. C. (1996). The categorization of serendipitous career development events. *Journal of Career Assessment, 4*, 91–98.

Bolles, R. N. (2001). *What color is your parachute? 2001.* Berkeley, CA: Ten Speed Press.

Bronfenbrenner, U. (1977). Toward an experimental ecology of human development. *American Psychologist, 32(7)*, 513–531.

Buehler, C. (1933). *Der menschliche lebenslauf als psychologiches problem.* Leipzig: Hirzel.

Cabral, A. C., & Salomone, P. R. (1990). Chance and careers: Normative versus contextual development. *The Career Development Quarterly, 39*, 5–17.

Cook, E. P., Heppner, M. J. & O'Brien, K. M. (2001). Career development of women of color and White women: Assumptions, conceptualizations, and interventions from an ecological perspective. *Career Development Quarterly.*

Davidson, P .E., & Anderson, H. D. (1937). *Occupational mobility in an American community.* Stanford, CA: Stanford University Press.

Fisher, I. (1989). *Midlife change.* Unpublished doctoral dissertation, Teachers College, Columbia University.

Flores, L. Y., & O'Brien, K. M. (in press). The career development of Mexican American adolescent women: A test of social cognitive career theory. *Journal of Counseling Psychology.*

Fouad, N., & Smith, P. L., (1996). A test of a social cognitive model for middle school students: math and science. *Journal of Counseling Psychology, 43,* 338–346.

Gainor, K. A., & Lent, R. W. (1998). Social cognitive expectations and racial identity attitudes in predicting the math choice intentions of Black college students. *Journal of Counseling Psychology, 45,* 403–413.

Gelatt, H. B. (1989). Positive uncertainty: A new decision-making framework for counseling. *Journal of Counseling Psychology, 36,* 252–256.

Ginzberg, E., Ginsburg, J. W., Axelrod, S., & Herma, J. L. (1951). *Occupational choice.* New York: Columbia University Press.

Gottfredson, G. D., & Cook, M. S. (1984). The psychology of everyday life: A theory of persons and environments with implications for social control. Unpublished manuscript.

Gottfredson, G. D., Holland, J. L., & Ogawa, D. K. (1982). *Dictionary of Holland occupational codes.* Palo Alto, CA: Consulting Psychologist Press.

Hackett, G., & Betz, N. E. (1981). A self-efficacy approach to the career development of women. *Journal of Vocational Behavior, 18,* 326–339.

Holland, J. L. (1977). *Manual for the Vocational Preference Inventory.* Palo Alto, CA: Consulting Psychologist Press.

Holland, J. L. (1997). *Making vocational choices.* Odessa, FL: Psychological Assessment Resources.

Holland, J. L., Daiger, D. C., & Power, P. G. (1980). Some diagnostic scales for research in decision-making and personality: Identity, information and barriers. *Journal of Personality and Social Psychology, 39,* 1191–1200.

Holland, J. L., Fritzsche, B. A., & Powell, A. B. (1994). *The Self-Directed Search technical manual.* Odessa, FL: Psychological Assessment Resources.

Holland, J. L., & Gottfredson, G. D. (1994). *Career Attitudes and Strategies Inventory.* Odessa, FL: Psychological Assessment Resources.

Holland, J. L., Powell. A. B., & Fritzsche, B. A. (1994). *The Self-Directed Search professional user's guide.* Odessa, FL: Psychological Assessment Resources.

Jordaan, J. P., & Heyde, M. B. (1979). *Vocational maturity during the high-school years.* New York: Teachers College Press.

Krumboltz, J. D. (1979). A social learning theory of career decision-making. In A. M. Mitchell, G. B. Jones, & J. D. Krumboltz (Eds.), *Social learning and career decision-making* (pp. 19–49). Cranston, RI: Carroll Press.

Krumboltz, J. D. (1998). Serendipity is not serendipitous. Journal of Counseling Psychology, 45, 390–392.

Landrine, H. (1995). *Bringing cultural diversity to feminist psychology: theory, research, and practice* (pp. 1–20). Washington, DC: American Psychological Association.

Lent, R. W., Brown, S . D., & Hackett, G. (1994). Toward a unifying social cognitive theory of career and academic interest, choice, and performance. *Journal of Vocational Behavior, 45,* 79–122.

Mitchell, K. E., Levin, A. S., & Krumboltz, J. D. (1999). Planned happenstance: Constructing unexpected career opportunities. *Journal of Counseling and Development, 77,* 115–124.

Morrow, S. L., Gore, P. A., & Campbell, B. W. (1996). The application of a sociocognitive framework to the career development of lesbian women and gay men. *Journal of Vocational Behavior, 48,* 136–148.

Niles, S. G. (2001). Using Super's career development assessment and counseling (C-DAC) model to link theory and practice. *International Journal for Educational and Vocational Guidance, 1,* 131–139.

Parsons, F. (1909). *Choosing a vocation.* Boston: Houghton Mifflin.

Prochaska, J. O., Norcross, J. C., & DiClemente, C. C. (1994). *Changing for good.* New York: Morrow.

Savickas, M. L. (1996) A framework for linking career theory and practices. In M. L. Savickas, & W. B. Walsh. *Handbook of Career Counseling Theory and Practice.* Palo Alto CA Davies-Block Publishing Company.

Schlossberg, N. K. (1984). *Counseling adults in transition: Linking practice with theory.* New York: Springer Publishing Company.

Schlossberg, N. K., Waters, E. B., & Goodman, J. (1995). *Counseling adults in transition: Linking practice with theory* (2nd ed) New York: Springer Publishing Company.

Shertzer, B., & Stone, S. C. (1980) *Fundamentals of Counseling* (3rd ed). Boston: Houghton Mifflin.

Super, D. E. (1942). *The dynamics of vocational adjustments.* New York: Harper-Collins.

Super, D. E. (1953). A theory of vocational development. *American Psychologist, 8,* 185–190.

Super, D. E. (1985). Coming of age in Middletown: Careers in the making. *American Psychologist, 40,* 405–414.

Super, D. E. (1990). A life-span, life-space approach to career development. In D. Brown, L. Brooks, & Associates. *Career choice and Development* (2nd ed.). San Francisco, CA: Jossey-Bass.

Super, D. E., Osborne, W. L., Walsh, D. J., Brown, S. D., & Niles, S. G. (1992). Development career assessment and counseling. *Journal of Counseling & Development, 71,* 74–80.

Super, D. E., & Overstreet, P. L. (1960). *The vocational maturity of ninth-grade boys.* New York: Teachers College Press.

Super, D. E., Savickas, M. L., & Super, C. M. (1996). The life-span, life-space approach to careers. In D. Brown, L. Brooks, & Associates. *Career Choice and Development* (3rd ed.). San Francisco, CA: Jossey-Bass.

Swanson, J. L. & Fouad, N. A. (1999). *Career Theory and Practice.* Thousand Oaks, CA: Sage.

Tang, M., Fouad, N. A., & Smith, P. L. (1999). Asian Americans' career choices: A path model to examine factors influencing their career choices. *Journal of Vocational Behavior, 54,* 42–157.

Williams, E. N., Soeprapto, E., Like, K., Touradji, P., Hess, S., & Hill, C. E. (1998). Perceptions of serendipity: Career paths of prominent women in counseling psychology. *Journal of Counseling Psychology, 45,* 379–389.

▶ 3

Empowering Life Choices

Career Counseling in Cultural Contexts

*If vocational counseling was born from the changing
demographics and economic needs of this century,
then clearly career counseling will need to change in
response to the changing needs of the coming century.*
—*(BINGHAM & WARD, 1994, P. 168).*

There are four major goals of this chapter. First, we will examine how the historical and social factors that provided the impetus for the birth of the field of career development resulted in five tenets based on western European cultural values which have through the century dramatically influenced our theory, research, and practice. Second, we will briefly discuss the demographic and ethical imperatives for expanding the field of career development. Third, we will examine three critical individual differences constructs which have major impact on the career development of racial and ethnic minorities: world view, racial identity development, and acculturation. And fourth, we will outline the role of cultural contexts in all aspects of career counseling from recognition of the need for assistance through post counseling follow-up.

(This chapter was written in collaboration with Helen A. Neville, Ph.D. Dr. Neville is an Associate Professor in Psychology at the University of Illinois)

It is important to note that there are a number of excellent books available that can provide information about the career development of racial and ethnic minority group members. For example, Walsh, Bingham, Brown, and Ward's (2001) book *Career Counseling for African Americans,* and Leong's (1995) book *Career Development and Vocational Behavior of Racial and Ethnic Minorities* are two of the growing body of resources that provide helpful information in this area.

DEFINITIONS OF TERMS

Although there appears to be considerable interchangeability in the literature related to word usage, in this chapter we will use the terms *ethnicity, race,* and *culture* as described below. In addition, since the construct of social class is contextually interwoven with that of race and ethnicity, we discuss how we define this construct as well. Ethnicity, or ethnic origin, refers to a group of people who share a unique sociogeographical and often cultural heritage. The sociogeographical customs (e.g., language, religion, food, dance, values, etc.) commonly associated with specific ethnic groups are passed down from one generation to the next. Examples of ethnic groups include Italian, Ethiopian, Sioux, Korean American, and African American.

On the other hand, race has been generally defined in the social science literature in two ways: natural/biological race and social race. The concept of natural race refers to a shared genotype or physiology that often is outwardly manifested in a group's phenotype or physical characteristics such as hair texture, body type, facial features, and skin pigmentation. Biologists and social scientists have long challenged the concept of natural races and have all but abandoned this usage. One reason for this desertion is the difficulty in defining a "pure" race; for example, the presence of offspring from "racially" different parents questions the validity of race as purely natural or biological. Moreover, social scientists have argued that one's physiology is not related to social behaviors or personality styles.

Currently, most social scientists view race as a social construct; that is, race is socially defined within a particular society or nation. Social race encompasses the shared sociohistorical experiences of a group of people (e.g., slavery and Black liberation movements for Blacks throughout the diaspora); shared experiences and social relationships between races significantly affect one's beliefs, behaviors, and sociopolitical and economic conditions. In the United States, five major "racial" groups have been constructed: Native American, Asian/Asian American, Black, Hispanic/Latina/o, and White. Within each of these social races are numerous ethnic groups such as Cherokee, Chinese American, African American, Chicano/Mexican American, and German American. White individuals have been identified as the majority race because they are the numerical majority in the United States and, more-over, they have political and economic power.

Culture is an important concept that is related, but not equivalent, to race and ethnicity. In general, culture refers to the attitudes, values, norms, and behaviors of a social group. Members of racial and ethnic groups often acquire or learn the values and behaviors of their social group through a pro-cess of enculturation or racial/ethnic socialization. However, just because someone is racially or ethnically in one group, he or she is not necessarily cul-turally affiliated with the attitudes, values, or norms commonly associated with that group. For example, a person who is ethnically Mexican American does not mean that he or she identifies with cultural customs commonly prac-ticed within Mexican-American communities.

Social class as a construct is intricately linked to one's race and ethnicity. Previously, social class has been almost exclusively defined around socioeco-nomic status and has included educational, occupational, and financial sta-tus. Recently there has been a call to go beyond defining social class as only socioeconomic status (Liu, Dunston, Hopps, Picket, & Soleck, 2001) and to include issues such as lifestyle, power, and prestige (Patterson, 2001). When one examines economic differences by race and gender, one sees that minority group members are overrepresented in the lower income categories at a rate three times that of majority group members (Leeder, 1996). Economic inequi-ties however do not tell the whole story of social class. Researchers (Lui, et al., 2001; Patterson, 2001) argue that only when we examine the combination of economic and social status variables (esteem, power, lifestyle) can we explain the effects of social class on a person's career aspirations, choice, and develop-ment.

One's social class has been demonstrated to affect many aspects of psy-chological functioning (Hill, 1996; Rubin, 1992) and a host of career-related variables as well as (Rojewski, 1994; Ryan, Tracy & Rounds, 1996). Although social class has until recently received little attention in the counseling psy-chology literature (Fouad & Brown, 2000), we view social class as a critical aspect in understanding the career development process of both minority and majority clients.

THE BIRTH OF THE FIELD

To understand the changes that Bingham and Ward (1994) allude to in the quote that begins this chapter, we need to provide a brief historical reminder about the roots of career counseling, and the assumptions and practices that developed out of those early roots. The vocational guidance movement was born in a time of tremendous transition for the country. This was a time when both economic turmoil and demographic change were coupled with the changes brought on by the Industrial Revolution, and thus the vocational guidance movement was centered primarily in the industrial cities of the Midwest and East Coast. Services were designed to help European immigrants find their place in this new and vast country. The great influx of these workers led to much worker abuse, employment discrimination, and poverty in the industrial cities. The career theories born out of these early conditions were meant to be applicable for White workers.

Thus, early vocational services were essentially services provided to White immigrants from western Europe. This was also a time of severe racial discrimination, with racial and ethnic minorities excluded from the vocational services being provided. It was reasoned that due to discrimination and prejudice, racial and ethnic minorities could not access most occupations, so it would be illogical to counsel them about nonexistent options (Jackson, 1995). For example, African Americans who did receive services were funneled into the narrow range of career fields that were open to them at the time (Aubrey, 1977), such as education, domestic service, and farming.

Five Key Tenets

The Europeans who received this early career guidance sought to assimilate into American culture, a culture that encouraged exchanging one's ethnic identity for another ethnic identity, that of the White American. These immigrants were striving to learn English and to blend into the American "melting pot," where western European cultures blended together to create a White culture. Out of this backdrop, many of the antecedents of our current tenets about career development were formed. Five key tenets, born out of this historical setting which focused on western European experiences and world view, dramatically influenced career theory, research, and practice in the United States. These five tenets include (a) individualism and autonomy, (b) affluence, (c) structure of opportunity open to all, (d) the centrality of work in people's lives, and (e) the linearity, progressiveness, and rationality of the career development process.

The Tenet of Individualism and Autonomy

A central tenet of career development theory, research, and practice is the importance of the individual. The individual makes choices that ultimately shape his or her destiny. Western psychological theories emphasize separation and individuation from the family unit as a key developmental task. Career theories are theories of the self: How can we find a match between the individual and the work world? How can we help the individual strive for self-actualization? How can we help the individual explore the full range of career paths? How can we help the individual decide on the critical matters of staying in school, choosing a major, or finding a career? In career counseling we encourage the "healthy" developmental step of the adolescent separating from family and beginning to trust one's own decision-making ability. Here, healthy is defined as part of the individuation process; that is, to be perceived as healthy one needs to separate from family. This tenet is reflected in our theories and in our interventions. Fouad and Bingham (1995), for example, point out that DISCOVER, the computerized career information system, has numerous questions assessing the individual's interest, attitudes and abilities, but no questions that examine the importance of the family or culture in career decision making. This criticism could be made of most, if not all, methods of career assessment in current use.

Yet, this tenet may not be relevant or meaningful for many racial and ethnic minority group members where a collectivist tenet is much more appropriate. In some racial and ethnic groups, membership in that group is of primary importance and members place great value and significance on their collective group membership. Decision making and life planning is done to a much greater extent with one's community in mind. Thus, for example, it may be a serious mistake to view this reliance on family support and collective decision making as being diagnostic of a developmentally delayed or immature Asian American. In fact, such "dependency" or reliance is perceived as a reflection of being a responsible and filial person, which is a very much respected and valued characteristic in many Asian cultures (Heppner & Duan, 1995). Career choices are thus weighed in terms of the potential contribution such choices would make to the group as opposed to autonomous choices made for the individual's actualization. Recent empirical data supports the observation that individualism and autonomy may not be as culturally relevant for some Asian Americans (Hardin, Leong, & Osipow, 2001).

The Tenet of Affluence

Another central tenet is that which assumes a certain level of affluence on the part of the career client. Career development theory has at its core the assumption that individuals are able to economically afford choice. The role of the career counselor is to assess interests, skills, and values and help match individuals with appropriate career options. Those career options then all have price tags, such as the cost of vocational–technical training, college, or relocating to where there are jobs in a chosen career field.

This tenet of affluence is not true for the majority of the world's population, nor is it true for many individuals in the United States. It is particularly not true for working class Whites and for racial and ethnic minorities across class lines. For many poor and working class individuals living near or below the poverty line, finding a job—any job—that pays for the basic needs of life is what is important. The luxury of choosing a career to fulfill one's personal or group identity is usually reserved for the college educated and/or wealthy. Very little is known about the interface between economic exploitation and racism experienced by racial and ethnic minorities and by whites on career interests and development. Much more research is needed that elucidates the interaction between race and class as well as disentangles race from class in order to more fully understand the applicability of this tenet to both racial and ethnic minorities and White individuals.

The Tenet of the Structure of Opportunity Open to All Who Strive

This tenet emphasizes the construct of individual control in the selection, attainment, and ultimate satisfaction in a career field. The assumption is made that the individual who works hard enough will be able to make any occupational dream a reality. This tenet is reflected in the "pull yourself up by your bootstraps" motto.

Color-blind racial ideology is a useful construct in underscoring the cultural relativity of the tenet of "Structure of opportunity." Specifically, individuals, groups of people, and systems that consciously or unconsciously operate from this ideological framework deny, distort, or minimize the role of racism on people's lives. Color-blind racial ideology, thus, helps to legitimize blaming people themselves and not structures of opportunity, for the inability to pull themselves out of poverty or pull themselves into exciting professional careers (Neville, Worthington, & Spanierman, 2001). In an ideal world, everyone would have the same opportunity to choose a career that would be personally meaningful, rewarding, and lucrative. Unfortunately, we do not live in an ideal world. We live in a society in which racism and class exploitation exists. These interlocking systems, in turn, help to structure individual career choice. A scale to measure colorblind racial ideologies, the Colorblind Racial Attitudes Scale (CBRAS: Neville, et al., 2000) has recently been developed and validated and serves as a useful tool for measuring this construct.

Thus, this tenet ignores the toll that racial discrimination has taken in the creation of social, psychological, institutional, political, and economic barriers that seriously erode the control that racial and ethnic minority group members have over various facets of their career choice and satisfaction. Racial and ethnic minority group members hold only 10 percent of the managerial and 13 percent of the professional positions in this country, even though they make up more than 30 percent of the population. A recent national study revealed that Black college graduates, on average, make 27.4 percent less than White college graduates (*USA Today*, 1995). The perception or awareness of institutional racism (e.g., disparity in income, glass ceiling) may limit one from examining some occupations or entire career fields.

Sue and Sue (1999) proposed a four-quadrant model of locus of control (i.e., internal vs. external explanations for creating one's fate) and locus of responsibility (i.e., person vs. system attribution for one's life condition) that is helpful for examining career counseling with both White and racial and ethnic minority clients. Most traditional career counseling follows the internal control, person responsibility philosophy. The belief of one's ability to "pull oneself up by the bootstraps" and of a meritocracy where anyone can achieve economic security with hard work and self-reliance exemplifies this philosophy. Given the existence of prejudice and racial discrimination, many racial and ethnic minority group members may legitimately perceive institutional barriers that may impede on their career development. However, little empirical research has examined both personality variables and perceived institutional racism on the career choices and satisfaction of racial and ethnic minorities. Thus, little is known about the interface between perceived locus of control and responsibility on the career development of racial and ethnic minority group members.

The Tenet of the Centrality of Work in People's Lives
This tenet assumes that work plays a central and pivotal role in people's lives, and thus it is critical to find a career that fulfills many of the person's needs. Work is thought to make up the core of a person's identity. Work provides the actualization humans need to feel whole.

Although the role of work is important in many people's lives, it may not have the center stage position many career theorists and researchers may give it. This lack of centrality may be the case due to (a) racism, (b) economic exploitation, and/or (b) cultural values. For example, racial and ethnic minority group members may experience institutional racism in the workplace and thus view it as a hostile or at least a non-affirming environment for them as individuals. Relatedly, because of institutional racism or because of class background, poor and working class individuals may feel their labor is being exploited, further adding to feelings of alienation from work. Cultural values might also create a greater tendency for other life roles or aspects, such as family, church, or leisure activities, to take on a more central role. In their work with Navajo people, for example, Morgan, Guy, Lee, and Cellini (1986) report that many American Indians view the home, family, and community as the center of their existence rather than their jobs. Little research has examined the role of culture in creating and emphasizing the salience of environments other than the work setting as providing centrality and identity affirmation in people's lives. In addition, the role that the intersection of poverty and racial discrimination plays in altering the importance work assumes in determining identity is a largely unexplored variable.

The Tenet of the Linearity, Progressiveness, and
Rationality of the Career Development Process
Career counseling itself and one's progress in the world of work are often described in orderly, rational, and linear terms. Consider, for example, Frank Parson's (1909) three-factor linear progression for making a wise vocational

choice: (1) "a clear understanding of yourself, your aptitudes, interests, ambitions, resources, limitations and their causes, (2) a knowledge of the requirements and conditions of success, advantages and disadvantages, compensation opportunities, and prospects in different lines of work, and (3) true reasoning on the relation of these two groups of facts leads to a wise vocational choice" (p. 5). This orderly progression has had a profound impact through the century and continues to provide the format of much of our current practice. In 1962, Gelatt presented his ideas about decision making, which he labeled "a totally rational approach to making decisions" (p. 242). Interestingly, Gelatt revised his model in 1989 to incorporate flexibility, intuition, and irrationality, and called into question the applicability of his earlier rational approach. Thus, the efficacy of a linear, progressive, and rational approach for all clients and particularly for racial and ethnic minority clients is an important consideration for career counselors. Fouad and Bingham (1995), for example, indicate that the linear and rational career planning process may not be valid for some racial and ethnic minority clients who do not experience career counseling as either linear or rational. They indicate that many Latina/o clients, as a case in point, tend to see counseling as circular rather than linear and may benefit from cycling through the career planning process a number of times. In examining the practices of traditional healers or Shamans, Lee, and Armstrong (1995) similarly indicate that "rather than merely considering the relationship between cause and effect as a linear sequence of connected events, healers in the universal shamanic tradition transcend this reasoning process and view problem etiology in a manner that stresses interconnectedness and may go beyond a linear time bound perspective" (p. 448).

Thus, the assumed linear nature of the world of work is becoming less true for all workers, but perhaps especially for those working-class racial and ethnic minorities who many times have relied on short-term, disrupted employment in whatever field had an available opportunity. As we will discuss in more detail later in the chapter, many of these assumptions born in the early part of the last century may no longer be true for the majority of workers of this century. If career counseling is to be truly empowering to the increasingly diverse workforce, we must examine the present-day accuracy of our basic operating tenets.

DEMOGRAPHIC AND ETHICAL IMPERATIVES

In contrast to a European American population that was the majority clientele of vocational development clinics of the last century, today's clientele is more diverse. The workplace itself is changing dramatically, and so are the individuals with whom career counselors work. We argue that both demographic and ethical imperatives indicate the need to use culture as a lens for examining all aspects of career development. The following statistics illuminate the changing demography in the United States, and the need to more fully attend to the career needs and development of racial and ethnic minorities:

- The decade of the 1980s experienced a dramatic increase in the number of Hispanic/Latina/o, with this population increasing by 48 percent compared to the 12 percent increase of the population as a whole (U.S. Bureau of the Census, 1991). The latest census data indicates that about 12 percent of the U.S. population is Latina/o.
- Although African Americans represent 12 percent of the population, their poverty rate in 1999 was 24 perecent, but generally hovers around 32 percent, with the average family income of African Americans being approximately 58 percent of Whites. In 2001, African-American teenagers had an unemployment rate that was triple that of White teenagers (Brown, 1995).
- The poverty rate of Native-American families is twice that of the general U.S. population. Only 56 percent of Native Americans and Alaskan natives over the age of 25 have completed high school, compared to 67 percent of the general population (U.S. Bureau of the Census, 1990).
- In the years 1986–2000, the African-American labor force is expected to grow by 29 percent, the Hispanic/Latina/o labor force by 74 percent, and Asian American workers by 12 percent. This is in stark contrast to White male workers who are expected to increase by a mere 15 percent (Johnson, 1987).
- Hispanic/Latina/o, and Asian Pacific Islanders report wishing they had received more career planning assistance (75 and 71 percent respectively; Brown, Minor, & Jepsen, 1991).

As these points suggest, the 21st century represents the creation of an increasing multiracial, multicultural society. Shortly after the turn of the millennium it is projected that the majority of the population in the United States will be people of color: Asian/Asian American, Black, Hispanic/Latina/o American, or Native American (Zunker, 1994). What emerges from these statistics is a dramatic and profound need for career assistance for racial and ethnic minorities as they more fully move into the schools and workplaces that have so long discriminated against and marginalized them. This is also especially important because the interface between race and class is demonstrated in the social reality that racial and ethnic minorities, particularly Blacks and Latina/o are over represented among the poor. This means that if the United States is going to compete globally, it will have to expand the development of its human resources, and this necessitates providing the majority of the population with information about and access to a broad range of career options.

Unfortunately, our knowledge base about the development of racial and ethnic minorities is limited at this time (Byars & McCubbin, 2001). Our research has been overwhelmingly conducted on an exceedingly small portion of the population: White, able-bodied, heterosexual, middle-class college students. We know considerably less about the bulk of the U.S. population, most notably racial and ethnic minorities. Research in this area is needed to assist in the development of culturally relevant theories and paradigms to describe the career development of a broad range of populations.

What is not explicitly articulated in the statistics just outlined is the ethical obligation to provide quality, culturally sensitive, and relevant career counseling to all clients. Psychologists have argued that the provision of "professional services to persons of culturally diverse backgrounds by persons not competent in understanding and providing professional services to such groups shall be considered unethical" (Korman, 1974, p. 105). In spite of this recognition, there is growing evidence that the services currently provided by the mental health care services delivery system have not been particularly helpful or sensitive to racial and ethnic minority group members. We now have data to indicate that racial and ethnic minorities are underrepresented in their use of both generic mental health services and career services (Brown, Brooks, & Associates, 1990; Burrell & Rayder, 1971; Parker & McDavis, 1983). We know that the likelihood of various racial and ethnic minority group members coming to counseling for one session and then prematurely terminating after one session is greater than for Whites (Sue & Sue, 1999). In searching for reasons for premature termination, researchers have found negative attitudes and perceptions toward counseling services on the part of minority group members (Cimbolic, Thompson, & Waid, 1981; Tucker, Chennault & Mulkeme, 1981; Vontress, 1970). These negative attitudes may be a result of encounters with poorly trained practitioners or culturally biased techniques or procedures.

There are several areas that should be considered to facilitate placing career counseling in cultural context(s) and to provide culturally sensitive services. Specifically, career counseling has been criticized for using culturally biased assessment tests that were originally normed on White Americans and that may or may not be valid for racial and ethnic minorities (Fouad, 1993). When assessing instrument validity, one should consider the following criteria: (a) the extent to which the items are culturally relevant for the population, (b) that the semantic meaning of the items is similar for each culture, and (d) that the interpretation for the instrument is similar across populations (Paniagua, 1994). Models of career development also have been criticized for not including the critical variables of immigration disruption, racial discrimination, or poverty (Brown, Brooks, & Associates, 1990; Leong, 1995). Some major career theories were built using primarily White middle-class men (e.g., Super's 1953 Middletown study). These theories, models, and assessments have been developed out of the Eurocentric world view and underlying tenets that characterized the field at its inception. The validity of many of these models for persons of color remains a largely untested hypothesis. Thus, it is our position that in order to provide ethical career counseling that truly has the welfare of the client as a paramount goal, counselors must become proficient at providing services within cultural contexts.

Thirty-five years ago Wrenn (1962) warned against cultural encapsulation that emphasizes a universal concept of what is healthy and normal behavior, and in the United States what has traditionally been considered healthy is centered on the Eurocentric tenets outlined in the beginning of this chapter. This Eurocentric stance disregards cultural variation and assumes rigid uniformity (Sue & Sue, 1999). Moreover, cultural encapsulation continues to characterize much of our current theory and practice in career development. This universal application of Eurocentric constructs must be overcome if all counselors, regardless of race or ethnicity, are to provide ethical and effective career counseling to all clients. A prerequisite to providing culturally sensitive career counseling is valuing and affirming cultural diversity; as Fouad and Bingham (1995) so aptly state: "The goal of career counseling is not to have all clients make the same choices but to help clients make career choices that are culturally appropriate" (p. 333).

INDIVIDUAL DIFFERENCE VARIABLES: WORLD VIEW, ACCULTURATION, AND RACIAL IDENTITY DEVELOPMENT

Given the tremendous amount of within-group variability among specific racial and ethnic populations, it is vital to consider individual difference variables when providing career counseling. Identifying culture-specific difference is pivotal because cross-cultural experts contend that the "defining issue determining the cross-cultural relevance" of traditional career theories, models, or constructs is the "degree to which any individual differs from the majority culture" (Leong & Brown, 1995, p. 154). Thus, the efficacy of our career interventions may also be heavily influenced by how similar or different from middle-class European-American culture each client approximates. In addition to within-group differences common across racial and ethnic groups, such as gender, age, and social class, several culture-specific individual difference variables are gaining considerable theoretical and empirical support, notably, world view, acculturation, and racial identity development. Understanding clients in terms of their world view, acculturation level, and racial identity development can lead to much more culturally relevant person-specific career counseling interventions. These individual difference variables may affect each stage in the career counseling process, from initial acknowledgment of the need for career assistance to the closure of career counseling. Some psychologists have contended that models of racial identity are applicable to all cultural groups (Helms, 1995), while others view acculturation as a more useful construct for certain ethnic groups (Choney, Berryhill-Paapke, & Robbins, 1995).

World Views

Probably the broadest of these three individual difference variables is the construct of world view. This construct is defined as a "frame of reference through which one experiences life. It is the foundation of values, attitudes and relations" (Fouad & Bingham, 1995, p. 335). World view is typically acquired via the enculturation process. That is, a person learns how to perceive his or her relation to self, community, and the world via ethnic and racial socialization. Although world view consists of several components, such as group identity (cultural consciousness), individual identity (individual vs. collective self-concept), beliefs (shared assumptions), and language (communication patterns) (Dana, 1993), critical elements of world view consistently discussed in the literature concentrate on value dimensions. According to noted anthropologist Florence Kluckhohn (1960), values orientation reflects cultural components of the problem-solving process. Common value dimensions or solutions to broader human problems discussed in the literature include the following (Dana, 1993; Sue & Sue, 1999):

1. Human nature, or the belief of human nature as inherently good, evil, or both.
2. Human activity that involves one of three modalities: being, being and becoming, and doing.
3. Social relations that consist of one of three dimensions: lineal or vertical (leaders and followers), collateral (collective and consultation with significant others), and individual (individualistic control of destiny).
4. Person/nature relationship that involves one of three affiliations: mastery, subjugation, or harmony with nature.
5. Time that consists of one of three foci of human life: past, present, and future orientations.

Assessments of components of world views can assist in conceptualizing between and within-group differences. Additionally, these broad world view differences may well influence many aspects of the career development process. For example, the five basic tenets described in the beginning of this chapter reflect the world view embraced by many western European cultures;

these tenets have, consequently, shaped current career research theory and practice. It is also important to examine one's world view or conceptual framework as it may influence the pace and timing of career choice and the actual occupational content of job choices. Illustratively, an American Indian woman seeking career counseling may have a present time orientation and value collateral relationships, whereas career counseling practice tends to focus on future time orientation and individual relationships. This difference may manifest itself if the career specialist encourages this client to identify potential future career options relying solely on individual-focused strategies such as interest inventories. A potentially more culturally sensitive strategy would be to assess current career realities relying on both individual and family-oriented interventions.

Acculturation

Compared to world view, acculturation is a more descriptive construct often employed to understand individual differences within a specific ethnic group. Acculturation has been largely defined as a multidimensional psychosocial process of learning the cultural values and practices of a new culture while maintaining some degree of cultural affiliation to one's traditional culture; acculturation is thus a "process of attitudinal and behavioral change undergone willingly or unwillingly, by individuals who reside in multicultural societies" (Casas & Pytluk, 1995, p. 171). Dimensions of culture affected by acculturation include language, friendship patterns and social affiliations, customs, music, and food preferences. Two essential components of acculturation are cultural awareness and cultural loyalty (Padilla, 1980), which are largely affected by one's age, geographical location, and generation. Because of the focus on learning a new culture, acculturation models and assessments generally have been developed to describe and measure the adaptation process of individuals that move to the United States from another country, including Mexico (Cuellar, Harris, & Jasso, 1980; Mendoza, 1989), Vietnam (Smither & Roderiquez-Giegling, 1982) and Japan (Pierce, Clark, & Kiefer, 1972); however, more recently acculturation also has been applied to American Indians (Choney et al., 1995), and African Americans (Landrine & Klonoff, 1996; Walsh, et al., 2001). Acculturation models in the psychology literature evolved fairly rapidly over the past 20 years (Kim & Abreu, 2001).

Berry (1980) has proposed a general model to describe varying degrees of an individual's acculturation level irrespective of national origin. According to this model, two broad queries help ascertain level of acculturation: (a) to what extent the person wishes to remain culturally as they have been with regard to their own language, self-identity, and way of life as opposed to giving that up to become part of the majority culture, and (b) to what extent the individual wants to have day-to-day interactions with the dominant culture as opposed to relating to one's own group. Responses to these queries help to place individuals in one of four quadrants defined as (a) integrationists, characterized by individuals who want to maintain their own culture while having daily interactions with other groups, (b) assimilationists, who wish to give up their own cultural identity to become more a part of the dominant group, (c) separationists, who want to retain their own cultural identity and not have interaction with the majority group, and (d) marginalists, who are neither interested in maintaining their own ethnic identity nor in interacting with the dominant group.

Another general acculturation model considers the multidimensionality of the adaptation process (Keefe & Padilla, 1987). In this model, numerous cultural dimensions or traits (e.g., language and food) are considered simultaneously. Individuals can selectively maintain or discard certain traits from their traditional and/or new cultures depending on the adaptive utility of the trait. For example, a young male who moved to the United States from Peru may choose to learn to speak fluent English to advance in his career while maintaining traditional childrearing practices to demonstrate cultural loyalty. The assumption here is that an individual may or may not be completely facile in one or both cultures.

Understanding more about an individual's level of acculturation may help describe and explain critical aspects of vocational behavior, such as career choice and adjustment. For example, researchers have found that acculturation influences both career choices (Tang, Fouad, & Smith, 1999) and career maturity (Hardin, Leong, & Osipow, 2001) among Asian American college students. Acculturation level may also explain critical aspects of the career counseling process, from differences in initial help-seeking behavior to racial or ethnic preference for a counselor. It is hypothesized that more "traditional" career interventions would be most appropriate for clients who are highly acculturated, whereas rooting career interventions in a cultural context would be essential for clients who more closely adhere to the practices of their traditional culture. For example, it seems appropriate to apply "traditional" career interventions with a fourth generation Chinese-American woman who was raised in a small predominantly White Midwestern community. However, this application does not preclude consideration of other race or culture-related concepts, such as racial identity development, in devising an intervention plan.

Racial Identity Development

A number of theorists and researchers throughout the last three decades have proposed and investigated various models of racial identity development (Atkinson, Morten, & Sue, 1993; Cross, 1971; Cross & Vandiver, 2001; Helms 1984, 1990, 1995; Phinney, 1992; Sue & Sue, 1999; Thomas, 1971). In the career field, racial identity theories are the most widely used culturally specific approaches to examine within group differences among racial and ethnic minority populations (Byars & McCubin, 2001).

Similar to acculturation, racial identity is a complex psychosocial process that encompasses race or ethnic related attitudes, beliefs, and behaviors. Acculturation, however, involves the adaptation to a new culture, whereas racial identity development entails understanding oneself in a racially oppressive environment. Also, racial identity development models tend to focus on race while acculturation models are often applied to specific ethnic groups. Also, these models assume that individuals "develop (or do not develop) healthy racial collective identities in environments in which their socially ascribed racial group has differential access to socio-political power" (Helms & Piper, 1994, p. 125). There are several Black, racial minority, and White racial identity development models that have received increasing attention over the past decade. Among these models are Helms' (1990; 1994; 1995) Black and White racial identity models and Atkinson and colleagues' (1989, 1993) minority models.

Black Racial Identity Development
Emerging from theories of Nigrescence (French, meaning the process of becoming Black) and building on the earlier work of Cross (1971), Helms (1990; 1995) developed a comprehensive model of Black racial identity. According to Helms (1994; 1995), racial identity is an interactive maturation process in which individuals increasingly become aware of racial oppression and themselves as racial beings; racial identity is a dynamic interplay between an individual's affective, cognitive, and behavioral attitudes and his or her environment. According to this model, Black racial identity development process can be described using the following five statuses:

- Contact (formerly pre-encounter), characterized by obliviousness to social races and reverence to White standards while devaluing Black standards
- Dissonance (formerly encounter), illustrated by ambivalence or confusion about one's racial identity typically ignited by a positive uplifting experience or a negative experience with racial discrimination
- Immersion/emersion, represented by high racial saliency and idealization of Black standards while denigrating White standards
- Internalization, depicted by positive racial commitment and an objective view of White society and standards
- Integrative awareness, characterized by both valuing one's own racial group and empathizing and understanding toward other oppressed groups.

It is important to note that these statuses are not mutually exclusive and that an individual has attitudes consistent with all of the statuses; however, the strength of these attitudes differ across the statuses and across environments. That means that individuals typically have stronger attitudes in one status compared to the others and that this strength of endorsement may differ depending on the environmental condition in which one is currently operating (e.g., predominantly White school environment or predominantly Black social environment).

Racial identity attitudes have been found to play an important role in the career development of African Americans. Findings from empirical investigations suggest that more developed racial identity attitudes (i.e., internalization status) are related to mature career interests and goals (Chretien & Neville, 1996; Manese & Fretz, 1984) and, conversely, less developed attitudes (i.e., the first two statuses) are associated with lower confidence in decision making (Thompson, 1985). Racial identity has also been found to be related to life role salience (Carter & Constantine, 2000). Research also suggests that racial identity attitudes predict, over and above demographic variables such as age and sex, career development among African-American students (Chretien & Neville, 1996). In addition, these statuses may theoretically affect all aspects of the career planning process. For example, clients who have strong attitudes that are consistent with the pre-encounter status may be largely oblivious to racial elements of the work world, whereas individuals with robust immersion/emersion attitudes may be distrustful of non-Black coworkers and, consequently, this may affect perceived job satisfaction. Helms (1994) discussed the role of racial identity development in the career development process and is an excellent source of information regarding specific ramifications of racial identity statuses on the career development process.

Minority Racial Identity Development

Atkinson and colleagues (1989) expanded Cross's (1971) Nigrescence model to describe the racial identity development process of racial minorities in general. The model is similar to the Black racial identity development model described earlier, and recent empirical data supports the link between minority racial identity and career development, specifically career development among Asian Americans (Carter & Constantine, 2000). The minority racial identity model consists of the following five stages:

1. Conformity, characterized by devaluing one's own racial group and other racial minority groups while appreciating White systems
2. Dissonance, denoted by conflict between appreciating and depreciating all racial groups

3. Resistance and immersion, illustrated by valuing one's own racial group and volatile support of other racial groups while denigrating White individuals and systems
4. Introspection, depicted by the (re)evaluation of and questioning the objectivity of previously held assumptions about one's own and other racial groups
5. Integrative awareness, characterized by a realistic appreciation of all racial minority groups and selective appreciation of White systems.

White Racial Identity Development

Many times social scientists fail to recognize that White individuals are also racial beings. To raise awareness and to highlight the importance of racial identity, several models designed to describe the racial identity development of White individuals in the United States have been proposed (Hardiman, 1982; Helms, 1984, 1990, 1995; Rowe, Bennett, & Atkinson, 1994). Helms' (1984, 1990, 1995) model has received the most attention in this literature. According to Helms (1995), the main developmental task for White individuals is the abandonment of perceived privilege or entitlement. This is contrasted to racial and ethnic minorities whose main developmental task is to disavow internalized racism, that is, to challenge and discard any negative racial representations projected by dominant culture that an individual may have internalized. White racial identity development process can be described using the following six statuses (Helms, 1995):

1. Contact, illustrated by obliviousness to social race and racial discrimination as well as one's active or passive involvement in it
2. Disintegration, denoted by confusion and conflict caused by questioning social race; torn between group allegiance and existence of institutional racism;
3. Reintegration, characterized by an idealization of Whiteness and denigration of other racial groups
4. Pseudo-independence, portrayed by an intellectual understanding of social race but subtle endorsement of White as normative
5. Immersion/emersion, illustrated by an honest appraisal of racism and one's socioracial privilege as well as a negotiating a positive redefinition of what it means to be White
6. Autonomy, characterized by a secure, positive, nonracist White identity that is informed by an understanding of other racial groups.

Few have theorized about the role racial identity development may play in the career process of White clients. The research on this individual difference variable has instead focused on the relationship between racial attitudes and sensitivity to racial and cultural issues. Examination of this relationship is extremely important because it has implications for the provision of culturally sensitive and relevant counseling interventions by White counselors offering services to racial and ethnic minority clients. Preliminary studies suggest that advanced racial identity attitudes are associated with more developed self-reported multicultural therapy competencies (Neville, Heppner, Louie, Thompson, Brooks, & Baker, 1996; Ottavi, Pope-Davis, & Dings, 1994). Researchers have also found a relationship among white racial identity attitudes, personality styles and racism (Silvestri & Richardson, 2001).

THE CAREER COUNSELING PROCESS THROUGH THE LENS OF CULTURE

We believe that culture is a critical factor in career counseling and should be used both as a filter, and hypothesized to be a factor in each phase of the process. What follows is a description of some of the culturally salient aspects of each phase in our career planning process outlined previously in Chapter 1. However, we also believe that it is vital for career counselors to first explore their own cultural values and how these values may influence their work with clients who are racially, ethnically, or culturally similar to or different from themselves. In addition, it is critical for counselors to identify their attitudes toward social class as these attitudes have been shown to relate to counselor preferences in working with clients (Leeder, 1996), and the perceived possibility of the benefit of counseling (Garb; 1997). To assist with this exploration process, we encourage readers to examine their world view, racial identity attitudes, internalized classism and, if appropriate, acculturation level(s).

Phase 1: Client Goal or Problem Identification, Clarification, and Specification

Identification—Opening

It is critical from the onset that counselors have an awareness of the myriad ways culture may potentially influence a person's career development. Given the vast array of different cultural contexts a client may bring to the career counseling session, perhaps the best advice is Leong's (1993) construct of creative uncertainty. Even if we are uncertain about each client's cultural background and values and how these may have influenced the career counseling process, Leong reminds us to remain creative in our approach to helping the client. The more our knowledge and awareness of culturally relevant factors can inform our practice, the more creative we can be.

Along with the need for creativity comes the need to develop a strong working alliance quickly with the client. As indicated earlier in this chapter, racial and ethnic minority clients terminate counseling after just one session at a rate much greater than that of Whites. Meara and Patton (1994) suggested that one reason for premature termination of career clients in general may be a lack of attention to the working alliance. Thus, regardless of the racial or ethnic background of the counselor and the client, there is a need to connect with the client in a way that helps the client feel rapport with the counselor and sets the stage for the collaboration and mutuality necessary for effective career counseling to take place. The working alliance may also be facilitated by the counselor communicating an understanding and validation of the client's life experiences, and by communicating a willingness and excitement about the client's life and future options.

At this opening phase in career counseling it may be helpful to try to assess the client's level of "racial salience," or to what extent the individual perceives race to be influential in the career planning process, including perceived work options, level of occupational stereotyping, and career decision making (Helms & Piper, 1994, p. 128). It is also important to examine the client's level of class salience and how their current or previous social class identity may impact their career development. This information can help shape the discourse of career counseling.

Clarification—Gathering Client Information

Gathering information about the client should include an assessment of culture-specific variables and individual differences discussed earlier. The Race/Gender Ecological Model of career development discussed in Chapter 2 provides a template for helping the client examine the systems from macro to micro affecting their career development. For example, an assessment of the client's racial identity status as a micro-system influence is very important to understanding many of the dynamics of the career counseling process. This assessment of racial identity status can be accomplished using one of the racial identity scales or through a less formal verbal assessment based on the counselor's thorough grounding in the various racial identity statuses. Counselors would benefit from reading recent chapters on the acculturation process of American Indians (Choney et al. 1995); the psychology of Nigrescence (Cross, 1995); ethnic identity of Asians (Sodowsky, Kwan, & Pannu, 1995); Helm's White and People of Color racial identity models (Helms, 1995); Hispanic identity development (Casas & Pytluk, 1995); and biracial identity development (Kerwin & Ponterotto, 1995). An issue of the *Journal of Career Assessment* was devoted to career assessment with racial and ethnic minorities (Walsh, 1994). As Helms (1994) indicated in this special issue, to understand a client's racial identity status, the counselor may be able to assess how the client integrates racial information into his or her career self-conception, which may be a critical factor in effectively providing career planning assistance. It is especially important to examine how the client's racial identity status might be effecting such constructs as racial salience in job selection, strategies for dealing with racism in the work environment, work adjustment, and work satisfaction.

In addition to gathering client information, this is also a phase of giving information that may be useful to the client. Particularly if the client is at a less developed racial identity status, he or she may be unaware of potential barriers to be faced in the career development process. Thus, it is important that the counselor help the client become aware of these barriers and also of ways to circumvent these obstacles should they occur. The counselor may also point out the role of the sociopolitical environment, the role of culture and social class, in helping to shape the current self-concept of the individual. This information will lay the groundwork for future discussion about how environmental and cultural factors may influence important aspects of this client's career development process.

Specification—Understanding and Hypothesizing about Client Information and Behavior

In attempting to gain greater specificity with the client, the counselor might explore, when appropriate, the role that poverty, sexism, racism, or discrimination may have on both the client's self-efficacy concerning his or her probability of succeeding in the traditional labor market and also in the outcomes he or she perceives to be possible. The counselor may also explore the client's perceptions of job availability and how these perceptions may themselves influence the client's vocational self-concept. The counselor may further explore how these perceptions of self may influence an individual to compromise his or her career choices in ways that may be detrimental. For example, if a client indicates low educational aspirations, the counselor may challenge those assumptions and seek to widen the educational and occupational options the client is considering. Or, for example, given the overrepresentation of African Americans in social occupations, the counselor may explore whether these are authentic interests or represent a process of compromise (Gottfredson, 1981). In addition, this phase of counseling may include the counselor testing hypotheses about culture-specific variables that may explain the client's vocational behavior. In particular, it may be helpful to examine how culture-specific variables can enhance the counselor and client's understanding of the career development process. Culture-specific variables can be examined as unique strengths that the client brings to the career planning process, and eventually to the workplace setting.

Phase 2: Client Goal or Problem Resolution

Taking Action

Some writers in the field of multicultural counseling (Sue & Sue, 1999) indicate that many racial and ethnic minority clients prefer directive and action-oriented approaches to counseling rather than insight or reflective-oriented approaches. Although there is some evidence that this preference may be related to level of acculturation, with the less acculturated clients preferring this directive style, the action phase may nonetheless be especially relevant to racial and ethnic minority clients. Given the tremendous impact environmental barriers have had on racial and ethnic minorities, it may be very important in this phase to help clients identify those aspects of the process that are within and beyond their personal control. This may be especially helpful for those racial and ethnic minorities who are living in poverty. It may also be very helpful to talk directly with clients about ways of overcoming certain barriers in the career planning and job search process.

In addition, it may be particularly helpful to provide opportunities for racial and ethnic minorities to take part in group interventions, as some writers indicate that this reinforces the collectivist rather than individualistic world view (Bowman, 1993). In the action phase, this may take the form of a career exploration group, or a job club, where individuals come together and provide support, leads, and resources, as well as a normalization of the fears and feelings that may accompany these important transitions in people's lives. This may also be an appropriate time to introduce the client to racially similar role models in a variety of career fields in order to expand awareness of possible career fields and to increase the self-efficacy beliefs of individuals by presenting them with role models similar to themselves.

It may also be beneficial to include the family in the action phase, either by directly involving them in parts of the process or by inquiring about how the family would view particular options the individual is considering. Clients might be encouraged to use their immediate family, extended family, or community as resources in their career planning process. Delivery systems might include holding career planning workshops in community centers and collaborating with community leaders in the design and implementation of career planning services. This may be particularly advantageous for people living in lower economic neighborhoods with little access to transportation.

Some writers have indicated the importance of the counselor emphasizing clients' abilities to generate knowledge about themselves and to act in their own behalf in locating appropriate role models and developing networks. While advocacy on the client's behalf is definitely warranted when the client is having difficulty negotiating the predominately White work environments, the more that counselors emphasize client-generated rather than counselor-generated knowledge, the more self-efficacy and strength the client is likely to feel (Hawks & Muha, 1991).

Developing an Individual Career Plan

The career counseling process continues with the development of an individual career plan. This specific plan can serve as a road map for clients as they try to navigate the action phase of the process. Here the counselor can help the client examine at a more micro level how to take action steps and how to overcome potential obstacles. For some of the action steps, the counselor may need to play the role of advocate for the client in the larger employment and educational system. The counselor can also help the client to creatively devise a repertoire of possible responses to situations of racism, classism, and discrimination that the client may face. At this stage, the lack of linearity to the process may become evident as the client sees the need to reevaluate and circle through previous steps again. It is especially important at this time that the counselor reinforce the client's decision-making style and unique strengths.

Evaluating and Closing the Relationship

This is the phase in which the counseling session is evaluated from both a content (what we did) and a process (how we did it) perspective. During this phase the counselor can emphasize the client's strengths and proficiency at various aspects of the career planning process. This is also a time to welcome clients back if they need further help or assistance. This is especially important for racial and ethnic minority clients for a couple of reasons. First, Fouad and Bingham (1995) argue that many times individuals from non-majority backgrounds may ascribe expert or even familial status to the counselor. Returning to counseling after termination may be perceived as a failure or loss of face, especially for Asian American clients, and thus be very difficult for the client. Thus, it is important that the counselor normalize coming back to counseling and help the client see it as simply a part of what often occurs in counseling relationships. Another reason for emphasizing the possibility of the clients return is the likelihood that the client will be met with race-related obstacles (racism, discrimination) and need further assistance. If a strong relationship has been built between counselor and client, this is a natural place for the client to return and get help instead of having to develop an entirely new relationship with another counselor.

In sum, it seems imperative that each phase of the career planning process be examined through the filter of culture. Although much of what is included in each phase may be similar, cultural contexts can bring different needs to these phases that, when attended to can lead to more effective and empowering career counseling. The more awareness and knowledge counselors have about racial and ethnic specific variables, the more equipped they will be to provide the best quality service and help empower the life choices of all people.

REFERENCES

Atkinson, D., Morten, G., & Sue, D. W. (1989). *Counseling American minorities: A cross-cultural perspective* (3rd ed.). Dubnque, IA: William C. Brown.

Atkinson, D., Morten, G., & Sue, D. W. (1993). *Counseling American minorities: A cross-cultural perspective* (4th ed.). Dubuque, IA: William C. Brown.

Aubrey, R. F. (1977). Historical developments of guidance and counseling and implications for the future. *Personnel and Guidance Journal, 55* (1), 288–295.

Berry, J. W. (1980). Acculturation as varieties of adaptation. In A. M. Padilla (Ed.), *Acculturation: Theory, models and some new findings* (pp. 9–25). Boulder, CO: Westview.

Bingham, R. P. & Ward, C. M. (1994). Career counseling with ethnic minority women. In W. B. Walsh and S. H. Osipow (Eds.), *Career counseling for women* (pp. 165–196). Hillsdale, NJ: Erlbaum.

Bowman. S. L. (1993). Career intervention strategies for ethnic minorities. *The Career Development Quarterly, 42,* 14–25.

Brown, D., Brooks, L., & Associates (1990). *Career choice and development: Applying contemporary theories to practice* (2nd ed.). San Francisco: Jossey-Bass.

Brown, D., Minor, C. W., & Jepsen, D. A. (1991). The opinions of minorities preparing for work: Report of the second NCDA National Survey. *Career Development Quarterly, 40,* 5–19.

Brown, M. T. (1995). The career development of African Americans: Theoretical and empirical issues. In F. T. Leong (Ed.), *Career development and vocational behavior of racial and ethnic minorities* (pp. 7–36). Mahwah, NJ: Erlbaum.

Burrell, L., & Rayder, N. F. (1971). Black and white students' attitudes toward white counselors. *Journal of Negro Education, 40,* 48–62.

Byars, A. M., & McCubin, L. D. (2001). Trends in career development research with racial/ethnic minorities: Prospects and challenges. In J. G. Ponterotto, J. M. Casas. L. Suzuki, & C. Alexander, (Eds.), *Handbook of multicultural counseling* (2nd Edition) (pp. 633–654). Thousand Oak, CA; Sage.

Carter, R. T., & Constantine, M. G. (2000). Career maturity, life role salience, and racial/ethnic identity among Black and Asian American college students. *Journal of Career Assessment. 8,*173–187.

Casas, J. M., & Pytluk, S. D. (1995). Hispanic identity development: Implications for research and practice. In J. G. Ponterotto, J. M. Casas, L. A. Suzuki, & C. M. Alexander (Eds.), *Handbook of multicultural counseling* (pp. 155–180). Thousand Oaks, CA: Sage.

Choney, S. K., Berryhill-Paapke, E., & Robbins, R. R. (1995). The acculturation of American Indians: Developing frameworks for research and practice. In J. G. Ponterotto, J. M. Casas, L. A. Suzuki, & C. M. Alexander (Eds.), *Handbook of multicultural counseling* (pp. 73–92). Thousand Oaks, CA: Sage.

Chretien, C. L., & Neville, H. A. (1996). *Predictors of African American college students' vocational identity and goal setting: An examination of racial identity attitudes and demographic variables.* Unpublished manuscript.

Cimbolic, P., Thompson, R. A., & Waid, L. R. (1981). A comparison of black and white student preference for help sources other than the university counselor. *Journal of College Student Personnel, 22,* 342–347.

Cross, W. E. (1995). The psychology of Nigrescence: Revising the Cross model. In J. G. Ponterotto, J. M. Casas, L. A. Suzuki, & C. M. Alexander (Eds.), *Handbook of multicultural counseling* (pp. 93–122). Thousand Oaks, CA: Sage.

Cross, W. E., Jr. (1971). The Negro-to-Black conversion experience. Toward a psychology of Black liberation. *Black World, 20,* 13–27.

Cross, Jr., W. E., & Vandiver, B. J. (2001). Nigrescence theory and measurement: Introducing the Cross Racial Identity Scale. In J. G. Ponterotto, J. M. Casas, L. Suzuki, & C. Alexander, (Eds.), *Handbook of multicultural counseling* (2nd ed.). Thousand Oak, CA; Sage.

Cuellar, I., Harris, L. C., Jasso, R. (1980). An acculturation scale for Mexican American normal and clinical populations. *Hispanic Journal of the Behavioral Sciences, 2,* 199–217.

Dana, R. H. (1993). *Multicultural assessment perspectives for professional psychology.* Boston: Allyn and Bacon.

Fouad, N. A. (1993). Cross-cultural vocational assessment. *Career Development Quarterly, 42,* 4–13.

Fouad, N. A., & Bingham, R. P. (1995). Career counseling with racial and ethnic minorities. In W. B. Walsh & S. H. Osipow (Eds.), *Handbook of vocational psychology* (pp. 331–366). Mahwah, NJ: Erlbaum.

Fouad, N. A., & Brown M. T., (2000). Role of race and social class in development: Implications for counseling psychology. In S. D. Brown, R. D. Lent (Eds.), *Handbook of counseling psychology* (pp. 379–408). New York. John Wiley & Sons.

Garb, H. N. (1997). Race bias, social class bias, and gender bias in clinical judgment. *Clinical psychology: Science and practice, 4,* (2). 99–120.

Gelatt, H. B. (1962). Decision-making: A conceptual frame of reference for counseling. *Journal of Counseling Psychology, 9,* 240–245.

Gelatt, H. B. (1989). Positive uncertainty: A new decision making framework for counseling. *Journal of Counseling Psychology, 36,* 252–256.

Gottfredson, L. S. (1981). Circumscription and compromise: A developmental theory of occupational aspiration. *Journal of Counseling Psychology, 28,* 545–579.

Hardiman, R. (1982). *White identity development: A process oriented model for describing the racial consciousness of White Americans.* Unpublished doctoral dissertation. University of Massachusetts, Amherst.

Hardin, E. E., Leong, F. T., & Osipow, S. H. (2001). Cultural relativity in the conceptualization of career maturity. *Journal of Vocational Behavior. 58,* 36–52.

Hawks, B. K., & Muha, D. (1991). Facilitating the career development of minorities: Doing it differently this time. *Career Development Quarterly, 39,* 251–260.

Helms, J. E. (1984). Toward a theoretical explanation of the effects of race on counseling: A Black and White Model. *The Counseling Psychologist, 12* (4), 153–165.

Helms, J. E. (Ed.). (1990). *Black and White racial identity: Theory, research and practice.* New York: Greenwood Press.

Helms, J. E. (1994). Racial identity and career assessment. *Journal of Career Assessment, 3,* 199–209.

Helms, J. E. (1995). An update of Helm's white and people of color racial identity models. In J. G. Ponterotto, J. M. Casas, L. A. Suzuki, & C. M. Alexander (Eds.), *Handbook of multicultural counseling* (pp. 181–198). Thousand Oaks, CA: Sage.

Helms, J. E., & Piper, R. E. (1994). Implications of racial identity theory for vocational psychology. *Journal of Vocational Behavior 44,* 124–136.

Heppner, M. J., & Duan, C. (1995). From a narrow to expansive world view: Making career centers a place for diverse students. *Journal of Career Development, 22,* 87–100.

Hill, M. (1996). We can't afford it: Confusions and silences on the topic of class. In M. Hill & E. D. Rothblum (Eds.), *Classism and feminist therapy: Counting costs* (pp. 1–6). Binghamton, NY: Harrington Park Press.

Jackson, M. L. (1995). Multicultural counseling: Historical perspectives. In J. G. Ponterotto, J. M. Casas, L. A. Suzuki, & C. M. Alexander (Eds.), *Handbook of multicultural counseling* (pp. 3–16). Thousand Oaks, CA: Sage.

Johnson, W. B. (1987). *Workforce 2000.* Indianapolis, IN: Hudson Institute.

Keefe, S. E., & Padilla, A. M. (1987). *Chicano ethnicity.* Albuquerque: University of New Mexico Press.

Kerwin, C., & Ponterotto, J. G. (1995). Biracial identity development: Theory and research. In J. G. Ponterotto, J. M. Casas, L. A. Suzuki, & C. M. Alexander (Eds.), *Handbook of multicultural counseling* (pp. 199–217). Thousand Oaks, CA: Sage.

Kim, B. S., & Abreu, J. (2001). Acculturation measurement: Theory, current instruments, and future directions. In J. G. Ponterotto, J. M. Casas, L. Suzuki, & C. Alexander, (Eds.), *Handbook of multicultural counseling* (2nd Ed.). Thousand Oak, CA; Sage.

Kluckhohn, F. R. (1960). A method for eliciting value orientations. *Anthropological linguistics, 2,* 1–23.

Korman, M. (1974). National conference on levels and patterns of professional training in psychology. *American Psychologist, 29,* 441–449.

Landrine, H., & Klonoff, E. A. (1996). *African American acculturation: Deconstructing race and reviving culture.* Thousand Oaks, CA: Sage.

Lee, C. C., & Armstrong, K. L. (1995). Indigenous models of mental health intervention: Lessons from traditional healers, In W. B. Walsh & S. H. Osipow (Eds.), *Handbook of vocational psychology* (pp. 441–456).

Leeder, E. (1996). Speaking rich people's words: Implications of a feminist class analysis in psychotherapy. In M. Hill & E.D. Rothblum (Eds.), *Classism & feminist therapy: Counting costs* (pp.45–58). Binghamton, NY: Harrington Park Press.

Leong, F. T. L. (1995). *Career development and vocational behavior of racial and ethnic minorities.* Mahweh, NJ: Erlbaum.

Leong, F. T. L., & Brown, M. T. (1995). Theoretical issues in cross–cultural career development: Cultural validity and cultural specificity. In W. B. Walsh & S. H. Osipow (Eds.), *Handbook of vocational psychology* (pp. 143–180).

Leong, F. T. L., Wagner, N. S., & Tata, S. P. (1995). Racial and ethnic variation. In Alexander (Eds.), *Handbook of multicultural counseling* (pp. 415–438). Thousand Oaks, CA: Sage.

Leong, F. T. L. (1993). The career counseling process with racial-ethnic minorities: The case of Asian Americans. *Career Development Quarterly, 42,* 26–40.

Liu, W. M., Dunston, K., Hopps, J., Pickett, T., & Soleck, G. (2001, March). New perspectives on social class: Social class world view model. In W. M. Liu (Chair) *Understanding social class in counseling psychology.* Symposium conducted at the meeting of the American Psychological Association 4th National Counseling Psychology Conference, Houston, TX.

Manese, J., & Fretz, B. (1984). *Relationship between Black students' racial identity attitudes and vocational exploration.* Paper presented at the 92nd Annual Convention of the American Psychological Association, Toronto, Canada.

Meara, N. M. & Patton, M. J. (1994). Contributions of the working alliance in the practice of career counseling. *The Career Development Quarterly, 43,* 161–177.

Mendoza, R. H. (1989). An empirical scale to measure type and degree of acculturation in Mexican-American adolescents and adults. *Journal of Cross-Cultural Psychology, 20,* 372–385.

Morgan, C. O., Guy, E., Lee, B., & Cellini, H. R. (1986). Rehabilitation services for American Indians: The Navajo experience. *Journal of Rehabilitation, 52,* 25–31.

Neville, H. A., Heppner, M. J., Louie, C. L., Thompson, C. E., Brooks, L., & Baker, C. E. (1996). The impact of multicultural training on White racial identity attitudes and therapy competencies. *Professional Psychology: Research and Practice, 27,* 83–89.

Neville, H. A., Lilly, R. L., Duran, G., Lee, R. M., & Browne, L. (2000). Construction and Initial validation of the Color-Blind Racial Attitudes Scale (CoBRAS). *Journal of Counseling Psychology, 47,* 59–70.

Neville, H. A., Worthington, R. L., & Spanierman, L. B. (2001). Race, power, and multicultural counseling psychology: Understanding White privilege and color-blind racial attitudes. In J. G. Ponterotto, J. M. Casas, L. Suzuki, & C. J. Alexander, (Eds.), *Handbook of multicultural counseling* (2nd Ed.) (pp. 257–288). Thousand Oak, CA; Sage.

Ottavi, T. M., Pope-Davis, D. B., & Dings, J. G. (1994). Relationship between White racial identity attitudes and self-reported multicultural counseling competencies. *Journal of Counseling Psychology, 41,* 149–154.

Padilla, A. M. (Ed.). (1980). *Acculturation: Theory, models and some new findings.* Boulder, CO: Westview.

Paniagua, F. A. (1994). *Assessing and treating culturally diverse clients.* Thousand Oaks, CA: Sage.

Parker, N. B., & McDavis, R. J. (1983). Attitudes of blacks toward mental health agencies and counselors. *Journal of Non-White Concerns in Personnel and Guidance, 11,* 89–98.

Parsons, F. (1909). *Choosing a vocation.* Garrett Park, MD: Garrett Park Press.

Patterson, E. K., Hathaway, S., Doan, T., & Arthur, E. (2001, March). The attitudes toward lower social classes scale: Initial development and factor analysis. Poster session presented at the American Psychological Associatation 4th National Counseling Psychology Conference, Houston, TX.

Phinney, J. S. (1992). The multigroup ethnic identity measure: A new scale for use with diverse groups. *Journal of Adolescent Research, 7,* 156–176.

Pierce, R. C., Clark, M., & Kiefer, C. W. (1972). A "bootstrap" scaling technique. *Human Organization, 31,* 403–410.

Rojewski, J. W. (1994) Career indecision types for rural adolescents from disadvantaged and nondisadvantaged backgrounds. *Journal of Counseling Psychology, 41,* 356–363.

Rowe, W., Bennett, S. K., Atkinson, D. R. (1994). White racial identity models: A critique and alternative proposal. *The Counseling Psychologist, 23,* 129–146.

Rubin, L. B. (1992). *Worlds of pain: Life in the working-class family.* New York: Basic Books.

Ryan, J. M., Tracey, T. J. G., & Rounds, J. (1996). Generalizability of Holland's structure of vocational interests across ethnicity, gender, and socioeconomic status. *Journal of Counseling Psychology, 43(3).* 330–337.

Silvestri, T. J., & Richardson, T. Q. (2001). White racial identity statuses and NEO personality constructs: An exploratory analysis. *Journal of Counseling and Development. 79,* 68–76.

Smither, R., & Roderiquez-Giegling, M. (1982). Personality, demographics, and acculturation of Vietnamese and Nicaraguan refugees to the United States. *International Journal of Psychology, 17,* 19–25.

Sodowsky, G. R., Kwan, K. L. K., & Pannu, R. (1995). Ethnic identity of Asians in the United States. In J. G. Ponterotto, J. M. Casas, L. A. Suzuki, & C. M. Alexander (Eds.), *Handbook of multicultural counseling* (pp. 123–154). Thousand Oaks, CA: Sage.

Sue, D. W., & Sue, D. (1999). *Counseling the culturally different: Theory and practice (3rd ed.).* New York: John Wiley & Sons.

Super, D. E. (1953). A theory of vocational development. *American Psychologist, 8,* 185–190.

Tang, M., Fouad, D. A., & Smith, P. L. (1999). Asian Americans' career choices: A path model to examine factors influencing their career choices. *Journal of Vocational Behavior, 54,* 142–157.

Thomas, C. W. (1971). *Boys no more.* Beverly Hills, CA: Glencoe.

Thompson, C. E. (1985). *Attitudes toward academic undecidedness and identity foreclosure among black students.* Unpublished master's thesis, University of Maryland, College Park, MD.

Tucker, C. M., Chennault, S. A., & Mulkeme, D. J. (1981). Barriers to effective counseling with blacks and therapeutic strategies for overcoming them. *Journal of Non-White Concerns in Personnel and Guidance, 9,* 68–76.

USA Today (1995, May 9). "Racial earning gap for college grads," p. 10D.

U.S. Bureau of the Census (1990). *Characteristics of American Indians by tribe and selected areas.* Washington, DC: U.S. Government Printing Office.

U.S. Bureau of the Census (1991). *The Hispanic population in the United States: March 1991* (Current Population Report, Series P-20, No. 455). Washington, DC: U.S. Government Printing Office.

Vontress, C. (1970). Counseling Blacks. *Personnel and Guidance Journal, 48,* 713–719.

Walsh, W. B. (Ed.). (1994). Special Feature: Career Assessment with Racial and Ethnic Minorities. *Journal of Career Assessment, 2* [Special issue] (3).

Walsh, W. B., Bingham, R. P. Brown, M. T., and Ward, C. M. (2001). *Career Counseling for African Americans.* Mahwah, NJ: Lawrence Eribaum.

Wrenn, C. G. (1962). The culturally-encapsulated counselor. *Harvard Educational Review, 32,* 444–449.

Zunker, V. G. (1994). *Career counseling: Applied concepts of life planning.* Pacific Grove, CA: Brooks/Cole.

► 4

Empowering Women's Life Choices

An Examination of Gender and Sexual Orientation

An impressive literature now exists that documents the vastly different gender contexts of women's and men's lives. Although evidence for biological differences between men and women remains small, learned differences are great. From birth, boys and girls are supported for dramatically different characteristics and behaviors (Matlin, 1996; Unger & Crawford, 1992). Men's lives are characterized by an occupational focus in which performance and mastery in competitive situations is valued. Thus, male self-esteem is a direct function of mastery level (Heppner & Heppner, 2001; Skovholt, 1993). Women's lives are characterized by a focus on relationships and connectedness with others (Gilligan, 1990a, 1990b) causing many young women to rule out occupations that they perceive would lessen the time and energy they have for home and family (Lips, 1992). Understanding the gender context of a client is critical to effective career counseling. In addition to gender, one's sexual orientation may also influence one's career development in many profound ways. Regardless of age or life stage, lesbian, gay, bisexual, and transgendered (LGBT) individuals may have unique issues that are critical to account for in the career planning process.

We start this chapter by highlighting key aspects of the gendered context and their gender-specific outcomes. Next, we provide an overview of these complex and varied issues. Whole texts (Betz & Fitzgerald, 1987; Walsh & Osipow, 1994) have been written on the topic of women's career development and should be consulted for a more in-depth analysis of these issues. Key issues are discussed here in order to highlight aspects of the gendered context and those specific to lesbian, bisexual, and transgendered individuals that may impact our clients most directly. The second part of this chapter will suggest specific assessments, techniques, and information to share with clients to make career counseling more empowering for lesbian, bisexual, transgendered, and heterosexual women. This part also discusses the impact of gender and sexual orientation on the different phases of career counseling outlined in Chapter 1.

As we begin this section, it is important to note that while we have attempted to integrate career research on lesbian, gay, bisexual, and transgendered individuals wherever possible, this body of literature remains quite small and incomplete. In addition, much of this research was conducted on one of the subgroups such as lesbian women, but not gay men. Although the literature on lesbian women and gay men is small, the literature on the career development of bisexual and transgendered individuals is virtually nonexistent. Thus, the reader is cautioned that our ability to discuss and offer assistance in working with LGBT clients is limited because of the limited research base. The designation of transgendered needs special caution as several different sexual identities are often grouped under this umbrella term. Therefore, one must use caution in assuming that what has been documented in the literature as explaining some aspect of the career development of lesbian women, would necessarily apply to transgendered individuals as well. We do however, believe that it is important for LGBT issues to be addressed in the mainstream career literature and thus, we have tried to include reference to this scholarship whenever possible.

Now we will briefly review the literature on critical gender and sexual orientation influences, presenting them in a thematic and developmental progression. They are, however, not exclusive categories, nor are they linear. Men and women, for example, continue to experience the impact of sex role socialization from birth to death. The thematic schema is meant to provide an organizing framework for typical developmental influences and includes sections on the gendered overlay: sex role socialization in childhood, the gendered context of adolescents, and the gendered workplace context.

THE GENDERED OVERLAY: SEX ROLE SOCIALIZATION IN CHILDHOOD

The overlay for all of the critical aspects of the gendered context that follow is the pervasive sex role socialization of boys and girls. How we interact with and are reinforced by others from a very young age dramatically alters how we view ourselves and our options. Our acquisition of gender-typed personality traits, interests, and behaviors starts early in life (Matlin, 1996) and is reinforced by parents, teachers, peers, the media, and the church, among others. Occupational stereotyping starts early. Gettys and Cann (1981) reported that children as young as two or three identified sex-stereotyped occupations for men and women. Matlin (1996) reported that children between kindergarten and fourth grade become increasingly rigid about which occupations they perceive that men and women can hold. These findings support Gottfredson's (1981) theory of circumscription and compromise in which she theorized that children's perceptions of appropriate occupations become circumscribed into a narrow range of acceptable sex-typed career options. This range is generally set by the time the child is six to eight years old and is difficult to modify once set.

Although this research on the narrowing of occupational options is distressing, it appears there are ways of broadening options. A primary influence may be role models. Similar-sex role models facilitate a widening of perceived acceptable opportunities. For example, in a study that compared schools with male or female principals, children were much more likely to think that both men and women could be principals when their school had a female principal (Paradise & Wall, 1986). These types of studies offer hope about our ability to broaden the range of career opportunities that girls will consider. However, the availability of role models for LGBT individuals are limited (Croteau, Anderson, Distefano, & Kampa-Kokesch, 2000; Fasinger, 1996).

The role of sexual orientation identity in the vocational development of lesbian and bisexual women has been the focus of some research over the past decade. In their chapter, Croteau, Anderson, Distefano and Kampa-Kokesch (2000) discuss two areas of research which have prompted the most scientific inquiry. First, gender role socialization influences the development of vocational interest in gay and lesbian individuals in a distinct manner from heterosexual individuals and second, gay and lesbian individuals internalize societal vocational stereotypes and use them to define their structures of opportunity.

Croteau et al. (2000) indicate that gay and lesbian individuals tend to be more gender non-traditional in their career interests than their heterosexual counterparts. This non-traditionality has two potential outcomes. If gay and lesbian children are discouraged from pursuing non-traditional paths, this may lead to increased indecision, restricted choices and less career satisfaction. There is some evidence, however, to suggest that lesbian women may be more likely to pursue non-traditional careers and that there may be more support for non-traditional career choice within the lesbian community (Fassinger, 1995, 1996).

In addition writers have indicated that LGBT individuals may internalize stereotypes about appropriate career fields and limit their choices to ones they believe are appropriate. For example, several studies have provided evidence that LGBT individuals restrict their opportunity for working with children (Crouteau, et al., 2000). Thus it appears that for heterosexual, lesbian, or bisexual women, early societal messages about what is gender appropriate may have powerful influences on their eventual career choice. This emphasizes the need for school counselors to play an active role in helping to change these messages before they become firmly implanted into the ways that boys and girls view the world of work.

THE GENDERED CONTEXT OF ADOLESCENTS

As children enter into adolescence, that critical transition period between childhood and adulthood, a number of important influences shape their view of themselves in relation to the occupational world. This time period is especially critical in the development of a sense of self-identity. Several researchers have looked to the school environment as a major socializing and self-concept forming influence.

A number of important studies have examined the differential treatment of boys and girls at all levels of their educational experience. In studies that examined gender bias in the classroom, researchers have observed bias at the grade school level (Sadker & Sadker, 1985) through the college level (Fischer & Good, 1994; Ossana, Helms, & Leonard, 1992; Hall & Sandler, 1982). Although some of the gender bias is blatant, such as professors telling sexist jokes, much of it is more subtle, such as the systematic ignoring of girls' and women's comments by professors, which leads them to feel devalued or invisible in the academic community. Freeman (1989) labeled this phenomena the null environment. A null environment is one that neither actively discourages or encourages, but rather ignores the individual. In Freeman's study of college students, she found that both women and men felt ignored by educational institutions, but that men felt more supported by friends and family. This process of ignoring women, which is so characteristic of the null environment, has been referred to as a form of passive discrimination (Betz, 1989).

Although the explicit pledge is equality of educational opportunity, there appears to be a hidden curriculum (Lee & Gropper, 1974) that reinforces sexist views of women and men and devalues women's experience. The impact of this devaluing on women's career aspirations is great. Clearly counselors and teachers at all educational levels have a responsibility to examine the many subtle ways in which their own restricted socialization contaminates the educational experiences of the next generation.

As awareness is growing on the part of teachers and counselors, blatant gender bias may be diminishing. As the Sadkers' (1985) research emphasized, however, even in classrooms with competent, aware, and well-meaning teachers, there is still differential treatment of girls and boys. A parallel situation may be true with school counselors. Although research in the 1970s indicated that there appeared to be some gender bias on the part of school counselors who were poorly informed about women's employment and who reinforced stereotypic options (Betz & Fitzgerald, 1987), few studies have been conducted since that time to examine current attitudes and practices. Although most counselors are probably now aware of the need to not sex-role stereotype occupational choices, it is unclear how more subtle messages are conveyed in the counseling context. Without behavioral research analogous to that conducted in classrooms by the Sadkers (1985), it will be difficult to determine what is actually being reinforced by school counselors. The few studies conducted in the last decade that have examined the role of gender bias in career and lifestyle planning unfortunately continue to find gender-biased attitudes and practices (Fitzgerald & Cherpas, 1985; Robertson & Fitzgerald, 1990).

Research also indicates that homophobic beliefs are common among a range of mental health professionals (DeCresenzo, 1985; Rudolph, 1988), and although no studies have been conducted that specifically assess the homophobia of career counselors, one would predict a similar occurrence. Counselors must be aware of their own homophobia and not encourage or discourage lesbian clients into certain careers based on stereotypic beliefs.

While adolescence is for some a time of identity development around tentative career choices, if the adolescent is also involved in the process of sexual identity development their vocational identity can be delayed. Included in one study lesbian women reported feeling behind their heterosexual counterparts due to the time and emotional energy devoted to their sexual identity development and the coming out process. For more information about LGBT adolescents, see Hershberger and D'Augelli (2000).

Kerr and Maresh's (1994) extensive research on academically gifted girls and women emphasized that even for this highly talented portion of the population, a lack of guidance and support can have drastic consequences. Kerr indicated that what happens to these young women can hardly be called career development, rather she describes it as "a gently downward spiral as gifted young women adjust their interests, aspirations, and achievements to fit their own perceived limitations" (Kerr & Maresh, 1994, p. 207).

Research has also indicated that even girls with appropriately high aspirations tend to compromise them when they enter colleges that promote what Holland and Eisenhart (1990) termed the "culture of romance." In their book, *Educated in Romance: Women, Achievement, and College Culture,* they follow the lives of a group of Black and White women in two southern universities as they experience college and enter the workforce. They found that in two-thirds of the women studied, their career aspirations declined as these women spent a larger portion of their time on dating and romantic relationships, eventually altering and subordinating their own career plans to those of their husbands'.

Thus, the gendered context of childhood and adolescence has a critical influence on the career aspirations of young men and women. As social–cognitive learning theory and research makes clear, the earlier these messages are encoded in the schema of the individual, the more difficult they are to alter. When the individual leaves the educational institution and pursues employment, research indicates that gender and sexual orientation biases continue to be reinforced. For lesbian and bisexual women and transgendered individuals these biases are compounded as the intersection of multiple minority statuses increases the likelihood that these women will face discrimination based not only on gender, but also on sexual orientation, in the forms of homophobia and heterosexism.

THE GENDERED WORKPLACE CONTEXT

Although more women are now working in the paid labor force, and some fields that once had no women are now sex integrated, gender bias and discrimination continue to plague the workplace. In 1977, Kanter discussed the phenomena of organizations and institutions stereotyping women workers into one of four gender-familiar roles: mother, child, iron maiden, or sex object. Unfortunately, research conducted 15 years later continues to support Kanter's categorizations (Garlick, Dixon, & Allen, 1992). These ways of viewing women result from traditionally male organizations attempting to find a familiar place for women that reinforces their long-held views and helps them feel more comfortable about having women in the workplace. Each of these roles diminishes women's professional competence and leads to structural discrimination in the workplace.

The mother role emphasizes women's nurturing and relational qualities. But instead of these being valued and reinforced with the prestige and status such important skills could receive, they are used to segregate women into stereotypical roles of support and care for others with little prestige and the lowest salaries. The child role, conversely, emphasizes the generally held view that women are less mature, less competent, more dependent, and in need of protection from others. These stereotypes reinforce the notion that because of these deficits it is acceptable to pay women less than men for the same job (Bureau of Labor Statistics, 1991).

The iron maiden view is that women who are hard driving and ambitious in the workplace are not really women, that to be a woman necessitates certain feminine characteristics. Women who are strong, assertive, and competitive—in short, who portray the male model they have been told they should emulate—are rejected for these very qualities.

Finally, the sex object is the stereotype that focuses on women's sex and sexuality. The existence of this stereotype is supported by research that indicates there is a great deal more attention paid to women's appearance in hiring and promotion decisions (Wood, 1994). This focus on women as sex objects has obvious implications for the sexual harassment of women, so prevalent in the workplace. If women are viewed as sex objects, verbal and physical harassment of women is a predictable outcome.

These gender-based roles for women may form the basis for the continued discrimination in hiring (Betz & Fitzgerald, 1987; Nieva & Gutek, 1981), in salaries (Eccles, 1987; O'Neil, 1985), and in sexual harassment on the job (Gutek, 1985) so consistent in the literature. Even if women do exceedingly well, there appears to be what some have referred to as a glass ceiling (Morrison, White, & Van Velsor, 1987) in which women can only rise so far on the corporate ladder, but not to top-level executive positions. Wood (1994), in her review of the current climate of organizations, emphasized that although there is increased awareness in organizations, hostile environments that devalue women still exist, informal networks that exclude women still predominate, and mentoring of women workers is still rare.

There is also convincing evidence that lesbian women experience significantly more employment discrimination than their heterosexual counterparts (Morgan & Brown, 1991). This is because, in addition to the bias they may receive due to their sex, they also must face the harassment and discrimination that comes from our heterosexist, homophobic society. Although it may have become somewhat less socially acceptable to be blatantly discriminatory against some minority groups, research indicates it is still acceptable to express hostility toward lesbians and gay men. Lesbians report fear of losing their jobs should they decide to be open about their sexual/affectional orientation (Brooks, 1981). Studies indicate that these fears are not unfounded (Levine & Leonard, 1984) and that lesbians do face considerable levels of employment discrimination based on their orientation (Morgan & Brown, 1991). From recent anti-gay legislation that was introduced in two states in 1992 and passed in one of them, it appears that there will be an uphill battle in helping to guarantee the basic employment rights along with all civil rights for lesbians and gays.

Croteau et al. (2000) reports that employment discrimination against LGBT individuals is widespread with between 25-66% of those studied reporting discrimination. This discrimination is often formal and involves discrimination in hiring, promotion, raises and limited benefits for partners, but may also be informal and include a hostile work environment and verbal harassment (Croteau, 1996).

The level of concealment of one's sexual orientation has been shown to relate to level of discrimination (Croteau & Lark, 1995). Griffin (1992) identified four categories of vocational identity management. These include (a) "passing" strategies where the individual leads others to believe they are heterosexual, (b) "covering" in which the individual tries to hide their orientation at work while not pretending to be heterosexual; (c) "implicitly out" where one is honest about one's life, but not actually describing themselves as lesbian and (d) "explicitly out" which involves openly labeling oneself as lesbian or bisexual at work. Griffin hypothesizes that the choice of strategy involves a tension between fear of discovering and need for self integrity (Croteau et al., 2000). The workplace environment and organizational policies of current and potential employers may be considered in the context of career counseling. Thus, it may also be important for us to discuss the continuum of possible identity management strategies with clients and determine at what level they want their sexual orientation identity known at work.

Clearly, the gendered context of the workplace and attitudes and practices realted to sexual orientation continue to have an impact on women workers. As we will see, that impact will have a variety of gender specific outcomes when women seek career planning services.

GENDER SPECIFIC OUTCOMES

The previous section was an overview of some of the career related aspects of the gendered environment that occur during early development, adolescence, and in the workplace. Learning more about aspects of this environment is an important step in improving career counseling for lesbian, bisexual, and heterosexual women. Only when counselors have adequate information about the extent of the gendered context and issues relevant to sexual orientation can we be effective in our interventions with clients. The following section discusses some of the most prevalent gender specific outcomes that may result from these environments and that may dramatically influence career counseling. Specifically, these outcomes are math avoidance, lower expectations for success, lower self-efficacy beliefs about nontraditional careers, relational focus, and role conflict.

Math Avoidance

Of all the gender-based outcomes that result from sex role stereotyping, arguably one of the most devastating to women's ultimate career attainment is math avoidance. This curious and occupationally devastating phenomenon has been well traced in the professional literature. Girls in elementary school outperform boys on math tasks. They report liking math more and believe that they are better at math than boys (Boswell, 1985). By early high school, girls have lost their competitive edge and score similarly to boys. By late high school, males have the clear advantage in advanced math skills. On tests like the SAT, which is used to predict performance in post-secondary education, boys score better than girls and consequently receive more offers of admission and more scholarship funds (Unger & Crawford, 1992). Evidence is accumulating that there is sex bias in the SAT scores, because although men tend to score better, women tend to do better in college classes including courses related to math and science.

The largest single predictor of girls' lower math performance appears to be the number of math classes taken. Researchers find that when the number and type of courses are controlled, differences in performance disappear (Chipman & Thomas, 1985). There is very little evidence to suggest that there is a hereditary basis for mathematical ability by gender and much evidence to suggest it is a strongly socialized phenomenon (Eccles & Jacobs, 1986). Again, teachers and counselors appear to play a pivotal role in shaping and reinforcing girls' self-confidence in math and science. Research indicates that even when girls have a belief in their own ability in math and science, teachers and other powerful adult figures who communicate a lack of confidence in their ability to do well can have a devastating effect on their willingness to pursue these areas (Greenberg-Lake, 1991).

But why is all of this so important when considering girls' and women's career development? Betz calls mathematics the "critical filter" (1994, p. 22) for women and presents compelling data indicating the continually narrowing career options that math avoidance creates. Consider the following:

- Women comprise 45% of the workforce but only 16% of scientists and engineers (National Science Foundation, 1990).
- When boys and girls leave high school with enough of the appropriate math classes to pursue a science major in college, 50% of the males, but only 20% of the females, do so (Betz, 1994).
- In a study of mathematically talented boys and girls at John Hopkins, Benbow (1988) reported that 42% of the boys, but only 22% of the girls, selected science or engineering related fields.
- In an early study (1973), Sells reported that only 8% of the first-year women, versus 57% of the men at the University of California–Berkeley, had taken four years of high school math. Only those who had taken the four years of math were able to consider 15 of the 20 major fields at Berkeley; the five remaining options were stereotypically female fields.

As society becomes more technologically advanced, math will become even more important in order to achieve higher paying, higher status jobs. Without intervention, women will continue to lose out on these potentially rewarding career options.

Lower Expectations for Success

A second pervasive outcome of the gendered context seems to be a consistent underestimation of abilities on the part of girls and women. Beginning at a very young age, girls perceive and report their career options to be much narrower than do boys. In a study reported by Unger and Crawford (1992), first- and second-grade children were asked the traditional question, "What do you want to be when you grow up?" Thirty-three boys and thirty-three girls responded. The boys came up with eighteen different occupational options, the girls only eight. Girls are significantly more likely to report that they aren't smart enough or good enough to attain their desired careers (O'Brien, Friedman, Tipton & Linn, 2000)

Studies report that college women also consistently indicate lower expectancies for success on exams and other measures of achievement in college (Matlin, 1996). This phenomena seems to continue throughout a woman's development, with adult women also reporting lower expectations for what they can achieve in their lives. In studies of sex-related differences in expectations, Meece and colleagues (1982) indicated that women not only reported lower estimates for their present abilities, but also for their performance and predictions of success in future situations. These underestimates were present even when the women's objective performance was found to be better than males.

Betz (1994) reported that lower expectations for success occur primarily on masculine stereotyped tasks. Specifically, lower expectations are found on tasks that have as components social comparison, competition, and social evaluation, and that lack clear performance feedback. As Betz argued, these are the very characteristics generally necessary for career success. Consequently, if women consistently underestimate their ability to perform in these situations, it is probably harmful to their overall career development.

A recent longitudunal study by O'Brien and her colleagues found that over the 5 years of the study the woman chose less prestigious careers and more traditional careers to those to which they aspired as high school seniors. In addition, these women chose careers that underutilized their abilities. (O'Brien, et al., 2000). Lesbian and bisexual woman may also express more limited expectation for success due to the perception they will be entering more prejudicial and discriminatory work environments. This perception may limit the range of careers they pursue (Croteau, et al., 2000).

Research also indicates that women's underestimation of ability is present in ability and interest inventories (Swanson & Lease, 1990). Swanson and Lease's (1990) research supports an earlier finding of Bailey and Bailey (1971) who reported that male college students rated themselves above a "typical male student" and women rated themselves below a "typical female student." These researchers urge career counselors to supplement self-ratings and to explore the authenticity of ratings whenever possible.

Lower Self-Efficacy Beliefs about Nontraditional Careers

In addition to research indicating that women tend to underestimate their skills and potential in general, this appears to be true also when predicting their ability for nontraditional career fields. Again, holding actual ability as a constant, women tend to report less ability to perform traditionally male activities and instead enter a narrow range of occupations characterized by low pay and low prestige. There have been numerous studies examining the antecedents of such career decisions. First, because many of these career fields require math and science background, women's traditionally lower perceived ability in these academic fields is seen as one primarily factor (Kimball, 1989).

The lack of role models in nontraditional career fields has also been the topic of ongoing research. Role models are a powerful force in shaping young women's self-efficacy in nontraditional fields (Betz, 1994; Eccles, 1987). Seeing someone else who has dealt with conflicts and met challenges in male dominated fields can be very helpful to other women. Female graduate students who had female professors as mentors reported being more confident and more career oriented (Gilbert, Galessich, & Evans, 1983). This lack of role model may be especially salient for lesbian and bisexual women as even if they find women role models it is unlikely they will find explicitly "out" role models.

Brooks (1988) proposed an expectancy-valence model to understand women's lack of participation in nontraditional fields and, further, how to intervene to help women into these career fields. Brooks contended that women must have the expectancy that they can succeed in the given career field and the field itself must have positive valence (attractiveness) for the woman. Both expectancy and valence must be positive for a nontraditional occupation to be chosen. That is, if a woman believes in her ability to be successful in a nontraditional field, but does not view that career field as positive or attractive for her, she will likely not pursue it. Conversely, if she views a nontraditional job field as highly attractive, but has no belief in her ability to attain that career, she will also not pursue it. Brooks proposed a number of strategies embedded in the expectancy–valence model to help women explore nontraditional fields.

Relational Focus

While traditional theories of human development have viewed autonomy and independence as critical to healthy and mature development, a growing number of theorists have questioned this basic tenent, especially as it applies to women. Specifically researchers and theorists have begun to uncover a fun-

damentally different form of development for girls and women. This difference has been referred to as the self-in-relation (Miller, 1991) orientation and
may have far-reaching importance for career counseling. Briefly, this theoretical work has been the result of both qualitative and quantitative research on
the development of girls and women. Gilligan (1980), for example, interviewed individuals from six to sixty and noted some important gender differences. "Male and female voices have typically spoken of different truths, the
former of the role of separation in development as it comes to define and
empower the self, the latter of the ongoing process of attachment that creates
and sustains the human community" (Gilligan, 1980, p. 18). These differences
were further articulated by Lyons (1983) who described women's ways of
relating as emphasizing responsiveness to the needs of others. There is an
identification with the other person in a relationship and an empathetic
response. Male patterns, according to Lyons (1983), are based more on reci-
procity and fairness between equal individuals. Chodorow (1978) and Gilligan (1982) indicated that these gender differences in relational components
originate in differing experiences of attachment and separation in the very
early years of life. Further empirical research on adolescent development consistently demonstrates greater relational salience for girls than for boys
(Bakken & Romig, 1992; Claes, 1992; Tannen, 1994; Stein, Newcomb, and
Bentler, 1992).

Forrest and Mikolaitis (1986) hypothesized that this relational component
may relate to the confusion many women feel about career choice, satisfaction, and adjustment in a given field. They contend that the individuation and
separation from others that is promoted in Western culture as the way to
healthy career development may not fit the development of girls and women.
In recent investigations by O'Brien and her colleagues (2000), separation from
parents was not found to have a direct effect on career self-efficacy and there
was some evidence that attachment to parents may lead to greater confidence
in pursuing career-related tasks. Although little empirical research has been
conducted to apply these constructs to the career development literature,
some related empirical investigations do exist. In a study of mid-life career
changers, for example, Henton, Russell and Koval (1983) emphasized the
impact of career transitions on the lives of family members. Although men in
their sample had made successful career changes, they did so with seemingly
little awareness of the impact such changes would have on their families.
Conversely, in a study of returning women students, Mohney and Anderson
(1988) suggested that the decision to return to college may not be so much a
matter of internal career motivation as one of timing and being responsive to
the needs of others. A prominent influence was whether these women felt
they could return to college without being disruptive to husbands, children,
and in some cases coworkers and employers. These two studies, although
studying unrelated career development constructs, are examples of men's

greater independence, and women's greater relational focus in career decision making.

Additional research indicates that women and men may actually emphasize different factors when initially choosing a career field (Lips, 1992). Women's valuing of relational factors was indicated in studies that found that men chose careers based on prestige and salaries, whereas women chose careers based on relational factors, such as whether they would like their coworkers (Neil & Snizek, 1987).

Although this outcome of the gendered context would seem to have positive valence in society, the reverse seems to be true. With the exception of some companies which are becoming more team-oriented, very little value is typically placed on the relational focus in America's capitalistic, individualistic, competitive society. Thus, the relational qualities of connectedness and communion are not those that girls and women are taught to value or that are valued monetarily in most work settings.

Role Conflict

As more and more heterosexual women have left the home to enter the paid labor force, one would expect changes in role expectations to have occurred in the home. Data indicates, however, that heterosexual women who work full-time outside the home continue to be responsible for 80 to 90 percent of the work within the home as well (Ferree, 1987; Russo & Denmark, 1884). This appears to be true across ethnic and cultural groups also (Hartzler & Franco, 1985). Research indicates that working two full-time jobs is creating great strain on women workers. In examining the role conflict of home and work responsibilities, lesbian couples were much more committed to an equitable division of home-related tasks than were their heterosexual counterparts (Blumstein & Schwartz, 1983). Unique role conflict may included dealing with partner differences in sexual orientation identity management at work and the issues of benefits being denied to partners (Croteau et al., 2000).

Among heterosexual couples, however, the pattern is quite clear. Betz and Fitzgerald (1987) conducted an extensive review of the literature on the relationship of marital status to career involvement and reported that there is a "strong inverse relationship between being married and number of children and every measurable criterion of career involvement and achievement" (Betz, 1994, p. 21). Betz & Fitzgerald (1987) indicated that based on their review, they believe that role conflict is "the most salient factor in women's career development" (p. 203). Thus, as we can see, the gendered context of women's lives has produced outcomes that directly impact what they will bring to the counseling context and give us many clues as to what might be helpful in career counseling.

ASSESSMENTS AND TECHNIQUES FOR EMPOWERING WOMEN'S CHOICES

The previous section examined several key aspects of the gendered context and their resultant gender specific outcomes. Now we turn to examining various assessments and techniques for promoting women's awareness and understanding how gender and sexual orientation have influenced their career development. We first describe assessment techniques for both counselor and client that will help you understand the impact of gender and sexual orientation on the change process in counseling. Then we discuss the importance of helping clients acquire information on which to make more authentic life choices.

Assessing Your Own Counseling Philosophy

As we ask you to assess your philosophy of counseling, it is important for us to clarify our own. Much of what we will suggest in actual career counseling strategies flows from this underlying philosophy. There appears to be a wide diversity of philosophies that guide career counseling. These philosophies can be placed on a continuum. At one end of the continuum are career counselors who view their role as matching individuals and occupational roles. These counselors would see their role as largely a technical one: assessing the skills, interests, and abilities of the client and matching that individual to an occupation that would best utilize those personal characteristics. These counselors would find assessment skills and knowledge of labor market information of most value to them. At the other end of the continuum, and more congruent with the current authors' philosophy, are career counselors who view their role as personal and societal change agents. These counselors use knowledge of assessment and occupational information, along with psychological knowledge and constructs, to understand how the environmental context may be limiting the range of options their clients are currently considering. Thus, the counselor examines and challenges underlying assumptions clients have about themselves and the world of work.

As this philosophy applies directly to the gender context of career planning, we believe it is important to focus on gender and sexual orientation as categories of analysis within the career counseling context. We view the role of the career counselor as helping clients to understand and work through the numerous societal obstacles that systematically keep women and men from envisioning and achieving economic security and balancing meaningful achievement and relational connectedness in their lives.

We recognize that gender socialization brings with it a host of problems for women, such as lower expectations for success, math avoidance, occupational stratification and segregation, and family and career conflict, which severely restrict women's aspirations and options. Similarly, as will be explored in greater depth in the next chapter, men's socialization brings with it performance anxiety, restricted emotional expressively, limited interpersonal relationships, and shortened life expectancy. Therefore, we view the role of the career counselor as one that challenges gender-based homophobic and heterosexist assumptions and helps clients recapture dreams and restore options that have been discarded along the way.

This philosophy also incorporates affirmative counseling practices. It recognizes homophobia and heterosexism as critical barriers to the lives of lesbians and bisexual women and seeks ways to affirm and enhance the lives of LGBT individuals through career counseling.

This philosophy challenges the counselor to go far beyond the maintenance of the status quo typified by the matching of people and jobs. It calls on each of us to ensure that our clients have information to make authentic life decisions. In doing so, some of our suggestions will run counter to the popular notion in career counseling that we must respect the client's own decision-making and career choices. Given the weight of gender socialization and the power of homophobia and heterosexism, we believe that many times women and men have not experienced the kind of environmental support and information necessary to lead them to authentic career decisions. This philosophy also emphasizes our role as change agents who are working for more humane and person-enhancing school and work environments. It views both our individual work with clients and our work in promoting change in the environment as being equally valid.

We urge you to clarify your own philosophy toward career counseling and to consider especially the role of gender and sexual orientation in that philosophy. Three orientations that emphasize the critical role of gender in the counseling process may provide a helpful starting point. They are briefly described here and referenced for more in-depth examination.

Nonsexist Counseling (Marecek & Kravetz, 1977; Travis, 1988)

The basic tenet of nonsexist counseling is that there should be equity in the treatment of men and women in counseling. This orientation recognizes the pervasiveness of sexism in society and argues that clients should be thought of as individuals rather than as one sex or the other. Nonsexist counselors emphasize the importance of counselors working out their own biases and becoming knowledgeable of both the blatant and subtle ways career counseling can reflect sexism. Nonsexist counselors work to avoid any differentiation between males and females in the counseling process.

Gender Aware Counseling (Good, Gilbert, & Scher, 1990)

There are five basic tenets of gender aware therapy: (1) the construct of gender is recognized as an integral part of counseling, career development, and overall psychological health; (2) client concerns are viewed within a larger societal context; (3) counselors actively address gender injustices; (4) the counselor and client work together in a collaborative relationship; (5) ultimately the client has the freedom to make his or her own life choices.

Feminist Counseling (Brooks & Forrest, 1994)

The two basic tenets of feminist counseling are: (1) society has shaped women's behavior, and thus the personal is political, and (2) counselors should be no more powerful than their clients. These two basic tenets have been expanded into a series of principles that further explicate the powerful interrelationship between society and the individual woman and that specifically address the power differential between counselor and client.

In addition to clarifying our philosophical view of the change process in counseling, it is also critically important that we as career counselors work on our own gender issues. Given the pervasive nature of sexism in American society, it is likely that as counselors, we have grown up with bias and gender-typed attitudes similar to our clients. Although we may pride ourselves on being gender aware, there are subtle and unconscious ways that we may communicate gender bias to our clients. It is vital that counselors at all professional levels receive supervision from gender-aware supervisors who can help with the awareness and change process.

LGBT-affirmativeness among heterosexuals is conceptualized as "the range of attitudes beliefs, emotions and behaviors that express and assert the positive valuing of the sexual identity of, and an understanding of the realities faced by LGBT individuals within an oppressive society" (Worthington, Savoy, & Vemaglia, 2001) Affirmative individuals are not only knowledgeable about LGBT issues, but they are also understanding of and comfortable with their own sexual identity and diverse sexual orientations. Contact and involvement with LGBT individuals is an important component of the process of becoming a LGBT-affirmative career counselor. This contact is presumed to occur not only in one's professional role, but also in other contexts, including personal, social and familial networks. The model describes five statuses: *Passive Conformity, Revelation and Exploration, Tentative Commitment, Synthesis and Integration,* and *Active Commitment.* Becoming LGBT-affirmative is a developmental process of movement from an unexamined, unconscious heterosexist and/or homophobic construction of the world, through a phase of intellectualized understanding of what it means to be LGBT-affirmative, and finally to a more fully integrated level of awareness and expression, in which knowledge achieved at earlier phases is incorporated into one's personal, professional and political spheres. LGBT-affirmative counselors utilize their self-awareness, knowledge, skills, and involvement with LGBT individuals to inform their practice with all clients, including lesbian, gay, bisexual, and heterosexual clients.

Similar to the assessment of our own philosophy regarding gender-related issues and sexual orientation, it is also important to assess various aspects of the client's perceptions and environment. Three types of assessments will be provided here: (1) a description of a theory of feminist identity development (FID) that can help to formally or informally assess where your client is in her own gender role development, (2) an environmental assessment of the early years of the gendered context, and (3) an assessment of the gendered work context. These assessments are each provided as a stimulus for your own thinking about ways to examine the impact of gender on our clients' lives.

FEMINIST IDENTITY DEVELOPMENT

Downing and Roush (1985) have proposed a five-stage model of feminist identity development. Depending on where career clients are in their own developmental process, they may view the same gendered context quite differently. A counselor's awareness of this model may promote greater understanding of the clients in the counseling session.

Stage 1: Passive Acceptance

In this first stage, the client has passively accepted the inherent sexism and discrimination of society and may believe it to be justified. Clients in this stage may say such things as:

I don't think women should be put in charge at the office. They really don't make very good leaders. I get along much better with men.

Yes, it does seem like our math teacher spends more time with the boys, but that is because they are more likely to go into math.

At this stage, there is an acceptance of traditionally held gender roles that support the superiority of males.

Stage 2: Revelation

The second stage may be triggered by a life event that jars the client into a realization that the oppression of women is not valid or right. The person may feel guilty about her own past actions and lack of awareness. You may hear this stage being expressed in statements like:

I could kick myself for the many times I have doubted or discounted other women when they were courageous enough to expose the harassment that was going on.

I never considered myself a feminist. I just went in, did my job, and that was that. But when I was passed over again for that job, I started realizing they weren't really making promotions based on competence or previous job performance.

Stage 3: Embeddedness—Emancipation

This stage is often characterized by a dichotomization of the sexes, with all men perceived negatively and all women positively. In this stage women may seek more communion with other women to the exclusion of men. Women may look for other women in the workplace who share their perceptions regarding gender inequity and bond with them for support and encouragement.

Men I have known are not trustworthy. I have given up on them. With women, they may not have as much power, but at least I know they have my best interests at heart.

I am looking for a more woman-centered place to work. Perhaps it is a man's world, but I don't have to work for or with them.

Stage 4: Synthesis

At this stage women evaluate men as individuals as opposed to an oppressive group. They value the uniqueness of other women and recognize the impact of internal and external factors that influence women's lives.

It seems as though I really underestimated my abilities. Some of what happened to me was a result of my own internal conflicts; other things were overt discrimination.

I've had good male bosses and some real abusive ones. I am a lot wiser now about identifying the losers earlier.

Stage 5: Active Commitment

When clients reach this stage they are ready to take a much more active role in shaping their own destiny and changing harmful environmental factors. These clients see the need to take on the role of making the world a more just place for themselves and other women. Although Downing and Roush (1985) believe that few women reach this stage, those that do can be especially exciting to work with in career counseling. As one recent client said in a session:

I have come to the conclusion that a part of this change is really up to me. During much of my life, I blamed others or waited for others to fix things. I now understand that I really need a job that promotes change for women and men at both the individual and societal levels.

Understanding feminist identity development may help us learn a great deal more about our clients' reactions to the gendered environment. A woman whose attitudes and beliefs are at Stage 1 may either be unaware or actually accepting of sex bias, whereas a client in the middle stages may prefer a female counselor and may benefit from processing the anger she feels about sexism in the classroom or workplace.

If a more formal assessment of a client's level of feminist identity development is desired, a scale is available (FIDS: Bargad & Hyde, 1991). FIDS is a 39-item measure that has five subscales that assess the five stages described here. Clients respond to questions on a five-point Likert scale, ranging from "strongly agree" to "strongly disagree" on items such as "Being a part of a women's community is important to me." This instrument may serve as a helpful discussion tool for examining clients' perceptions of the influences of gender-related issues in the career development process.

Environmental Assessment of the Gendered Context

Although research indicates that sex role socialization is pervasive, there are numerous individual differences in both the extent of exposure and its impact. We recommend that an assessment be done to examine the level to which each client has been influenced. This assessment should include an examination of the various sources of active support and discouragement, as well as neutral treatment that has influenced the client's life journey and perceived choices. Although these assessments will vary depending on life circumstances, the following questions provide a starting point:

- Think back to your childhood. What messages did you receive about the career options you might pursue?
- Who most actively supported the development of your interests and skills? What form did that active support take?
- Can you think of any discouragement you received regarding a potential interest area? What form did the discouragement take?
- In grade school (high school, college), did you feel support, discouragement, or a neutral atmosphere for the development of your interests?
- Were you more actively encouraged to pursue sex-role appropriate interests than nontraditional interests?
- If you were to graph your own sense of personal self-efficacy throughout your life, how would that graph look?

- Can you think of occupational areas you once dreamed of that you discarded at some point in your life? What were they, and what do you remember about the reasons why you discarded them?

This assessment can be done as part of the career counseling session or provided as a homework assignment for the client to ponder and write about independently. You may also want to use some variation of these questions while conducting a career genogram (see Chapter 10). The client can then process these reflections in the following sessions.

Environmental Assessment of the Gendered Context of Work

Much of the literature in career development focuses on adjustment or adaptation to the work environment. Fitting into the work culture, and sharing similar interests and skills as those currently employed in the field have all been seen as valued career skills. While not questioning their overall importance, researchers have begun to point out the toxic quality of some work environments, which promote neither the physical nor the psychological health of their workers (Carayon, 1993). In this chapter, we point to research on sexual harassment, the glass ceiling, lack of mentoring and support, and stereotypical definitions of working women as sex objects or iron maidens. Thus, fitting into these environments cannot be seen as an appropriate goal. Research indicates that these unhealthy environments may be especially detrimental to individuals who have previously been underrepresented and marginalized in particular work fields. Women and men who work in nontraditional fields may find themselves being asked to adapt to environments that may not value their uniqueness and in which they might suffer bias, discrimination, and harassment. Thus, it may be vitally important that career counselors help clients analyze the work environment. Is it an environment in which the goal of adaptation is a healthy choice? Or does the environment support a culture that is basically unhealthy for the individual worker? Although these assessments will vary greatly depending on the individual circumstances of the work environment, the following questions might be a starting point:

- In general, how does your work environment feel to you? Warm and friendly? Cold and hostile? What words would you use to describe your work atmosphere?
- What messages have you received in your work environment about what options you might pursue within the organization. Do they seem limited because of your sex?; sexual orientation?
- What are the signs that your environment at work is healthy for the individuals who work there?

- Are your skills and interests being actively promoted and developed within the organization?
- Are the unique aspects that characterize you (which may not be characteristic of the environmental culture) valued in your work environment?
- Can you think of subtle or blatant experiences of harassment or discouragement experienced in your work environment that have diminished your sense of personhood?
- Have there been times when you felt singled out or ignored because of your sex?; and sexual orientation?

Once an environmental assessment of this kind has been conducted, the counselor's role involves helping the client determine whether fitting in, becoming a change agent, or getting out of the system is the most healthy and functional life choice.

Thus, these assessments are all ways of helping you gain information about the influences of the gendered context on the individual. While they should be adapted to fit the individual circumstances of the situation, they are provided here to stimulate your thinking about ways of addressing gender-related and sexual orientation issues in the career counseling sessions.

Increasing the Authenticity of Career Decision Making through Knowledge

It is our view that career counselors have an obligation to both challenge gender-based beliefs, homophobia, and heterosexist practices and provide information to increase the authenticity of career decisions. While a variety of knowledge bases might be appropriate given the individual clients needs and situation, five areas that are generally salient are presented here: (1) Inform the client about the rewards and costs of gender role traditionality, (2) Teach clients how to alter gender- and heterosexist-based self-efficacy beliefs, (3) Inform clients about the importance of continuing in math and science careers and in considering nontraditional career fields, (4) Reinforce the importance of valuing the unique characteristics that women traditionally possess, and (5) Use specific awareness and skills to work with the unique issues of lesbian and bisexual women.

Inform Women about the Rewards and Costs of Occupational Gender Role Traditionally

Research on the importance of achievement through paid employment in the lives of men and women is important knowledge to share with clients. Data is compelling that women who do not have outlets for achievement outside the homemaker role are more likely to suffer from psychological distress (Bernard, 1972; Radloff, 1975) and lower self-esteem (Ferree, 1987) than their employed counterparts. Although respecting our clients' ultimate choices is important, it is critical to examine the authenticity of those choices. Authentic choices can only be made through knowledge of both the costs and rewards of choices.

In addition to the psychological benefits of meaningful paid employment, women need to know about the likelihood that they will be economically independent during their lifetimes. Over two-thirds of women in the United States are divorced, widowed, separated, single, or married to men whose income is below the poverty level (U.S. Department of Labor, 1988). Although most young women optimistically approach relationships with a vision of an economically stable future, they should be aware of the reality of many women's lives.

Similarly, the reality for most lesbians is that they will be economically independent. Research indicates that most lesbians work in the paid labor force, ranging from 85 to 92 percent in various samples reported by Morgan and Brown (1991). Research also indicates that in most lesbian relationships individuals do not assume the financial dependence of their partner (Clunis & Green, 1988). The likelihood of lesbian women needing to work to support themselves is therefore especially great. In addition to the salary disparity experienced by women in general, research indicates that all other factors being held constant, lesbian women earn less than their heterosexual female counterparts (Bradford & Ryan, 1987).

Thus, women need more information about adherence to traditional gender role prescriptions and the occurrence of psychological distress as well as financial need. The career counselor is in a unique role to explore how much the client already knows about these costs and rewards, and to furnish additional information as needed.

Teach Clients How to Alter Gender- and Homophobic-Based Self-Efficacy Beliefs

Self-efficacy has been defined as "people's judgments in their capabilities to organize and execute courses of action required to attain designated types of performance" (Bandura, 1986, p. 391). Self-efficacy has been shown to predict choice of behavioral activities, effort expended on these activities, persistence despite obstacles, and actual performance (Bandura, 1977). The development of self-efficacy beliefs has been demonstrated to be facilitated by the following conditions: (a) performance attainment, or trying a behavior and having success with it, (b) verbal persuasion, being told by others that you can do it, (c) vicarious reinforcement, seeing others similar to oneself successfully perform a behavior, and (d) physiological input, bodily sensations that give us information about how we are doing (Bandura, 1977, 1982).

Although gender-based self-efficacy beliefs may be embedded in how clients view themselves, it is important that career counselors provide information about the changeable nature of these beliefs. If men and women know that these beliefs can be altered, and the procedures needed for change, they are in a better position to decide whether to alter these beliefs. Hackett and Betz (1981) hypothesized that Bandura's theoretical framework would have particular relevance to the area of women's career development, sparking a plenitude of important research on the impact of self-efficacy beliefs on career-related behavior. In the first empirical test of the application of Bandura's theory to women's career development, Betz and Hackett (1983) demonstrated considerable support for its application. Additional research has demonstrated that self-efficacy was related to performance in a myriad of other domains, such as academic performance (Bores-Rangel, Church, Szendre, & Reeves, 1990; Multon, Brown, & Lent, 1991), math performance (Pajares & Miller, 1995) and work-related behavior (Sadri & Robertson, 1993). Recently, Lent, Brown, and Hackett (1994) also expanded Bandura's work by advancing a social cognitive theory of career and academic interest, choice, and performance. Using meta-analytic data, they suggested a direct relationship between self-efficacy and performance in academic and vocational areas. Social cognitive theory has also been applied to LGBT individuals (Morrow, Gore, & Campbell, 1996).

Career counselors can promote women's self-efficacy through a variety of theoretically based strategies. Performance attainment as a source of self-efficacy can be facilitated through women being encouraged to try out a variety of experiences and roles similar to one they might be considering. Internships, part-time jobs, and volunteer experiences provide valuable ways for women to realize that they are capable of more than they had thought was in their realm of possibilities. Verbal persuasion may come from any significant person in a woman's life, including her counselor. Letting the client know that you believe in her ability to accomplish her goals can be a powerful message. Vicarious reinforcement involves seeing other women who are similar to oneself succeed in roles the client is considering, another important source of self-efficacy beliefs. Career counselors can help locate such role models and make arrangements for formal or informal contact. Thus, it is important that career counselors let women know that it is possible to alter their gender-based interest and behavior patterns. Giving clients specific information about how they can alter their beliefs in their abilities is an important step toward empowering them.

Inform Clients about the Importance of Pursuing Math and Science

Although the evidence reported earlier in this chapter about the occupational importance of continuing on in math and science courses has been in the professional literature for a number of years, there is little evidence that parents and children are aware of this data.

Career counselors can take an active role in helping girls and women understand the role of mathematics and science in their career development. Four specific techniques career counselors might use are:

1. Girls should be presented with specific data, perhaps in graphic form, that depicts the continually narrowing range of options available to those who lack math and science backgrounds.

2. Because research (see Beurk, 1985) has shown that women often do not take mathematics courses because they feel alienated by the teaching methods, it may be useful to help girls and women locate innovative new programs that facilitate their growth and competence in science and math. Many of these programs incorporate work in groups and use examples that are more relevant to the lives of girls and women.

3. There is also considerable evidence that girls and women believe math to be unfeminine, unattractive, and generally incompatible with being a wife and mother (Sherman, 1983). Thus, it would seem highly beneficial for girls and women to be exposed to mathematicians who break that stereotype. Career counselors can help identify such role models and facilitate these encounters for their clients.

4. The perception of how sociable people in the math and science fields are has also been the subject of investigations. For example, Lips (1992) found that subjects who believed that scientists are sociable were more likely to enjoy math and science courses and stated more interest in pursuing math and science related careers. This data would highlight the importance again of counselors exposing clients to role models who can help break pre-existing stereotypes about mathematical and scientific occupations.

Valuing What Is Female: Integrating the Self-in-Relation Theory into Career Counseling

One of the gender-related outcomes presented earlier in this chapter is that self-concept may be formed differently for men and women, with the relational component more critical to women's identity formation than to men's. This difference has a host of implications for both the process and content of our work with female clients.

1. Perhaps one of the most critical roles for the career counselor is helping clients to value their uniqueness as women. From the earliest years, and across cultures, there is a valuing of masculine traits over feminine ones and of boys over girls (Basow, 1992). This phenomena continues throughout life in environmental situations where female characteristics are not

valued, often resulting in a devaluing of self. Therefore, it is important that the counselor value the strong preferences women may have for connectedness and relationship and reinforce these characteristics as unique strengths rather than, as traditionally has been the case, signs of immature dependency.

2. The counselor might help the client explore whether dissatisfaction in a work setting is a result of a lack of perceived connection with others. It may be especially important to help the client determine the advantages and disadvantages of various courses of action. Do I try to find a different work environment that better meets my relational needs, or do I try to change my need for connection from 9 to 5 and fit into the work environment? Do I try to change my work environment to make it a place that better fits my needs? Each of these courses of action requires additional assistance; for example, if the woman decides to change her work environment, the counselor can help her identify work environments that may promote a greater sense of relationship.

3. While it seems critically important to overtly demonstrate that you value your client's need for connection and her relational competence, especially given how devalued these characteristics are in society, it is still important that clients examine the benefits as well as the costs of both the separate and connected perspectives when making career decisions (Hotelling & Forrest, 1985). The predominance of women in social occupations (nursing or teaching, for example) may enable women to meet needs for connection and relationship, but due to the devalued status of these occupations, they may not provide the income needed to sustain a household. The counselor can also help the client identify when her emphasis on connection may lead to role overload and conflict because of too many relational demands. Especially during the stressful time of a career transition, the counselor may also need to emphasize to the client the importance of caring for her own wants and needs.

4. During the career counseling process, a client's relational perspective may mean that she would benefit from greater connection with you as the counselor (Nelson, 1996) and she may wish for more self-disclosure from you about your own career and life-planning decisions. This may be one way of building a strong working alliance with the client. Conversely, they may react negatively to, and find little benefit in, vocational exploration tools that they perceive as lacking human connection (e.g., computerized career information systems, batteries of vocational assessment instruments, etc.). As one client recently characterized her career counseling experience, "They just took my data, referred me to some boxes, and shuffled me out the door—no human connection. This is my life I am wanting help with."

5. Although "the mainstream of vocational theory includes the implicit assumption that a career is a vehicle or opportunity leading to realization of self" (Forrest and Mikolaitis, 1986, p. 86), clients may benefit from a close examination of how their career choices also affect others in their relational community. It may, therefore, be beneficial for you to examine the importance the client perceives her career-planning decisions will have on others in her environment (partner, children, employer, etc.). This self-versus-relational focus formed the theoretical bases for one of the factors on the Career Transitions Inventory, which is discussed in depth in Chapter 11. One factor, called decision independence, includes such items as "career choices affect others and I must take the needs of others into account when making a career transition." The Career Transitions Inventory may be helpful in assessing a client's relational focus as it relates to her career decision making.

These ways of altering our view of healthy identity development to include the relational component may influence career counseling from both a content and a process perspective. The relational component emphasizes the importance of the life career perspective (McDaniels & Gysbers, 1992) in career counseling, in which one's vocation is only a part of the total life career.

In addition, this knowledge may be useful to clients to help them make the most well-informed decisions possible. Other information may be valuable given the specific demographics or situation of the client. The Walsh and Osipow (1994) text provides in-depth research on a variety of topics, such as counseling gifted girls and women, women in management, women in science and engineering, dual career relationships, and so forth. This type of current information is indispensable when helping clients sort through gender-related life issues.

In Chapter 1 we outlined a process of career counseling that consists of two major phases and a number of subphases. In the next section of this chapter we will discuss ways of integrating the issues relevant to the gendered context into this broad career planning process. Although more generic issues related to this model are presented in Chapters 8 through 18 of this book, this section will highlight those aspects of each phase that may have gender-related implications for girls and women.

Competence on Working with Lesbian and Bisexual Women

Although most of the recommendations made for working with girls and women in general are salient for lesbian and bisexual women, a host of unique skills and areas of awareness also need our attention. The following four areas seem critical in becoming an effective career counselor for LGBT clients.

1. Understanding sexual orientation identity development and its role in influencing career development. Excellent chapters have been written to aid in this understanding (see: Broido, 2000; Reynolds & Hanjorgiris, 2000; Fukuyama & Ferguson, 2000) In addition it may be helpful to examine classic models of identity development including those of Cass (1979) and Troiden (1988). More recently McCarn and Fassinger (1996) have developed a model of lesbian development and Fassinger and Miller (1996) have developed a model of sexual minority identity formation.

2. Understanding and helping clients with issues of workplace discrimination and sexual identity management (see Croteau et al., 2000; Griffin, 1992).

3. Understanding how societal messages about sexual orientation influence career interests, choices and perceptions of the Structure of Opportunity for LGBT clients (Croteau et al., 2000).

4. An awareness of the counselors own homophobic or heterosexist prejudices and active steps to overcome them and develop LGBT affirmative attitudes. The work by Worthington, Savoy, and Vernaglia (2001) represents important new contributions in the area of LGBT affirmativeness.

THE CAREER COUNSELING PROCESS: PLACING THE GENDER ISSUES WITHIN THE EXISTING COUNSELING PROCESS

Client Goal, or Problem Identification, Clarification, and Specification

Identification—Opening

The opening phase of career counseling has as its central goals (a) the identification of the clients' goals or problems and related internal thoughts and feelings, (b) the formation of a working alliance, and (c) defining and clarifying the client–counselor relationship and responsibilities. In planning this phase with the gendered context in mind, the counselor should:

- Help the client examine her goals with a gender and sexual orientation filter. Which goals are motivated out of socialization needs? What presenting problems result from environmental pressures or a diminished sense of self? Are internal thoughts and feelings the result of socialized feelings of devaluation or lowered efficacy? Does the client appear to be setting authentic goals based on a full knowledge of relevant information? Are there references to discarded dreams?

- As you begin to develop the working alliance, you should be especially aware of the client's level of feminist identity development and what impact that might have on the relationship you are building. If a client is in the embeddedness–emancipation phase, for example, it may be particularly important for her to work with a gender-aware female counselor. A gender-aware male may also be acceptable, depending upon her current level of anger and separatism. Building the working alliance means building a bond of collaboration and hope. The client needs to see you as someone who understands her situation and relates to her concerns. Self-disclosure of relevant and appropriate information from your own life may help to build the bond. As you begin building the working alliance, this is also a time to reinforce client strengths and to stress the importance of valuing unique, traditionally female characteristics.

As you work with lesbian and bisexual clients be aware of their sexual orientation identity development and how this may impact their career development. This knowledge is also important in helping the counselor gauge what interventions may be helpful. For example, if the client is at a very early stage in their sexual identity development they may not be ready to discuss how their sexual identity influences their career development. Additionally, awareness on the part of the counselor is important in communicating LGBT-affirmative attitudes and behaviors. Consideration of heterosexist assumptions, use of language (partner versus spouse), and behaviors are essential to establish a safe, trusting working alliance.

- When clarifying the client–counselor relationship and each individual's responsibilities, it is important to discuss your philosophy of counseling, particularly those aspects that relate to counseling women. If you prefer a feminist or gender-aware counseling relationship—a collaborative working relationship emphasizing equality—then this needs to be communicated. Because many clients come to counselors seeking an expert who will give them advice, this collaborative relationship may be foreign. The role of the environment in shaping the individual may also be an important philosophical issue to discuss. If you believe it is your responsibility to challenge gender-based and heterosexist assumptions, the client should know this. The client has a right to informed consent in the choice of a career counselor. The counselor's philosophical base is an important consideration for a client when making that choice.

Clarification—Gathering Client Information
The clarification and information-gathering subphase of the career counseling process has as its central goal learning more about the client.

- Here, any or all of the assessment measures discussed earlier in this chapter can be used to supplement other standardized or nonstandardized assessment measures you consider appropriate to use. The Assessment of Feminist Identity Development, Assessment of the Gendered Context, or Assessment of the Gendered Context of Work all would be appropriate ways of gathering information about the client's experiences that may have an impact on her career planning process.

- If standardized tests are used, it will be important to discuss issues related to test bias and how women typically underestimate their ability on such measures.
- Card sorts (see Chapter 11) are recommended as a way to understand more about how the client is processing her interests and skills related to each career field, and allow the counselor to challenge beliefs regarding the clients abilities in nontraditional career fields.

Specification—Understanding and Hypothesizing about Client Information and Behavior

The specification subphase of the career counseling process has as its central goal understanding the client more fully and hypothesizing about her unique dynamics and the psychological and environmental forces at work.

- This phase probes deeper to understand more about how clients make meaning out of themselves and their occupational world. As we look through the gender filter, we try to understand the life choices from both an individual and an environmental perspective. We try to assess the authenticity of the client's earlier choices, and those she has ahead of her.
- In this phase, providing knowledge to the client to help her understand the impact of gender is appropriate. Depending on the situation, this may involve talking about the importance of continuing in the math and science fields, the ways in which self-efficacy beliefs about nontraditional fields can be altered, or what we know about the costs and benefits of traditional gender-role beliefs.
- This is an important phase in helping lesbian clients understand how various aspects of their sexual orientation may influence the career planning process. It is also important that the counselor understand the phenomena of internalized homophobia and help the client recognize whether she has internalized heterosexist messages and beliefs. It is important for the counselor to recognize that sexual identity development represents an "emergent continuous life process" (Reynolds & Hanjorgiris, 2000, p. 36).
- Techniques like the geneogram (presented in Chapter 10) may be used in this phase of counseling to understand better the client's gender-influenced life choices from a family systems perspective. This may also be the time to have the client construct a lifeline to help her understand issues such as how her self-efficacy beliefs have changed over time, or the role compromise has played in her life choices. This may be the time to have

the client take the Career Transitions Inventory (Chapter 13). She may want to take the instrument results home to use as stimulus for journal writing about both the psychological resources and barriers she is bringing to her current career transition.

Client Goal or Problem Resolution

This second phase of the career counseling process is one of action taking. Here we move from gathering and evaluating aspects of the gendered environment and their resultant gender-specific outcomes to actually taking steps to act on this information. Getting to this phase means that you have worked through all the major aspects of the client's situation and that she is in a position to make an authentic life decision based on as complete a set of information about herself and the work world as possible.

Taking Action

Whether the action is deciding to attend a vocational–technical school for auto body repair training, change from a pre-med student to a nursing program, join the Peace Corp to improve the lives of Third World women, or start one's own business importing ethnic textiles and baskets, a variety of gender-related issues should be explored. A few examples of these are:

- The client should practice interviewing skills so that she will not devalue herself in the job interview and can recognize sex bias and homophobia in the interview and early signs of an unhealthy work environment.
- The client should learn the importance of networking with other women to gain support, and find women role models who have dealt with similar situations.
- A strong, self-enhancing resume must adequately represent her skills and background. Women tend to underestimate their abilities on resumes, and, to make matters worse, evidence also shows that women's resumes are given less favorable ratings by employers when only the names are changed from male to female. Thus, it is critical that women have the strongest written presentation of their credentials as possible.

Developing Client's Individual Career Plans

In this subphase, the client benefits from a variety of interventions that help her develop an individual career plan. This happens when all the individual pieces gained from the earlier phases of counseling are brought together and integrated into a unique plan. This plan helps to make the step from the nurturing environment of the counseling setting to the outside world a little less frightening. When a plan is made and small, manageable steps are identified, the client can begin to feel a sense of confidence in her ability to make changes in her life. In addition to identifying the steps the client will take, it is also important to identify potential stumbling blocks along the way and develop plans for overcoming them. This is a time for talking about the "what ifs": What if your boss refuses to discuss your request for additional training? What if you suffer harassment after you choose to come out about your sexual/affectional preference at work? What if you don't get into the vocational technical program you desire? By having a plan of action, clients feel more confident in this phase of the process. In addition to identifying barriers, it is also important to identify the strengths that each woman brings to the situation, and to find ways of reminding her about these strengths.

Evaluating Results and Closing the Relationship

The closure session is a time for evaluation of goal progress and process. When examining the closure session through a gender filter, consider the following:

- Reflect on the journey the career counseling process has taken—what the client brought in to the first session and how the goals of the sessions changed over time. This is an important time to reinforce what the woman brought to the session—her strengths, openness, and courage to explore the roots of some of her beliefs and choices, so that she owns her part in what made this counseling process successful.
- Discuss the relationship between the counselor and client over time. How did the working alliance develop? How were tears in the alliance mended? How do both parties feel about termination?
- Let the client know of your willingness for her to return if she wants more help, or just to let you know how things are going. It may be especially important for women clients, given their greater relational focus, to know that the support system you have provided during counseling will remain available should she have difficulties after counseling.

Fortunately, a great deal has been written over the last decade about the career development of women. While less has focused specifically on the career development of lesbian and bisexual women, there has been significant progress made in this field as well (Croteau, et al., 2000).

We have referred to numerous sources of both empirical and conceptual literature in this chapter. The purpose of this chapter has been to highlight key aspects of the gendered context, to identify their resultant outcomes in women clients, to discuss strategies and assessments for integrating knowledge of the gendered environment into the counseling sessions, and, specifically, to indicate key issues of relevance at each stage of the career planning process for lesbian, bisexual, and heterosexual women. In doing so, we hope to have prepared the counselor to feel more personal efficacy in empowering the choices of women through career counseling.

REFERENCES

Bailey, R. C., & Bailey, D. G. (1971). Perceived ability in relation to actual ability and academic achievement. *Journal of Clinical Psychology, 27*, 461–463.

Bakken, L., & Romig, C. (1992). Interpersonal needs in middle-class adolescents: Companionship, leadership, and intimacy. *Journal of Adolescence, 15*, 301–316.

Bandura, A. (1977). *Social learning theory.* Englewood Cliffs, NJ: Prentice Hall.

Bandura, A. (1982). Self-efficacy mechanism in human agency. *American Psychologist, 37*, 122–147.

Bandura, A. (1986). *Social foundations of thought and action: A social cognitive theory.* Englewood Cliffs, NJ: Prentice Hall.

Bargad, A., & Hyde, J. S. (1991). Women's studies: A study of feminist identity development in women. *Psychology of Women Quarterly, 15*, 181–201.

Basow, S. A. (1992). *Gender: Stereotypes and roles* (3rd ed.). Pacific Grove, CA: Brooks/Cole.

Benbow, C. P. (1988). Sex differences in mathematical reasoning ability in intellectually talented preadolescents: Their nature, effects, and possible causes. *Behavioral and Brain Sciences, 11*, 169–232.

Bernard, J. (1972). *The future of marriage.* New York: World Publishing.

Betz, N. E. (1989). The null environment and women's career development. *Counseling Psychologist, 17*, 136–144.

Betz, N. E. (1994). Career counseling for women in the sciences and engineering. In W. B. Walsh & S. H. Osipow (Eds.), *Career counseling for women.* Hillsdale, NJ: Erlbaum.

Betz, N. E., & Fitzgerald, L. F. (1987). *The career psychology of women.* Orlando, FL: Academic Press.

Betz, N. E., & Hackett, G. (1983). The relationship of career-related self-efficacy expectations to perceived career options in college women and men. *Journal of Counseling Psychology, 28*, 399–410.

Beurk, D. (1985). The voices of women making meaning in mathematics. *Journal of Education, 167 (3)*, 59–70.

Blumstein, P., & Schwartz, P. (1983). *American couples: Money, work, sex.* New York: William Morrow.

Bores-Rangel, E., Church, A. T., Szendre, D., & Reeves, C. (1990). Self-efficacy in relation to occupational consideration in minority high school equivalency students. *Journal of Counseling Psychology, 39*, 498–508.

Boswell, S. L. (1985). The influence of sex-role stereotyping on women's attitudes and achievement in mathematics. In S. F. Chipman, L. R. Brush, & D. M. Wilson (Eds.), *Women and mathematics: Balancing the equation* (pp.175–198). Hillsdale, NJ: Erlbaum.

Bradford, J., & Ryan, C. (1987). *National lesbian health care survey: Mental health implications.* Richmond: Virginia Commonwealth University Research Laboratory.

Broido, E. M. (2000). Constructing identity: The nature and meaning of lesbian, gay, and bisexual identities (pp. 13–34). In R. M. Perez, K. A. DeBord, and K. J. Bieschke (Eds.). *Handbook of counseling and psychotherapy with lesbian, gay and bisexual clients.* Washington, DC: American Psychological Association.

Brooks, L. (1988). Encouraging women's motivation for nontraditional career and lifestyle options: A model for assessment and intervention. *Journal of Career Development, 14 (4),* 223–241.

Brooks, V. R. (1981). *Minority stress and lesbian women.* Lexington, MA: Lexington Books.

Brooks, L., & Forrest, L. (1994). Feminism and career counseling. In W. B. Walsh & S. H. Osipow (Eds.), *Career counseling for women.* Hillsdale, NJ: Erlbaum.

Carayon, P. (1993). Effect of electronic performance monitoring on job design and worker stress: A review of the literature and conceptual model. *Human Factors, 35,* 3–11.

Cass, U. C., (1979). Homosexual identity formation: A theoretical model. *Journal of Homosexuality, 4,* 219–235.

Chipman, S. F., & Thomas, V. G. (1985). Women's participation in mathematics: Outlining the problem. In S. F. Chipman, L. R. Brush, & D. M. Wilson (Eds.), *Women and mathematics: Balancing the equations* (pp. 1–24). Hillsdale, NJ: Erlbaum.

Chodorow, N. (1978). *The reproduction of mothering.* Berkeley: University of California Press.

Claes, M. E. (1992). Friendship and personal adjustment during adolescence. *Journal of Adolescence, 15,* 39–55.

Clunis, D. M., & Green, G. D. (1988). *Lesbian couples.* Seattle: Seal Press.

Croteau, J. M.(1996). Research on the work experiences of leasbian, gay, and bisexual people: An integrative review of methodlogy findings. *Journal of Vocational Behavior, 48,* 195–209.

Croteau, J. M., Anderson, M. Z., Distefano, T. M., & Kampa-Kokesch, S. (2000). Lesbian, gay, and bisexual vocational psychology: Reviewing foundations and planning construction (pp. 383–408). In R. M. Perez, K. A. DeBord, and K. J. Bieschke (Eds.). *Handbook of counseling and psychotherapy with lesbian, gay and bisexual clients.* Washington DC: American Psychological Association.

Croteau, J. M. & Lark, J. S. (1995). On being lesbian, gay or bisexual in student affairs: A national survey of experience on the job. *NASPA Journal, 32,* 189–197.

DeCrescenzo, T. A. (1985). Homophobia: A study of the attitudes of mental health professionals toward homosexuality. In R. Schoenberg, R. Goldberg, & D. Shore (Eds.), *With compassion toward some: Homosexuality and social work in America* (pp. 115–136). New York: Harrington Park.

Downing, N. E., & Roush, K. L. (1985). From passive acceptance to active commitment: A model of feminist identity development for women. *The Counseling Psychologist, 13,* 695–709.

Eccles, J. S. (1987). Gender roles and women's achievement related decisions. *Psychology of Women Quarterly, 11,* 135–172.

Eccles J. E., & Jacobs, J. (1986). Social forces shape math participation. *Signs, 11,* 367–380.

Fassinger, R. E. (1995). From invisibility to integration: Lesbian identity in the workplace. *Career Development Quarterly, 44,* 149–167.

Fassinger, R.E. (1996). Notes from the margins: Integrating lesbian experience into vocation psychology of women. *Journal of Vocational Behavior 48,* 160–175.

Fassinger, R. E., & Miller, B. A. (1996). Validation of an inclusive model of sexual minority identity formation on a sample of gay men. *Journal of Homosexuality, 32,* 53–78.

Ferree, M. M. (1987). She works hard for a living: Gender and class on the job. In B. B. Hess & M. M. Ferre (Eds.), *Analyzing gender: A handbook of social science research* (pp. 322–347). Newbury Park, CA: Sage.

Fischer, A. R., & Good, G. E. (1994). Gender, self, and others: Perceptions of the campus environment. *Journal of Counseling Psychology, 41* (3), 343–355.

Fitzgerald, L. F., & Cherpas, C. C. (1985). On the reciprocal relationship between gender and occupation: Rethinking the assumptions concerning masculinity and career development. *Journal of Vocational Behavior, 27,* 109–122.

Forrest, L., & Mikolaitis, N. (1986). The relational component of identity: An expansion of career development theory. *Career Development Quarterly, 35,* 76–88.

Freeman, J. (1989). How to discriminate against women without really trying. In J. Freeman (Ed.), *Women: A feminist perspective* (2nd ed., pp. 194–208). Palo Alto, CA: Mayfield.

Fukuyama, M. A., & Ferguson, A. D. (2000). Lesbian, gay, and bisexual people of color: Understanding cultural complexity and managing multiple oppressions (pp. 81–106). In R. M. Perez, K. A. DeBord, and K. J. Bieschke (Eds.). *Handbook of counseling and psychotherapy with lesbian, gay and bisexual clients.* Washington, DC: American Psychological Association.

Garlick, B., Dixon, S., & Allen, P. (Eds.). (1992). *Stereotypes of women in power: Historical perspectives and revisionist views.* Westport, CT: Greenwood Press.

Gettys, L. D., & Cann, A. (1981). Children's perceptions of occupational sex stereotypes. *Sex Roles, 7,* 301–308.

Gilbert, L. A., Galessich, J. M., & Evans, S. L. (1983). Sex of faculty role model and students' self-perceptions of competency. *Sex Roles, 9,* 597–607.

Gilligan, C. (1980). Restoring the missing text of women's development to life cycle theories. In D. G. McGuigan (Ed.), *Women's lives: New theory, research, and policy* (pp. 17–33). Ann Arbor: University of Michigan Press.

Gilligan, C. (1982). *In a different voice.* Cambridge, MA: Harvard University Press.

Gilligan, C. (1990a). Prologue. In C. Gilligan, N. P. Lyons, & T. J. Hanmer (Eds.), *Making connections* (pp. 1–5). Cambridge, MA: Harvard University Press.

Gilligan, C. (1990b). Preface. In C. Gilligan, N. P. Lyons, & T. J. Hanmer (Eds.), *Making connections* (pp. 6–29). Cambridge, MA: Harvard University Press.

Good, G. E., Gilbert, L. A. & Scher, M. (1990). Gender aware therapy: A synthesis of feminist therapy and knowledge about gender. *Journal of Counseling & Development, 68,* 376–380.

Gottfredson, L. S. (1981). Circumscription and compromise: A developmental theory of occupational aspirations. *Journal of Counseling Psychology, 28,* 545–579.

Greenberg-Lake, The Analysis Group, Inc. (1991). *Shortchanging girls, shortchanging America.* Washington, DC: Author.

Griffin, P. (1992). From hiding out to coming out: Empowering lesbian and gay educators. In K. M. Harbeck (Ed.), *Coming out of the classroom closet* (pp.167–196). Binghampton, NY: Harrington Park Press.

Gutek, B. A. (1985). *Sex and the workplace.* San Francisco: Jossey-Bass.

Hackett, G., & Betz, N. E. (1981). A self-efficacy approach to the career development of women. *Journal of Vocational Behavior, 18*, 326–339.

Hall, R. M., & Sandler, B. R. (1982). *The classroom climate: A chilly one for women?* Project on the status and education of women. Washington, DC: Association of American Colleges.

Hartzler, K., & Franco, J. N. (1985). Ethnicity, division of household tasks and equity in marital roles: A comparison of Anglo and Mexican-American couples. *Hispanic Journal of Behavioral Sciences, 7*, 333–344.

Henton, J., Russell, R., & Koval, J. (1983). Spousal perceptions of mid-life career change. *Personnel and Guidance Journal, 61*, 287–291.

Heppner, M. J., & Heppner P. P. (2000). Addressing the implications of male socialization for career counseling (pp. 369–386). In G. R. Brooks & G. E. Good (Eds.). *The new handbook of psychotheory and counseling with men.* San Francisco, CA: Jossey-Bass.

Hershberger, S. L., & D'Augelli, A. R. (2000). Issues in counseling lesbian, gay, and bisexual adolescents (pp. 225–248) in R. M. Perez, K. A. DeBord & K. J. Bieschke (Eds.). *Handbook of counseling and psychotherapy with lesbian, gay and bisexual clients.* Washington, DC: American Psychological Association.

Holland, D. C., & Eisenhart, M. A. (1990). *Educated in romance: Women, achievement, and college culture.* Chicago: University of Chicago Press.

Hotelling, K., & Forrest, L. (1985). Gilligan's theory of sex role development: A perspective for counseling. *Journal of Counseling and Development, 64*, 183–186.

Kanter, R. M. (1977). *Men and women of the corporation.* New York: Basic Books, 198–214.

Kerr, B., & Maresh, S. E. (1994). Career counseling for gifted girls. In W. B. Walsh and S. H. Osipow (Ed.), *Career counseling for women.* Hillsdale, NJ: Erlbaum.

Kimball, M. M. (1989). A new perspective on women's math achievement. *Psychological Bulletin, 105*(2), 198–214.

Lee, P. C., & Gropper, N. B. (1974). Sex-role culture and educational practice. *Harvard Educational Review, 44*, 369–407.

Lent, R. W., Brown, S. D., & Hackett, G. (1994). Toward a unifying social cognitive theory of career and academic interest, choice, and performance. *Journal of Vocational Behavior, 45*, 79–122.

Levine, M. P., & Leonard, R. (1984). Discrimination against lesbians in the work force. *Signs: Journal of Women in Culture and Society, 9*, 700–710.

Lips, H. M. (1992). Gender- and science-related attitudes as predictors of college students academic choices. *Journal of Vocational Behavior, 40*, 62–81.

Lyons, N. P. (1983). Two perspectives: On self, relationships and morality. *Harvard Educational Review, 53*, 125–145.

Marecek, J., & Kravetz, D. (1977). Women and mental health: A review of feminish change efforts. *Psychiatry, 40*, 323–329.

Matlin, M. (1996). *The psychology of women.* New York: Holt, Rinehart, & Winston.

McCarn, S. R., & Fassinger, R. E., (1996). Revisioning sexual minority identity formation: A new model of lesbian identity implications for counseling and research. *The Counseling Psychologists, 24*, 508–534.

McDaniels, C. & Gysbers, N. C. (1992). *Counseling for career development.* San Francisco: Jossey-Bass.

Meece, J. L., Parsons, J. E., Kaczala, C. M., Goff, S. B., & Futterman, R. (1982). Sex differences in math achievement: Toward a model of academic choice. *Psychological Bulletin, 91,* 324–348.

Meyerding, J. (1990). Letter to the editor. *Lesbian Resource Center Newsletter, 15,* p. 5.

Miller, J. B. (1991). *Women's Growth in Connection: Writings from the Stone Center.* New York: Guilford.

Mohney, C., & Anderson, W. (1988). The effect of life events and relationships on adult women's decision to enter college. *Journal of Counseling and Development, 66,* 271–274.

Morgan, K. S., & Brown, L. S. (1991). Lesbian career development, work behavior, and vocational counseling. *The Counseling Psychologist, 19,* 273–291.

Morrison, A. M. , White, R. P., & Van Velsor, E. (1987). *Breaking the glass ceiling: Can women reach the top of America's largest corporation?* Reading, MA: Addison-Wesley.

Morrow, S. L., Gore, P. A., & Campbell, B. W. (1996). The application of sociocognitive frameworks to the career development of lesbian women and gay men. *Journal of Vocational Behavior, 48,* 136–148.

Multon, K. D., Brown, S. D., & Lent, R.W. (1991). Relation of self–efficacy beliefs to academic outcomes: A meta-analytic investigation. *Journal of Counseling Psychology, 38,* 30–38.

National Science Foundation. (1990). *Women and minorities in science and engineering.* Washington, DC: Author.

Neil, C. C., & Snizek, W. E. (1987). Work values, job characteristics, and gender. *Sociological Perspectives, 30* (3), 245–265.

Nelson, M. L. (1996). Separation versus connection, the gender controversy: Implications for counseling women. *Journal of Counseling and Development. 74,* 339–344.

Nieva, V. F. & Gutek, B. A. (1981). *Women and work: A psychological perspective.* New York: Praeger.

O'Brien, K. M., Friedman S. M., Tipton, L. C., & Linn S. G. (2000). Attachment, separation and women's vocational development: A longitudinal analysis. *Journal of Counseling Psychology 47,* 301–315.

O'Neil J. (1985). The trend in the male–female wage gap in the United States. *Journal of Labor Economics, 3,* S91–S116.

Ossana, S., Helms, J., & Leonard, M. M. (1992). Do "womanist" identity attitudes influence college women's self-esteem and perceptions of environmental bias? *Journal of Counseling and Development, 70,* 402–408.

Pajares, F., & Miller, M. D. (1995). Mathematics self-efficacy and mathematics performances: The need for specificity of assessment. *Journal of Counseling Psychology, 42,* 190–198.

Paradise, L. V., & Wall, S. M. (1986). Children's perceptions of male and female principals and teachers. *Sex Roles, 14,* 1–7.

Perez, R. M., DeBord, K .A. & Bieschke, K. J. (Eds). *Handbook of counseling and pscyhotherapy with lesbian, gay, and bisexual clients.* Washington, DC: American Psychological Association.

Phillips, J. C. (2000). Training issues and considerations (pp. 337–358) in R. M. Perez, K. A. DeBord, and K. J. Bieschke (Eds.). *Handbook of Counseling and psychotherapy with lesbian, gay and bisexual clients.* Washington, DC: American Psychological Association.

Radloff, L. S. (1975). Sex differences in depression: The effects of occupation and marital status. *Sex Roles, 1*, 249–265.

Reynolds, A. L., & Hanjorgiris, W. F. (2000). Coming out: Lesbian, gay, and bisexual identity development (pp. 35–56) in R. M. Perez, K. A. DeBord & K. J. Bieschke (Eds.). *Handbook of counseling and psychotherapy with lesbian, gay and bisexual clients.* Washington, DC: American Psychological Association.

Robertson, J., & Fitzgerald, L. F. (1990). The (Mis) Treatment of men: Effects of client gender roles and life-style on diagnosis and attribution of pathology, *Journal of Counseling Psychology, 37*, 3–9.

Rudolph, J. (1988). Counselors' attitudes toward homosexuality: A selective review of the literature. *Journal of Counseling and Development, 67*, 165–168.

Russo, N. F., & Denmark, F. L. (1984). Women, psychology, and public policy: Selected issues. *American Psychologist, 39*, 1161–1165.

Sadker, M. P., & Sadker, D. M. (1985). The treatment of sex equity in teacher education. In Siklein (Ed.), *Handbook for achieving sex equity through education.* Baltimore: Johns Hopkins University Press.

Sadri, G., & Robertson, I. T. (1993). Self-efficacy and work-related behavior: A review and meta-analysis. *Applied Psychology: An International Review, 42*, 139–152.

Sells, L. (1973). High school mathematics as the critical filter in the job market. In *Developing opportunities for minorities in graduate education. Proceedings of the conference on minority graduate education.* Berkeley: University of California, Berkeley.

Sherman, J. A. (1983). Girls talk about mathematics and their future: A partial replication. *Psychology of Women Quarterly, 7*, 338–342.

Skovholt, T. M. (1993). Career themes in counseling and psychotherapy with men. In D. Moore & F. Leafgren (Eds.), *Men in conflict.* Alexandria, VA: American Association for Counseling and Development.

Stein, J. A., Newcomb, M. D., & Bentler, P. M. (1992). The effect of agency and communality on self-esteem: Gender differences in longitudinal data. *Sex Roles, 26*, 465–483.

Swanson, J. L., & Lease, S. H. (1990). Gender differences in self-ratings of abilities and skills. *The Career Development Quarterly, 38*, 346–359.

Tannen, D. (1994). *Gender and discourse.* New York: Oxford University Press.

Travis, C. B. (1988). *Women and health psychology: Mental health issues.* Hillsdale, NJ: Erlbaum.

Troiden, R. R. (1988) Homosexual identity development. *Journal of Adolescent Health Care, 9*, 105–113

Unger, R., & Crawford, M. (1992). *Women and gender.* New York: McGraw Hill.

U.S. Department of Labor. (1988). *Facts on U.S. working women* (Fact sheet 88–1). Washington, DC: Office of the Secretary, Women's Bureau.

U.S. Department of Labor, Bureau of Labor Statistics. (1991). *Employment and earnings, February 1991.* Washington, DC: U.S. Government Printing Office.

Walsh, W. B., & Osipow, S. H. (1994). *Career counseling for women.* Hillsdale, NJ: Lawrence Erlbaum Assoc.

Wood, J. T. (1994). *Gendered lives: Communication, gender, and culture.* Belmont, CA: Waldsworth Publishing Co.

Worthington, R. L., Savoy, H. B., & Vernaglia, E. R. (2001). Beyond tolerance: An integrative model of LGB-affirmativeness. Unpublished manuscript.

▶ 5

Empowering Men's Life Choices

An Examination of Gender and Sexual Orientation

In 1977, Leona Tyler wrote, "Much of what we know about the stages through which an individual passes as he [sic] prepares to find his [sic] place in the world of work might appropriately be labeled 'The Vocational Development of Middle Class Males'" (Tyler, p. 40).

With Tyler's commonly held view as the backdrop, the question quickly becomes: Why include a chapter on empowering men's career choices when the whole field of career psychology was, until the last few decades, concerned almost exclusively with male career development?

Men's career patterns were, until very recently, considered the norm. Our theories of career development, our assessment measures, even our normative work patterns were all developed from a male perspective. If women worked in the male world, they were implicitly instructed to try to be like men. No one gave much thought to the specifics of the male condition. No one thought much about the unique gendered context from a male perspective, or the consequences of living the "norm" on the individual male (Heppner & Heppner 2001).

Much has been written about the dramatic effect of the women's movement on the lives of women. Much less has been written documenting the profound effect of societal changes born out of the women's movement on the lives of men. The women's movement and the subsequent men's movement pushed men to examine their own gendered context individually and aspects of the male condition more generally (Rabinowitz & Cochran, 2002). Men began to question the quality of their lives, particularly their work lives. Were they satisfied with the cultural definitions of success? Was competition with others the way they wanted to get ahead? Was it healthy that so much of their definition of who they were was dependent on what they did for a living? For heterosexual men was having all the stress of the breadwinner role necessary? What does the seven-year-shorter life span between men and women have to say about career and lifestyle choices?

The women's movement also created dramatic changes in relationships and family structures. In addition, the changing economy also changed the role of men and women in the workforce. Dual-career relationships increased. Working outside the home themselves, women encouraged men to take on a greater role in rearing children and in performing the domestic responsibilities of making a home. These changes continue to create both turmoil and opportunity in men's lives.

Because male socialization has taught men that work is primary (Dubois & Marino, 1987) and everything else is secondary, and that male identity is almost solely defined through work (Skovholt, 1990), the changes brought on by the women's movement as they relate to the role of work in men's lives were of paramount importance. Understanding more about these changes and the broader gendered context from which our male clients come is critical to providing effective career counseling. Career counseling that decontextualizes the client's experiences does not provide the richness of information necessary for informed career planning.

One form of decontextualization that has occurred in the career literature over the years is the separation of love and work, especially for gay and bisexual men. As we mentioned in the last chapter, it is important to note that while we have attempted to integrate career research on lesbian, gay, bisexual, and transgendered individuals wherever possible, this body of literature remains quite small and incomplete. In addition, much of this research was conducted on one of the subgroups such as lesbian women, but not gay men.

Although the literature on lesbian women and gay men is small, the literature on the career development of bisexual and transgendered individuals is virtually nonexistent. Thus, the reader is cautioned that our ability to discuss and offer assistance in working with LGBT clients is limited because of the limited research base. The designation of transgendered needs special caution as several different sexual identities are often grouped under this umbrella term. Therefore, one must use caution in assuming that what has been documented in the literature explaining some aspect of the career development of gay men, would necessarily apply to transgendered individuals as well. We do however, believe that it is important for LGBT issues to be addressed in the mainstream career literature and thus, we have tried to include reference to this scholarship whenever possible.

The first purpose of this chapter is to highlight key aspects of the gendered context and their resultant gender-specific outcomes. The first section is an overview of these complex and varied issues. The last decade has brought a flurry of excellent texts on issues related to men and gender role development (Brooks & Good, 2001; Levant & Pollack, 1995; Moore & Leafgren, 1990). In addition, a landmark book, *The Handbook of Counseling and Psychotherapy with Lesbian, Gay, and Bisexual Clients* by Perez, DeBord and Bieschke (2000), has also been published and should be consulted for a more in-depth analysis of these and other issues. Particular constructs are discussed here in order to highlight key aspects of the gendered and heterosexist context in childhood, adolescence, and the adult workplace that most directly influence male clients who come for career counseling. The second part of this chapter suggests particular assessments, techniques, and areas of knowledge to share with clients to make career counseling more empowering for men. Finally, we provide an overview of the impact of gender and sexual orientation identity on the different phases of career counseling discussed in Chapter 1.

THE GENDERED OVERLAY: SEX ROLE SOCIALIZATION IN CHILDHOOD

The gendered context for males begins when parents first learn their child is a boy. Whole interaction patterns begin to be established. Boys are given different toys than girls. Boys are much more likely to be played with in a rough and aggressive way. They are told not to cry, or express sadness or hurt feelings. The male role models in their children's books and cartoons are aggressive, dominant, and always in control: they can fix any situation, rescue any damsel in distress. Research has demonstrated that because traditional fathers have been raised in environments that foster autonomy and independence, they in turn perpetuate this pattern by emotionally distancing themselves from their sons (Chodorow, 1978; Gilligan, 1982). These early experiences with sex-role socialization lay a firm groundwork for the gender-based characteristics they portray throughout life. Although much has been written about the problems girls encounter in childhood, much less attention has been devoted to boys. "We have a cultural blindness to the problems of boys, in part because of our assumption that males should be self-sufficient, and in part because boys are required to keep their problems to themselves" (Levant, 2001, p. 355). This early socialization influences initial perceptions of occupational options.

In their very early years, boys are already able to sex-role stereotype occupational fields as women's work and men's work (Gettys & Cann, 1981) with these views becoming more and more rigid from kindergarten to fourth grade (Matlin, 1993). For boys, the need not to identify with anything feminine, including traditionally feminine occupations, is paramount. The worst fear is to be called a sissy, so boys repress the side of themselves that is vulnerable or scared and put on the facade of toughness (Rabinowitz & Cochran, 1994).

THE GENDERED CONTEXT OF ADOLESCENCE

Adolescence is a time of trying to fit in and finding a place in the world. It is a time when peer pressure is great. Many adolescent boys are trying to figure out who they are and how they can "be someone" in the world. This can mean joining groups who are interested in particular activities such as sports, chess clubs, or cars, or joining gangs. There is great pressure to conform to group norms and to prove manhood through these activities.

Sports provide a major socializing experience for boys, and is one that has direct connection to attitudes and behaviors in the workforce. Boys play games that have clear winners and losers. They are taught to compete and win. They are socialized to the rules of the game, similar to the traditional rules of the adult, male-centered workplace: teamwork, appropriate competitiveness, a facade of invulnerability. In Skovholt's (1990) analysis of the socializing force of sports in men's lives, he suggests that emotional intimacy is as dysfunctional as extreme individualism is in most sports. Boys need to learn a certain level of cooperation, but resist any real connectedness with other boys. Thus, adult men tend to say they have many acquaintances and people who they can cooperate with on projects, but that they lack close intimate connections, especially with other men. The messages of the football field live on in the corporate office building, with socialized life scripts being perpetuated and reinforced through time.

Consequently, through sports and other activities adolescence continues to be a time of restricted emotionality for boys. They learn to be tough and not express their tender or vulnerable sides (Levant, 2001). They are, in effect, further severing the feeling side of themselves. Demonstrating masculinity through sexual conquest with girls is of utmost importance, making these years particularly hard for gay adolescents who feel they have to fit in to the heterosexual world or risk being ostracized, or becoming victims of verbal and physical abuse (Hershberger & D'Augelli, 2000). For adolescents who are struggling with sexual identity issues, their vocational identity may be delayed (Croteau et al., 2000).

While much of the literature focuses on the negative harmful aspects of traditional male socialization, it is important, on the other hand, for the counselor to understand and reinforce traditional male strengths as well. As Levant argues, this same traditional adolescent socialization also plants the seeds for adult male strengths—the ability to persist in difficult situations until problems are resolved, and the ability to strategize, think logically, solve problems, take risks and stay calm in the face of danger (Levant, 1996). Both the positive aspects as well as the more detrimental aspects of the traditional male role are important for the counselor and the client to understand.

THE GENDERED WORKPLACE CONTEXT

Often young men begin carving out their identity in the adult world in their first job. Keen (1991) spoke of the first job as a boy's rite of passage into manhood. It is a role he has been training for since birth. Achievement, competition, and goal orientation are all familiar concepts to him. Thus, work begins to form identity, to the point where, for many men, the two become virtually inseparable.

As Skovholt expressed it, "Painting a picture of men's lives often results in a work-dominated landscape" (Skovholt, 1990, p. 39). Once in the work environment, males tend to strive for those elusive characteristics that define success. The definition usually includes a predominately materialistic component: owning a home, a car, providing for a family, nice vacations (Skovholt & Morgan, 1981). The dream for many men is a middle-class professional job with all its inherent rewards, as portrayed repeatedly on television.

Men have many traditional role models of "the way you do a life" (Skovholt, 1990, p. 42). Fathers and grandfathers, male neighbors and friends all provide information to young men about appropriate work behaviors. The message is clear: Men are supposed to work outside the home throughout their lives. "Whether the job is loved, hated, intrinsically satisfying, or boring is much less relevant than the expectation that a man will work. A long-term nonworking male adult violates this strong male principle and is usually shunned and rejected" (Skovholt, 1990, p. 42).

If a man chooses a nontraditional life pattern, however, role models may be more sparse than those available for nontraditional women. In the words of Betty Friedan, 1981 (quoted in Skovholt, 1990), "The trouble is, once they disengage from the old patterns of American masculinity and success—John Wayne, Lindbergh, John Kennedy—men today are just as lost for role models as women are" (p. 140).

Gay men are particularly limited in terms of visible role models to increase their awareness of occupational possibilities and to demonstrate and discuss work-related issues specifically in relation to their sexual/affectional orientation. Although all minority groups suffer from lack of role models, the invisibility of gays, in some cases even to each other, compounds the problem. Thus "gay men may need to make career decisions without awareness of how other gay men employed in the occupations under consideration made their decisions and how their choices were implemented" (Hetherington, Hiller-brand, & Etringer, 1989, p. 453).

In addition, discrimination against LGBT workers is very prevalent. Twenty-five to 66 percent of respondents across three studies reviewed by Croteau (1996) reported experiencing discrimination in the workplace due to sexual orientation. Thus, the gay or bisexual worker has this added pressure in his work life which may be highly influential in his decision about whether to be "out" with regard to his sexual orientation at work.

Many men work to get ahead and be "on top." A substantial portion of their identity is related to being "on top." Unfortunately, many men are finding there is very little room at "the top." Very few men will be able to achieve this dream. Only 8 percent of the total male population work in white-collar professional jobs (Dubois & Marino, 1987). Thus, a large portion of male identity is tied up in striving for an unlikely outcome. There are few other avenues for male identity than the worker role, and the likelihood of failure in this role leading to disillusionment and stress related illnesses is great (Pleck, 1987). The empirical literature also indicates that gender-role conflict is related to a variety of indices of psychological distress (Sharpe & Heppner, 1991).

Although the traditional male role in the workplace can result in harmful physical and psychological costs, the behaviors and beliefs embedded in this role can also be strengths. As Levant (1996) illustrated, these traditional male roles exemplify men's willingness to sacrifice personal needs in order to provide for others, their willingness to withstand hardship to protect others, and their ability to express love through action—doing things for others. Levant pointed out that these positive aspects of the traditional male role are often unrecognized and undervalued.

COUNSELOR ROLE WITH MALE CLIENTS

Given the likelihood of psychological distress in males, it seems likely that they would seek counseling for both career and psycho-social concerns. Studies of gay men, particularly, indicate that they have more uncertainty and confusion about their careers than either lesbian women or heterosexual men or women (Hetherington, Hillerbrand, & Etringer, 1989). Unfortunately, the constellation of traditional male characteristics, which include emotional restrictedness and strong need for control, may keep men from seeking mental health or vocational services. It has been demonstrated that males underutilize all forms of social services, including career planning assistance, as compared to females. While unfortunate, given male socialization this is to be expected (Good, Dell, & Mintz, 1989).

There has been encouragement from some recent writers to rethink traditional counseling to make it more male-friendly (Kiselica, 2001). While primarily aimed at school-aged boys, many of Kiselica's suggestions seem fitting for men of all ages. These suggestions include: (a) reexamining the 50-minute hour, (b) reexamining the formal office setting, (c) using humor and self-disclosure, and (d) using rapport-building tactics that build on male strengths (Kiselica, 2001). These suggestions are attempts at closing the gap between the personality of many men and the "personality" of most counseling sessions. Being sensitive to what will make for a more natural and comfortable counseling environment for boys and men is an important counselor issue.

The counselor's role in the perpetuation of the status quo has been studied extensively with women who choose nontraditional employment options. A parallel examination of the impact of men's nontraditional choices on counseling process and outcome is sparse. Fitzgerald and Cherpas (1985) reviewed literature indicating that parents were more concerned about male children who exhibited sex-inappropriate [sic] attitudes and behaviors than female children. This is similar to other research that indicates that sex-role deviant [sic] behavior is considered more problematic and dealt with more severely when it occurs in men rather than women (Silverberg, 1986). Only one or two empirical studies have examined the role of nontraditionality in male clients' process or outcome in counseling. Fitzgerald and Cherpas (1985) reported that counselors in training perceived male clients who selected nontraditional career choices more negatively.

In an interesting analog study, Robertson and Fitzgerald (1990) found that with regard to nontraditional male clients, counselors (a) considered them to have more severe pathology, (b) behaved differently toward them, (c) were more likely to attribute their depression to their nontraditional choices, and (d) were more likely to target their nontraditional behavior as a focus for counselor intervention. Robertson and Fitzgerald concluded: "...it is still somewhat startling to find that a group of experienced mental health professionals is likely to diagnose severe pathology essentially on the basis that a client has chosen not to engage in the good provider role" (p. 8). Therefore, it seems that in initial exploratory studies, the same gender-role bias identified in counseling with nontraditional women may also be true with nontraditional men. For men who are trying to break away from cultural norms to find new and more healthy paths for themselves, it is disturbing that sex-role bias exists among the counseling profession.

In addition, it is important for counselors to practice LGBT-affirmative counseling. LGBT-affirmativeness (Worthington, Savoy, & Vernaglia, 2001) among heterosexuals is conceptualized as "the range of attitudes, beliefs, emotions and behaviors that express and assert the positive valuing of the sexual identity of, and an understanding of the realities faced by LGBT individuals within an oppressive society" (Worthington, Savoy, & Vernaglia,

2001). Affirmative individuals are not only knowledgeable about LGBT issues, but they are also understanding of and comfortable with their own sexual identity and diverse sexual orientations. Contact and involvement with LGBT individuals is an important component of the process of becoming a LGBT-affirmative career counselor. This contact is presumed to occur to only in one's professional role, but also in other contexts, including personal, social, and familial networks. The model describes five states: *Passive Conformity, Revelations and Exploration, Tentative Commitment, Synthesis and Integration,* and *Active Commitment.* Becoming LGBT-affirmative is a developmental process of movement from an unexamined, unconscious heterosexist and/or homophobic construction of the world, through a phase of intellectualized understanding of what it means to be LGBT-affirmative, and finally to a more fully integrated level of awareness and expression in which knowledge achieved at earlier phases is incorporated into one's personal, professional, and political spheres. LGBT-affirmative counselors utilize their self-awareness, knowledge, skills and involvement with LGBT individuals to inform their practice with all clients, including lesbian, gay, bisexual, and heterosexual clients.

GENDER-SPECIFIC OUTCOMES

The previous section provided an overview of some of the career-related aspects of the gendered environment that occur during early development, adolescence, and in the adult workplace for gay, bisexual, and heterosexual men. Learning more about aspects of this environment is an important step in improving career counseling for all men. Only when counselors have adequate information about the extent of the gendered context can we be effective in our interventions with clients. The following section discusses some of the most prevalent gender-specific outcomes that may result from these environments and that may dramatically influence the career counseling process.

The Relationship of Gender-Related Behaviors to Mortality and Morbidity

Probably one of the most tangible results of the gendered context on male lives is that, on average, women live seven years longer than men (Courtenay, 2000). Although a variety of biological factors are involved in determining longevity, Harrison, Chin, and Ficarrotto (1989) have studied mortality rates across the life span and conclude that biological factors alone cannot account for these dramatic and consistent differences in longevity. Other researchers have argued that as much as 75 percent of the differences in longevity between men and women can be attributed to the gender role behaviors of men (Waldron, 1976). A growing body of literature links traditional masculinity and men's beliefs about what it means to be a man to greater health risk (Courtenay, 2001).

The Relationship of Gender-Role Ideologies to Stress and Coping

The relationship of gender-role ideologies to stress and coping has been examined by Eisler and Blalock (1991). These researchers applied Lazarus and Folkman's (1984) work on the role of cognitive appraisal of events in predicting stress and coping reactions to the issue of male gender-role stress. Specifically, Eisler and Blalock (1991) predict that strong adherence to traditional gender-role ideology may result in a restriction of the type of coping strategies men feel are available in stressful situations. For example, when experiencing stressful events at work, such as a rumored downsizing of the company, men may need more social and emotional support, but feel that it is inappropriate for them to ask for it. The kinds of thinking emphasized by Kiselica's (2000) male-friendly counseling and what Courtenay (2001) refers to as humanizing help-seeking seem like critical changes that could greatly enhance men's ability to seek needed support and services.

In order to test these hypotheses about the relationship of adherence to the male role and the way men cope with stressful life events, Eisler and Skidmore (1987) developed the Masculine Gender Role Stress scale (which is reviewed later in the assessment portion of this chapter). They proposed that excessive commitment to the male gender role tends to severely limit men's flexible responses to stressful events. Eisler and Blalock outlined four broad gender-related coping mechanisms that men use which tend to promote dysfunctional coping. These are discussed under their general topic heading of (a) commitment to masculinity, (b) reliance on aggression, power, and control, (c) importance of performance, achievement, and success, and (d) emotional inexpressiveness. The interested reader is referred to the Eisler and Blalock (1991) article for a more specific description of these coping strategies. The current discussion will apply each copying strategy to career and work-related issues of relevance to the career counselor.

Commitment to Masculinity

Eisler and Blalock (1991) contended that one aspect of a rigid adherence to sex-typed masculine ideology is a fear of femininity and subsequently anything that is considered feminine. This aspect may be reflected in career counseling in a number of salient ways. It may be reflected initially in men's avoidance of help seeking, and in their rational and logical presentation style.

The desire to appear masculine and in charge while asking for assistance is a difficult balancing act.

Because anger expression is much more acceptable for men than expression of distress or vulnerability, the career counselor is likely to be presented with the expression of anger, if not toward the counselor then toward others in the man's environment. Eisler and Blalock have found anger is more frequently associated with masculine gender role stress and conjecture that it may lead to the prevalence of Type A behavior in the workplace. Type A behavior is described as consisting of "an aggressive, time-urgent, competitive orientation to task with a hostile, impatient interpersonal style" (Eisler and Blalock, 1991, p. 54). Eisler and Blalock proposed that the pervasive aura of hostility so characteristic of Type A behavior may be "due to the frustration of trying to live up to unrealistic definitions of masculine achievement and success" (p. 52). Type A behavior is found to be much more prevalent in males, and the sex-linked nature of the Type A construct can be traced back to as early as kindergarten (Matthews & Angulu, 1980; Waldron, 1976).

In the workplace, too, this commitment to masculinity may be reflected in the conflict and stress men feel when working with women as colleagues or bosses. Because males tend to control most managerial positions within organizations, this adherence influences the whole culture of the organization and has profound negative consequences on women and nontraditional men who work in these environments. Consequently, career counselors are more likely to see clients who are suffering the effects of working in environments run by men who have an excessive commitment to masculine ideology and thus create a rigid environment that reinforces male characteristics and punishes feminine qualities. These work environments can also be very difficult for gay and bisexual men whether "out" in the work environment or not; the fear of formal and informal harassment is great. If the workplace is dominated by men who exhibit rigid adherence to sex-typed masculine ideologies, the environment can be even more stressful and difficult for gay and bisexual men.

Reliance on Aggression, Power, and Control

As a result of the sex role socialization process, aggression, power, and control are evident in all domains of a man's life, including the workplace. Men have learned that to be respected and valued they need to display these characteristics. Obviously, some measure of these characteristics is functional; however, the "unrelenting reliance on competitive and aggressive coping behaviors to solve problems consistent with rigid masculine schemata is likely to produce stress" (Eisler and Blalock, 1991, pp. 52–53).

Career counselors may deal with this coping mechanism from both a process and content perspective. The process of career counseling may be effected if men feel the need to use their power and control mechanisms to be comfortable in the counseling context. Demanding counselor credentials, unrealistic expectations of the counselor, or attempts to control the course of counseling may all be process outcomes of this coping strategy.

The content of the career counseling itself may also be shaped by men's use of aggression, power, and control. The workplace is currently in a state of transition from a strict hierarchy characterized by a dominant, aggressive leader and compliant workers to a more egalitarian work culture that emphasizes greater cooperation and group consensus. This change may create great stress and career conflicts for the traditional male who was comfortable with and felt competent in the old workplace structure.

Importance of Performance, Achievement, and Success

Because male self-identity is inextricably tied to the worker role, much importance is placed on performance and achievement in men's career lives. The importance given to the work role at the expense of other life roles can be conceptualized as an obsession (Eisler & Blalock, 1991). As a result, it is likely that the career counselor will see men when some aspect of this performance achievement success paradigm breaks down. Examining strictly environmental changes in the work setting, we see many opportunities for this breakdown to occur. As will be discussed in Chapter 7 on the changing workplace, companies are downsizing to become "leaner and meaner," different kinds of skills are needed and valued, and lateral career moves occur more often than vertical ones. All of these changes affect a man's ability to feel successful and gain identity in the workplace.

Emotional Inexpressiveness

Eisler and Blalock (1991) contended that the construct of emotional inexpressiveness "results in their frequent appraisal of certain types of interpersonal situations as stressful, restricts the range of coping behaviors available to them, and impairs the success of their relationships" (p. 55). Although Eisler and Blalock focused almost entirely on the consequences of this construct on romantic relationships and friendships, one can clearly see the role of emotional inexpressiveness in the workplace and career counseling setting as well. By restricting emotional expression, males may appraise the variety of interpersonal interactions at work as much more stressful than their female counterparts who may be more likely to express their emotional reactions at work to resolve differences. Workers' ability to cooperate, hear others' perspectives, and problem-solve to reach consensus, all require the ability and willingness to express one's feelings more than ever before in the workplace.

The theoretical and empirical work of Eisler and Blalock (1991) appears to have much relevance to understanding men's coping mechanisms in stressful situations. Applying these constructs to work-related issues helps career counselors understand and interpret behavior and provide more effective career counseling.

Search for Meaning

For adult men who have spent a great share of their lives striving to achieve in the work world, there often comes a time where their perspective changes from asking "Can I do it?" to "What meaning does this have for me?" Adult developmental theorists call this a change from a search for competence to a search for meaning. The man may come to the realization that he can do many things; he then asks himself whether what he is doing is important in the bigger picture of his life. He may also begin questioning the impact of his striving on his health, friendships, and family connectedness. Some men decide that their current jobs no longer provide what they need and are propelled into a career transition. Given the paramount role that work has in men's lives, being in this ambiguous transition time can be especially stressful. If they are also questioning gender role attributes, even more conflicting feelings can arise.

Themes in Men's Experience of Career Transitions

O'Neil and Fishman (1986) identify four central gender-specific outcomes that emerge during times of occupational transition. These four themes are: (a) discrepancy and incongruity, (b) devaluation, (c) restriction, and (d) violation.

Discrepancy and Incongruity

Discrepancy and incongruity occur when men realize a difference between their real and ideal self concepts. Especially during times of career transition, men may feel they are not living up to the idealized notion of what a man should be. Depending on the circumstances of the transition, men may feel inadequate, depressed, angry, and may exhibit self-hatred. Although O'Neil and Fishman (1986) appeared to be primarily describing males who equated the traditional male role as the ideal, the discrepancy could also occur when men are awakened to a new, less traditional mode of living but feel they are not able to measure up to that ideal either.

Devaluation

Devaluation occurs as a result of self blame and blame deriving from others, such as spouses, partners, or family members. Self blame usually occurs when men do not feel they are measuring up to the masculine ideal. They may be in a career transition because of losing a job, and feel that they are not providing for their family by being the proper breadwinner. This self blame can lead to fear and anger, a loss of confidence in themselves, and depression.

Restriction
Restriction occurs when traditional masculine roles limit the flexibility men have in their work or family roles. When restricted men exhibit rigid roles at home and work, this leaves little room for self growth and much room for interpersonal conflict and stress.

Violation
Violation occurs when men's rights are taken away and they are forced to conform to the rigid patterns of male achievement and success in the workplace. If men question or reject the masculine standards of success, they may become alienated or ostracized in the work environment.

ASSESSMENTS AND TECHNIQUES FOR EMPOWERING MEN'S CHOICES

Now we turn to an examination of various assessments and techniques for promoting men's awareness and understanding how gender has influenced men's career development. Fortunately, the last decade has seen the development of a variety of assessment measures that examine various aspects of the male gender role. Thompson and Pleck (1995) provided a review of instruments available on men and masculinity-related constructs. It is imperative that counselors be aware of their own gender-related biases, the conflicts they may feel with their own gender role, and how these biases and conflicts may influence their work with clients. As we have seen, the few empirical studies that have been conducted uncovered gender bias on the part of counselors in their treatment of non-traditional male clients. Thus, we discuss four instruments that we have found particularly useful in applying male gender-role concepts to the career counseling process. These may be helpful for counselors to use to assess themselves, and may also be helpful in assisting male clients to make more authentic life-planning decisions.

Gender Role Conflict Scale (O'Neil, Helms, Gable, David, & Wrightsman, 1986)
This scale measures the construct of gender role conflict, which is defined as "a psychological state arising from the inherently contradictory and unrealistic messages within and across the standards of masculinity. Gender role conflict exists when masculinity standards result in personal restriction and

devaluation." (Thompson & Pleck, 1995, p. 150). This 37-item scale measures four constructs: (1) Men's concerns with success, power and competition; sample item: "Moving up the career ladder is important to me," (2) restrictive emotionality; sample item: "I have difficulty expressing my emotional needs to my partner," (3) restrictive affectionate behavior between men; sample item: "Expressing my emotions to other men is risky," and (4) the conflicts in work/family relations; sample item: "My need to work or study keeps me from my family or leisure more than I would like."

Masculine Gender Role Stress Scale (Eisler & Skidmore, 1987)
This inventory was constructed to measure stressful life situations that are more common in men's than women's lives, given their gender role socialization. The instrument measures five areas of gender linked stress: (1) situations that demonstrate physical inadequacy; sample item: "Losing in a sports competition," (2) expressing tender emotions; sample item: "Telling someone that you feel hurt by something she/he said," (3) placing men in subordination to women; sample item: "Letting a woman take control of the situation," (4) threatening a male's intellectual control; sample item: "Working with people who are brighter than yourself," and (5) revealing performance failures in work and sex; sample item: "Finding you lack the occupational skills to succeed."

Male Roles Scale (Brannon & Juni, 1984; Thompson & Pleck, 1986)
The original creation, development, and psychometric work on this scale was conducted by Brannon and Juni (1984) as a scale to measure men's approval of the norms and values associated with the male role. The original form is known as the Brannon Masculinity Scale. Thompson and Pleck conducted factor analysis on the Brannon and developed a shorter (26-item) three-factor scale they call the Male Role Norms Scale. The three factors composing this scale are (1) status norms, (2) toughness norms, and (3) antifemininity norms.

Gender Role Journey Measure (O'Neil, Egan, Owens, & McBride, 1993)
This measure was constructed to help both men and women explore the stage they are in with regard to their own gender role changes and transitions. The scale is based on the idea that individuals can grow and change in their gender role ideology, moving from stages of traditional and rigid sex segregated social worlds to more flexible and less restrictive views. The five original theorized stages were collapsed into three factors that make up the current instrument. These three stages are: (1) acceptance of traditional gender roles; sample item: "Men should be in charge at work," (2) Gender role ambivalence, anger, confusion, and fear; sample item: "I sometimes feel confused

about gender roles," and (3) personal–professional activism that promotes social change; sample item: "I have taken some action in my personal life to reduce sexism."

As assessment tools, these four instruments provide a context and a language to discuss the complex issues of gender and career planning. By using them with male clients, the counselor can open up a dialog with the client in which gender role constructs become a category of analysis within the career counseling process.

In addition to using assessment measures in the career counseling process, a number of other interventions may be helpful. We discuss three strategies that may be particularly helpful to male clients in their exploration of gender-role and career: (1) expressiveness training, (2) the use of *Man Alive: A Primer of Men's Issues,* and (3) the use of a gender-focused journal especially designed for men to examine career-related issues.

Expressiveness Training

Because restricted emotionality is one of the most pervasive outcomes of men growing up in the gendered context, interventions aimed at helping men become more expressive have been advocated (Dosser, 1982; Kahn & Greenberg, 1980; Zunker, 1994). Zunker describes two goals of expressiveness training. First, the client needs to learn situations where the expression of emotion is appropriate in the workplace, and second, the specifics of how to express a variety of emotions.

A host of counseling techniques can be creatively applied to expressiveness training, including the use of role play, where group members play the roles of key figures in the work environment while men practice appropriate ways of expressing themselves with those individuals. The Gestalt technique of the Empty Chair may also be a powerful tool in expressiveness training (Kahn & Greenberg, 1980). For example, one client identified a situation from the past where he wished he had been able to express appropriate emotion. His secretary was emotionally distraught over the loss of her husband to cancer. He had managed to tell her to take as much time off as she needed, but had been unable to express his empathy for her loss. Through using the Empty Chair technique, the client was able to practice ways of speaking to her, and to switch roles to feel how she would have felt in response to both his nonexpressive and expressive modes. Skillful counselors can help men explore the full range of their emotions and thus have a much wider repertoire of responses from which to choose.

Man Alive: A Primer for Men's Issues
(Rabinowitz & Cochran, 1994)

This book can be used either as a self-help guide or as part of ongoing individual or group work to assist male clients in understanding and working through key aspects of the male role that might be destructive to their mental, physical, or spiritual health. It contains chapters on a range of topics including early socialization messages, male health issues, and work, money, and male identity. Each chapter has a narrative that examines some aspect of the male role, followed by exercises designed to help men reflect on and explore these aspects of their lives. Some of these are consciousness-raising exercises; others are personal development ones. Additional readings are also provided for men to fully explore each topic.

Deepening Psychotherapy with Men (Rabinowitz & Cochran, 2002) is a new and very helpful resource that integrates theory, research, and practice in helping counselors deepen their relationship with male clients. Robinwitz and Cockran also provide in depth case studies which demonstrate ways of helping men understand important issues in their lives and more deeply connect with who they are and what they want from their lives.

Gender-Focused Journal

The use of journal writing in counseling and psychotherapy has been helpful to many clients (Progoff, 1975). Through reflection and writing, male clients may come to a new understanding of themselves and their work. While the technique of journalling has been used most with women clients (Kahn & Greenberg, 1980), it would seem appropriate for addressing the internal and introverted characteristics of many men. The autonomy and independence that journalling allows may be particularly appealing to men. Writing about one's thoughts and feelings may also be a good preparatory step to discussing them in the counseling session. It is recommended that the counselor give the client stimulus questions, quotes, or ideas to explore in the journal. For example, men could be asked to trace their heroes and role models through time, from their earliest memories to present day and to analyze characteristics consistent in their role models and those that changed over time. Kahn and Greenberg suggest asking men to display graphically how they spend their time, or asking them to draw a lifeline to highlight the peaks and valleys of their life experiences. Planning and developing exercises to help male clients explore how their gender role has facilitated and hindered their career development can be a creative process for the counselor. The stimulus issues for the journal should be carefully planned to match the particular needs of the client.

THE STRUCTURE OF CAREER COUNSELING: PLACING GENDER ISSUES WITHIN THE COUNSELING PROCESS

In Chapter 1 we outlined the structure of career counseling, which consisted of two major phases and a number of subphases. In the next section we discuss ways of integrating the issues relevant to the gendered context for men into this structure and process. This section will highlight those aspects of each phase that may have gender-related implications for gay, bisexual, and heterosexual clients.

Client Goal or Problem Identification, Clarification, and Specification

Opening

The opening phase of career counseling has as its central goals: (a) identifying of the client's goals or problems and the internal thoughts and feelings that might be involved, (b) beginning formation of the working alliance, and (c) defining and clarifying the client–counselor relationship and responsibilities. In planning this phase with the gendered context in mind, the counselor should consider the following issues:

- You should help the client examine his goals through a gender filter. Which goals are motivated out of socialization? What presenting problems result from environmental pressures and a need to prove some aspect of the traditional male role? Is the client able to express emotions honestly, even if they include feelings of vulnerability? Does the client appear to be setting authentic goals based on a full knowledge of relevant information?
- As you begin to develop the working alliance, you should be especially aware of the client's level of gender-role identity and sexual identity orientation and what impact that might have on the relationship you are building with him. It is critically important not to assume a heterosexist stance, but rather to use inclusive terminology when building the working alliance and finding out about the man's situation. Small signs such as whether there is a place to indicate "partnered" as opposed to married communicates a gay-bisexual sensibility, important to building a strong alliance.

It is very difficult for most men to admit that they need help. Men's training fosters self-reliance. Thus, if a man actually comes to counseling, it may be important to recognize the likelihood that he is experiencing a fair amount of turmoil and pain. Building a strong working alliance is paramount. Little has been written about how best to establish a strong working alliance with a traditional male. An understanding of the typical male socialization process tells us that building a relationship of honesty and collaboration with a male client will often be difficult. If the counselor is male, often the male client is confused by the unfamiliar intimacy with another man, and may have homophobic reactions. Ettkins (1981) contended that most traditional men dread being known, and this dread of being known severely hampers the formation of the working alliance.

Building the working alliance involves building a bond of collaboration and hope. The client needs to see the counselor as someone who understands his situation and will relate to his life experiences. Appreciating the pride of the man and empathizing with his discomfort and inadequacy is critical for a working alliance to form. Self-disclosure of relevant and appropriate information from the counselor's own life may help model the appropriate expression of emotion and help to build the bond. As you build the working alliance, client strengths should be reinforced, because the client may feel that he has no strength of his own if he has reached the point of needing help. This is a time when emphasizing the strengths that are part of the traditional male role is especially important. Helping the client understand that his development has fostered such positive characteristics as integrity, steadfastness, loyalty, and the ability to persevere (Levant, 1996), for example, can help build self-esteem and increase the bond between counselor and client.

Recognize that counseling settings may not be a comfortable place for men to be. Talking about feelings directly, sitting for 50-minutes, being asked to be vulnerable are not behaviors that most men relate to. It may be important to alter the typical counseling session to better meet the needs of male clients. When clarifying the client–counselor relationship and responsibilities, it is important to discuss your philosophy of counseling and particularly those aspects that relate to counseling men. If you concur with the feminist or gender-aware counseling position discussed in Chapter 4—seeing the client–counselor relationship being one of equality, a collaborative working relationship—then that needs to communicated. Because many clients come to counselors seeking an expert who will give advice about their lives, this characterization of a collaborative relationship may be foreign. Men often view the counselor as an answer dispenser. They expect to go in and "get fixed," not to work in a collaborative relationship that emphasizes self-awareness. Also, the role of the environment in shaping the individual may also be an important philosophical issue to discuss. If you believe it is your responsibility to challenge gender-based assumptions, this should also be communicated. The client has a right to informed consent in the choice of a career counselor. Knowing where you stand and your philosophical base is important information in making that choice. As discussed in Chapter 4, it is also important for counselors to be aware and knowledgeable about sexual identity development of men and how this may impact their vocational development. The reader is referred to Chapter 4 for more information and resources about sexual identity models that may be helpful.

Gathering Client Information
The clarification and information gathering subphase of the career counseling process has as its central goal learning more about the client.

- Here, any or all of the assessments discussed earlier in this chapter can be used to supplement any other standardized or nonstandardized career related assessment measures. The Gender Role Conflict Scale, Masculine Gender Role Stress Scale, Male Role Norms Scale, and the Gender Role Journey are all appropriate ways of gathering information about the client's experiences that may impact his career planning process. It is important to discuss your rationale for choosing a particular measure with the client. You might say something like:

Career development for men is often intertwined with how they see themselves as men. This scale helps you assess your own gender role and how aspects of this role might affect your career planning.

These instruments have also been used effectively when clients have brought their test results home, reflected on them, and written about how these fit their perceptions of themselves. For example, the following is a portion of a client's writing after taking the Male Role Norms Scale:

I hadn't really realized how driven toward status and material things I have become. As a product of the sixties, I always prided myself on living the simple life, but now I find myself working three jobs in order to be able to afford things I use to ridicule people for wanting.

The assessment of gender role constructs can also be very helpful when the results of such an assessment are integrated with more traditional career assessments, as this case example illustrates:

Lester had a very low, flat profile on the Self-Directed Search, with strong scores only in the realistic area. His scores on the Gender Role Journey Measure indicated that he was at the second stage, characterized by gender role ambivalence, confusion, anger, and fear. By talking through the antecedents of his ambivalent feelings, it became clear that he wanted to be more open to broader roles, but never felt his social skills were good enough to do other kinds of occupations. Thus, the path of counseling was shifted slightly toward examining ways of improving interpersonal skills in order to feel that he had greater career options.

Understanding and Hypothesizing Client Behavior

The specification subphase of the career counseling process has as its central goal understanding clients more fully and hypothesizing about their unique dynamics and the psychological and environmental reasons behind their actions.

In this phase, it is important to probe deeper to understand more about how the client makes meaning of himself and his occupational world. As we listen through the gender filter, we are trying to understand the life choices from both an individual and an environmental perspective. We are trying to help the client explore the gender-based career choices he has made and to evaluate how they are working for him at this point in his life.

As a counselor, your awareness of gender-role constructs can also be used during this phase to assess their influence on men's lives in more informal ways. The instruments can provide you with language and constructs to use as filters when talking to male clients. They can help you build hypotheses about the client's behavior, such as:

Mike is talking a lot about his anger toward his coworkers, how they aren't measuring up. I want to check out whether this is out of his own need to feel superior, or whether he feels angry at himself for being at the office every night, or whether there is another explanation for why he feels so upset by their behavior.

Another hypothesis might be that his anger at others is masking his feelings of inadequacy that result from his feeling inferior to his coworkers.

These hypotheses can then be tested in various ways so that the counselor and client can become more aware of the underlying gender-related dynamics that may be creating certain behaviors and attitudes.

In this phase it is appropriate to provide knowledge to the client to help him understand more about the impact of gender on people's lives. Depending on the client's situation, this may mean talking about such issues as the importance of learning to define success on your own terms, expressing emotions rather than withholding them, ways of replacing the importance of achievement in defining one's identity with other more balanced life options, and what we know about the costs and rewards of traditional gender role beliefs on psychological and physical well-being.

This may be an important phase for helping gay clients understand how various aspects of their sexual orientation may be influencing the career planning process. The counselor must also understand the phenomena of internalized homophobia and help the client recognize if he has internalized heterosexist messages and beliefs. Some bisexual and gay men need to spend an enormous amount of energy in "passing" for heterosexuals at work. Understanding more about where the client is in terms of his coming out process can be a vital aspect of helping to understand and negotiate various career-related issues and transitions.

Finally, this may also be the phase to use techniques such as the geneogram (presented in Chapter 10) to understand more specifically about the client's gender-influenced life choices from a family systems perspective. At this time, the client might construct a lifeline to help him understand issues such as how his achievement orientation was manifested over time. He could take the Career Transitions Inventory (Chapter 13), and then take the results home to use as inspiration for journal writing about the psychological resources and barriers he is bringing to his career transition. It might also be helpful for the client to reflect on O'Neil and Fishman's (1986) gender-related themes that men experience during times of transition to see how they fit the client's own experience.

Client Goal or Problem Resolution

This second major phase of the career counseling process involves action taking. Here we move from gathering and evaluating aspects of the gendered environment and their resultant gender-specific outcomes to actually taking steps to act on this information. Reaching this phase means that you have worked through all the major issues surrounding the client's situation and he is now in a position to make an authentic life decision based on as complete a set of information about himself and the work world as possible.

Taking Action
Taking action is sometimes an easier phase of the counseling process for men than women, because it is ingrained in their gender role training more than talking about themselves is, as in the earlier stages of the process. For the male client, action may be the quickest way to quell anxiety. It is important, therefore, to be sure men have the necessary self-knowledge and occupational knowledge to make career decisions before charging ahead with the process. A poignant personal memory comes to mind that may help to highlight this point.

> *Having come into the career center where I work, I saw a man in his late 50s sitting on the bench waiting for me. There was a young woman, maybe in her early 20s, with him. He was dressed like a college student, and had carefully combed his little remaining hair over the large bald spot on top of his head. As he began the session with me, he explained that he had just lost his job, his wife had left him, and he wanted to get into another career field as quickly as possible. Even though he had built up a financial nest egg, his anxiety was clearly driving him to jump into another life as quickly as possible. The young woman with him was his new romantic relationship whom he had started dating one week after his wife had left him.*

So, as this situation illustrates, it is important to try to help the client slow down and learn to live with the ambiguity of the career transition in order to increase the odds of making better choices.

Developing Career Goals and Plans of Action

Individualized career plans are particularly important when helping male clients incorporate parts of their gender role ideology into the career planning process. Carefully examining each step of the process with an eye to how the client is likely to handle particular action steps given his gender-role upbringing can be invaluable to him. Different aspects will be important given the uniqueness of each man's situation. For example, when counseling a traditional man who is likely to appear arrogant when interviewing with women, building his awareness about the consequences of various interpersonal styles might be helpful. When helping a gay man apply for positions in a potentially discriminating employment setting, discussing each choice point he has in the job application, and interview process would be vitally important. This also emphasizes the need for counselors to be aware of laws protecting and discriminating against gays in employment settings, as well as issues related to HIV testing in the workplace (Hedgepeth, 1979/1980).

Evaluating Results and Closing the Relationship

The closure session is a time for evaluating whether goals have been met and what the process was like for the counselor and the client. When examining the closure session through a gender filter, the following issues are important:

- Reflect on the journey the career counseling process has taken. For many males this may have been the first time that they identified the need for help and sought counseling. It is important to reflect on and reinforce the courage of that act. It may be helpful to the client to see the experience of asking for help as a sign of strength rather than a weakness.
- Discuss the relationship between the counselor and client over time. How did the working alliance develop? How were tears in the alliance mended? How are both parties feeling about termination? Developing intimate relationships that often develop between a counselor and client are difficult for all clients, but especially for males. It is helpful to talk about how the counseling relationship developed, how communication became more honest, how trust developed, and how all of this felt from the client's perspective. You can point out that the strengths of the client that helped to foster this relationship are transferable to other relationships in the man's life.
- Let the client know that you are here should he wish to return for more counseling, or just to let you know how things are going. Men clients should know that the support system you have provided during counseling will remain should he have difficulties after counseling has closed, because this may be one of the few support systems he really has.

In each phase of the counseling process there are important gender-related issues to incorporate. If you plan each session knowing the individual man's life experience and its many gender socialized aspects, the career counseling process is more likely to be an empowering and reinforcing one. In sum, the purpose of this chapter has been to highlight key aspects of the gendered context, to identify their resultant outcomes in male clients, to discuss strategies and assessments for integrating knowledge of the gendered environment into the counseling sessions, and, specifically, to point out key relevant issues at each stage of the career planning process. We have also tried to integrate the much more limited literature on the unique career-related issues of gay and bisexual men. In doing so, we hope to have prepared the counselor to feel more personal efficacy in empowering the choices of all men through career counseling.

REFERENCES

Brannon, R., & Juni, S. (1984). A scale for measuring attitudes toward masculinity. *JSAS Catalog of Selected Documents in Psychology, 14,* 6. (Ms 2012).

Brooks, G. R., & Good, G. E. (Eds.) (2001). *The New handbook of psychotherapy and counseling with men.* San Francisco, CA: Jossey Bass.

Chodorow, N. (1978). *The reproduction of mothering.* Los Angeles, CA: University of California Press.

Courtenay, W. H. (2001). Counseling men in medical settings: The six-point health plan, pp. 59–91 in G. R. Brooks & G. E. Good (Eds.). *The New handbook of psychotherapy and counseling with men.* San Francisco, CA: Jossey Bass.

Croteau, J. M., Anderson, M. Z., Distefano, T. M., & Kampa-Kokesch, S. (2000). Lesbian, gay, and bisexual vocational psychology: Reviewing foundations and planning construction. In R. M. Perez, K. A., DeBord, & K. J. Bieschke (Eds.). *Handbook of counseling and psychotherapy with lesbian, gay and bisexual clients,* pp. 383–408. Washington, DC: American Psychological Association.

Crouteau, J. M. (1966). Research on the work experiences of lesbian, gay and bisexual people: An integrative review of methodology and findings. *Journal of Vocational Behavior, 48,* 195–209.

Dosser, D. A. (1982). Male inexpressiveness: Behavioral interventions. In K. Solomon & N. B. Levy (Eds.), *Men in transition,* pp. 343–432. New York: Plenum.

Dubois, T. E., & Marino, T. M. (1987). Career counseling with men. In M. Scher, M. Stevens, G. Good, and G. A. Eichenfild (Eds.), *Handbook of counseling and psychotherapy with men,* pp. 68–82. Newbury Park, CA: Sage.

Eisler, R. M., & Blalock, J. A. (1991). Masculine gender role stress: Implications for the assessment of men. *Clinical Psychology Review, 11,* 45–60.

Eisler, R. M., & Skidmore, J. R. (1987). Masculine gender role stress: Scale development and component factors in the appraisal of stressful situations. *Behavior Modification, 11,* 123–136.

Ettkins, L. (1981). Treating the special madness of men. In R. A. Lewis (Ed.), *Men in difficult times: Masculinity today and tomorrow.* Englewood Cliffs, NJ: Prentice Hall.

Fitzgerald, L. F. & Cherpas, C. C. (1985). On the reciprocal relationship between gender and occupation: Rethinking the assumptions concerning masculinity and career development. *Journal of Vocational Behavior, 27,* 109–122.

Friedan, B. (1981). *The second stage.* New York: Summit Books.

Gettys, L. D., & Cann, A. (1981). Children's perceptions of occupational sex stereotypes. *Sex Roles, 7,* 301–308.

Gilligan, C. (1982). *In a different voice.* Cambridge, MA: Harvard University Press.

Good, G. E., Dell, D. M., & Mintz, L. B. (1989). Male roles and gender role conflict: Relationships to help seeking in men. *Journal of Counseling Psychology, 3,* 295–300.

Harrison, J., Chin, J., & Ficarrotto, T. (1989). Warning: Masculinity may be dangerous to your health. In M. S. Kimmel & M. A. Messner (Eds.), *Men's lives* (pp. 296–309). New York: Macmillan.

Hedgepeth, J. M. (1979/1980). Employment discrimination law and the rights of gay persons. *Journal of Homosexuality, 5* (12), 67–78.

Heppner, M. J., & Heppner, P. P. (2001). Addressing the implications of male socialization for career counseling. In G.R. Brooks and G. E. Good (Eds.). *The New handbook of psychotheory and counseling with men,* pp. 369–386. San Francisco, CA: Jossey-Bass.

Hershberger, S. L. & D'Augelli, A. R. (2000). Issues in counseling lesbian, gay, and bisexual adolescents. In R. M. Perez, K. A., DeBord, & K. J. Bieschke (Eds.). *Handbook of counseling and psychotherapy with lesbian, gay and bisexual clients,* pp. 225–248. Washington, DC: American Psychological Association.

Hetherington, C., Hillerbrand, E., and Etringer, B. D. (1989). Career counseling with gay men: Issues and recommendations for research. *Journal of Counseling and Development, 67,* 452–454.

Kahn, S. E., & Greenberg, L. S. (1980). Expanding sex role definitions by self-discovery. *The Personnel and Guidance Journal, 49,* 220–225.

Keen, S. (1991). *Fire in the belly: On being a man.* New York: Bantam Books.

Kiselica, M. S. (2001). A male-friendly thereuputic process with school age boys in G. R. Brooks & G. E. Good (Eds.). *The New Handbook of Psychotherapy and counseling with men,* pp. 43–58. San Francisco, CA: Jossey Bass.

Lazarus, R. S., & Folkman, S. (1984). *Stress, appraisal and coping.* New York: Springer.

Levant, R.F. (2001). The Crisis of Boyhood (pp. 355–368) in G. R. Brooks & G. E. Good (Eds.). *The New handbook of psychotherapy and counseling with men.* San Francisco, CA: Jossey Bass.

Levant, R. F. (1996). Masculinity reconstructed. *The Independent Practitioner, 16,* 1. APA, Division 42. Bulletin of the Division of Independent Practice.

Levant, R. F., & Pollack, W. S. (1995). *A new psychology of men.* New York: Basic Books.

Matlin, M. (1993). *The psychology of women.* New York: Holt, Rinehart, & Winston.

Matthews, K. A. & Angulu, J. (1980). Measurement of the Type A behavior pattern in children: Assessment of children's competitiveness, impatience, anger, and aggression. *Child Development, 51,* 466–475.

Moore, D., & Leafgren, F. (1990). *Men in conflict.* Alexandria, VA: American Association for Counseling and Development.

O'Neil, J. M., Egan, J., Owens, S. V., & McBride, V. (1993). The gender role journey measure: Scale development and psychometric evaluation. *Sex Roles, 28,* 167–185.

O'Neil, J. M., & Fishman, D. M. (1986). Adult men's career transitions and gender-role themes (pp. 132–162.). In Z. Leibowitz & D. Lea (Eds.), *Adult career development: Concepts, issues and practices*. Alexandria, VA: National Career Development Association.

O'Neil, J. M., Helms, B. J., Gable, R. K., David, L., & Wrightsman, L. S. (1986). Gender-role conflict scale: College men's fears of femininity. *Sex Roles, 14*, 335–350.

Pleck, J. H. (1987). The contemporary man. In M. Scher & M. Stevens (Eds.). *Handbook of counseling & psychotherapy with man*. Thousand Oaks, CA: Sage Publications, Inc.

Perez, R. M., DeBord, K. A., & Bieschke, K. J. (Eds). *Handbook of counseling and pscyhotherapy with lesbian, gay, and bisexual clients*. Washington, D.C.: American Psychological Association.

Progoff, I. (1975). *At a journal workshop: The Basic text and guide for using The Intensive Journal*. New York: Dialogue House Library.

Rabinowitz, F. E., & Cochran, S. V. (1994). *Man alive: A primer of men's issues*. Pacific Grove, CA: Brooks/Cole Publishing.

Rabinowitz, F. E., & Cochran, S. V. (2002). *Deepening psychotherapy with men*. Washington, DC: American Psychological Association.

Robertson, J., & Fitzgerald, L. F. (1990). The (Mis) Treatment of men: Effects of client gender roles and life-style on diagnosis and attribution of pathology. *Journal of Counseling Psychology, 37*, 3–9.

Sharpe, M. J., & Heppner, P. P. (1991). Gender role, gender-role conflict, and psychological well-being in men. *Journal of Counseling Psychology, 38*, 323–330.

Silverberg, R. A. (1986). *Psychotherapy for men: Transcending the masculine mystique*. Springfield, IL: Charles C. Thams.

Skovholt, T. M. (1990). Career themes in counseling and psychotherapy with Men. In D. Moore and F. Leafgren (Eds.), *Men in Conflict*. Alexandria, VA: American Association for Counseling and Development.

Skovholt, T. M., & Morgan, J. I. (1981). Career development: An outline of issues for men. *The Personnel and Guidance Journal, 60*, 231–236.

Thompson E. H., & Pleck, J. H. (1995). Masculinity ideology: A review of research instrumentation on men and masculinity. In R. F. Levant and W. S. Pollack (Eds.), *A New Psychology of Men*. (pp. 129–163). New York: Basic Books.

Thompson, E. H., & Pleck, J. H. (1986). The structure of male role norms. *American Behavioral Scientist, 29*, 531–543.

Tyler, L. E. (1977). *Individuality*. San Francisco: Jossey-Bass.

Waldron, I. (1976). Why do women live longer than men? *Journal of Human Stress, 2*, 1–13.

Worthington, R. L., Savoy, H. B., & Vernaglia, E. R. (2000, August). Beyond tolerance: An integrative model of LGB affirmativeness. Unpublished manuscript.

Zunker, V. G. (1994). *Career counseling: Applied concepts of life planning*. Pacific Grove, CA: Brooks Cole.

▶ 6

An Empowerment Approach to Career Counseling with People with Disabilities

BY JOHN F. KOSCIULEK

The world of work is changing at a rapid pace and the changes are likely to accelerate during the twenty-first century. Employment arrangements such as temporary employment, short-term hires, contractual positions, leased workers, and on-call and part-time workers have and will continue to influence the career development of all workers (Institute on Rehabilitation Issues, 1999). These changes are having a substantial impact on the life roles of individuals with disabilities, the settings in which they live and work, and the events that occur in their lives. At the same time, current disability policy in the United States focuses on the inclusion, independence, and empowerment of people with disabilities (Kosciulek, 2000). Thus, career counseling of people with disabilities must be a dynamic, creative, and highly individualized process. Effective career counseling can be instrumental for empowering the life choices, inclusion, and independence of people with disabilities. In turn, empowerment, inclusion, and independence will lead to high-quality employment and fulfilling careers for individual with disabilities (O'Day, 1999).

John F. Kosciulek, Ph.D, CRC, is an Associate Professor, Office of Rehabilitation and Disability Studies, Department of Counseling, Educational Psychology, and Special Education, Michigan State University.

The purpose of this chapter is to help you expand and extend your vision of career counseling and your counseling repertoire to include those skills and techniques necessary to effectively serve people with disabilities. It will enable you to assist individuals with disabilities in becoming empowered to achieve their career goals and resolve their career problems. To this end, the following topics will be presented: (a) the current employment and career status of people with disabilities, (b) a career counseling empowerment framework, and (c) the career counseling structure applied to people with disabilities.

CURRENT EMPLOYMENT AND CAREER STATUS OF PEOPLE WITH DISABILITIES

Assisting people with disabilities in finding suitable employment is becoming an increasingly difficult task due to the ever-changing nature of work. Major trends such as globalization of the American economy, technology, and population shifts are changing the nature of work and worker skill requirements (Ryan, 1995). Despite rehabilitation efforts, a majority of Americans with disabilities between the ages of 16 and 64 are not employed and their numbers have not changed since 1986, despite the fact that a majority of non-employed people with disabilities in the working age population wants to work (National Organization on Disability, 2000; Taylor, 1994). Given that work is a central force in peoples' lives, dramatically high rates of unemployment and underemployment can adversely affect not only economic and social status of individuals with disabilities, but also their self-image. Disability, therefore, is a risk factor that should be carefully considered when providing career planning, preparation, and counseling services to individuals with disabilities (Szymanski & Hanley-Maxwell, 1996).

SPECIFIC DIFFICULTIES FACED BY PEOPLE WITH DISABILITIES

Providing career development services to people with disabilities presents a challenge to career counselors. In general, the vocational adjustment of people with disabilities has been characterized by limited salable work skills, low income, underemployment, and unemployment (Curnow, 1989). In addition, according to Harrington (1997), students with disabilities frequently leave school without marketable skills or the ability to function independently. The discouraging report on the vocational preparation and employment outcome for people with disabilities (Roessler, 1987; Wolfe, 1997) highlights the need for improved career counseling services for this population. A distinct set of challenges encountered by many people with disabilities that can be used as a reference point for the practicing career counselor includes: (a) limitations in early life experiences, (b) decision-making difficulties, and (c) a negative worker self-concept as a result of castification processes in service delivery systems.

Limitations in Early Experiences

Frequently, people with disabilities arrive at adulthood with few career options (Chubon, 1995). Limited early vocational and social experiences encountered by people with disabilities restrict the array of career options they perceive, impede decision-making ability, and impair future vocational development. The effect of limited early vocational experiences has been described by Holland (1985) as a precursor to the development of career-related problems. Specific career development problems resulting from limited vocational experiences may include the failure to develop a consistent and differentiated personality pattern, a clear vocational identity, and the establishment of a career in an incongruent occupation (Holland, 1985). Unfortunately, such developmental patterns are not unusual among people with disabilities.

Decision-Making Ability

Lack of opportunities to participate in decision-making, to form a perception of oneself as a worker, and to test self-competencies can be the outcome of limited early experiences and can impede career development. The poorly defined self-concept, ambivalence about obtaining work, and limited occupational information reported by people with disabilities (Curnow, 1989) is indicative of distortions that could result in unrealistic vocational aspirations or decisions. Harrington (1997) has aptly described how many individuals with disabilities have had little opportunity for successful experience in decision-making and, therefore, lack competence in making decisions.

Negative Worker Self-Concept Resulting from Castification Processes

Lack of experience and difficulty in decision-making are not solely the result of disability, but also an outcome of social attitudes and stereotypes. Social attitudes toward disability may be as important as the disability itself in that the negative attitude of others plays a part in shaping the life role of the individual with disability. The outcome of this long-term exposure to prejudicial attitudes may result in a negative self-appraisal and a negative worker self-concept.

Society generally holds diminished expectations for people with disabilities (Schroeder, 1995). These attitudes are pervasive; they influence all of us to some degree. As a class, people with disabilities have suffered discrimination. Individuals with disabilities (Fine & Asch, 1988), similar to members of racial and ethnic minority groups (Trueba, 1993), face common social problems of stigma, marginality, and discrimination. Further, given that disability rates among racial and ethnic minority group members are proportionally higher than rates in the population overall (Rehabilitation Services Administration, 1993), many individuals with disabilities face double jeopardy.

Szymanski and Trueba (1994) maintained that at least some of the difficulties faced by people with disabilities are not the result of functional impairments related to the disability, but rather are the result of castification processes embedded in societal institutions for rehabilitation and education and enforced by well-meaning professionals. Castification processes have their roots in a determinist view in which people who are different are viewed as somehow less "human" or less capable (Trueba, Cheng, & Ima, 1993). Problems of castification plague services to people with disabilities because the same categories of impairment and functional limitation (constructed mostly by people without disabilities) are used to determine eligibility for services, to prescribe interventions, and on occasion, to explain failure. The constructs and those who use them become agents of castification (Szymanski & Trueba, 1994).

The disempowering nature of these classification systems is often all too apparent to people with disabilities applying for rehabilitation services in an effort to enhance self-sufficiency and personal independence (Scotch, 2000). Rather than being treated as adults with free or equal status, they may be confronted by able-bodied persons asserting a right to determine what kinds of services they need. Thus, it is critically important that career counselors reject paternalistic castification processes and actively work to foster empowerment among their clients with disabilities. To aid you in accomplishing this task, below is presented an empowerment framework useful for providing career counseling services to people with disabilities.

EMPOWERING PEOPLE WITH DISABILITIES THROUGH CAREER COUNSELING

Three milestone pieces of federal legislation passed in the 1990's set a tone of empowerment and choice regarding service provision to people with disabilities and rejuvenated the consumer movement among people with disabilities originally begun in the 1960's. These pieces of legislation are the Americans with Disabilities Act of 1990 (ADA), the 1992 Rehabilitation Act Amendments, and the Ticket to Work and Work Incentives Improvement Act of 1999.

Americans with Disabilities Act of 1990

Barriers to employment, transportation, public accommodations, public services, and telecommunications have imposed staggering economic and social costs on U.S. society and have undermined our well-intentioned efforts to educate, rehabilitate, and employ individuals with disabilities. The intent of the ADA is to break down these barriers and, thereby, enable society to benefit from the skills and talents of individuals with disabilities (Pardeck, 2001). The ADA gives civil rights protections to individuals with disabilities similar to those provided to individuals on the basis of race, color, sex, national origin, age, and religion. It guarantees equal opportunity for individuals with disabilities in public accommodations, employment, transportation, state and local government services, and telecommunications (U. S. Equal Employment Opportunities Commission, 1992).

The practices and activities covered by the employment nondiscrimination requirements of the ADA are of particular importance to career counselors. The ADA prohibits discrimination in all employment practices, including job application procedures, hiring, firing, advancement, compensation, training, and other terms, conditions, and privileges of employment. In addition, it applies to recruitment, advertising, tenure, layoff, leave, fringe benefits, and all other employment-related activities. Employment discrimination is prohibited against "qualified individuals with disabilities." This includes applicants for employment and employees. An individual is considered to have a "disability" if he or she has a physical or mental impairment that substantially limits one or more major life activities, has a record of such an impairment, or is regarded as having such an impairment. The Society for Human Resource Management (2000) has found that the ADA has been beneficial in all phases of the employment process for both employers and individuals with disabilities seeking employment and/or needing accommodations in an existing position.

1992 Rehabilitation Act Amendments

In the opening of the 1992 Rehabilitation Act Amendments, similar to information in the ADA and other data provided earlier in this chapter, Congress reported that individuals with disabilities continually encounter various forms of discrimination in such critical areas as employment, housing, public accommodations, education, transportation, communication, and recreation. The explicit purpose of the Amendments is therefore to empower individuals with disabilities to maximize employment, economic self-sufficiency, independence, and inclusion and integration into society (Rehabilitation Services Administration, 1993). A particular focus of the legislation is the increased emphasis on client choice in the service provision process. The choice provisions go beyond simply the right of a client to be involved actively in the selection of a service provider. The Act also broadens a client's participation in the selection of a vocational goal (Schroeder, 1995). Following passage of the 1992 Amendments, a state vocational rehabilitation (VR) agency must consider an individual's unique strengths, resources, priorities, concerns, abilities, and capabilities in the selection of an employment outcome.

In this way, Congress made a clear statement that the purpose of the VR program is not simply to find a person a job, but a good job with a promising future that will allow the individual to raise him or herself out of poverty and to live a life of real dignity. In other words, the responsibility of the vocational rehabilitation system is to help impart an elevated expectation for people with disabilities coming to the system for help. While focused on the services provided through the state-federal VR system, the philosophical tenets and practical implications of the Act are useful and valid for any counselors providing career services to people with disabilities. The goal of empowering people with disabilities to live independently, enjoy self-determination, make choices, contribute to society, and pursue meaningful careers should be a common one for all professionals serving individuals with disabilities.

Ticket to Work and Work Incentives Improvement Act of 1999

The Ticket to Work and Work Incentives Improvement Act of 1999 (Ticket to Work) is the most significant disability-related legislation since the ADA. It is federal legislation related to increasing employment opportunities for individuals with disabilities who are Social Security Disability Insurance (SSDI) and Supplemental Security Income (SSI) recipients. The Ticket to Work is designed to remove the primary disincentive that prevents people with disabilities from entering or re-entering the workforce, which is loss of health insurance benefits. In addition, this legislation makes real the opportunity for client choice in the employment and rehabilitation process. The driving forces behind the Ticket to Work are (a) that SSDI recipients do not often get off public rolls and become disability benefits recipients for life and (b) that the state-federal vocational rehabilitation system is not effective in getting people with disabilities back to work once they become SSDI or SSI recipients.

The Ticket to Work, consistent with an empowerment philosophy of career counseling, encourages client choice in the selection of employment-related rehabilitation services. Essentially, the Ticket to Work represents the deregulation of vocational rehabilitation because it mandates client choice of rehabilitation service providers. In a deregulation sequence, choice, in turn, is followed by increased competition, increased variety of services, increased quality of services, increased client satisfaction with services, and reduced costs of services. In sum, the Ticket to Work enhances the employment services system and increases the significance of the role of the career counselor by introducing a voucher system and extending Medicare and Medicaid coverage for people with disabilities.

AN EMPOWERMENT PHILOSOPHY

The ADA, Rehabilitation Act Amendments of 1992, and Ticket to Work have served to fuel the expansion of an empowerment philosophy in disability and rehabilitation services. While some people with disabilities may receive vocational services exclusively from the state-federal VR system, it is important that all career counselors be aware of the philosophical tenets related to the disability empowerment movement and develop a framework for providing career counseling services from an empowerment perspective.

Empowerment of individuals with disabilities may be viewed as possession of the same degree of control over one's own life and the conditions that affect life as is generally possessed by people without disabilities (Harp, 1994). It is the transfer of power and control of values, decisions, choices, and directions of human services such as career counseling from external entities to individuals themselves (Bolton & Brookings, 1996). Thus, as hypothesized and tested by Kosciulek and Merz (2001), the career counselor committed to an empowerment approach to service delivery should facilitate and maximize opportunities for individuals with disabilities to have control and authority over their own lives.

Emener (1991) has described the philosophical tenets necessary for an empowerment approach to rehabilitation. Extended, these tenets provide a valuable philosophical framework for the provision of career counseling services to people with disabilities. The four tenets are paraphrased as follows:

1. Each individual is of great worth and dignity.
2. Every person should have equal opportunity to maximize his or her potential and is deserving of societal help in attempting to do so.
3. People by and large strive to grow and change in positive directions.
4. Individuals should be free to make their own decisions about the management of their lives.

From an empowerment perspective based on the above philosophical tenets, career counseling is not something that can be done to or for a client. Rather, it is a process in which clients must become active, informed participants who learn and control a planning process that they use for short- and long-term career development (Szymanski, Hershenson, Enright, & Ettinger, 1996). In addition, the lifelong, developmental nature of the process means "unless we plan to work with an increasingly dependent client again and again across the decades, our professional responsibility is to assure that each person learns the [career planning] process" (Mastie, 1994, p. 37).

Active client involvement is the key element of successful career counseling interventions (Ettinger, Conyers, Merz, & Koch, 1995). In an empowerment approach to career counseling, clients are actively involved in: (a) gathering information, including self-assessment and learning about occupations and the labor market; (b) generating alternative courses of action and weighing those alternatives; and (c) formulating a plan of action. The final section of this chapter applies the structure of career counseling to people with disabilities. The information and structure provided allows you to develop the skills necessary to provide efficacious services to people with disabilities from an empowerment perspective.

APPLYING THE CAREER COUNSELING
STRUCTURE TO PEOPLE WITH DISABILITIES

Unfortunately, reports on the current employment and career status of people with disabilities are discouraging (National Organization on Disability, 2000; Taylor, 1994). Many people with disabilities are either unemployed or underemployed. Career challenges encountered by people with disabilities often result from a combination of limitations in life experiences and decision-making difficulties. In addition, individuals with disabilities may feel disempowered as a result of long-term exposure to prejudicial attitudes from castification processes in service systems. The need for improved career counseling for people with disabilities cannot be overstated. An empowerment approach to career counseling is necessary to assist people with disabilities to achieve their career goals and resolve their career problems. In the section that follows, the career counseling structure is applied to people with disabilities to aid you in developing the skills necessary to effectively serve this population. By applying this structure to a disability context, you can be instrumental in empowering the life choices, inclusion, and independence of people with disabilities.

Client Goal or Problem Identification,
Clarification, and Specification

Phase 1 of career counseling involves client goal or problem identification, clarification, and specification. In this phase, the counselor and client proceed mutually from forming the working alliance to gathering client information to understanding and hypothesizing about client information and behavior.

Opening—Forming the Working Alliance

It is important to note at this juncture that, at least theoretically, career counseling for people with disabilities should not differ from career counseling for any other client. In practice, however, this is less than totally true, primarily because the person with a disability presents unique issues that were not presented by the population of individuals without disabilities on whom career counseling approaches were developed (Hershenson, 1996). For example, in forming the working alliance with a client with a disability, it is important to distinguish those whose onset of disability was pre-career (e.g., congenital or in early childhood) from those whose onset of disability was after the person had entered upon a career. As summarized by Goldberg (1992), past research has shown that people with acquired disabilities tend to choose occupations consistent with their pre-disability plans, while the people with pre-career disabilities tend to choose occupations consistent with their parents' aspirations and social class. It is critical from the onset that you have an awareness of the myriad ways disability may potentially influence a person's career development. Awareness of such disability-related factors is a critical ingredient in establishing an effective working alliance (Kosciulek, Chan, Lustig, Pichette, & Strauser, 2001).

In the opening stage of Phase 1 of career counseling, the counselor and client identify initial client goals or problems and the internal thoughts and feelings and underlying dynamics that may be involved. Ryan (1996) emphasized the importance of forming an effective working alliance in counseling people with disabilities by clearly identifying presenting problems and defining the client-counselor relationship and responsibilities. In order for an effective and useful career counseling process to occur, clients should be encouraged to be active participants in the counseling process (Kosciulek et al., 2001). An empowerment approach to forming the working alliance in career counseling includes elements that both clients and counselors bring to the relationship. Primary client elements include that clients (1) take responsibility for their own actions and consequences of their actions and (2) are responsible for their own decision-making. Counselor elements in the working alliance show the following characteristics: (1) counselors know and admit their limitations (e.g., lack of knowledge of a specific disability condition) and (2) counselors display unconditional positive regard for the clients they serve (National Institute on Disability and Rehabilitation Research [NIDRR], 1994). Specific counseling techniques that contribute to client empowerment and the development of an effective working alliance also include the following:

- Treating all clients as adults regardless of the severity of the disability condition
- Using age-appropriate language and techniques
- Placing emphasis on client strengths
- Respecting client values and beliefs

Gathering Client Information

Following the development of an effective working alliance and the establishment of an empowerment approach to career counseling, you should proceed to gather information about the client's specific situation. A series of questions may be helpful in the information gathering process. It may be beneficial to inquire about the client's overall worldview. For example, asking clients how they view themselves, others, and the world may provide valuable starting point for the career exploration process. Another question that applies directly to people with disabilities relates to the personal and environmental barriers or constraints within which a client operates. The data generated from responses to this question may give the career counselor clues about the primary difficulties encountered by a client including limitations in life experiences and feelings of disempowerment as a result of castification processes in previous educational and vocational pursuits. A third question important to address with clients with disabilities relates to their decision-making styles. Simply asking a client about his or her decision-making processes and the life matters on which they make decisions may elicit valuable information about the client's comfort with decision-making regarding career planning.

Understanding and Hypothesizing Client Behavior

The final stage of Phase 1 of career counseling involves understanding and hypothesizing about client information and behavior. Following the development of an empowering working alliance and gathering information about client worldviews, personal and environmental barriers, and decision-making patterns, the counselor and client are prepared to hypothesize how this information relates to the client's career development process. At this stage, it may be instructive for you to apply the language and constructs from career development, counseling, and personality theories, and the literature and research concerning individuals with disabilities to understand and interpret client information and behavior. Identification of the specific disability-related variables (including interaction with the client's family, social, and labor market environments) that may be contributing to a career-related problem or inhibiting maximal career growth may be particularly useful for the client and counselor to focus potential actions and interventions.

Client Goal or Problem Resolution

Phase 2 of career counseling involves taking action, developing career goals, and evaluating and closing the relationship. In this phase, the counselor and client undertake actions that will begin to foster positive career progress, identify specific career goals, close the counseling relationship to the extent necessary, and plan appropriate services for monitoring progress and assessing goal attainment.

Taking Action

Career counseling with people with disabilities, as with all individuals, may best proceed into an action phase by using theory-based counseling and assessment procedures. Empowerment counseling assists clients with striving to achieve their goals or resolve their concerns in a positive atmosphere created by an effective working alliance. It is important to remember that empowerment career counseling with people with disabilities involves treating all clients as adults, using age-appropriate language and techniques, and respecting client values and beliefs.

For example, a 20-year-old client seeking job placement assistance may present with cognitive limitations due to mental retardation. In this case, you should address the individual as you would any other 20 year-old, respecting their goals, and making accommodations as necessary for individual needs. In addition, assessment processes must be comprehensive and individualized so that you can understand client needs, wants, skills, and weaknesses. It is also particularly important to remember that client strengths play a major role in their empowerment. Assessment procedures should focus on identifying and capitalizing on these strengths in the goal-development process. Protocols should also be tailored to individual needs and preferences to avoid castification and disempowering service processes. For example, standardized assessment batteries that did not include individuals with disabilities in the development and norming process may further accentuate disability limitations rather than identify individual strengths.

Finally, client disabilities affect their families, spouses, friends, and other individuals who can be assets to counseling and its outcomes. In the past, many professionals underutilized these valuable resources. You may wish to include a family member or friend in some aspect of the career counseling process (e.g., intake, client homework) to facilitate integration of information and goal-directed behavior outside of counseling sessions. Involving "significant others" (with client consent) in counseling can be a critical element in creating empowering relationships (NIDRR, 1994) and facilitating client career development.

Developing Career Goals and Plans of Action

Career counseling is an active process that must be done in an empowering context. Successful goal-development and interventions require active client involvement in all phases of the process. When developing career goals, clients with disabilities must be encouraged to take responsibility for (a) gathering and integrating information about themselves, occupations, and the labor market; (b) generating and evaluating alternatives; (c) making decisions and formulating plans of action; (d) implementing career plans; and (e) and evaluating their results (Szymanski & Hershenson, 1997).

A wide range of career interventions is available to assist counselors and their clients with disabilities with effective goal planning. General interventions include career planning systems, assessment tools, career classes and workshops, including those specially designed for people with disabilities, and career portfolios. Career interventions which may accompany school-to-work transition, adult training, and direct job placement programs include apprenticeship, cooperative education, school-based enterprises/entrepreneurship, internships and practica, and community-based volunteerism. As discussed by Wolfe (1997), the use of a combination of both individual and group-based career counseling and job search interventions has a positive effect on the employment status of individuals with disabilities.

Two major rehabilitation approaches are also highly applicable to the career counseling goal-identification and development of people with disabilities. One of these is supported employment, which provides ongoing, work-related supportive services that permit persons with severe disabilities to engage in competitive employment. A second approach is job accommodation, in which job tasks and job sites are modified to make them accessible to workers with disabilities (Hershenson, 1996). By allowing for exploration and attending to specific disability-related factors that may be adversely affecting career growth, supported employment and job accommodation processes may greatly assist clients and counselors with identifying realistic and satisfying career options. As people with disabilities are a heterogeneous population, no single counseling, assessment, or intervention approach will be applicable to all individuals with disabilities. Therefore, as with all career counseling clients, the focus should be eclectic, that is, on identifying and meeting individual needs, removing specific barriers, expanding the person's range of options, and supporting the person through his or her transition to work (Szymanski & Hershenson, 1997).

Evaluating Results and Closing Relationships

As previously stated, active client involvement is the key element of most successful career counseling interventions. A critical question at the close of a career counseling relationship with individuals with disabilities is whether the client was actively involved in (a) gathering information, (b) generating alternative courses of action and weighing those alternatives, and (c) formulating a plan of action. The quality of the working alliance, level of empowerment generated, usefulness of interventions, and appropriateness of career goals identified are likely to be closely related to the answer to this question.

A critical ingredient for successful career development of people with disabilities is effective follow-along and follow-up services. Thus, when closing the career counseling relationship, counselors and clients may want to establish a monitoring process to ensure achievement of established career plans (e.g., completion of an educational or vocational training program, or successful job maintenance). Follow-along services that are not intrusive but continue to support empowerment can be critical for achieving desired long-term outcomes. Counselors should recognize that clients might choose to discontinue ongoing supports at any time. Counselors should not foster dependency, because clients may see too much follow-up as lack of confidence. An empowered client will feel free to re-initiate counseling contacts if the need arises (NIDRR, 1994).

Once clients leave counseling, their success may depend on their ability to access community resources. Counselors can enhance self-reliance by teaching clients how to get information and tap into supportive workplace and community networks. Clients who discover and utilize community-based resources will be more independent and transfer their personal empowerment beyond the counseling arena into all realms of life.

CLOSING THOUGHTS

Due to the ever-changing nature of the world of work and service system castification processes, assisting people with disabilities to achieve positive, challenging, and stimulating career development is an increasingly difficult task. Effective career counseling can thus be instrumental for empowering the life choices and career success of your clients with disabilities. The information provided in this chapter should help you expand your counseling repertoire to include those skills and techniques necessary to effectively serve people with disabilities. Applying the career counseling structure within an empowerment framework will enable your clients with disabilities to become active, informed participants who learn and control a planning process that they use for both short- and long-term career development. In this manner, you will promote opportunities for your clients with disabilities to have control and authority over their own lives.

REFERENCES

Bolton, B., & Brookings, J. (1996). Development of a multifaceted definition of empowerment. *Rehabilitation Counseling Bulletin. 39* (4), 256–264.

Chubon, R. A. (1995). Career-related needs of school children with severe physical disabilities. *Journal of Counseling and Development, 64,* 47–51.

Curnow, T. C. (1989). Vocational development of persons with disability. *The Career Development Quarterly, 37,* 269–278.

Dart, J. (1992, September). *Toward equality and empowerment.* Paper presented at the IBM Conference on Full Participation in a Modern Society, Tokyo, Japan.

Emener, W. (1991). Empowerment in rehabilitation: An empowerment philosophy for rehabilitation in the 20th century. *Journal of Rehabilitation, 57* (4), 7–12.

Ettinger, J., Conyers, L., Merz, M. A., & Koch, L. (1995). *Strategies and tools for counselors, educators, and consumers.* (Working Paper No. 3). Madison, WI: University of Wisconsin-Madison: Rehabilitation Research and Training Center.

Fine, M., & Asch, A. (1988). Disability beyond stigma: Social interaction, discrimination, and activism. *Journal of Social Issues, 44,* 3–21.

Goldberg, R. T. (1992). Toward a model of vocational development of people with disabilities. *Rehabilitation Counseling Bulletin, 35,* 161–173.

Hagner, D., & Marrone, J. (1995). Empowerment issues in services to individuals with disabilities. *Journal of Disability Policy Studies, 6* (2), 17–36.

Harp, H. T. (1994). Empowerment of mental health consumers in vocational rehabilitation. *Psychosocial Rehabilitation Journal, 17,* 83–90.

Harrington, T. F. (1997). *Handbook of career planning for students with special needs.* Austin, TX: Pro-Ed.

Hershenson, D. B. (1996). Career counseling. In Dell Orto, A. E., & Marinelli, R. P. (Eds.), *Encyclopedia of disability and rehabilitation* (pp. 140-146). New York: Simon & Schuster Macmillan.

Holland, J. L. (1985). *Making vocational choices: A theory of vocational personalities and work environments* (2nd ed.). Englewood Cliffs, NJ: Prentice-Hall.

Holmes, G. E. (1993). The historical roots of the empowerment dilemma in vocational rehabilitation. *Journal of Disability Policy Studies, 4* (1), 1–19.

Institute on Rehabilitation Issues. (1999). *Meeting future workforce needs.* Stout Vocational Rehabilitation Institute, University of Wisconsin-Stout, Menomonie, WI.

Kosciulek, J. F. (2000). Implications of consumer direction for disability policy development and rehabilitation service delivery. *Journal of Disability Policy Studies, 11* (2), 82–89.

Kosciulek, J. F., Chan, F., Lustig, D., Pichette, E., & Strauser, D. (2001, October). *The working alliance: A critical element in the rehabilitation counseling process.* Paper presented at the Alliance for Rehabilitation Counseling Symposium, St. Louis, MO.

Kosciulek, J. F., & Merz, M. A. (2001). Structural analysis of the consumer-directed theory of empowerment. *Rehabilitation Counseling Bulletin, 44,* 209–216.

Mandeville, K., & Brabham, R. (1992). The federal-state vocational rehabilitation program. In R. M. Parker & E. M. Szymanski (Eds.), *Rehabilitation counseling: Basics and beyond* (2nd ed., pp. 43–71). Austin, TX: Pro-Ed.

Mastie, M. M. (1994). Using assessment instruments in career counseling: Career assessment as compass, credential, process and empowerment. In J. T. Kapes, M. M. Mastie, & E. A., Whitfield (Eds.), *A counselor's guide to career assessment instru-*

ments (3rd. Ed., pp. 31–40). Alexandria, VA: The National Career Development Association.

National Institute on Disability and Rehabilitation Research. (1994). Empowerment counseling: Consumer-counselor partnerships in the rehabilitation process. *Rehab Brief, 16* (6), 1–4.

National Organization on Disability. (2000). *Survey of the status of people with disabilities in the United States: Employment.* Washington, DC: Author

O'Day, B. (1999). Policy barriers for people with disabilities who want to work. *American Rehabilitation, 25* (1), 8–15.

Pardeck, J. T. (2001). An update on the Americans with Disabilities Act: Implications for health and human service delivery. *Journal of Health & Social Policy, 13* (4), 1–15.

Rehabilitation Services Administration. (1993). *The Rehabilitation Act of 1973 as amended by the Rehabilitation Act Amendments of 1992.* Washington, D.C.: Author.

Roessler, R. T. (1987). Work disability and the future. Promoting employment for people with disabilities. *Journal of Counseling and Development, 66,* 188–190.

Ryan, C. P. (1995). Work isn't what it used to be: Implications, recommendations, and strategies for vocational rehabilitation. *Journal of Rehabilitation, Oct./Nov./Dec.,* 8–15.

Schroeder, F. K. (1995, November). *Philosophical underpinnings of effective rehabilitation.* Sixteenth Mary E. Switzer Lecture, Worcester, MA.

Scotch, R. K. (2000). Disability policy: An eclectic overview. *Journal of Disability Policy Studies, 11* (1), 6–11.

Society for Human Resource Management. (2000). *The ADA at work: Implementation of the employment provisions of the Americans with Disabilities Act.* Washington, DC: Author.

Szymanski, E. M., & Hanley-Maxwell, C. (1996). Career development of people with developmental disabilities: An ecological model. *Journal of Rehabilitation, 62,* 48–55.

Szymanski, E. M., & Hershenson, D. B. (1997). Career development of people with disabilities: An ecological model. In R. M. Parker & E. M. Szymanski (Eds.), *Rehabilitation counseling: Basics and beyond* (3rd Ed., pp. 273–304). Austin, TX: Pro-Ed.

Szymanski, E. M., Hershenson, D. B., Enright, M. S., & Ettinger, J. M. (1996). Career development theories, constructs, and research: Implications for people with disabilities. In E. M. Szymanski, & R. M. Parker (Eds.), *Work and Disability: Issues and strategies in career development and job placement* (pp. 79–126). Austin, TX: Pro-ed.

Szymanski, E. M., & Trueba, H. T. (1994). Castification of people with disabilities: Potential disempowering aspects of classification in disability services. *Journal of Rehabilitation, July, Aug., Sept.,* 12–20.

Taylor, H. (1994). N.O.D. survey of Americans with disabilities. *Business Week,* special advertising section.

Trueba, H. T. (1993). Castification in multicultural America. In H. T. Trueba, C. Rodriguez, Y. Zou, & J. Contron, *Healing multicultural America: Mexican immigrants rise to power in rural California* (pp. 29–51). Philadelphia: Falmer.

Trueba, H., Cheng, L., & Ima, K. (1993). *Myth or reality: Adaptive strategies of Asian Americans in California.* London, England: Falmer.

U.S. Equal Employment Opportunity Commission. (1992). *The Americans with Disabilities Act: Questions and Answers.* Washington, DC: Author.

Wolfe, K. E. (1997). *Career counseling for people with disabilities.* Austin, TX: Pro-Ed.

► 7

Helping Clients Understand and Respond to Changes in the Workplace and Family Life

The worlds of work and family are changing at a rapid pace and the changes are likely to accelerate as we enter the 21st century. Changing workplaces (globalization, deregulation, downsizing, upsizing, free trade, mergers), increasing diversity in society and the workplace, extended life expectancy, lifelong learning, and changing family structures with the challenges, tensions, stress, and anxiety they bring about in individuals and society are not abstractions. They are real. They are challenging and changing the traditional rules that have governed life in the workplace and family. As a result, they impact substantially the life roles of individuals, the settings where they live and work, and the events that occur in their lives. Many of the problems clients bring to career counseling are manifested in their life roles, settings, and events, and are caused directly or indirectly by one or more of these changes (Allcorn, 1994; Beehr, 1995; Kurzman & Akabas, 1993; Peterson & Gonzalez, 2000; Statt, 1994).

This chapter focuses on how to help your clients respond to the challenges and consequences of these changes through career counseling. First, we focus on changes that are occurring in the workplace and family life, followed by a discussion of the problems your clients may be facing as a result of the challenges and consequences of these changes. Next, we present four major areas of required knowledge to guide your selection of interventions to use with clients. Finally, the chapter closes with a checklist of roles that are critical to the success of career counseling as we help our clients understand and respond to changes in the workplace and family life.

CHANGES IN THE WORKPLACE AND FAMILY LIFE

Changes in the workplace and in family life have been underway for some time. Some commentators have used the term *revolutionary* to describe them, while others have used the term *evolutionary*. Whichever term you prefer, the changes taking place now in these two worlds will continue into the foreseeable future. What are some of these changes?

Changes in the Workplace

The workplace of today continues to undergo significant restructuring. It is being reinvented and reengineered so that it can compete successfully both nationally and internationally. Terms such as globalization, downsizing (rightsizing), upsizing, outsourcing, deregulation, and technology describe various forces at work that cause this ongoing restructuring. "America's workplace revolution isn't over. It has only just begun" (Boyett & Boyett, 1995, p. xi).

What are the consequences of such forces on the workplace? Although a number of writers have offered their views on these consequences (Boyett & Boyett, 1995; Bridges, 1993; Solmon & Levenson, 1994), there is consensus on the following points:

1. As globalization and mergers occur, some workers lose their jobs.
2. The U.S. labor force continues to grow. More jobs are being created in service industries than in goods-producing industries.
3. Flexibility, creativity, adaptability, and education/training will count more than seniority.
4. Job security is no longer assured in many sectors of the economy. Pressure on workers to produce and feelings of insecurity among workers will increase.
5. "Employees and employee teams, who for the past decade have focused their problem-solving and process-reengineering efforts on quality, service, speed, and cost containment, will find their efforts redirected to the constant pursuit of innovation" (Boyett & Boyett, 1995, p. xi).
6. Outsourcing work to other companies is a major force in workplace change. Companies are staying with what they do best; they outsource the rest.
7. "A major trend is the shift to a more temporary workforce" (Altman & Post, 1996, p. 57). The use of temporary workers to handle company business is creating increased involuntary part-time employment (Tilly, 1996).

8. "The shape of work—how people organize themselves and each other—is obviously shifting, and shifting is becoming the shape of work" (Arthur & Rousseau, 1996, p. 371).

9. "Family issues resonate strongly with younger Americans and, most notably, with young men. Most Americans are optimistic about their economic future, although one-quarter report they are earning just enough to get by, and two-thirds lack confidence that they will be able to retire comfortably. More than half of all workers report that they are very loyal toward their employers, but that they do not believe that this loyalty is reciprocated. Finally, workers see technology as both a blessing and a curse: It can make it easier to integrate work and family, but it can also make life more stressful" (The Radcliffe Public Policy Center, 2000, p. 1).

Given these consequences, what implications do they have for people? "People come and go; jobs stay. Well, no, not quite. Jobs come and go too, but only specific jobs—jobs in this industry and that. Jobs-as-a-concept stay. They form the bedrock of our economic planet" (Bridges, 1993, p. 30). Job security is increasingly in the person, not in the job.

In addition to these forces at work that are reshaping the workplace, another powerful force is at work. This force is the dramatic demographic changes occurring in our society that produce an increasingly diverse labor force. So, not only are forces at work changing the very nature and structure of the workplace, but also the people who do the work are changing as well, mirroring the diversifying demographics of our society. Here are some examples:

- The U.S. workforce will become more diverse by 2008. White, non-Hispanic persons will make up a decreasing share of the labor force, from 73.9 to 70.7 percent. Hispanics, non-Hispanic blacks, and Asians and other racial groups are projected to comprise an increasing share of the labor force by 2008—10.4 to 12.7 percent, 11.6 to 12.4 percent, and 4.6 to 5.7 percent, respectively. However, despite relatively slow growth, white non-Hispanics will have the largest numerical growth in the labor force between 1998 and 2008, reflecting the large size of this group.
- The number of men and women in the labor force will grow, but the number of men will grow at a slower rate than in the past. Between 1998 and 2008, men's share of the labor force is expected to decrease from 53.7 to 52.5 percent while women's share is expected to increase from 46.3 to 47.5 percent.
- The youth labor force, ages 16 to 24, is expected to slightly increase its share of the labor force to 16 percent in 2008, growing more rapidly than the overall labor force for the first time in 25 years. The large group of workers, 25 to 44 years old, who comprised 51 percent of the labor force

in 1998, is projected to decline to 44 percent of the labor force by 2008. Workers 45 and older, on the other hand, are projected to increase form 33 to 40 percent of the labor force between 1998 and 2008, due to the aging baby-boom generation (U.S. Department of Labor, 2000, p. 1-2).

Changes in Family Life

As changes continue to take place in the work world, so, too, do changes continue to occur in family life. Work life and family life are intertwined. "Work and family are the major life roles for most employed adults" (Burke, 1996, p. 213).

> *As America approaches the twenty-first century, it is clear that the traditional demarcation between public economic activity and private domestic activity—between "bread winning" and "care giving"—has all but broken down. So has the allocation of these activities along strict gender lines. If it is no longer possible for employees to neatly separate work and family, career and the rest of life, then it is equally unrealistic for employers to expect their employees to do so. The family baggage, like it or not, sits right there on the factory floor or in the middle of the office. And there is a lot of baggage, because the American family is in big trouble (Boyett & Boyett, 1995, p. 84).*

Whether we agree or disagree that the American family is in big trouble, most commentators on families in America do agree that family structures are changing. The traditional family structure of two parents and two or more children with only the father working is no longer in the majority. It has been displaced by a wide variety of family combinations, including dual-career families, dual income-earners, and single-parent families.

- Composition of the labor force. The expanding number of women entering the labor market is resulting in more persons (particularly women) combining family care and employment. Today there are more dual-earner couples as well as more employed single parents. Furthermore, future growth in the labor market will result in a labor force that is younger and more ethnically and racially mixed.
- Changes in the nature of work. With the impact of technological advances and global competition, skill and performance have become generally more valued than loyalty and tenure in the U.S. workplace. Many workers are experiencing more autonomy with increased demands and responsibility.
- Family and gender roles. Despite tremendous demographic change, several facets of U.S. life have remained relatively constant—for example, the central role of the family and the continued relevance of gender in the dis-

tribution of family-care responsibilities (Fredriksen-Goldsen & Scharlach, 2000, p. 13).

Another trend in the family–work arena is the emergence of what a number of writers have called the "sandwich generation" (Boyett & Boyett, 1995; Fredriksen-Goldsen & Scharlach, 2000; Kugelmass, 1995). This phrase describes families that must pay for the education of their children while needing to pay for nursing home care of an aged parent. "Elder care strains a fifth of the work force, and many are in the 'sandwich generation' earning for both children and elders" (Kugelmass, 1995, p. 9).

CHANGING WORKPLACE AND FAMILY LIFE CHALLENGES AND CONSEQUENCES

What are some of the challenges and consequences individuals face as a result of the changes that are occurring in the workplace and in family life? What impact do these changes have on their worker and family roles? This section focuses on some of these issues.

Worker Role Loss

Layoffs, plant closures, and company mergers will continue to be a fact of economic life. Two out of three Americans will lose their job at some time during their working life. For some the effects will be minimal, particularly if they possess marketable skills or live in areas where there are plentiful work opportunities. For others, such as those with strong emotional investment in their work or limited financial resources, employment may have a major impact on activities, relationships, and physical and emotional well-being (Kates, Greiff, & Hagen, 1993, p. 157).

A major consequence for some individuals as the workplace undergoes changes is job loss. When workers lose their jobs due to downsizing, for example, they lose a major anchor in their lives; they lose part of their identity. They feel devalued as individuals and often the feelings that result affect every aspect of their lives, all of their life roles.

Job loss has economic meanings as well as social and psychological meanings. The loss of steady income; daily social contacts, friendships, and support; and the loss of identity and self-worth accompany job loss. Correspondingly, often increased stress creates strains in individuals (anger, frustration, anxiety) and in family life and family relationships (Beehr, 1995).

A number of writers (Bridges, 1993) have adapted Elizabeth Kubler-Ross's (1969) five stages of grieving to describe what happens to individuals who experience job loss. First, there is denial: "They made a mistake." "They must mean somebody else." Then comes anger: "It was that free trade agreement." "It's Washington's fault." This is followed by bargaining: "Things don't have to be like this." "Let's all get together and maybe we can lick this situation." Then comes despair: "All hope is gone." "There is nothing out there for me." Finally, after these progressively deeper stages of grieving, individuals reach Kubler-Ross's final stage of acceptance: "I am ready to get on with it." "I miss what I did, but I can't sit around waiting." Not all workers who go through job loss go through these stages. But when they do, written descriptions of the stages cannot begin to touch their thoughts, emotions, and feelings.

Although all of the stages are connected and are important, the anger stage merits special attention because of the possible consequences of behavior at this stage that individuals may exhibit in the workplace or at home (Daw, 2001; Heskett, 1996). The anger stage also needs attention because anger may be expressed in the workplace or at home as a result of incidents other than job loss.

Confrontation and dialogue usually form part of the normal working environment. Workers and managers are confronted on a daily basis with their personal and work-related problems. They have to face the anxieties and frustration of coworkers, organizational difficulties, personality clashes, aggressive intruders from the outside, and problematic relations with clients and the public. Despite this, dialogue usually prevails over confrontation, and people manage to organize efficient and productive activities within the workplace. There are cases, however, where dialogue fails to develop in a positive way, where relationships between workers, managers, clients, or the public deteriorate, and the objectives of working efficiently and achieving productive results are affected. Violence may enter the workplace and turn a previously benign environment into a hostile and hazardous setting (Chappell & DiMartino, 2000).

Sometimes workers bring anger to work. At other times they become angry because of work and then take this anger home. While job loss may be the precipitating event, there may be any number of other reasons, some rooted in an individual's past and others in the present. "Aggression is a common way anger is acted on. Someone acts offensively; offense is perceived to have occurred; anger is felt and is acted out by perhaps striking back; the offender stops the offense; balance is restored" (Allcorn, 1994, p. xiii).

What are the thoughts and feelings that may lead clients to become angry and act on that anger? Suppose you are working with clients who are expressing anger because they did not get promoted to their next job level. What sequence of thoughts and feelings might you anticipate? Allcorn (1994, pp. 29–30), quoting the work of Hauck (1973, p. 44–54), suggests that you can anticipate the following: First, they might express feelings of frustration because they expected to be promoted but were not. This could be followed by thoughts that not being promoted is terrible, and that they should have been treated more fairly. Now, as anger builds, they may begin to think that they should not be treated that way. Finally, they may think that the bosses who denied them their promotions should be punished severely, because people in management deserve severe punishment.

Given the previous example, how should you respond? Allcorn (1994, p. 56) recommended the following responses: Address anger directly by listening. Try to determine the source of the anger. Try to determine if the anger being expressed is covering up something, such as feelings of helplessness and powerlessness. As you listen, begin to focus on solutions. Help clients shift and sort, separating facts from fantasies.

Worker Role Gain

Much attention in the literature is devoted to the individual and societal consequences of job loss. It is important to remember, however, that along with job loss there is also job gain. Our economy is expanding. The labor force is growing. "Employment in 2008 is expected to reach 160.8 million, an increase of 20.3 million—14 percent above the 1998 level" (Kelinson & Tate, 2000, p. 2).

It also is important to understand which industries will be affected by these projected employment increases. According to the Bureau of Labor Statistics (U.S. Department of Labor, 2000), employment in service-producing industries will increase but will decline in goods-producing industries. This shift in employment affects which occupations are available and the salary and wages paid. New workplace entrants and those seeking to reenter the workplace will need to understand these shifts, because they impact the type of work available, salary or wages paid, and one's general standard of living.

Work–Family/Family–Work Role Connections

Given the changes in work life and family life described previously, how can the challenges and consequences individuals face in family life roles be understood? After an extensive review of the literature, Zedeck and Mosier (1990) describe five ways to understand and explain the complexities and dynamics of the work–family relationship. As you will see, they focus more on individuals in families than on families as units.

The first way is called spill-over theory. According to spill-over theory, there are no boundaries between work and family; what happens at work spills over into the family sphere, and vice versa. Job satisfaction or dissatisfaction is seen as directly related to life satisfaction or dissatisfaction. Work is viewed as a socializing force providing workers with skills and views about self, others, and the world that carry over into family life (Zedeck and Mosier,

1990). There can be a negative side; for example, people may have to respond to the work conflicts and strain experienced by family members, thus diverting energy that could have been used more positively elsewhere.

The second approach is compensation theory, which hypothesizes that work and family roles are inversely related. Because individuals invest differently in their work roles and family roles, they may compensate in one for what is missing in the other. Zedeck and Mosier (1990, p. 241), building on the work of Crosby (1984), point out that "events at home provide 'shock absorbers' for disappointments at work, and vice versa."

The third way is segmentation theory, which suggests that work and family roles can exist side by side without influencing one another. In other words, people can compartmentalize their lives. Zedeck and Mosier (1990, p. 241) state that "the family is seen as the realm of effectivity, intimacy, and significant ascribed relations, whereas the work world is viewed as impersonal, competitive, and instrumental rather than expressive."

The fourth approach is instrumental theory, wherein one role is used as a means of obtaining the necessities and luxuries that are deemed important for another role. Individuals work to obtain goods for family life. They also work to finance the purchase of goods and services for leisure activities, such as a boat, sports equipment, or a media center for the home.

Finally, Zedeck and Mosier (1990) describe conflict theory. This theory postulates that success in one role may mean making sacrifices in another role. Or, even more directly, responding to family obligations may require individuals to be absent from their job, to sometimes arrive late, or to not work efficiently on the job because of family obligations. In summing up this theory, Zedeck and Mosier (1990, p. 241) observed that "the two environments [work and family] are incompatible because they have distinct norms and requirements."

Another perspective on understanding the challenges and consequences individuals face in family life roles is provided by Morrison and Deacon (1993) in their descriptions of the impact of family problems on the workplace. They point out that there is little research and limited clinical data that focus specifically on how family problems can have organizational consequences. Most of the literature available describes the impact of the workplace on the family, rather than the other way around. To respond to this imbalance in perspectives, they identified four family problems and their consequences at work. The problems they identified include loss of family support, family needs interfering at work, workplace as a substitute for unmet family needs, and motivation to work is family driven. Then, for each problem, they list some possible behavioral and attitudinal consequences of each. Let's look more closely at each of these problems and their possible consequences.

When individuals lose family support, what attitudes and behaviors might we see at work? Morrison and Deacon (1993, p. 220) suggest that workers with low emotional energy might sometimes appear to be preoccupied. They may exhibit anger through aggressive behavior, may have difficulty forming and maintaining relationships with other workers, and may appear depressed and detached.

What about family needs interfering at work? How will this problem affect worker behavior and worker attitudes? According to Morrison and Deacon (1993, p. 220), workers may seemingly not want to reach their potential. In fact, they may actually sabotage their own advancement. They may appear to be uncommitted or lacking confidence. They may be vulnerable to burnout. In effect, the worker role is undermined by the family role.

Next is the problem of the workplace serving as a substitute for unmet family needs. What attitudes and behaviors might workers with this problem exhibit in the workplace? Morrison and Deacon (1993, p. 220) suggest that the demands of the workplace might be subverted by personal needs. Workers might exhibit guilt and shame concerning their work behavior because they are using work to respond to unmet family needs. Finally, they suggest that family role problems may damage self-esteem, which could spillover to the workplace.

Finally, the last problem identified by Morrison and Deacon (1993, p. 220) is that motivation to work is family driven. Work is secondary to family. The family unit takes precedence over individual family members. The family controls what happens outside of the home, including the workplace. This problem may result in discord with colleagues, lack of commitment to work and the workplace, and unfulfilled workplace potential because commitment is focused solely upon the home, not upon work.

RESPONDING TO WORKPLACE AND FAMILY LIFE PROBLEMS THROUGH CAREER COUNSELING

A Life Career Development Perspective

As we stated earlier, many of the problems clients bring to career counseling are caused directly or indirectly by one or more of the changes that occur in the workplace and in family life. They are often complex problems interwoven with personal, emotional, family, and work issues. Because they are often complex, a holistic perspective of your clients is beneficial so that problem issues can be seen collectively as well as individually. The holistic perspective we advocate is the concept of life career development as described in Chapter 1.

The concept of life career development provides you and your clients with the language of life roles, life settings, and life events. It becomes a shared language because you can use it to identify, analyze, and understand clients' work and family problems, and clients can do the same. While you provide clients with these constructs, they are easily personalized by clients because they can link them to their real life work and family situations. These provided constructs can be responded to from clients' "own personal experience and individualized vocabulary" (Neimeyer & Leso, 1992, p. 333).

In responding to clients' work and family problems, use of the shared language of life roles, settings, and events provides ways to place and understand work and family problems in context. The use of shared language opens the door to joint (you and your clients together) learning about and understanding of clients' problems so that interventions can be chosen and used to help clients solve their problems. Thus, career counseling becomes a "unitary action" with clients and counselors working together (Young, Valach, & Collin, 1996, p. 501).

Major Areas of Required Knowledge

Helping clients respond to workplace and family life problems requires the selection and use of appropriate interventions. While the specific interventions you choose to use with your clients will depend upon your hypotheses, major areas of knowledge are presented here to remind you of the important problems that often require your attention when dealing with clients' workplace and family concerns. Hotchkiss and Borow (1996) list several areas, including learning about labor markets, combating gender stereotyping, and reducing racial and ethnic barriers. To their list we add combating barriers for the disabled and dealing with work–family/family–work problems.

Learning about Labor Markets

"Clients must be helped to understand something of the complexity of the world of work and the economic order" (Hotchkiss & Borow, 1996, p. 317). Because the work world is dynamic and ever-changing, individuals often have a difficult time understanding it. To many clients who come for career counseling, the work world has few boundaries. It is difficult to grasp. It is overwhelming. This can be true for clients who are first-time job seekers as well as for clients who have been employed in the workplace but have lost their jobs. When we add to this other possible client problems in career counseling that are connected to work but related to race, culture, religion, gender, age, and family, the complexity and interrelatedness of the issues involved in career counseling increases substantially.

Many client problems addressed in career counseling originate in the work world and then spill over into other arenas of life. For example, some clients have presenting problems of finding and getting jobs for the first time or finding and getting other jobs after industry downsizing. This problem is often directly related to their worker roles, but then can spill over into other life roles, such as spouse, family, parent, and learner. Client gender, ethnic and racial identity, sexual orientation, age, religion, and socioeconomic status may also be involved. If clients have experienced any form of discrimination previously in the workplace or in other situations, these experiences may effect the job search. Even if clients have not experienced direct discrimination, the anticipation that discrimination may occur, based on clients' identity group history, may also effect the job search.

Given all of these possible dynamics and connections in clients' presenting problems of finding and getting jobs, a starting point is needed. Because their problems are connected to the work world, starting there makes sense. Helping clients learn a way to negotiate the work world can be a first step. By providing clients with the concept of labor markets, they will have a way to describe, label, and negotiate the work world. They will have a starting point to connect themselves directly to the workplace, one which plants the seed of hope that there is a way to begin to solve their problems.

So, what are labor markets? Ettinger (1991) described them as follows:

Labor markets bring together buyers and sellers seeking to exchange one thing of value for another. Sellers are individuals seeking work, and buyers are employees offering wages and other benefits in exchange for work. Through the operation of the market, employers obtain the labor needed to transform raw materials into goods and services, and workers earn an income to support themselves and others. Labor markets are dynamic and constantly changing. They tend to be more complicated than other kinds of markets. There are many interacting variables that influence supply and demand in a labor market. The commodity being sold, the labor supply, is controlled by human beings with individual values and abilities who are free to make choices about education, training, occupation and geographic location. Moreover, workers can even choose to work for themselves and become their own employers (p. 4).

The occupational opportunity structure available to clients depends in part upon where they live, how far they are willing or able to travel to work, and if they are willing to move to a new location. "Understanding labor markets and job opportunities begins with an awareness of their basic relationship between where people live and where they work. For this reason any discussion of a labor market has geographical implications" (National Occupational Information Coordinating Committee, 1991, p. 69). This means we can describe labor markets as being local, regional, national, or global.

An exception to this are internal labor markets. Instead of being described in geographic terms, internal labor markets exist within employing firms. Internal labor markets are characterized by organizational rules that define how employees are hired and promoted and how jobs are structured. Mace (1979) describes some of these rules. Many jobs are filled only by promotions from within the firm. New employees are hired for only certain lower-level jobs. Movement is largely vertical within families of jobs; lateral mobility among jobs of similar status is restricted. Skills are acquired through on-the-job training. A worker's occupational position and wage rate is more likely to be determined by seniority than by productivity. Explicit rules govern seniority and pension benefits. Wages are attached to particular jobs, and are not determined by the productivity of the workers.

Client knowledge about internal labor markets is important because of these rules that govern employment. New employees are hired for only certain lower-level jobs. Once inside, movement is mostly vertical, and on-the-job training is featured. So, in organizations where internal labor markets are operating, clients need to be aware that even though they may have skills for higher level positions, the entry point is where they must begin. Then the rules presented apply.

Combating Gender Stereotypes

"Deeply rooted socialization processes perpetuate rigid sex role perceptions that limit career options" (Hotchkiss & Borow, 1996, p. 318). Because of such socialization, it is imperative that female and male clients so affected be helped to overcome gender stereotype limitations, including initial occupational selection, earnings, rank, and job responsibilities. Chapters 4 and 5 of this book cover this topic in detail, so further attention will not be given here. This reminder is placed here, however, to highlight the importance of the topic.

Reducing Racial and Ethnic Barriers

Due to the increasingly diverse population of the United States and the reflection of this diversity in the labor force, attention to racial and ethnic barriers is critical. We must appreciate and respond to the variety of racial and ethnic backgrounds that clients bring to career counseling, as well as their experiences with discrimination. Understanding their personal and group histories, their world views, their identity status, and their levels of acculturation will lay the foundation for the working alliance and the effective selection of appropriate action intervention strategies. Chapter 3 provides you with extensive background and practical action intervention strategies, so more attention to the topic is not provided here; we simply want to remind you of its importance.

Combating Barriers for the Disabled

Due to greater awareness of the needs of people with disabilities, as well as federal mandate, more and more individuals with disabilities are seeking employment. It is critical that counselors understand the unique issues facing people with disabilities and to work toward their inclusion, independence, and empowerment. Counselors can be critical links in helping foster greater skill development and exploration for clients with disabilities. Counselors can also serve as change agents with employers, helping to open more doors for employment in a wider variety of occupations. Chapter 6 provides specific information on the current employment status of people with disabilities, an empowerment framework, and specific issues relevant to the career counseling process when working with this client group.

Dealing with Work–Family/Family–Work Problems
As individuals become adults, many must deal with work–family/family–work problems.

> . . . *what happens at work often affects other aspects of their life, just as other commitments often affect employment attitudes and behaviors. One of the common refrains is the desire to balance work and other commitments more successfully. The most familiar version of this challenge occurs with parents of young children. However, the challenges do not cease when parents move into the middle years. In fact, family involvement often becomes more complex, with marital, parental, grandparental, and filial roles competing with work for energy (Sterns & Huyck, 2001, p 469).*

The life career development perspective presented in Chapter 1 and discussed earlier in this chapter, with its concepts of life roles, life settings, and life events all interacting over the life span, is a useful way of dealing with work–family/family–work problems. As suggested earlier, the concepts of life roles, settings, and events provides you and your clients with a shared language to break apart, identify, and label the issues and contexts surrounding work and family problems. As this is accomplished, concepts derived from the work of Zedeck and Mosier (1990) and Morrison and Deacon (1993) can be applied to help explain the dynamics of work–family relationships and the possible consequences of family–work problems.

A beginning point in this process is to translate clients' work and family problems into life roles, life settings, and life events terminology. Worker roles, family roles (parent, spouse), the workplace, home, work-related events, and family-related events become the vocabulary used to analyze, specify, and understand client work–family/family–work problems. Clients' presenting problems and possible underlying problems, originally global and fuzzy, now can take on specificity. A vocabulary is available to clarify issues and pinpoint concerns, the vocabulary of life roles, settings, and events.

The specifying and labeling process described helps you and your clients to begin to sort out, explain, and understand the complexities and dynamics of work–family relationships. As you listen to clients describe their presenting problems, and as underlying dynamics emerge in the gathering information phase of career counseling, does what happens (event) at work (work setting, worker role) spill over into family life (family setting, parent role, spouse role)? Does what happens (event) at work (work setting, worker role) as a result of spillover cause conflict in family life (family setting, parent role, spouse role)? Does compartmentalization occur where clients try to separate these two worlds? (Zeddeck & Mosier, 1990).

A CHECKLIST OF COUNSELOR ROLES

The opening phase of the career counseling process, with its beginning development of the working alliance, is crucial. While you focus your attention on presenting goals or problems, there is awareness that these may expand into other goals or problems as the process of career counseling continues. Then, with the establishment of the boundaries of the career counseling process, the gathering information phase is underway. This involves learning more about your clients and their problems using quantitative and qualitative procedures and instruments so that hypotheses can be generated. Using interventions based on your hypotheses to help your clients achieve their goals or resolve their problems follows. Then, when clients' goals are achieved or their problems are resolved, closure ends the career counseling process and relationship.

As these phases of the career counseling process are unfolding, the working alliance (Meara & Patton, 1994) between you and your clients is being further developed and strengthened. The use of shared language facilitates statements of clear goals to be achieved and specifies the tasks to be carried out to achieve these goals. This, in turn, creates a joining together of you and your clients, creating the foundation for developing bonds of mutual trust and respect.

Given the phases of the career counseling process that you and your clients will go through together and the importance of the working alliance, what are some important roles for you to consider when helping your clients understand and respond to changes in the workplace and family life? Here is a beginning list.

1. Help clients view themselves and their situations and problems holistically so that they can see connections and relationships in their lives, their families, and their work.
2. Help clients understand and deal with the intertwined issues of psychological adjustment and career adjustment.
3. Help clients appreciate diversity of all kinds including race, ethnicity, gender, and sexual orientation in the workplace.

4. Help clients appreciate changing gender roles in the workplace.
5. Empower clients with disabilities.
6. Help clients understand and work through the stages of life transitions.
7. Help clients separate their successes and failures at work and at home from who they are as people.
8. Help clients develop support systems to buffer workplace and family stresses and strains.
9. Help clients recognize that grief and loss are natural reactions to change.
10. Help clients deal with resistance to change.
11. Help clients turn workplace and family frustration and anger energy toward positive solutions.

A FINAL NOTE

Helping clients understand and respond to changes in the workplace and family life through career counseling requires knowledge, understanding, and skill. This chapter was designed to provide you with an overview of workplace and family life changes and to highlight needed foundation knowledge required to understand and respond to client problems that occur as consequences of these changes. To understand and respond appropriately, we recommended viewing client problems from a holistic view of human development called life career development.

The life career development perspective, as well as our understanding of the career counseling process, was described in Chapter 1. The chapters that follow highlight foundation knowledge and application skills needed when dealing with gender, racial, ethnic, and disability issues. Then the rest of the book focuses on the career counseling process, demonstrating how all of these issues and concerns are interwoven from the opening phase through closure. Throughout the entire book you will see the concept of the active, involved counselor at work. We firmly believe in the necessity of your active involvement in the career counseling process. "Counselors should...be encouraged to consider constructive intervention when barriers loom that clients cannot surmount unaided" (Hotchkiss & Borow, 1996, p. 318).

REFERENCES

Allcorn, S. (1994). *Anger in the workplace.* Westport, CN: Quorum Books.
Altman, B. W., & Post, J. E. (1996). Beyond the "social contract." In D. T. Hall & Associates (Eds.), *The career is dead—long live the career* (pp. 46–71). San Francisco: Jossey-Bass.
Arthur, M.B., & Rousseau, D.M. (1996). Conclusion: A lexicon for the new organiza-

tional era. In M.B. Authur & D.M. Rousseau (Eds.), *The boundaryless career* (pp. 370-382). New York: Oxford University Press.

Beehr, T. A. (1995). *Psychological stress in the workplace.* New York: Routledge.

Boyett, J. H., & Boyett, J. T. (1995). *Beyond workplace 2000.* New York: Dutton.

Bridges, W. (1993). *Job shift: How to prosper in a workplace without jobs.* Reading, MA: Addison-Wesley.

Burke, R. J. (1996). Work experiences, stress and health among managerial and professional women. In M. J. Schabracq, J. A. M. Winnubst, & C. L. Cooper (Eds.), *Handbook of work and health psychology.* New York: Wiley.

Chappell, D., & DiMartino, V. (2000). *Violence at work* (2nd Ed.). Geneva: International Labour Office.

Crosby, F. (1984). Job satisfaction and domestic life. In D. M. Lee & R. N. Kanungo (Eds.), *Management of work and personal life* (pp. 41–60). New York: Praeger.

Daw, J. (2001, July/August) Road rage, air rage and now 'desk rage'. *Monitor on Psychology, 32,* 52-54.

Ettinger, J. M. (Ed.). (1991). *Improve career decision making in a changing world.* Garrett Park, MD: Garrett Park Press.

Fredriksen-Goldsen, K.E., & Scharlach, A.E. (2000). *Families and work: New directions in the twenty-first century.* New York: Oxford University Press.

Hauck, P. (1973). *Overcoming frustration and anger.* Philadelphia: Westmenter Press.

Heskett, S. L. (1996). *Workplace violence: Before, during, and after.* Boston: Butterworth-Heinemann.

Hotchkiss, L., & Borow, H. (1996). Sociological perspective on work and career development. In D. Brown, L. Brooks, & Associates (Eds.), *Career choice and development.* (3rd ed.). San Francisco: Jossey-Bass.

Kates, N., Greiff, B. S., & Hagen, D. Q. (1993). Job loss and employment uncertainty. In J. Kahn (Ed.), *Mental health in the workplace* (pp. 156–176). New York: Van Nostran Reinhold.

Kellinson, J.W. & Tate, P. (Spring 2000). The 1998-2008 job outlook in brief. *Occupational Outlook Quarterly, 44* (1), 2.

Kubler-Ross, E. (1969). *On death and dying.* New York: Macmillan.

Kugelmass, J. (1995). *Telecommuting.* New York: Lexington Books.

Kurzman, P. A., & Akabas, S. H. (Eds.). (1993). *Work and well-being.* Washington DC: National Association of Social Workers.

London, M. (1998). *Career barriers: How people experience, overcome, and avoid failure.* Mahwah, NJ: Lawrence Erlbaum Associates, Publishers.

Mace, J. (1979). Internal labour markets for engineers in British industry. *British Journal of Industrial Relations, 17* (1), 49–62.

Meara, N. M., & Patton, M. J. (1994). Contributions of the working alliance in the practice of career counseling. *The Career Development Quarterly, 43,* 161–177.

Morrison, D. E. & Deacon, D. A. (1993). Organizational consequences of family problems. In J. Kahn (Ed.), *Mental health in the workplace* (pp. 218–238). New York: Van Nostrand Reinhold.

National Occupational Information Coordinating Committee. (1991). *Improved career decision-making through the use of labor market information: participants workbook.* Washington, DC: Author.

Neimeyer, G. J., & Leso, J. F. (1992). Effects of occupational information on personal versus provided constructs: A second look. *Journal of Counseling Psychology 39*, 331–334.

Peterson, N., & Gonzalez, R.C. (2000). *The role of work in peoples lives*. Belmont, CA: Wadsworth/Thomson Learning.

Solmon, L. C. & Levenson, A. R. (Eds.). (1994). *Labor markets employment policy & job creation*. Boulder, CO: Westview Press.

Statt, D. A. (1994). *Psychology and the world of work*. New York: New York University Press.

Sterns, H.L., & Huyck, M.H. (2001). The role of work in Midlife. In M.E. Lachman (Ed.), *Handbook of Midlife Development* (pp. 447-486). New York: John Wiley & Sons, Inc.

Tilly, C. (1996). *Half a job: Bad and good part-time jobs in a changing labor market*. Philadelphia: Temple University Press.

The Radcliffe Public Policy Center. (2000). *Life's work: Generational attitudes toward work and life integration*. Cambridge, MA: Author

U.S. Department of Labor. (2000). *Occupational Outlook Handbook 2000-2001*. Washington, DC: Author.

U.S. Department of Labor. (1995). *Occupational Outlook Quarterly, 39* (2), Washington, DC: Author.

Young, R. A., Valach, L., & Collin, A. (1996). A contextual explanation of career. In D. Brown, L. Brooks, & Associates (Eds.), *Career choice and development* (3rd ed.). San Francisco: Jossey-Bass.

Zedeck, S., & Mosier, K. L. (1990). Work in the family and employing organization. *American Psychologist, 45* (2), 240–251.

▶ 8

Opening Phase of the Career Counseling Process: Forming the Working Alliance

There is much to consider as we begin the career counseling process, but nothing is more important than an emphasis on building strong working alliances with our clients. We will define what is meant by a working alliance, clarify how important these alliances are to achieving successful outcomes in career counseling, and include ideas on how to build alliances. Statements from clients will illustrate the importance of the alliance as seen through their eyes.

THE WORKING ALLIANCE

Establishing a solid working alliance is presented in Chapter 1 as a necessary first step in making things happen in career counseling. Skovholt, Ronnestad and Jennings (1997, p. 362) summarizing the research on counseling, emphatically state: "If we had to choose the single most important research-based counseling/psychotherapy domain, it would be the ability to establish a very positive working alliance with clients." The clearest definition of a working alliance was offered in the late 1970s by Edward Bordin (1979). He suggests that three parts in the relationship are essential and need our constant attention:

1. Agreement between the client and the counselor on the goals to be achieved in counseling.
2. Agreement on the tasks involved

3. The bond necessary between client and counselor that establishes the importance to both of them of goals and tasks

More recent research evidence (Gelso & Carter, 1985) supports this way of conceptualizing the relationship and further emphasizes the importance of establishing it early in counseling. The outcomes of (career) counseling may be very dependent not only on establishing this alliance early but maintaining it throughout the duration with our clients. Krupnick and colleagues (Krupnick, Sotsky, Simmmens, Moyer, Elkin, Watkins & Pilkonis, 1996) are quoted in the Skovholt et al. article (p. 363) as having an exhaustive review of research on the therapeutic alliance, finding that " . . . mean alliance ratings had a very large effect on outcome . . ." Other modalities looked at did not. We probably can't overstate the importance of the working alliance. However, were it entirely up to us to establish this alliance, we might move easily to ways to establish it, but it is clear that we describe a dynamic relationship that draws heavily on both what we say and do and what the client says and does. Meara and Patton (1994) describe the alliance as that part of counseling that can be characterized as collaboration, mutuality, and cooperation of two working together. Gelso and Hayes (1998) identify two fundamental components in the alliance: collaboration and attachment or bonding. It is this interdependence that makes it both complicated and fascinating. Like any good relationship, it demands work from both parties.

Establishing a Mutuality of Goals

First, then, we must establish a mutuality of goals for career counseling. We do not do this following any particular format or with a clear set of predetermined goals. Rather, we begin by being a good listener. We must be careful to first let our clients express what they believe they want from counseling. Listening well will provide an early basis for establishing a set of goals, and will allow time and opportunity to learn whether the client comes with well-established goals. If so, we must determine whether they are reasonable goals that can properly be addressed in career counseling. We can't have agreement on goals if a client is not clear about them at the outset, and often clients are not. We may have problems establishing these goals early, but a good alliance is dependent on both counselor and client, through an ongoing effort working to establish and modify goals as appropriate. This is an important component of building a working alliance and should be repeatedly assessed as we proceed with the other two components of the working alliance—tasks and the bond. Let us look next at what we mean by task.

Finding Tasks in Support of the Working Alliance

There are numerous tasks in counseling that can contribute to successful outcomes. We encourage talk, reflection, openness, honesty, commitment to trying various creative stimulus activities—interest inventories, tests, card sorts, fantasy trips, genograms, journalling, networking, creating personal narratives, reading books or articles—all kinds of activities that might move one along in thought or action toward agreed-upon goals. Although there may sometimes be good reasons for not engaging in these tasks, it is always important to work at reaching mutual agreement on what would be helpful and why. The tasks that lead to successful outcomes should be agreed upon up front so that there is a shared agenda for proceeding in career counseling. Just as we establish mutually agreed upon goals, we are aided by agreeing upon a set of tasks to accomplish these goals. Our experience, aided by our understanding of our clients when they come to us, can go a long way toward assuring that our counseling time together is truly productive.

Working at Bonding as Part of the Alliance

Finally, the working alliance depends on establishing a bond with our clients. Theorists give us a wealth of ways to conceptualize, understand, and even measure this bond (Barrett-Lennard, 1986; Gelso & Carter, 1985; Orlinsky & Howard, 1986; Rogers, 1961; Truax and Carkhuff, 1967), but they diverge in their thinking about what is essential, necessary, or sufficient. They do seem in agreement that there must be some kind of a bond between counselor and client—an attachment that includes caring and trust, for without it there is evidence that efforts (tasks) directed toward accomplishing goals will be compromised. Disregarding small differences of opinion presented in the research, it is difficult to have a constructive relationship if trust and support are not offered and felt by both parties.

We know that counselors need to be skillful at establishing good working relationships. What hasn't been as clear is how to do it. Are there essential conditions as Carl Rogers (1961) suggested, or can bonding be achieved in other ways? Are there other equally effective relationships that promote desired change? Should we give more or less attention to the importance of goals and tasks? The most recent evidence is that all three need attention in order to establish what we term a good working alliance. We define a good working alliance as attending to the establishment of mutually well-defined goals in our relationships, finding mutually agreed-upon tasks to promote pursuit of these goals, and equally important, creating an effective bond in the relationship to make the most constructive use of the therapeutic time together. When this is done early in career counseling, we can provide appropriate direction for our clients and, ultimately, we can expect better outcomes from our efforts.

BUILDING SUCCESSFUL WORKING ALLIANCES

In an effort to build successful working alliances, we should listen to what clients say about their good experiences in counseling. We hear what they like to have happen in counseling. Sometimes they come with preconceived ideas about what they want or what should happen, but these preconceived ideas must be incorporated into the process as mutually agreed-upon goals. Listen as we offer some summary statements from clients. Listen carefully to what each has to say, and then we can determine whether these statements can help provide a basis for ideas about what constitutes a good working alliance.

Client: *I didn't know what to expect from career counseling. The counselor made it clear from the beginning that we were going to work together to clarify my concerns, and that seemed good to me. She also said we would work out a plan of action by the next session and while that seemed ambitious at first, I came to see the importance of it and actually began to see myself as up to the challenge of doing it. It wasn't what I expected, but I liked the idea. I could tell she knew a lot about careers from what she said in response to my questions, but more important, she seemed really interested in me as a person. I respected her and I thought here was someone who was going to listen to me and help me plan some next steps. I left excited and optimistic.*

The client first tells us she didn't know what to expect from career counseling; this is typical, given that many clients only know secondhand about what to expect. Having been told we would be working together on issues, it was not what she expected, but it was acceptable to her. Then, the counselor suggested a task of eventually having a plan of action by the next session; that was viewed as an unexpected task and, upon reflection, as a challenge. We can see the goals and tasks being negotiated and agreed upon in a satisfactory way. Finally, the client lets you know she respects the counselor's competence as a expert and a good listener, so she left excited and optimistic. This suggests that the client believes that a healthy bond is developing. All that she has said, we think, might be offered as descriptive of a good bond between the client and the counselor.

Client: *I was completely lost and came for career counseling. At the time, I would have done whatever was suggested. I just wanted to get on with my life—get out of my job and my marriage. I don't think I received much advice at first, but I did find I could tell her all that was going on in my life, and she listened until I seemed to be getting clearer about my own situation. I came back regularly for weeks because I liked her and we seemed to be making progress with some things I hadn't thought about when I first came for help. I found myself becoming more focused on what I needed to do with my life. We both seemed invested in my finding some alternatives, and I have some now. I'm just not ready to act on them yet.*

Again, you hear loudest the importance of the relationship. The counselor did not take over or act on the expressed concern, as might have been the initial expectation of the client. The client moved toward a modified goal and then talked about the strength of her relationship with the counselor. She indicated that weeks later there was a shift in focus to her career concerns. Seemingly, the breakup of her marriage and thoughts of leaving her job were intertwined. This had to be dealt with before attending to the more specific goal of finding a new job. Clearly, an agenda can be brought to the interview, modified, and strengthened in a mutually agreed-upon manner. However, to effectively move toward mutually agreed-upon goals, there will need to be a strong bond or neither will hear the other's input.

Client: *It was a fascinating session. I had taken numerous tests and read various books on careers, and I had some vague ideas about what I wanted to do, but I knew I didn't have enough information or anyone to talk to about what I was thinking. I was ecstatic to find someone who would listen and at the same time offer to help with my dreams. The counselor didn't suggest that finding answers would be easy, but she was encouraging and I felt she knew more than she was telling me. We decided during the interview that this would be a real opportunity for me to put things together. We agreed to work toward my choosing a new career within the next six months and she made clear some of what I would have to do if I was to be successful at it. I liked the way she made me state my goal, and then she helped me define what I needed to do to make it happen.*

Clearly, the client is describing what it is like to have a good working alliance with a counselor. They have attended to goals and tasks, and seemingly have bonded in a relationship. You can hear that she is motivated to work, likes the counselor, is impressed with the agreed-upon tasks and, is likely headed toward some agreed-upon and well thought out changes in her life.

We do not intend to suggest that establishing the working alliance is easy in career counseling, only that it is important. Heppner and Hendricks (1995) in a qualitative study of career counseling, carefully document this fact. Horvath and Greenberg (1994) have complied an extensive collection of articles further supporting its importance. Too many times, counselors find themselves confused by reluctant clients or early terminations, and we seek explanations. We wonder if perhaps the client wasn't ready for counseling, wasn't properly motivated, found it difficult to commit the time, or some similar explanation. But first we should examine how well we were able to establish a good working alliance in that first interview. It might not be easy, but it clearly must be a goal for us if we are to deliver effective services.

A COUNSELOR'S CHECKLIST ON BUILDING THE WORKING ALLIANCE

So much of what we do in the initial session to establish a working alliance depends on the individual, but we can offer a list of questions that the counselor should consider before and after the first session and subsequent sessions. These are not in order of importance, and this is not an all-inclusive list, but these basic questions should spark our thinking about how attending to the various parts of the working alliance can make a difference.

- Have I given optimal time to the three parts of the relationship, goals, tasks, and bond?
- Have I clearly established a set of goals to work on?
- Do we have agreement on these goals?
- Am I sure the client sees these as reasonable goals?
- Have I established the tasks that will move us toward these goals?
- Am I comfortable that there is agreement on the tasks involved, and have we discussed how easy or difficult it will be to accomplish these tasks?
- Do I sense the beginning of a strong working relationship between us? Has this been discussed? Is it a sufficient bond to carry us through the previously described tasks?
- Is there mutual optimism about working together?
- Is the nature of the time and commitment to the career counseling process clear?
- Am I sure there is a clear plan, with appropriate assignments for the next session and beyond?
- Can I speak with optimism about initial progress with the three parts of the alliance: goals, tasks, and bond?
- If I have reservations about any of the three parts, do I have a plan for discussing them at the next session?

Answers to the questions above should help you assess how you are doing with the working alliance. You might ask the client to complete a set of questions similar to those we provide in our Career Counseling Progress Report (CCPR) (Table 8-1), a form routinely used at the University of Missouri-Columbia Career Center. You could use a more formal and psychometrically sound approach such as the Working Alliance Inventory—Form T (Horvath & Greenberg, 1989). There is also one that you can ask the client to complete, the Working Alliance Inventory—Form C (Horvath & Greenberg, 1989). These inventories help to focus on the developing relationship that is so important in career counseling. Use these instruments, but do not overlook the more obvious way of plotting or assessing the nature of the relationship: Ask the client regularly, "How are we doing?" Clients will often be forthright and helpful if asked.

TABLE 8–1   Career Counseling Progress Report (CCPR)

It might be helpful for both of us, but you in particular, in preparing for the next session, to indicate where you are after this interview. I would appreciate your completing it while the session is still fresh in your mind.

1. How clear are you about the *goals* we decided on in the session?

   Not clear   Somewhat clear   Quite clear

   1............2............3............4............5

2. How *reasonable* are these goals?

   Not reasonable   Somewhat reasonable   Quite reasonable

   1............2............3............4............5

3 How *comfortable* are you with these tasks?

   Not comfortable   Somewhat comfortable   Quite comfortable

   1............2............3............4............5

4. How *clear* are you about the *time, commitment,* and *direction* for the next session?

   Not clear   Somewhat clear   Quite clear

   1............2............3............4............5

5. How *optimistic* are you *about working together* on the above goals and tasks?

   Not optimistic   Somewhat optimistic   Quite optimistic

   1............2............3............4............5

Are there othe items you want clarified or discussed in the next session?

Leave this form at the front desk in the envelope provided with my name on it and marked *confidential.* I will review it before our next session. Thanks.

Your Career Counselor   Your name

REFERENCES

Barrett-Lennard, G. T. (1986). The relationship inventory now: Issues and advances in theory, method, and uses. In L. Greenberg and W. Pensoff (Eds.), *The psychotherapeutic process*. New York: Guilford.

Bordin, E. S. (1979). The generalizability of the working alliance. *Psychotherapy: Theory, research and practice, 16*, 252–260.

Gelso, C. J., & Carter, J. A. (1985). The relationship in counseling and psychotherapy: Components, consequences, and theoretical antecedents. *The Counseling Psychologist, 13*, 155–243.

Gelso, C. J., & Hayes, J. A. (1998). *The psychotherapy relationship: Theory, research, and practice.* New York: Wiley.

Heppner, M. J., & Hendricks, F. (1995). A process and outcome study examining career indecision and indecisiveness. *Journal of Counseling and Development, 73,* 426-437.

Horvath, A. O., & Greenberg, L. (1989). The development of the working alliance inventory. *Journal of Counseling Psychology, 36* (2), 223–233.

Horvath, A. O., & Greenberg, L. S. (1994). *The working alliance: Theory, research and practice.* New York: Wiley.

Krupnick, J. L., Sotsky, S. M., Simmens, S., Moyer, J., Elkin, I., Watkins, J., & Pilkonis, P. A. (1996). The role of the therapeutic alliance in psychotherapy and pharmacotherapy outcome: findings in the National Institute of Mental Health Treatment of Depression Collaborative Research Program. *J. Consult. Clin. Psychol. 24,* 532-539.

Meara, N. M., & Patton, M. J. (1994). Contributions of the working alliance in the practice of career counseling. *The Career Development Quarterly, 43,* 161–177.

Orlinsky, D. E., & Howard, K. I. (1986). Process and outcome in psychotherapy. In Garfield & Bergin (Eds.), *Handbook of psychotherapy and behavior change (3rd ed.).* New York: Wiley.

Rogers, C. R. (1961). The characteristics of a helping relationship. *On becoming a person* (pp. 39–58). Boston: Houghton Mifflin.

Skovholt, T. M., Ronnestad, M. H., & Jennings, L. (1997). Searching for expertise in counseling, psychotherapy, and professional psychology. *Educational Psychology Review, 9* (4), 361-369.

Truax, C. B., & Carkhuff, R. R. (1967). *Toward effective counseling and psychotherapy.* Chicago: Aldine.

▶ 9

Life Career Assessment

A Structured Interview to Gather Client Information

Qualitative assessment procedures are particularly useful in the gathering information subphase of career counseling. They are useful because as Goldman (1990) suggested, they "foster an active role for the client" (p. 205), "emphasize holistic study of the individual" (p. 206), and "emphasize the concepts of learning about oneself" (p. 206). The Life Career Assessment (LCA), a qualitative assessment procedure, is a structured interview that can be used with clients during the gathering information subphase of career counseling. It is particularly useful when working with clients of all ages and differing cultural and ethnic backgrounds; when dealing with women's and men's issues; and when dealing with disability issues, because clients' world views, environmental barriers, racial identity status, and levels of acculturation can be addressed directly and naturally. The LCA is very time flexible. The entire structured interview can be completed in 20 to 30 minutes or, if desired, a more in-depth interview can be conducted over several sessions with clients.

The LCA is designed to focus on clients' levels of functioning in their life career development and the internal and external dynamics that may be involved. The LCA helps form working alliances with clients, because an atmosphere of concern and caring can be created by the nonjudgmental, nonthreatening, conversational tone of the LCA process. Printed forms, booklets, and paper-and-pencil instruments—which some clients may associate negatively with school, training, and evaluation—are not used. The LCA is a person-to-person process that allows clients to explore and talk about themselves by focusing on their own experiences.

The LCA helps to increase clients' career planning abilities. Clients' strengths, the environmental barriers they may face, and their levels of functioning in various life roles are discussed, followed by suggestion of goals, and, finally, action to reach these goals. These discussions may uncover the need for other career assessment tools (such as standardized tests) by revealing areas that need further exploration (such as environmental barriers and disability issues) and may also uncover skills and abilities that may require further evaluation.

This chapter opens with a discussion of the theoretical foundations of the LCA; then the structure of the LCA is presented in detail. The chapter closes with some points about the use of the LCA, including how it can be adapted for use with a wide variety of people and issues. This is illustrated by a description of how the LCA can be adapted for work with younger clients.

THEORETICAL FOUNDATION

The LCA is based in part on the Individual Psychology of Adler (Dinkmeyer, Pew, and Dinkmeyer, 1979). Adler divided individuals' relations to the world into three life arenas: work, society (social relations), and sex (friendships). According to Adler, the three cannot be dealt with separately because they are intertwined, a change in one involves the others. Difficulty in one part of life implies comparable difficulties in the rest of a person's life.

Individuals tend to solve problems and attempt to obtain satisfaction in a similar manner in all three arenas. We use the phrase life career themes to describe these consistent ways of negotiating with the world. We define themes as the ways people express ideas, beliefs, attitudes, and values about themselves, others, and the world—in general, their world views. (For a detailed discussion of life career themes, see Chapter 13.) The themes individuals use can be considered to constitute a lifestyle. Individuals are not always aware of their approach toward life or the themes by which they operate, and they may not recognize the underlying consistencies that exist (Mosak, 1971). They may choose, rather, to dwell on specific, superficial feelings that serve to further obscure the ways in which they are developing.

In the following dialogue, a client is talking about her past job experiences. The client in this interview is a 25-year-old woman. Notice the possible themes that can be identified from this brief discussion.

Dialogue	*Possible Themes*
CO: *Let's find out about your work experience. Could you tell me about your last job?*	
CL: *It was with a small insurance company. I was in the claims department. I sent out form letters and payment checks.*	
CO: *What did you like about the job?*	
CL: *The people were real nice even though they were older. I liked talking on the phone to all the different people. That's mainly why I got into claims, so that I could talk to people and wouldn't be all by myself. I liked working downtown where there's a lot of places to go and I liked the insurance business.*	Likes social contact.
CO: *Did you?*	
CL: *Yeah, I don't think I'd like car insurance, but I liked life and health insurance. It was pretty interesting. There were many different plans, and they were interesting to read.*	Likes variety.
CO: *What are some of the things you didn't like about the job?*	
CL: *I just had a set thing that I did everyday. I'd check the mail, and I hated doing that and the form letters. I got to where that's all I could type were form letters. If I tried to type a letter that was handwritten, I just couldn't do it because I just wasn't used to it. It was just dull.*	Dislikes routine.
CO: *What about the job you had before that?*	
CL: *It was with a floral company. I liked it real well. Mom had gone to school with the owners. I really liked those people. They were a lot of fun. I loved to work with flowers. When I was on delivery I got to go out and run around and I liked that. That was a pretty fun job.*	Contact with people is important.
CO: *What about when you worked at the garment factory?*	

Dialogue	*Possible Themes*
CL: *Oh, I hated that. That was terrible. I worked at night. I went to school all day long and I worked until 1:00 in the morning. I just don't like to do all that routine stuff, that'll make a person go crazy. And I was on my feet all day long, and we got a 10-minute break and a half hour for lunch. It was just too much work.*	Does not like to be closed in.

Recurring themes from this dialogue suggest that this client enjoys working around people to meet some of her social needs. She probably dislikes routine kinds of tasks but can adapt to them if she is receiving other satisfaction. As important as learning about what jobs she has held is learning what kind of working environment is most reinforcing for her. A major purpose of the LCA in information gathering is to begin the process of helping clients identify and clarify their life career themes and the ways these themes guide their behavior.

Assessing clients' approach as to work, society (social relations), and sex (friendships) provides a concrete way of analyzing and synthesizing their movement in their life career development. This assessment is a cooperative endeavor that not only helps you understand your clients, but also helps them better understand their own life career themes that reveal their unique sense of the meaning of life. By identifying such themes through the LCA, you and your clients can begin to understand their approaches to life and do so in a comfortable and straightforward manner.

LCA STRUCTURE

The LCA structure is presented below in outline form. As you will see, there are four major sections: Career Assessment, Typical Day, Strengths and Obstacles, and Summary. Each section is covered in detail in subsequent discussion in this chapter, but for now, an important point to notice is that by following this format you can gather several types of information about your clients. One type is relatively objective and factual regarding your clients' work experiences and educational achievements. Another type is your clients' self-estimations of the skills and competencies they possess. Still another type is inferences made by you of your clients' skills and abilities. These inferences are based on life career themes and are derived from the kinds of activities your clients are involved in at work, at home, in school or training, or at leisure. Another kind of information obtained concerns your clients' opinions of their value as persons and their awareness of self.

Although the LCA format is suggested for you to follow, there is no one prescribed way to use the format. You will need to discover your own personal style of using the LCA. In fact, it is preferable for you to integrate the LCA structure into your own style as well as the style of your clients to keep the process from becoming mechanical and to make the gathering information subphase of career counseling as meaningful as possible.

Career Assessment

1. Work experience (part/full-time, paid/unpaid)
   * Last job
   * Liked best about
   * Disliked most about
   * Same procedure with another job

2. Education or training progress and concerns
   * General appraisal
   * Liked best about
   * Disliked most about
   * Repeat for levels or types

3. Recreation
   * Leisure time activities
   * Social life (within leisure context)
   * Friends (within leisure context)

Typical Day

1. Dependent–independent
   * Relies on others
   * Insists on someone else making decisions

2. Systematic–spontaneous
   * Stable and routine
   * Persistent and attentive

Strengths and Obstacles

1. Three main strengths
   * Resources at own disposal
   * What do resources do for clients

2. Three main obstacles
   * Related to strengths
   * Related to themes

Summary
1. Agree on life themes.
2. Use client's own words.
3. Relate to goal setting or problem solving.

Career Assessment Section of the LCA

The Career Assessment section of the LCA is divided into three parts: work experience, education or training, and recreation. Descriptions of each part of the Career Assessment section follow.

Work Experience

To assess work experience, ask your clients to describe their last job or their current job. The jobs can be part-time or full-time, paid or unpaid. Ask your clients to describe the tasks performed, and then relate what they liked best and least about the jobs. Listen for and discuss client world views, environmental barriers, and levels of acculturation as these topics may emerge. As likes and dislikes are discussed, the life career themes that become apparent should be repeated, clarified, and reflected so that your clients are aware of the consistencies that run through them. Examining your clients' domestic responsibilities, such as mowing the lawn, caring for a younger sibling, or doing household chores, also can be revealing and is especially useful when clients have had little or no work experience. This process is illustrated by the following interview with a 30-year-old client in which his work experience was discussed.

Dialogue	**Possible Themes**
CO: *The county hospital was the last job you had? You were working in the kitchen. You worked there quite awhile?*	
CL: *Right, two years.*	
CO: *What was your job exactly?*	
CL: *I worked a tray line, a patient tray line. Afterwards, I'd clean up and then we'd have odds and ends to do, like go up on the floors and take the patients ice cream, milk, bread, or fruit. We weighed fruit for the next meal, just little odds and ends that you could get done*	Takes care of details so that he can contact others.

Dialogue	*Possible Themes*
once you knew what you were doing. They had a time schedule set, but me, once I got the hang of it, it didn't take me the time they had scheduled for me, so I just went from one thing to the next. I'd get done at 3:00 or 2:30; sometimes I'd get done at 2:00. Then I'd help the other people, and we'd all sit around till 4:30 till the next meal.	
CO: *You really like to keep busy. It seems that you like to have something to show for your work.*	Completion of tasks is important.
CL: *Yes, otherwise I get bored with it.*	

The client's job priorities and life career themes begin to emerge in this short excerpt, although there is still much to learn. Note that his need for variety may interfere with his performance in a routine job. This is something to discuss with him later when you to look at occupational options.

Education and Training

To begin this section of the interview, ask your clients for a general appraisal of their educational or training experiences. You can provide further structure by asking what your clients liked best and liked least about these experiences. Usually life career themes begin to appear as likes and dislikes. These themes should be repeated, clarified, and reflected so that your clients are aware of the consistencies or inconsistencies running through them.

After clients give you some general impressions about their educational background or their training experiences, you can begin to ask more specific questions about preferences for subjects, teachers, instructors, and learning conditions. This type of focusing will yield several types of information. One kind is factual, surface information, such as "I like science and math, and dislike art and English" or "I like Mr. Jones and Mrs. Green, but don't get along well with Mr. Smith." Another type of focusing is on the themes discussed earlier in their work experience, some of which will appear again and again throughout the LCA. You also can obtain clues regarding your clients' learning styles from this section as well as the possible impact that gender, race, and ethnicity issues and disability status may have had on your clients' experiences in education and training.

The following is an excerpt from an interview in which a client's school experience is discussed:

Dialogue	*Possible Themes*
CO: *Tell me about your school experience.*	
CL: *I liked it, until I got into eighth grade. Then I just lost interest. Right around eighth grade.*	
CO: *What happened then to make you lose interest?*	
CL: *I have no idea. I guess I just kinda thought I knew everything and started running around.*	
CO: *When you think back to elementary school, you said you liked it pretty well. What were some things that you remember liking, what was good?*	
CL: *Um, I can always remember third and fourth grade...spelling and capitalization and stuff like that. We always had special games to make it a lot more fun, you know. The spelling bee. If you completed so many words right we got a star on the board. Things like that. I remember how the teacher always pointed me out as being the one person who always got the stars. I guess the things that I got rewards for made it more interesting.*	Seeks rewards and recognition. Approval from adults is important.
CO: *You felt like you could see that you had done something good....*	
CL: *She would have me help other people.*	Seeks acceptance.
CO: *You must have felt very worthwhile. Now tell me what you did not like about school.*	
CL: *Well, my worst class was fifth grade.*	
CO: *What was so bad about it?*	
CL: *The teacher was mean. I'm not kidding! Can you imagine somebody reading, what was it...the story Gone With the Wind. I had to read that story in the fifth grade. That thing was about this thick and then she had me write a report.*	Large assignments can be overwhelming.
CO: *She made you do that as a punishment?*	
CL: *We got off to a bad start, and when she did that to me it just made it worse. I went to the library and me and some girls were passing*	Attention from adults is important. Acts out for revenge. Needs involvement.

Dialogue	Possible Themes

notes, so as a punishment she gave us all these real big books to read ... real hard books to read. Then I stuck a tack underneath her chair and somebody told on me. So for a month she would send home progress reports to my father, and he would make me sit and write "I am sorry" ... 500 times each night. But sixth grade was a lot of fun. My teacher in sixth grade liked to get outdoors and she always took us on field trips to the parks, made a whole afternoon of it. On the weekends she had this nice place out of town and she would always ask us if we wanted to come out on Saturday or Sunday. We would always go out there, if we needed help.

CO: *Seemed like she really cared.*

CL: *Yeah, she was real nice. I think she left the next year.*

CO: *You said when you got to junior high you kind of lost interest.*

CL: *Seemed like once I got to junior high school nobody really took interest in what you were doing. That might have been part of it. I was used to the one class and everything. I'm kinda old fashioned.*

    Lacks assertiveness skills. No adult attention brings loneliness.

CO: *You felt you were left on your own with no one to go to for help.*

CL: *That was a lot of it, because I need a lot of help with the short time you've got there and all the students. I would leave class and still have questions. I wouldn't know what to do the next day. So I just got further and further behind. I'll have something to say, but I never say it until it's too late. I remember I talked to my counselor.*

    Lacks confidence and is dependent.

CO: *What did your counselor suggest you do?*

Dialogue	*Possible Themes*
CL: *Hang in there. And whenever I had a question walk up to them and say, "Hey, I need some help." And I did it for awhile when I got my nerve up, and I would say, "Hey, I need help over here." It was okay for awhile.*	Asking for assistance is difficult.

As this client enters into new educational experiences, it will be important for someone to be available to discuss progress and focus on positive experiences. Assertiveness training or related counseling may be needed so that the client can begin to learn how to take more responsibility.

Recreation

To assess recreation, ask your clients about how they spend their leisure time. It is important to note whether themes in the recreation section are consistent with the life career themes discussed in the work and education sections of the LCA or are in contrast with them. This also is a good time to explore love and friendship relations. Exploring clients' social lives within the context of how they spend their leisure time is a relatively nonthreatening way to explore this sometimes sensitive area. The goal is to discover how social relations themes may reflect themes identified in work and education settings. Does the client have many friends? Few? None? Does the client make decisions about leisure activities or does the client follow the suggestions of others?

In the following portion of the LCA, leisure and social activities are explored with a client.

Dialogue	*Possible Themes*
CO: *Now that you're out of high school, what do you do with your leisure time?*	
CL: *Well, we have horses and most of the time I ride them. I have two horses and I ride each of them two hours a day. Really, I don't have much time to do anything else.*	Intense interest and commitment.
CO: *Four hours of horseback riding a day?*	
CL: *Uh-huh, I get up at 6:00 in the morning and ride until 8:00. Now I'll have to ride them both when I get home. I guess I'll have to cut down to an hour apiece. But I've got to ride them during the week, because they're not worth a darn if I don't ride them during the week for the shows on the weekend.*	

Dialogue	**Possible Themes**

CO: *So you show them on the weekends.*

CL: *We go all over and show them.*

CO: *So that takes up most of your time?*

CL: *Yeah, quite a bit of it, and I got a Doberman pinscher that I'm trying to train, and he's about to drive me crazy. I spend most of my time with animals. We did raise Dobermans. Two years ago we had 13 of them and we sold all of them. Now we only have one, this little baby.*

CO: *So most of your time is spent with your horses and animals. What about friends?*

CL: *Most of my friends live in town, and they usually come out and see me. So it's just whoever comes out and somebody's usually out there all the time. I run around with my friends at night. Our horse shows last till about 7:30, then I come home and go to the dances or whatever parties are going on.*   Friends come to her.

CO: *What about weekends?*

CL: *Well, our shows are on Sunday, so I usually spend the whole day Saturday with mom. I don't get to see her too much during the week. I see her every once in awhile at night, but on Saturdays we go shopping. We go to breakfast first and then we shop. Sometimes we go to lunch. My mom and I are real close.*   Her mother is important to her.

CO: *You feel responsible for her in a way.*

CL: *Yeah, because she's done real well in spite of having to raise all us kids. I know my mom is just a lot of fun, I have more fun with her than I do most of my friends.*

CO: *She's a mother and a friend?*   Mom is someone to go back to.

CL: *Yeah, we're real close, but the problem is that I am thinking about moving to look for a job. If I move to California my sister may want me to live with her. If I stay here, I'd probably*   Relationship with mother may interfere with moving to where jobs are.

Dialogue	Possible Themes
move to someplace close so I could run back and forth to see Mom.	
CO: *One of the things holding you back is your mother.*	
CL: *I guess. She's married and my stepdad works an awful lot and I hate for her to be by herself all the time. I just enjoy seeing her. I'm kind of used to it, I guess.*	Will she be able to leave home?

It is relatively simple to move from leisure activities to social relationships. In the above example, the client's dependency on her animals and her mother for emotional support may interfere with career exploration. This conflict may have to be faced later in career counseling.

Typical Day Section of the LCA

Many of the themes that emerge during the LCA have natural opposites, such as active–passive and outgoing–withdrawn. Each of these opposite pairs can be considered a personality dimension. There are at least two personality dimensions that should be examined during the typical day portion of the LCA. These are dependent–independent and spontaneous–systematic.

Dependent–Independent
- Relies on others
- Insists that someone else makes decisions

Spontaneous–Systematic
- Stable and routine
- Persistent and attentive

The purpose of the typical day exploration is to discover how clients organize their lives each day. This assessment can be done by asking them to describe a typical day in a step-by-step fashion. The dependence–independence dimension can be explored by asking, "Do you get yourself up in the morning or rely on someone else to wake you?" "Do you do things alone or insist on having someone with you at all times?" Similarly, you need to determine whether your clients organize their lives systematically or respond to each day spontaneously. For example, systematic individuals tend to do the same thing day after day in a fairly stable routine (for example, eating raisin bran cereal every morning), while spontaneous individuals may rarely do the same thing twice.

An understanding of the life career themes that emerge from the typical day assessment can be very helpful to clients, for these themes sometimes cause problems in school, training, or on the job. For example, if a client confides that she just can't get up in the morning, you may foresee problems with punctuality and attendance on the job; this should be explored later in the career counseling sessions. As life career themes are identified, they should be repeated, clarified, and reflected so that clients begin to gain a clearer understanding of how they effect their behavior.

The following is a portion of the LCA in which a client's typical day is discussed. Notice that the client and counselor explore activities that are common to all people, such as eating and sleeping, as well as those that are more unique to this particular female client.

Dialogue	*Possible Themes*
CO: *I'd like you to think for a minute about what a day is like for you. It's time to get up. Does an alarm get you up, does somebody wake you up, or do you just wake up?*	
CL: *I wake up myself, get up, and go downstairs. I've already taken my shower the night before, so I just wash my face, put on a little make-up, find something to put on, get dressed, fix myself something to eat, and drink lots of milk because my stomach is upset when I get up. I have an ulcer.*	Responsible, systematic
CO: *You fix your own breakfast?*	
CL: *Yeah. Eggs or toast . . . then the phone usually rings and I talk.*	
CO: *Who's calling you?*	
CL: *One of my girlfriends.*	
CO: *Let's say you got up and you didn't have anything to do. You could do anything you wanted to do.*	
CL: *You want to know what I'd do? I'd grab a blanket, go downstairs, get something to eat, turn on the TV; I would just sit there and watch TV.*	Passive, seeks pleasure in the immediate environment.
CO: *You like TV?*	
CL: *Uh-huh.*	

Dialogue	Possible Themes
CO: *Daytime TV? Nighttime TV?*	
CL: *It depends. I like three soap operas. At night I really don't like TV that much unless it's really a good show or a movie. Other than that I don't watch too much, unless I really like it.*	
CO: *What do you like about soap operas?*	
CL: *Just the story itself, uh, the suspense of what's going to happen next, who's gonna find out what. And, um, who's getting married and whose daughter's pregnant (laughter).*	Social interests.
CO: *Can you ever put yourself in their place? Do you ever think that it's happening to you?*	
CL: *I get so mad that I stomp my feet, saying, "Stop! Stop!" or crying, I end up crying. And I get so mad. You see somebody behind a curtain with a gun and you're saying, "Don't go that way, don't go that way! Call the police." It's really exciting. Sometimes you get so mad and sometimes you get so happy you start crying.*	Identifies with and relates to others easily.

The client indicates that she likes a systematic routine in her daily living. However, it also sounds as though she is dependent on others and could get caught up in social relationship problems. She seems passive, and TV could be a pacifier for her.

Strengths and Obstacles Section of the LCA

The strengths/obstacles section of the LCA consists of asking clients what they believe to be their three main strengths and three main obstacles.

Three Main Strengths
- Resources at own disposal
- What resources do for them

Three Main Obstacles
- Relate to strengths
- Relate to themes

This part of the LCA gives direct information about the problems that your clients are facing, their possible environmental barriers, and the resources they may have at their own disposal to help them. Information is gathered by asking clients to look at the roles they play, such as mother, father, learner, or worker, and the skills they use to carry out these roles. After they name their three strengths, it is useful to probe deeper by asking them what these strengths do for them. For example, if a client lists persistence as a strength, further probing might disclose that it is a strength because it makes him keep trying.

The same kind of probing and clarification also should be done for obstacles. For some clients it is easier to come up with obstacles, perhaps because of past failure or low self-esteem. For such clients, you should look at their obstacles and strengths together. For example, how can strengths be used to offset obstacles? This may help them start thinking in light of the abilities, competencies, and skills they already possess.

The following is a portion of the LCA in which strengths and obstacles are pinpointed:

Dialogue	*Possible Themes*
CO: *What would you say would be some of your main strengths?*	
CL: *Oh, I'm a pretty good typist, especially with a little practice. I can run office machines. I've never had any trouble with any kind of office machine. I'm good over the telephone.*	Feels confident of her skills. Uses her social skills on the telephone.
I can always keep things pretty well organized. I can get things set up, so that if somebody came into the job they'd know exactly what to do. I always make a list of the things I do every day.	Well organized.
CO: *That's a good list. Now describe some of the obstacles you may need to overcome to be more employable.*	
CL: *Well, I probably talk too much. If I get started on something, it's hard for me to get off the subject and I probably do run my mouth too often. Another thing is that I don't pace my*	Must control social needs. Concern about being better organized is really a strength.

Dialogue   **Possible Themes**

*time right. Either I'm too fast or I'm not fast
enough. I never can get everything to work
out just right in the amount of time I'd like. I'd
always have things done an hour early, or I
won't have them done at all. If I could just get
things in a better order.*

CO: *Then it's important for you to be organized?*

CL: *Uh-huh, I like to be organized. And I don't
think that there would be anything else that I
would have any trouble with.*

During the strengths and obstacles section of the LCA, clients may not be able to respond to a request to list three strengths or three obstacles. In such cases, break down the task into smaller parts by asking them to list just one strength or obstacle. After one has been discussed, ask for another. This approach takes the pressure off clients to come up with a quick list of things and allows time to come up with more details.

You also may encounter clients who give short answers or answers that contain little information in response to the strengths and obstacles section. For example, a client may give as a strength "I'm a good worker." This response does not reveal much information. To gain more information, you can ask, "What does being a good worker mean to you?" or "What do you believe are the best things about the way you work?" Vague answers may be encountered in other sections of the LCA as well. In describing a typical day, a client may state, "I get up, go to work, come home, eat, and go to bed." Again, little information can be gleaned from this statement. Instead, ask, "How do you wake up? Does an alarm clock wake you or does someone else get you up? How do you get breakfast?" Continue examining the client's day in similar detail.

Another situation to which you should be ready to respond is a client who cannot think of any strengths. One strategy is to simply move on to the obstacles section and then be especially sensitive to strengths that may be hidden. For example, a client who lists as an obstacle "I work too slow" may reveal on further probing, "I pay a lot of attention to detail and want to be sure everything is right." Another strategy is to recall and reflect some of the themes expressed in other parts of the LCA. You might say to the client, "When you were talking about your typical day, you explained that your schedule was different each day depending on the schedule of other people in your family. Yet you seem to be able to get done what you need to each day. It seems to me that you are very flexible and adaptable." Such statements help clients discover strengths that they can bring to a job, that can result in greater self-esteem, and that may stimulate clients to think of other strengths.

One final strategy that you should consider whenever a client seems unwilling to talk freely is to examine your career counseling style. Although even the most skillful helpers encounter clients who do not open up to them, all counselors need to check their use of human relationship skills when their interaction with clients seem to be unproductive. Are you using good attending and listening skills? Good perceiving skills? Are helpful response styles present?

Summary Section of the LCA

The summary section is the last portion of the LCA. There are two primary purposes for conducting a summary. One purpose is to emphasize the information that has been gained during the interview. During the summary, it is not necessary to review every bit of information obtained, but prominent life career themes, strengths, and obstacles should be repeated. It is helpful to ask your clients to summarize what they have learned from the session first. Having them take the lead in expressing what has been learned increases the impact of the information, thus increasing self-awareness. It also lets you know what your clients have gained and, in some cases, missed. When your clients have finished, you can add any points that may have been omitted. It is important that you and your clients reach agreement about their life career themes. This agreement is effective particularly when it can be reached using your clients' own words and meanings.

The second major purpose of the summary is to relate the information gained to goals that you and your clients may work to resolve their problems. The life career themes that have been revealed may suggest possible internal dynamics that require further exploration and environmental obstacles that will need to be overcome. From the strengths and obstacles discovered, positive aspects of your clients may have been revealed that can be developed further. Then, too, obstacles that need to be overcome may be apparent; if so, together you can decide to establish goals and form plans of action to reach these goals.

The following example is a summary of an LCA interview. Notice that the counselor attempts to highlight important life career themes, skills, competencies, and obstacles; allows the client to express what has been learned; attempts to reach agreement with the client on the client's life career themes and skills using the client's own words; and relates the information gained to goals and possible courses of action.

CO: *Pam, we've been talking for awhile about a number of issues and I now need to bring this all together for you and look at what we have talked about. What do you see yourself learning from today? What is it that you have learned about yourself that you didn't know before?*

CL: *Well, I'm not real sure.*

CO: *Look back at when we talked about your daily routines, doing the same things, being organized. What do you think that tells you about your abilities?*

CL: *Well, I guess I'm organized. I guess I'm kind of responsible.*

CO: *Responsible in what way?*

CL: *I'm real concerned for Jill, my daughter. I do want to raise her well. My mom is always giving me a hard time about making sure to bring her up right. So, I think I am responsible with her.*

CO: *When we talked about your strengths, we came up with things like you were very dependable. We talked about how you hadn't missed very many days at work, that you are really conscious about getting to work on time, not being absent, that kind of thing. From your typical day, it sounds like you are very organized and have things at hand as to what you're going to do, and I get the feeling that you are responsible, too. How do you see that working to your advantage in the training program you are enrolled in?*

CL: *Well, I think it will be useful for me especially in my work experience, at the law office, you know. I think that I am going to be able to handle some of the things that they give me to do there.*

CO: *It is a chance to apply some of the skills you have.*

CL: *I've really enjoyed the typing that they give me to do, but I'm still kind of scared about whether I'm going to be able to pass the GED.*

CO: *I can understand your concern about that. It is a big step. It sounds like the certificate is important to you since you didn't get a chance to graduate.*

CL: *Yeah, it is. If I'm going to go on and become a legal secretary, I think that maybe I would need my GED.*

CO: *Well, I think we've got a good start here today. One concern that you have is passing your GED. We can work on that next time we meet.*

SOME CLOSING POINTS

Using Transitions

The LCA will be most effective if you use a conversational tone of voice. One way to help maintain a conversational atmosphere is to use transitional statements. These are signals to clients from you that the focus or topic of the LCA is going to change. By using transitional statements, you let clients know that the topic is being be changed and what the new topic is.

One way you can accomplish smooth transitions from one section of the LCA to another is to pay attention to wording. Make the first part of your statement a brief response to something your client has said in the last section. The second part of your statement is an introduction to the next topic, such as,

"Well, it seems that working has been enjoyable for you and you see it as valuable. Did you have these same feelings about being in school, or did you have a different outlook there?"

When introducing a new topic, another helpful strategy is to avoid long introductions that could break the conversational tone. In the following example, the counselor briefly describes the areas covered, signals to the client that a change in focus is coming, and lets the client know what the new topic is, all using a minimum of words: "Okay, we've talked about work and school and about how you spend your free time. I'd like to shift now and ask you to describe your typical day."

At what points in the LCA are transitions likely to be needed? Usually transition statements will be needed whenever you wish to move from one major section of the LCA, such as the typical day, to another, such as strengths and obstacles. Transitions also will be helpful when moving from one area to another within a major section, such as between work experience, education or training, and recreation.

Adapting the LCA

As we mentioned earlier, the LCA is useful in working with clients of all ages and circumstances. It is particularly useful because the four sections of the LCA are very broad, allowing you and your clients to structure the content and interactions involved by the choice of leads you use and the topics you and your clients choose to discuss. In the Career Assessment section, for example, opening leads or follow-up leads that explore possible workplace barriers resulting from clients' gender, race, ethnicity, culture, age, or disability flow directly and naturally as clients share their likes and dislikes concerning work and education. The Typical Day section provides additional opportunities for you and your clients to discuss possible gender, racial, cultural, ethnic, age, and disability issues that are present in their everyday lives. The Typical Day section is particularly suited for this purpose not only because it focuses on typical work days, but also extends beyond work into home, family, and community life. The focus of the last two sections of the LCA also can be adapted to clients of diverse needs in a similar manner.

To illustrate the adaptability of the LCA, we have chosen to show how it can be used with younger clients. Goals for using the LCA with younger clients may differ from those for older, more mature clients. For example, older clients may possess a higher level of career maturity and may be in need of help in acclimating to a specific work setting, remediation of past inappropriate work habits, or expanding their career options. As younger clients' experiences are generally more limited, your goals may include such items as introducing the world of work, appropriate work habits, and beginning to explore a variety of occupations as a prerequisite to occupational choice.

The LCA can be adapted easily for younger clients. These adaptations are listed by LCA section as follows:

Career Assessment

Work Experience. It is likely that younger clients have not had paid work experience. Many young people perform tasks at home, however, and these can be used in the same way that jobs are used with adults. Domestic responsibilities such as mowing the lawn, caring for a younger brother or sister, or doing the dishes are examples of these tasks.

Educational Experience. This is an important area to cover with younger clients and should be done in essentially the same manner as with older clients. Special emphasis should be placed on teachers, counselors, and administrators that younger clients liked or disliked and why. This provides information regarding the types of people they respect, emulate, or have difficulty cooperating with. Subject matter preferences also are important considerations to help explore later job placement possibilities and possible occupational interests, and to help determine future school subject choices related to eventual occupation choice.

Recreation. The area of recreation can be examined in terms of family recreational activities. It may be of interest to look at what kind of family activities are undertaken to understand family ties. Another area to explore is hobbies. Do your younger clients enjoy activities such as stamp collecting or more adventurous endeavors such as skateboarding or exploring? Ask them to describe a best friend or friends to help determine the kind of peer influence that exists.

Typical Day
The typical day section can be explored in much the same way as it is for older clients. Again, you are looking for independent–dependent, systematic–spontaneous tendencies. Who gets younger clients up in the morning? Do they have a set schedule? Do they have daily chores? If so, are responsibilities monitored? Are privileges contingent on fulfilling responsibilities? What is the home environment like?

Strengths and Obstacles
This section also is done much the same as it is for older clients. The focus is on recognizing strengths used to overcome obstacles. By having their strengths reinforced, clients may become more cognizant of the skills they possess.

Summary

The summary is done by asking younger clients what they learned from the session. It is important to instill an awareness of likes and dislikes and to organize strengths and obstacles to show how these form an overall method of operation or lifestyle. For example, do younger clients like teachers because they give encouragement? This may indicate a need for reinforcement in order to carry out tasks most efficiently. Such points are important revelations that can have implications for future occupational and personal success.

APPLYING WHAT HAS BEEN LEARNED

The LCA is a structured interview technique designed to help you and your clients gather information in a systematic way in a relatively short period of time. Please note the words *structured interview*. As such the LCA is a point of departure for the next steps in career counseling, because it helps to form positive working alliances with clients from which future career counseling activities can take place.

The structure of the LCA provides stimuli, which in turn evoke client responses. You acknowledge and dignify those responses by helping your clients identify and describe their responses in life career theme form. Together, you apply that knowledge to possible next steps such as testing, counseling, educational and occupational information gathering, and career planning and decision making.

You will find that as you use the LCA, it sets the stage for test taking and test interpretation, because the process used in the LCA teaches clients beginning skills in making observations, inferences, and hypotheses about themselves through life career theme identification. These beginning skills can have direct carryover because the language used to identify and describe client life career themes is the same language often used in test interpretation.

As you use the LCA you also will find that it sets the stage for the phases of career counseling that follow. It provides a comfortable, nonthreatening way to begin to bring a variety of issues to the surface, including women's and men's issues, racial issues, age issues, and disability issues. The LCA also will bring to the surface the ways clients gather and process information about themselves and the world in which they live. The styles they use may have implications for the kind of career counseling interventions you use.

The LCA supports and reinforces a holistic approach to career counseling. It helps begin a discussion of the life-role arenas of worker, student, leisure, and family and their relationships. This is important in career counseling because, as Berman and Munson (1981) pointed out,

Significant career involvements do not exist in isolation of, nor can they be understood apart from, other life ventures. People can be helped to identify areas of meaningful individual–environment dialogue and to examine their work life experiences in conjunction with family, community, school, and other important roles (p. 96).

REFERENCES

Berman, J. J., & Munson, H. L. (1981). Challenges in a dialectical conception of career evolution. *The Personnel and Guidance Journal, 60* (2), pp. 92–96.

Dinkmeyer, D. C., Pew, W. L., & Dinkmeyer, D. C. (1979). *Adlerian counseling and psychotherapy.* Monterey, CA: Brooks/Cole.

Goldman, L. (1990). Qualitative assessment. *The Counseling Psychologist, 18,* pp. 205–213.

Mosak, H. H. (1971). Life style. In A. G. Nikelly (Ed.), *Techniques for behavior change* (pp. 77–81). Springfield, IL: Charles C. Thomas.

► 10

Career, Multicultural, and Marital Genograms

Gathering Information About Career–Family–Socialization Connections

DeMaria, Weeks, and Hof (1999) group genograms into two types. The first type is called the basic genogram. It is the full genogram that contains all aspects of family system work. The second type is called the focused genogram. It uses the framework of the basic genogram but emphasizes specific topics such as:

Attachment: bonding, temperament, and attachment

Emotions: sadness, loss, and grief; fear; and pleasure

Anger: anger, family violence, and corporal punishment

Gender and sexuality: gender, sexuality, and romantic love

Culture: race, ethnicity, and immigration; religious orientation; socioeconomic status (DeMaria, Weeks, & Hof, 1999, p.10).

In this chapter a focused genogram called the career genogram is featured first. It uses the framework of the basic genogram but emphasizes career. Later in the chapter, two other focused genograms are presented, namely, a multicultural genogram and a marital genogram.

The career genogram is a qualitative assessment procedure that can be used in the gathering information subphase of career counseling. It provides a format and process for drawing a picture of a client's family over three generations. Career genograms, when completed, display "family information graphically in a way that provides a quick gestalt of complex family patterns...." (McGoldrick & Gerson, 1985, p. 1). As we will see, however, the process used to achieve a completed career genogram is as important as the final product.

The career genogram is an adaptation of the work of Bowen (1980) in family counseling. In family counseling the word career is not used with the word genogram, because the emphasis is more on specific family issues and concerns. When the word *career* is added, many other avenues of exploration are available for you and your clients in the gathering information subphase of career counseling (Brown & Brooks, 1991; Dagley, 1984; Gysbers & Moore, 1987; Isaacson & Brown, 1997; Okiishi, 1987; Penick, 2000; Thorngren & Feit, 2001).

The career genogram is particularly useful because it provides a direct and relevant framework for use with clients to shed light on many topics, including their world views, possible environmental barriers, personal–work–family role conflicts, racial identity status and issues, and levels of acculturation. It has substantial face validity for clients because it provides them with an opportunity to tell their story within the career counseling context. Clients have a chance to talk about themselves and their childhoods from a perspective they know well. The career genogram encourages trust and curiosity and helps to create the bond necessary in the working alliance.

> In career counseling, a genogram could help the counselor and client determine the individuals in the client's family who may have been significant to the formation of the client's career expectations. Also, the counselor could better understand the client's view of the world of work. Possible barriers posed by significant others or perceived by the client to be restrictions could be identified, and sex role stereotypes could be pinpointed (Okiishi, 1987, p. 139).

In presenting the career genogram, Chapter 10 first provides a rationale for its use in career counseling. This is followed by the details of the administration of career genograms. Three steps are involved in the administration, including presentation of the purpose, the actual construction of career genograms by the clients, and questions clients respond to upon completion of their career genograms. Chapter 10 closes with discussion of how you and your clients can analyze and use the information and insights gained through the career genogram process as well as adapt the genogram for a variety of uses.

RATIONALE

Dagley (1984) summed up the rationale for the career genogram by suggesting that clients often can be understood best in the context of their sociological, psychological, cultural, and economic heritage—their family. Heinl (1985) stated that a genogram "may provide pointers towards transgenerational and individual psychodynamic issues and may therefore contribute to fruitful therapeutic work" (p. 227). The career genogram can provide you and your clients with a process to connect clients' understanding of the past to the present in order to better understand the dynamics of the present.

The career genogram is particularly useful with clients who are struggling with work–family–socialization-identity issues, concerns, and stresses. McGoldrick and Gerson (1985) made this point by stating that: "Genograms make it easier for a clinician [counselor] to keep in mind family members, patterns, and events that may have recurring significance in a family's ongoing care. Just as language potentiates and organizes our thought processes, family diagrams that map relationships and patterns of functioning may help clinicians [counselors] think systematically about how events and relationships in their clients' lives are related to patterns of health and illness" (p. 2).

Because the career genogram process unfolds naturally, it is a comfortable procedure for you and your clients to use. As you show interest in and respond to the life experiences and life histories of clients, the bond within the working alliance is strengthened. Not only do you gain knowledge and understanding about clients, but clients learn about themselves as well. Clients often, for the first time, gain insights into their internal thoughts and feelings about themselves, others, and their worlds. The career genogram provides clients with a structure to integrate information about themselves and their growing up experiences in ways they had not thought of before.

ADMINISTRATION

There are three steps involved in using career genograms with clients. Step 1 involves sharing with clients the purpose of career genograms. Step 2 explains the process of how clients construct their own unique career genograms. And Step 3 focuses on how you and your clients can analyze and understand the meaning of clients' career genograms through a series of questions posed by you and the interaction and discussion that follows.

Step One: Purpose

The first step in the administration of career genograms is to share with your clients the purpose of career genograms. This can be done by explaining that the technique will provide them with insights into the dynamics of their families of origin, including grandparents. You can explain that it will provide them with insights into such issues as the career, work, gender, and cultural socialization they experienced while growing up, environmental barriers if any, and how they have integrated and dealt with various life roles. Many other issues of relevance to clients' situations also can be explored as the career genogram process unfolds depending upon the concerns clients may have, including clients' world views and racial identity status. How and why clients' current world views and racial identities were formed through the socialization process in their families and community can come into sharp focus through the construction and analyses of career genograms.

Step Two: Construction

The second step is to explain to your clients how to construct their own career genograms. The following directions can be used to fit your clients and their situations: Career genograms can help us understand you and your families of origin, including grandparents. Please draw a picture of your family of origin beginning with your mother and father. Draw it on the sheet of newsprint that is on the table in front of you. (A chalkboard or other comparable writing surface also could be used.) Place the following symbols (McGoldrick & Gerson, 1985) for your mother and father about two-thirds of the way down the sheet. Write in their names under the symbols (Figure 10–1).

Then, just above these symbols place the birthdates of your mother and father. If either of your parents died, put an X within their symbol and put the year of their death next to their birthdate. Next, add yourself to the picture and any brothers or sisters. Make sure you place their names under the appropriate symbols. Suppose for the purposes of this career genogram you have a brother and a sister. Your name is Justin, your sister's name is Melissa, and your brother's name is Samuel. Then, add birthdates for yourself and your brother and sister to the diagram. Now the diagram will look like Figure 10–2.

The next task is to add grandparents to the picture and any aunts or uncles from both sides of your family. Add names, birthdates, and dates of death if you know them for all of the people you add to your career genogram. Also add the titles of the occupations in which the members of your family of

FIGURE 10–1   Parents' Names

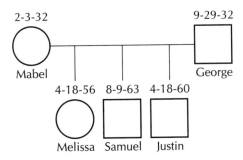

FIGURE 10–2   Parents and Brothers and Sisters

origin and extended family members are or were employed. Now your career genogram may look something like Figure 10–3.

At this point in the construction of your clients' career genograms it is important to remember that there are many different kinds of family patterns today—single-parent families, blended families, step-families, and two-parent families. Divorce, death, illness, remarriage, and no marriage have created these and other family pattern variations. Because many family pattern variations exist, some additional symbols are required to adequately construct career genograms. Figure 10–4 shows various career genogram symbols that can be used to represent the many variations in family patterns. Make sure these symbols are available and explained to your clients as appropriate and needed.

Step Three: Analysis

Once your clients' career genograms have been constructed and information (birthdates, deaths, divorces, occupations, and the like) about family members (brothers and sisters, parents, and grandparents) has been recorded, the next step is to use the structures to explore with your clients what it was like growing up. The questions that are used in the exploration process depend in part on your clients' presenting problems and their internal thoughts and feelings. Rita and Adejanju (1993) suggested that:

> In the session, the counselor can facilitate the exploration of "what happened?" (identification of facts/events), "what was the impact upon your people and the family?" (analysis), and "what generalizations can be made?" (specific learnings), regarding the relationship of the "there and then" (one's living history), to the "here and now" issues which are the focus of the exploration.

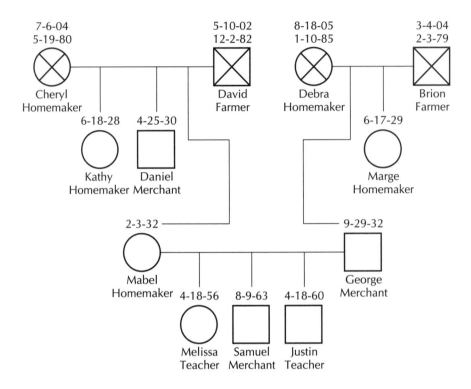

FIGURE 10–3 Extended Family

The counselor endeavors to help the student [client] fill in gaps, make affective connections between significant events, perceive overt and covert patterns, and recall dormant positive images that have helped bond one person with others in the unique family. Verbal and nonverbal clues are carefully observed and, where deemed appropriate, explored to help make connections. The feelings, thoughts, and dreams experienced in the process completed are also examined (p. 21).

Because the career genogram is not a standardized procedure, there is flexibility as to the questions asked as you and your clients make decisions about what would be most helpful to explore and discuss. Here are some general questions that could be asked as starters.

- How would you describe the family in which you grew up?
- If you grew up in a two-parent family, what is/was your father's occupation? What is/was your mother's occupation? (Also ask about your

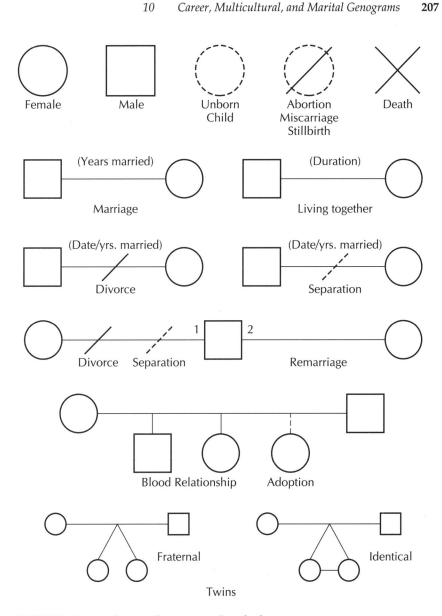

FIGURE 10–4   Career Genogram Symbols

clients' parents, other work experiences, education or training, career satisfaction, and unfulfilled dreams.)

- What are/were your mother and father like? What adjectives would you use to describe them? What is/was the nature of their marital relationship (responsibilities)?
- What are the occupations of your brothers and/or sisters? What do your younger siblings aspire to be? Where do your brothers and sisters live? Describe the lifestyle of each. (Also ask whether the family lives close by, and explore cousin relationships such as competitiveness for grandparents' approval.)
- What is/was your grandmother's occupation? Grandfather's?
- What do your aunts and uncles do?
- What is/was your role in the family (now and when growing up)?
- What is/was your relationship with your mother, father? (Ask about their career aspirations for you.)
- Who are you most like in your family? (Ask about who took care of whom, coalitions.)
- What is your spouse's relationship with your family?

Dagley (1984) suggested another set of questions to be used in developing a career genogram.

- What are the dominant values in the family of origin?
- Vocationally, are certain "missions" valued?
- Are there any "ghosts or legends" that serve either as anchor points or "rightful roles" for the family?
- Are there myths or misconceptions that seem to transcend generations?
- Are there any psychological pressures or expectations emanating from "unfinished business" of the family?
- How does the individual's description of economic values and preferences fit in with family's history?
- How has the family addressed the three boxes of life (learning, working, and playing)? Are there any imbalances?
- What family interaction rules and relationship boundaries have been passed along through generations?
- Are there any voids in the client's memory of family? Is there significance to those voids?
- Does the client have a sense of "owing" family traditions?
- How have the primary life tasks of love, work, and friendship been addressed by the family?
- What vocational patterns emerge, in terms of choices, as well as the choice and development process?

If you and your clients were focusing on educational/training issues, Rita and Adejanju (1993) recommended the following line of questions.

1. What are the overt/covert messages in this family regarding education, academic success?
2. Who said/did what? Who was conspicuously silent/absent in the area of academic striving, academic success?
3. Who was the most encouraging/discouraging in terms of academic striving, and in what ways?
4. How was academic achievement encouraged? Discouraged? Controlled? Within a generation? Between generations?
5. What questions have you been reluctant to ask regarding academic success in your family tree? Who might have the answers? How would you discover those answers?
6. What were the "rules," "secrets," "myths" in your family regarding success (e.g., dangers, cut-off from family)?
7. What do the other "players on the stage" have to say regarding these questions? How did these issues, events, and experiences impact upon you? Within a generation? Between generations? With whom have you talked about this? With whom would you like to talk about this? How would you do it?
8. How would you change this genogram (including who and what) to meet your wishes regarding academic striving and success (p. 22)?

CAREER GENOGRAM COMMENTARY

As stated earlier, career genograms provide real-life frameworks on which clients can visually organize and map perceptions of personal, work, and family concerns, tasks, and stresses into meaningful representations in the context of overall family life and family history. Career genograms are stimulus devices that provide clients with a natural, direct, and comfortable way for them to share their background and their life experiences. "Since individuals carry the history of past experiences with them continually, in understanding psychological aspects of development it may be more important to understand the individual's interpretations of his/her experiences rather than to have objective information about these experiences" (DeVries, Birren, & Deutchman, 1990, p. 4).

Although the analysis section follows the construction and discussion of clients' career genograms in this chapter, analyses actually begin as soon as clients undertake the construction of their career genograms. Tentative hypotheses about clients' presenting problems and the underlying dynamics that may be involved are formed fairly early, with the understanding that they are to be modified or discarded and new ones added, as new information and insights are gained from the career genogram interaction process. As this process unfolds, other issues or problems in addition to or in place of the presenting problem or issue may emerge. As Borgen (1995) suggested:

> *Assessment, ideally conducted in a counseling context, becomes a dynamic process. It stimulates dialogue between client and counselor, through which are merged the expert perspectives each brings. Together they construct a narrative, but often one that is in process, tentative, and incomplete (p. 438).*

As you interact with clients as they are telling their stories through the structure of their career genograms, it is important to listen to the words and phrases clients use in addition to considering the emotional weight they may carry. Some words and phrases may carry special meanings. For example, clients may talk in hushed voices about growing up in families with alcoholic parents. Other clients may describe experiences with mentors and you can hear in the words they use, and in their tone of voice, how significant these mentors were to them. In addition, listen for any affective tones which may "reveal unconscious longings which, with the therapist's [counselor's] help can be used to establish new goals and directions" (Wachtel, 1982, p. 340).

We also recommend that you observe closely how your clients construct their career genograms. Pay particular attention to the amount of detail your clients put into their career genograms, the time it takes for them to complete the task, and the spacing between generations (Heinl, 1985). How your clients record the details of their personal and family histories may provide clues as to their internal thoughts and feelings. In turn, these clues can provide you with possible leads to further clarify client concerns and issues.

It is important to remember at this point that a major goal of career genograms is to gather qualitative information about clients' growing up—their socialization and the impact that it had on how they view themselves, others, and their world. As career genograms are completed, more people of significance to clients are available for consideration so that "family scripts or legacies of an intergenerational nature" (Rita & Adejanju, 1993, p. 23) become visible and can be discussed. It is important to look for repetitive themes in the stories that clients tell.

Making family–socialization issues visible, putting them on the table out in the open, offers the opportunity for you and your clients to discuss them openly. Once information is gathered using the career genogram and added to client information collected in other ways, the counseling task is to use the tentative hypotheses that have been emerging to begin to consider interventions that may help clients achieve their goals or resolve their problems.

Sometimes questions are raised about the use of career genograms with resistant clients. Will resistant, defensive clients respond to information gathering devices such as career genograms? Wachtel (1982) suggested that genograms do work with such clients. In fact, according to Wachtel (1982), genograms actually assist such clients in loosening up:

> *It is often quite helpful to use the genogram, particularly with rigidly defensive people who have trouble knowing and opening up about their feelings. Reassured by the structured questioning and by the illusion that they are merely telling the "facts," these guarded and controlled individuals gradually begin to loosen up. Impressions of interest and sympathy on the therapist's [counselor's] part as the "facts" are gathered helps further emotional expressiveness. Since they are dealing with "past history" and supposedly "distant" relatives, they often do not feel the need to defend as much as when talking about what seems more obviously personally relevant (p. 336).*

ADDITIONAL USES OF THE GENOGRAM

The genogram is a versatile technique that can be used to gather information on a variety of issues in addition to the ones described earlier. Two additional uses are presented here as examples. The first focuses on clients who may wish to explore their racial/ethnic/cultural backgrounds (Sueyoshi, Rivera, & Ponterotto, 2001). The second focuses on the genogram's use with clients who may be experiencing marital difficulty with resulting impact on work and family life roles.

Multicultural Genogram

DeMaria, Weeks, and Hof (1999) suggested that the purpose of multicultural genograms "is to examine the impact of race, immigration, and ethnicity, religious orientation, and class upon individuals" (p. 177). The multicultural genogram can help individuals think about their racial/ethnic backgrounds and how these backgrounds may have influenced aspects of their lives. You and your clients can use multicultural genograms to note and reflect on clients' families' racial/ethnic heritage. The procedures to administer and construct these genograms are the same as presented earlier. The difference is in the analysis part, in the questions you use to assist clients to analyze their multicultural genograms.

The following questions can assist your clients to explore their roots and the meanings these roots may have for their present and future lives.

1. What are your ethnic and racial roots?
2. What parts of this heritage do you most identify with today?

3. Have certain career behaviors or occupations been part of your ethnic or racial heritage?
4. What personal characteristics do you attribute to your racial or ethnic heritage?
5. What biases/prejudices/forms of racism have you experienced because of your racial/ethnic background?
6. What biases/prejudices/forms of racism did you see demonstrated by family members toward other groups?
7. What biases/prejudices/forms of racism do you find yourself carrying with you that are first learned in your family of origin?
8. How does your cultural background serve both as a strength and a hindrance in your work?

Marital Genogram

The genogram also can be modified to work with clients who may be experiencing marital difficulty that is possibly linked to work and family issues. Using the marital genogram, your client's marriage can be explored beginning with the courtship phase to the time a child was born. You would explain the purpose of the marital genogram and instruct your client on how to construct it. The process might unfold as follows as you say: On the large sheet of paper in front of you please draw the following symbols as noted below. Then write in your first name and your spouse's first name underneath the appropriate symbols (see Figure 10–5).

As we go through this process I will be asking you some questions to help us gather information about the marital difficulties you are experiencing and any possible links to your work and family roles if these are of concern to you. Let's start with your courtship.

• What was the length of your courtship?
• What attracted you to each other?
• How much time did you spend together as a couple and how was this decided? (Inquire about who may have pursued for more togetherness or time apart in the relationship.)
• When your relationship became exclusive, how did you handle your individual friendships?

FIGURE 10–5   Wife and Husband

- How did your parents view your relationship?
- Were either of you previously married? Are there children from these marriages?

Let's now move to the time when you were married but before the birth of your child.

- What prompted you to get married when you did?
- How would you describe your relationship during this time?
- Describe the amount and nature of individual time and time with friends?
- As for your lifestyle, how much social, financial, and educational time is spent with in-laws?

Now let's add your child to the marital genogram (Figure 10–6).

Let's talk a bit more about your family now that your child has entered the picture.

- What entered into your decision to have a child when you did?
- How did marital relationship change with birth of child?
- How did your individual roles change?
- Describe each child for me, from oldest to youngest.
- Who takes care of whom, plays with whom, fights or argues the most, is the most different, is the most alike?

By going through the marital genogram process to unfold the history of a marriage through the time a child was born, husband and wife behaviors and possible stress and strain points may be revealed. This may provide you and your client with possible hypotheses about the specific issues involved. At the very least, these issues can be discussed openly. Possible links to work world and family life behavior also can be seen, understood, and addressed.

Keep in mind that in this scenario you hear the story of these events from only one person. It would be useful to add the perceptions of the other spouse.

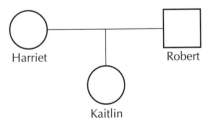

FIGURE 10–6   Wife, Husband, and Child

In fact, the marital genogram could be used in couples counseling, in which case the marital genogram could be constructed jointly.

SOME CAUTIONS

The focused genogram may not be an appropriate qualitative information gathering technique for some clients. "The genogram construction or information may seem cumbersome, superfluous, or even distasteful to some counselors and clients" (Okiishi, 1987, p. 142). Other clients, because of their cultural, ethnic, racial, or religious backgrounds, may view the use of career, multicultural, and marital genograms as invasions of privacy. For them, family issues and family history are private matters that are not to be discussed in public. Some counselors may be concerned about the time it takes to gather information using a focused genogram and wonder whether or not the process is worth the work. Clients, too, may be concerned about the time, believing that action steps are more important than spending time gathering information toward what they think may not produce results.

We feel the focused genogram is a useful qualitative information-gathering technique when used appropriately. It is your responsibility, with the advice of your clients as you share the purpose of genograms with them, to decide whether or not to use the technique. When it is explained clearly to clients, most will respond positively to the experience, and it will yield meaningful information that will be useful in the later phases of career counseling.

REFERENCES

Borgen, F. H. (1995). Leading edges of vocational psychology: Diversity and vitality. In W. B. Walsh & S. H. Osipow (Eds.), *Handbook of vocational psychology* (2nd ed., pp. 427–441). Hillsdale, NJ: Erlbaum.

Bowen, M. (1980). *Key to the genogram*. Washington, DC: Georgetown University Hospital.

Brown, D., & Brooks, L. (1991). *Career counseling techniques*. Boston: Allyn and Bacon.

Dagley, J. (1984). *A vocational genogram* (mimeograph). Athens, GA: University of Georgia.

DeMaria, R., Weeks, G., & Hof, L. (1999). *Focused genograms: Intergenerational Assessment of individuals, couples, and families*. Philadelphia, PA: Taylor & Francis.

DeVries, B., Birren, J. E. & Deutchman, D. E. (1990). Adult development through guided autobiography: The family context. *Family Relations, 39,* 3–7.

Gysbers, N. C., & Moore, E. J. (1987). *Career counseling: Skills and techniques for practitioners*. Englewood Cliffs, NJ: Prentice-Hall.

Heinl, P. (1985). The image and visual analysis of the genogram. *Journal of Family Therapy, 7,* 213–229.

Isaacson, L. E., & Brown, D. (1997). *Career information, career counseling, and career development.* Boston: Allyn and Bacon.

McGoldrick, M., & Gerson, R. (1985). *Genograms in family assessment.* New York: W.W. Norton.

Okiishi, R. W. (1987). The genogram as a tool in career counseling. *Journal of Counseling and Development, 66* (3), 139–143.

Penick, N. (2000). The genogram technique. In N. Peterson & R.C. Gonzalez (Eds.), *Career counseling models for diverse populations* (pp. 137-149). Belmont, CA: Wadsworth/Thomson Learning.

Rita, E. S., & Adejanju, M. G. (1993). The genogram: Plotting the roots of academic success. *Family Therapy, 30* (1), 17–28.

Sueyoshi, L.A., Rivera, L., & Ponterotto, J.G. (2001). The family genogram as a tool in multicultural career counseling. In J.G. Ponterotto, J.M. Casas, L.A. Suzuki, & C.M. Alexander (Eds.), *Handbook of multicultural counseling* (2nd ed., pp. 655–671). Thousand Oaks, CA: Sage Publications

Thorngren, J.M., & Feit, S.S. (2001). The career-o-gram: A post modern career intervention. *The Career Development Quarterly, 49,* 291–303.

Wachtel, E. F. (1982). The family psyche over three generations: The genogram revisited. *Journal of Marital and Family Therapy, 8,* (3) 335–343.

▶ 11

Gathering Client Information Using an Occupational Card Sort

Using Occupational Titles As Stimuli

As can be seen from the previous two chapters, there are a variety of ways to do career assessments. The life career assessment and the career genogram can both help us gather information that can be helpful to us and to our clients. We cannot, however, rely on any one approach, as each client may require something different. Goldman (1983) makes a convincing case for how the card sort can be a most effective approach with some clients. What should become obvious as you read the previous chapters is how varied the approaches are to gathering information. Some approaches are quite objective and may provide information and norms that make them truly unavailable through any other source. Other assessments that are somewhat more objective, for example, the genogram, are more dependent on the client producing information and then having it interpreted with the help of the counselor. Still other assessments, like card sorts, are more subjective in nature and their effectiveness depends on our ability to help the client arrive at insights and ideas from the process.

This chapter overview introduces and then describes a process for using an occupational card sort in career counseling. We suggest ways it might help with clients who resist, don't need, or already have explored more objective sources of information about themselves. We describe the benefits that seem particularly helpful with a card sort and then take you through use of it with a client. We conclude with an observation about how the card sort may help expand your understanding of your clients' ways of thinking about themselves.

OCCUPATIONAL CARD SORTS

In general, card sorts are nonstandardized approaches to sorting almost any array of ideas. For career counseling purposes, they involve the client sorting occupational titles from which all kinds of themes, ideas, issues, values, or feelings emerge. Unlike most standardized instruments, card sorts do not usually produce scores or have norms. The sort we describe consists of occupational titles listed on small cards, for example, and the client is simply asked to sort them into three piles: those they like, those they are indifferent to, and those they dislike. A next step then might be to ask the client to take one of the piles and sort it into smaller piles based on any common themes that might have influenced her placing them in the broader category. For example, a client may look at the cards in one pile and see that prestige or status or potential earnings seem to be common in some of the titles. Another theme might be recognizing that several occupational titles involved using math or numbers. The theme possibilities are limitless, and often are best suggested by the client rather than the counselor. This is one reason this approach remains nonstandardized—each person has a unique way of organizing his or her thoughts.

Card sorts usually depend on clients' ability to verbalize and eventually make sense of patterns they use to think about their world. This often depends more on your skill as a counselor than the client's predisposition to verbalize. The card sort may help clients better understand life patterns as they talk about themselves and where they want to go with their careers.

Overview of Card Sorts

In the final analysis, individuals must act for themselves. We can offer information, advice, and assessments that substantiate their thinking, but however we do it, eventually the individual must live with the consequences and own the ideas. Card sorts begin with the assumption that individuals have ideas about what they want to do but need to talk about them, and through the counseling process come to some insight or appreciation for how they can resolve issues for themselves.

A card sort is a semistructured way of sorting out or prioritizing the interests, skills, needs, values, or any predetermined array of ideas for a client. You can start from scratch and create some array of items, or you can simply use one of the many already published sorts. They exist for occupations (Hansen, Johnston and Wong, 2002, Holland et al., 1980, Jones, 1979), skills (Knowdell, 1995a), college majors (Garson & Johnston, 2001) and values (Knowdell, 1995b).

The number of cards may vary, as may the amount of information provided on the cards. But the cards are to be sorted by some predetermined procedure into piles that usually have clients describing their identification with, their possession of, their need for, or the importance of the items in their lives. So, for example, the cards might each have an occupational title with some brief description on it of what the title means, and the client may be asked to sort the cards into three piles depending on whether they like, are neutral toward, or dislike the occupation. That process of sorting reveals much about the client's facility with words, ideas, concepts, his approach to tasks, his style and comfort with thinking about a complex task, his decision-making style, and a host of other things that may help you to understand and assess the status of the client at a later point. If given early, the card sort may help you predict the client's receptivity to more objective data later provided from standardized tests.

It is difficult to describe all the nuances of a good card sort or a good card sort administration. No two are alike nor do they need to be. Good use depends on the particular needs of the client and your own style or need in choosing to administer it. You may only see it as a tool for getting acquainted—an easy format or structure for talking about one's self and career concerns. Or, you may see it as a way of helping one see relationships or priorities with items that may need to be considered in any career decision. It can be almost entirely open-ended or it can be very structured. It can be used as structure for conversation or for producing a fairly complete list of occupations, interests, values, or themes in much the same way you would from a standardized test of the same material.

We devote a complete chapter to occupational card sorts because they open so many possibilities. With practice, the possibilities become endless and the opportunities to help clients explore using their own existing resources become enormous.

General Benefits of Card Sorts

There are many types of card sorts, each of which has certain benefits that can be useful at particular times. Here we will cover some of the common benefits of all sorts, and then focus on one example of a card sort most applicable to career planning.

Benefit Number 1: Provide Structure

Card sorts provide structure, and usually comfort, in dealing with a sometimes difficult or complex task. Almost everyone finds it easy, and often fun, to deal cards, perhaps because of earlier associations with card games. Structure usually makes it easier to approach a difficult and/or unfamiliar task. Like with a puzzle, when you begin to see all the parts come together to form a picture, a complex task has become not only manageable but rewarding. To see patterns and closure with any difficult task, however, takes thought and sustained persistence with the task. A card sort may provide that for a confused client who at that particular moment may need a step-by-step way of approaching a complex problem.

Benefit Number 2: Promote Bonding

The card sorting process, as opposed to other tasks one might select early in career counseling, can be immediately engaging and contribute directly to the bonding that is so important in establishing a solid working alliance on an interpersonal level. Alternatives, such as computerized career systems, paper and pencil inventories, or reading career materials, demand less interpersonal contact or may be initiated without contributing in any way to the bonding between you and the client. In Chapter 8 we emphasized the importance of establishing a bond with the client as early as possible. You find that the card sort not only addresses your intention to work on developing a bond in the relationship, but it enables you to engage yourself in a process that will help you become much clearer about your client's needs, motivations, preferred ways, exploring style, and so forth. If clients are not engaged with the process, as may be the case when they take the initial steps with standardized tests, you will know it immediately, and you can correct or modify the intervention accordingly.

Benefit Number 3: Authenticate Choices

In the process of sorting cards, and as you encourage clients to express their opinions or reasons for putting cards in particular piles, you also receive cues about the strength or logic of choices or discards. Clients, for example, may dismiss some occupations for weak or illogical reasons, but you will hear that part of their thinking. This is insight you would not necessarily obtain when immediately asking clients to complete the typical interest inventory. In short, it helps you begin a process of authenticating choices.

Benefit Number 4: Promote Feedback

Feedback can be immediate and ongoing. You can continually incorporate new data as it is generated and constantly test it against data previously generated. If you have the time, a card sort will assure that your later interpretation and use of objective data will mesh with what the client is thinking—you will have already established what this is.

Benefit Number 5: Promote Understanding in Communication

The card sorting process continually confirms what is being said and heard. A continual undercurrent in career counseling is knowing for sure that what you are saying is what the client is hearing. You build a model for what is happening in the client's head, but you always want confirmation of it. In the proper administration of a card sort, there is continual verbalization and confirmation of what is being heard from what is being said. If this is done in a safe, nonthreatening atmosphere, it is likely to be an accurate reflection as well.

Benefit Number 6: Minimize Dependency

A card sort minimizes the risk of a client depending too much on the counselor. By reinforcing what the client is saying, you are recognizing those perceptions as the ones that are most important. You can always add your perceptions, but you are building on what you have been told rather than the other way around.

Benefit Number 7: Promote Inclusivity

Card sorts may be especially helpful with ethnic or nonethnic minority groups. In today's increasingly multicultural world where the norming of standardized instruments lags somewhat behind, and where we are increasingly raising questions about a client's sense of identity with particular groups, card sorts offer another striking advantage. Interpretations are not dependent on norms and, in fact, lacking norms, we are more inclined to listen carefully to our client's perceptions of what something means. We can't know what it is like to be raised in someone else's culture, one that may be unfamiliar with particular occupational titles or with different impressions of some occupations, to think as one who is disabled, or as one who has restrictive impressions of her roles. In all of these areas we must continually learn and appreciate someone else's perceptions or prior experiences in a decision-making process. The card sort has both counselor and client exploring and learning anew.

Benefit Number 8: Easily Tailored to Clients' Needs

Finally, you can easily tailor the experience for the client. A reluctant or skeptical client can be coached to explore more, while a verbal client can be coached to be more focused. One that wants a lot of structure can be asked to write or make lists of observations or career possibilities, while a client who would do better without structure can be left free to talk without much interruption.

Few will argue against using any card sort; those who do question using it may prefer a more standardized measure. We prefer to use it as another form of assessment—a particularly good one—which with practice both clients and counselors can improve their ability to make more effective use of the information provided.

THE CASE OF TANYA

At this point you may be asking when to choose to use a card sort. We can best answer that with a case that shows its value when you have already used a standardized test, or when a client comes to you disappointed with the results of the usual standardized instruments.

Tanya had come for career counseling before when she was a sophomore in college. She was the first in her family to go to college. Everyone had high expectations for her. She was a bright and articulate
African-American woman and could recall early on that her mother
told her she should go to college, become a doctor, and return home
and take care of the medical needs of the family. Her mother said the
town needed a good doctor and she was sure that would be her
daughter. Tanya had gone along with this idea until her sophomore
year in college. She enrolled in science courses, volunteered time at a
local hospital, joined the pre-med club, and began talking with others
who were in pre-medicine. She was bothered that they all seemed so
different from her. They liked their science classes and she didn't,
although she did quite well in them. She found them competitive as
they talked about their classes and she did not see herself that way.
She felt they were too concerned about what their salaries might be
and not very concerned about the practice of medicine. She began to
doubt her choice. She started thinking that maybe she had missed out
on some experience that should have clarified her career directions
earlier. Her roommate had taken a test at the career center that confirmed she did not have interests like those of others in her major, so
she was going to try something else. Tanya thought maybe a career
test would help her as well. She took it with high expectations that she
would find a new career for herself, but was disappointed. In fact, the
counselor said the test did not suggest she had interests like the people in any particular profession. She was not only disappointed, she
left discouraged and did not return for a follow-up interview even
though the counselor strongly urged her to do so. A year later she still
did not know what to do. She was doing well in classes, but she knew
deep inside she was not happy. She opted to try career counseling
again. Maybe another test would help this time.

The above story is not atypical. Clearly Tanya was trying to fulfill the family dream. She had no other strong interests so she simply went along with
their wishes. She received continued reinforcement from family and friends
and really didn't give it all that much thought as she was completely involved
with school. Good in science and all her classes, Tanya was voted most likely
to succeed in college. She listed pre-med as her expected major. It would have
been hard to not think of going into medicine without disappointing many
others. She enjoyed the support and encouragement they offered, but when it
came time to study, she didn't find much support for herself. She knew somehow it just was not right.

It is not likely she would find another interest inventory of help. She indicated she would be willing to try one but was not enthusiastic about it. The

initial conversation suggested the results would probably be somewhat like they were before. Would this not be a good time for a card sort? She was skeptical of the value of more tests and she seemed eager to talk about her situation. We opted for an occupational card sort here and while we used a particular one—the Missouri Occupational Card Sort (Hansen & Johnston, 1980)—you might use any of those listed in the references at the end of the chapter.

THE MISSOURI OCCUPATIONAL CARD SORT (MOCS)

This card sort is particularly helpful with traditional-aged college students, but it can easily be adapted to a younger or older population (Heim & Johnston, 1991). A discussion of its development will make obvious what you might do to tailor a card sort for your particular clients.

We developed this occupational card sort for use at a large land grant university that has many undeclared students and a great diversity of possible majors for them. It also incorporated the Holland schema, which helps clients to learn about their personal identification with the six Holland personality types and their respective environments while sorting the cards. We listed most of the popular majors available at the university and then sorted them into piles in accordance with how they match with the six environments. For example, firefighter was sorted into the realistic pile, anthropologist into the investigative pile, musician into artistic, career counselor into social, buyer/ purchasing agent into enterprising, and accountant into the conventional environment. We then took approximately an equal number of these occupations for each of the six areas. In all, we chose a total of 90 occupations, about the number we thought could be easily sorted in 30 minutes. We also wanted titles to be the more popular or easily identifiable ones, so we worked in somewhat arbitrary fashion to choose about 15 from each pile.

Because we also assumed clients would learn things about titles as they sorted, we put the titles on one side of each card and on the back of each we provided a three-letter Holland code for the title, a *Dictionary of Occupational Titles* reference number, and the primary activities and responsibilities of the occupation. The back of a typical card in the deck is shown in Figure 11–1 along with a key (Figure 11–2) to the information on each card. All the cards are described in the manual provided with the card sort (Krieshok, Hansen, & Johnston, & Wong, 2002).

In a session with a client like Tanya, you might begin the interview using a format like this:

"In front of you is a deck of cards. On each of the cards is the name of an occupation. These occupations will vary from unskilled to professional. Some

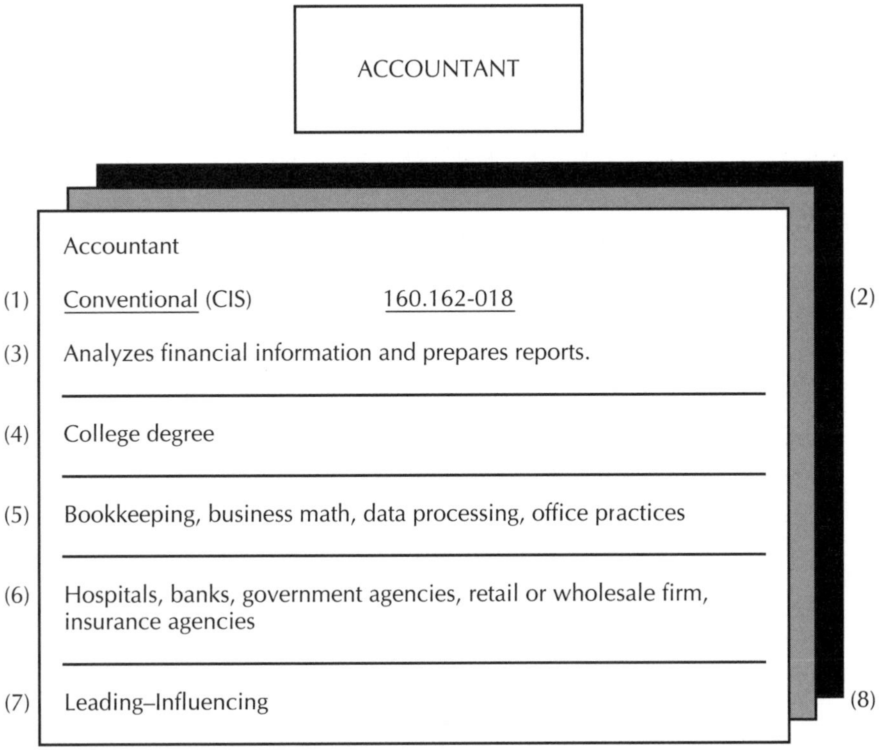

ACCOUNTANT

	Accountant
(1)	Conventional (CIS) 160.162-018 (2)
(3)	Analyzes financial information and prepares reports.
(4)	College degree
(5)	Bookkeeping, business math, data processing, office practices
(6)	Hospitals, banks, government agencies, retail or wholesale firm, insurance agencies
(7)	Leading–Influencing (8)

FIGURE 11–1   Back of a Typical Card (Accountant) in the Missouri Occupational Card Sort

of them you will have an interest in and some you will not. Go through the cards and sort them into three piles: one pile for those you feel you would like to do (LIKE pile), one for those you would dislike or not chose to do (DISLIKE pile), and a third pile for those you are unsure about or could go either way with (UNDECIDED/NEUTRAL pile). If you can talk about why you are putting them in each pile as you go along, I'll take some notes that might serve as the basis for our discussion of these choices later on. This is not a timed activity, but your first impressions are probably the more important ones, so don't deliberate too long on any one of the cards."

If you want more structure or want to provide a written report on this activity for the client, you can follow or provide the client with the six step handout outlined in Figure 11–3.

With some clients, looking over their shoulder may be too intimidating, so allow that person to get involved in the process on his own, and then check

(1) The primary Holland type of that occupation followed by the 3-letter code.

(2) The 9-digit reference number of that occupation from the *Dictionary of Occupational Titles*.

(3) The primary activities and responsibilities of the occupation.

FIGURE 11–2   A Key to Information on the MOCS Card

---

in on his progress a little later. This often provides the same outcome and allows you to do other things.

Most times, however, we recommend that you stay with your clients as they sort the cards. We suggest you make mental note of the speed or decisiveness with which the cards are sorted. Sometimes you may need to prod a bit or suggest that clients deliberate a little less. Sometimes you can easily detect that a client is clear about what not to do, or that another is very focused on one occupation so that dismissing most occupations seems reasonable, although that problem might need discussion or clarification before the client gets too far into the process. You also can pick up on how much or how little the client knows about the various occupations by the number of times she resorts to turning over the cards or asking you questions about particular titles. With practice, you become more and more astute at observing significant influences in the pattern used by each client. You become more effective at probing for thoughts that may lie just below the level of consciousness, or are at perhaps a conscious level but not yet at a spoken level. Remember, probably no one before has objectively spent this much time with the client on this topic. You may be taking the conversation further than anyone before you has because you are not encumbered by any previous agenda.

Once the sorting process is completed, you would ask Tanya to put the LIKE and NEUTRAL piles aside, and have her begin to categorize the DISLIKE pile into several piles based on her reasons for not liking or choosing each occupation. Here is where themes begin to emerge. Tanya may say, "I couldn't do that kind of work, it's too physical" or "It would mean I'd have to work with others on a team and that's not for me." You might probe for what she means by that; she may not be able to articulate it. In particular, we look for what clients can offer as themes, although sometimes you may need to help them find the themes. Sometimes you may have to point out inconsistencies in what they are saying. It is a subtle process; you hope first to reinforce what emerges in their minds and then help them see how this relates to what they may have

Name _____   Date _____

Step 1:

In front of you, you have a pack of cards. On each one of the cards is the name of an occupation. These occupations will vary from skilled to professional. Some of them you will have an interest in, and some you will not. Go through the cards and sort them into *three piles.*

On the right, you should place the occupations that you might actually choose, that have some specific appeal to you, or that seem appropriate for a person like you—your "Like" pile.

On the left hand side, you should place the cards that have occupations that you are not interested in, that you would not choose, or do not seem appropriate for a person like you—your "Dislike" pile.

Then a third pile should be placed in the middle. These should be occupations that you are indifferent to, are uncertain about, there is some question about, or you do not know if you would like or not—your "Undecided/Neutral" pile. (You will not use this middle group any further.)

Begin sorting into the three piles.

Dislike   Undecided/   Like
                   Neutral

Step 2:

Now take the cards that have occupations you "Dislike" and move the other two piles of cards out of the way. Spread the cards of occupations you "Dislike" out in front of you and group together occupations where the reasons for not choosing are the same or similar. You may have as many groups as necessary. One occupation can be considered a group.

Begin grouping your "Dislike" cards.

After you have formed the groups, write the names of the occupations in the various groups below. It makes no difference which group is listed first. You do not have to have as many groups as are shown below. If you have more than five groups, then indicate the additional groups on the back of the page. Start by listing the occupations in group One below:

Dislikes

Group 1: _____   _____

            _____   _____

            _____   _____

FIGURE 11–3   Missouri Occupational Card Sort

What is similar about this group?

Why are you not choosing this group? What do you not like about these occupations? Be as explicit as possible!

Themes: What generalitites or themes do the above contents suggest?

Group 2: _____   _____
            _____   _____
            _____   _____

What is similar about this group?

Why are you not choosing this group? What do you not like about these occupations? Be as explicit as possible!

Themes: What generalities or themes do the above contents suggest?

Group 3: _____   _____
            _____   _____
            _____   _____

What is similar about this group?

Why are you not choosing this group? What do you not like about these occupations? Be as explicit as possible!

Themes: What generalities or themes do the above contents suggest?

FIGURE 11–3 *Continued*

Group 4: _____   _____
         _____   _____
         _____   _____

What is similar about this group?

Why are you not choosing this group? What do you not like about these occupations? Be as explicit as possible!

Themes: What generalitites or themes do the above contents suggest?

===

Group 5: _____   _____
         _____   _____
         _____   _____

What is similar about this group?

Why are you not choosing this group? What do you not like about these occupations? Be as explicit as possible!

Themes: What generalitites or themes do the above contents suggest?

===

Now, do you want to make any changes in your "Dislike" group? Do you see any occupations that do not really belong in the same group? Indicate below any changes you would like to make and why.

Step 3:

Now take the cards that have occupations you "Like" and group them together where the reasons for choosing are the same or similar. It makes no difference which group is listed first. You do not have to have as many groups as are shown below. If you have more than five groups, then indicate the additional groups on the back of the page.

After you have found the groups, check them again and make any necessary changes. Now begin by writing the names of the occupations in Group 1 below.

FIGURE 11–3 *Continued*

Likes

Group 1: _____   _____

_____   _____

_____   _____

What is similar about this group?

Why are you choosing this group? What do you like about these occupations? Be as explicit as possible!

Themes: What generalities or themes do the above comments suggest?

Group 2: _____   _____

_____   _____

_____   _____

What is similar about this group?

Why are you choosing this group? What do you like about these occupations? Be as explicit as possible!

Themes: What generalities or themes do the above comments suggest?

Group 3: _____   _____

_____   _____

_____   _____

What is similar about this group?

Why are you choosing this group? What do you like about these occupations? Be as explicit as possible!

Themes: What generalities or themes do the above comments suggest?

FIGURE 11–3   *Continued*

Group 4: _____   _____

_____   _____

_____   _____

What is similar about this group?

Why are you choosing this group? What do you like about these occupations? Be as explicit as possible!

Themes: What generalities or themes do the above comments suggest?

Group 5: _____   _____

_____   _____

_____   _____

What is similar about this group?

Why are you choosing this group? What do you like about these occupations? Be as explicit as possible!

Themes: What generalities or themes do the above comments suggest?

Now, do you want to make any changes in your "Like" groups? Do you see any occupations that do not really belong in the same group? Indicate below any changes you would make and why.

Step 4:

Spread your "Like" occupation cards out in front of you and place them in rank order from 1 to 10 as to the occupations you most prefer. Take all relevant factors into account in the ranking of these occupations.

FIGURE 11-3 *Continued*

(Copyright, all materials regarding the Missouri Occupational Card Sort (MOCS), the MOCS Manual, and this guide sheet, Board of Curators, University of Missouri, 1989.)

Your Top Ten Occupations

	Occupation	Values	Holland code
1.	_____	_____	_____
2.	_____	_____	_____
3.	_____	_____	_____
4.	_____	_____	_____
5.	_____	_____	_____
6.	_____	_____	_____
7.	_____	_____	_____
7.	_____	_____	_____
8.	_____	_____	_____
9.	_____	_____	_____
10.	_____	_____	_____

Indicate below any occupations that you also would like to include with the above list.

Step 5:

Go back to your list of Top Ten Occupations and write a short phrase or word to the right of each occupation that best indicates why *you* value that specific occupation. For example:

Physician	makes lots of money, uses science, challenging
Lawyer	prestige, public speaking, utilizes detail
Nurse	helps people, uses science, good job market
Teacher	the working hours, works with youth, summers off
Artist	independent, being creative, works with hands

Step 6:

Again, go back to your list of Top Ten Occupations and write down the three-letter Holland code for each occupation. These codes can be found on the back of each card.

Now summarize your Holland codes by counting how many times each letter appears on your list. Indicate the numbers below:

_____	_____	_____
Most Frequent Code (Highest Number Above)	Second Most Frequent Code (2nd Highest Number)	Third Most Frequent Code (3rd Highest Number)

What additional occupations do these Holland codes suggest? (To identify related occupations, you might use the Holland Booklet, Occupational Finder, or the Dictionary of Holland Occupational Codes.)

FIGURE 11–3   *Continued*

said earlier. It is not unlike a counseling interview in which you help the client to see patterns in what they are saying that may not be obvious to them. You would have Tanya sort all the titles in the DISLIKE pile before trying to sum up with her what seems to be emerging themes as reasons for not entering these occupations. As Tanya reports the themes, you make notes for a later discussion. When the client isn't clear about a particular occupation, you may try to help place it in an appropriate category. The less articulate client or a particularly confused client may need more help with this process. The challenge is to tailor the process to the particular needs of your client. Initially, you may follow the six steps outlined in Figure 11–3, but with practice you can adapt your style to the particular needs of each client.

You then repeat the process with the LIKE pile of occupations. You might argue for starting with this pile rather than the DISLIKE pile, but usually it is best to end with these themes that will determine eventual choices, not the ones being rejected. An initial inspection of the size of the three piles may tell you where best to begin as well. Sometimes there will be too few in the LIKE pile and a large NEUTRAL pile or DISLIKE pile. That may favor starting with the NEUTRAL pile in an effort to tease some of those into the LIKE pile. While we outline the usual procedures, we must emphasize again that there is no right way to proceed with a card sort. Experiment and decide what works best for you and a particular client. We suggest you vary the process so that you are able to choose the best process for each client.

A typical card sort interview might last an hour. If shorter, you may not be getting all you should from the process; if much longer, you may need to break it into parts. Here you would work only with the LIKES one time, the DISLIKES another time, and maybe even try to tie it all together in a third interview. You must be convinced that the process will yield some helpful data and you must convey that impression to the client as well. While Tanya may be skeptical about another standardized assessment, typically one comes convinced that is what she wants. Clients are apt to have doubts about these less standardized approaches. This is especially true considering that you are trying to convince them that they know best what they should do, and they come to you believing you know the answers.

You may or may not be able to convince the client of the value of the process, but you should be convinced yourself. You should be comfortable knowing that you are trying to build on what the clients already know about themselves and that you are doing it through a process that should be helpful to them as they incorporate new information about occupations. There is evidence that this process of sorting out occupations may be the same process the clients use for sorting ideas about other things like jobs, friends, mates, places to live or goods to buy. All decisions may involve a similar decision-making process and a client may become more skillful in one area as she learns more about the process in another area. You certainly minimize her dependence on you while optimizing the opportunity for her to use you as a resource. There is no waiting for scoring, and no age, sex, ethnic or cultural bias in the construction of the instrument. Contrary to what you might find with a standardized instrument, there is no need to conform to a set of rigid practices regarding the administration.

Let us provide some hypotheses about why this process might better help Tanya at this particular point. She obviously felt she learned little from the earlier process with a standardized test. She had the most difficult of profiles to interpret—the flat profile. Her interests were not like the interests of any particular group, which is not very helpful to one looking for an alternative. You can say further exploration will probably change the profile, but that isn't too helpful to her right now. You can say that having marked too many items as neutral or uncertain may have contributed to the flat profile, but again, that isn't too helpful. You can say we are not sure how well the inventory represents the interests of minorities, but that too is not what Tanya needs to hear. None of these reservations apply to a card sort. It is likely that from the sorting process Tanya can begin to verbalize many themes that are likely to surround her sense of uneasiness about her career choice. She will find it helpful to express that she wants something different: perhaps something less competitive, something that rewards more individual initiative rather than team effort, promotes the theme of helping others but in a more people oriented-way, and where money is a less important goal. You expect these and others ideas, given a supportive counseling relationship, are apt to emerge and be considered as important variables in her ultimate career decision. These are not variables that emerge as easily from the usual format employed in interpreting a standardized interest inventory. We expect that Tanya will at this point be better served by this process of talking through her concerns rather than again measuring her interests.

It is well known that students like Tanya know more about themselves than they think. Standardized interest inventories probably do little better at predicting career choices than simply asking a client what they want to do. Building on this evidence, there is good reason to believe that you can be quite helpful with card sorts in helping clients uncover what they already know but have not been able to put together for themselves. Combined with the more standardized instruments, you strengthen your ability to build good working alliances with your clients and you make the other standardized test information more understandable and interpretable.

A CONCLUDING THOUGHT

One may be initially concerned that finding the themes with a client will be difficult, but we think you will be surprised. We offer a list of some of the common themes and subthemes that have surfaced from various sessions (See Figure 11–4).

As you can see, the list is almost endless. More important, you'll be surprised at how easy it is for your client to come up with themes—often ones you would not think to include if you were attempting to standardize the process. It is precisely for this reason that we urge you to let the themes flow from clients and then try to help them make sense of them as presented. More attention is given the process of identifying themes in Chapter 14.

1. ACHIEVEMENT
Sense of accomplishment. Attain goals. Need to be successful. Fear of failure. See results. Making a contribution.

2. ADVANCEMENT OPPORTUNITIES
Mobility upwards. Dead-end jobs. Menial (no upward movement).

3. AUTONOMY
Be my own boss. Use my own initiative. Choose and direct my own lifestyle. Self-sufficiency. Manage my own time. Doing someone else's work.

4. BENEFITS
Vacations. Unions. Retirement plans.

5. CHALLENGING/BORING
Physically (works body hard). Mentally stimulating. Meeting others needs or demands. Very hard to be successful. Need for competition. Boring.

6. CREATIVITY
Use my hands. Express myself. Use my imagination.

7. DIVERSITY/REPETITIONS
Different tasks. Different people. Different places. Different things. Too much repetition.

8. EARLY INFLUENCES
Fantasy. Parents. Others.

9. EFFORT REQUIRED
Too much manual labor. Not enough manual labor. Occupation comes naturally.

10. EXCITEMENT
Adventure.

11. GEOGRAPHIC BOUNDS
Tied to hometown. Tied to one type of location (city, country, suburbs).

FIGURE 11–4   Classifiers and Sub-Classifiers-Derived from the MOCS

12. GENUINENESS/DISSONANCE
Feels false doing this. Makes me go against my values. Lets me be myself. Honesty in my work. Religious reasons.

13. JOB MARKET
Occupation in demand. Occupation not in demand.

14. LIFESTYLE
Family life. Night life. Farm. Settled. Familiarity.

15. MEANINGFUL/MEANINGLESS
Practical. Superficial. Not needed.

16. MONETARY REWARD
Pays well. Doesn't pay well.

17. PACE OF WORK
Slow. Fast. Just right for me. Steady. Sporadic.

18. PAST EXPERIENCE
Previous job. Previous education. People in occupation.

19. PHOBIA/REPULSION
All animals. Snakes. Blood. Audiences. Sick people. Dirty hands. Pain. Flying. Physical contact. Guns. Doctors.

20. POWER
Control or direct others. Authoritarian role. Change society. Influence others.

21. PREPARATION REQUIRED
Too long. Too demanding. Not enough payoff for investment. Realistic.

22. PRESTIGE
Do something important. Care about how others view me. Get attention from others. Dislike being a "peon." "Professional" stereotype. Menial occupation.

23. RESPONSIBILITY
Immediate. Delayed. Physical. Mental. Too much or too little responsibility.

24. SAFETY OR HEALTH
Occupation would cause physical harm. Occupation would give me ulcers. Occu-

pation would make me crazy. Occupation would keep me healthy.

25. SECURITY
Monetary. Job. Position.

26. SELF JUDGEMENT
Ability. Talent. Personality (high, low, ok, questionable, patience, outgoing, introverted, aggressive, manipulative, perfectionist).

27. STEREOTYPE
Sex. Parental. Previous experience. Ability. Occupation as seen in general. Gay. Age-role. Inconsiderate people in occupation.

28. STRESS
Makes me nervous. I'm too emotional.

29. STRUCTURE
Structured. Flexible. Ambiguity. Orderly (hours, task, supervisor relations, goals, lifestyle).

30. TRAVEL
Excitement. Diversity. New culture. Away from home. Discovery. Fantasy. Relaxing.

31. VIRTUE
Altruism. Holier than thou. Don't like to force others. Lack of respect. Most in occupation do it for money. Help needy.

32. UNDERSTANDING
Self. Others. World. Existential questions. How things work. Know how (get feedback, help others, their culture).

33. WORKING ENVIRONMENT
Outdoors. Indoors. Alone. Social (too dirty, can't take the elements, close to nature, office too confining).

34. WORKING WITH CONCEPTS
Researching, investigating. Using my head. Math or physics. Ambiguity. Foreign language. Science.

FIGURE 11–4   *Continued*

REFERENCES

Garson, R. A., & Johnston, J. A. (2001) *College major finder sort.* Columbia, MO: Career Center, University of Missouri-Columbia.

Goldman, L. (1983). The vocational card sort technique: A different view. *Measurement and Evaluation in Guidance, 16* (2), 107–109.

Hansen, R. N., Johnston, J. A., & Wong, S. C. (2002). *Missouri occupational card sort,* 3rd ed. Columbia, MO: Career Center, University of Missouri-Columbia.

Heim, L. L., & Johnston, J. A. (1991). *Missouri Occupational Card Sort. Community/Junior College Edition.* Columbia, MO: Career Center, University of Missouri-Columbia.

Holland, J. L. and Associates. (1980). *The Vocational Exploration and Insight Kit* (VEIK). Palo Alto, CA: Consulting Psychologists Press.

Jones, L. K. (1979). Occu-Sort: Development and evaluation of an occupational card sort system. *Vocational Guidance Quarterly, 28,* 56–62.

Knowdell, R. L. (1995a). *Motivated skills card sort kit.* San Jose, CA: Career Research and Testing.

Knowdell, R. L. (1995b). *Values card sort planning kit.* San Jose, CA: Career Research and Testing.

Krieshok, T. S., Hansen, R. N., Johnston, J. A., & Wong, S. C. (2002). *Missouri occupational card sort manual,* 3rd ed. Columbia, MO: Career Center, University of Missouri-Columbia.

▶ 12

Gathering Client Information Using Selected Standardized Tests and Inventories

An In-Depth Approach

The evidence for how tests improve the process by which clients understand themselves and their fit with particular environments, is compelling (Holland, 1985). Not only do tests improve the process and the outcomes of career counseling, but the use of such assessments promotes a more scientific orientation and gives us ways to support and confirm what might otherwise be little more than good speculation. While many decisions are explained as leaps of faith, most clients want to make decisions with prior support from hard evidence. Clients expect us to employ the best tools that are available to help them in their exploration. We want to do that as well, especially when we find that it not only enhances the outcome but provides us with better data to help other clients resolve their problems and reach their goals.

FINDING THE RIGHT STANDARDIZED TESTS

It is estimated that there are hundreds of assessment instruments that might be of help in career counseling. There are interest, aptitude, and ability tests, personality and values inventories, environmental assessments, state and trait measures, survey forms, card sorts, computerized assessments, and the list goes on and on. Current reviews of most of these can be found in Kapes and Whitfield's (2002) *A Counselor's Guide to Career Assessment Instruments*

(4th Edition), a publication of The National Career Development Association. It is our belief, however, that counselors typically learn to use well only a select number of assessments in career counseling. These are ones that best support or affirm their point of view, and with practice and experience, ones they become more and more proficient at using. These are usually the tests they learned to use in their graduate training, and once on the job, they simply continue with these rather than learn about new ones that might be better or more useful.

We applaud the use of a particular group of tests but caution against deciding on that number and not being open to learning about new instruments, because many good ones are still being developed or at least were developed after many counselors finished their graduate training. Further, as we learn more about the appropriateness of tailoring tests to particular populations and developing gender, ethnic origin, race, spirituality, sexual orientation, and social class specific norms, the profession is questioning the value of many of our earlier approaches to assessment. It is a burgeoning area and one can expect it will continue to change fairly dramatically in the next few years.

We can, however, be relatively sure that it will continue to be appropriate to use a variety of assessments to help us better understand where a typical client is in the career counseling and planning process. We need to confirm results from one assessment with results from another. We also need to recognize that many of our traditionally accepted measures may not be appropriate for many clients from non-majority populations that now are becoming more frequent users of career services. This is one more reason for remaining open to new measures. We may continue to rely heavily and even become dependent upon a small number of instruments, but we should still remain vigilant about our own assessment of new or additional ones that might better complement the career counseling process.

In this chapter, we will first suggest criteria for selecting appropriate standardized tests and then identify and focus on a small battery of assessment tools that have proven particularly effective in our professional practices and settings. It is important to keep in mind your orientation and employment setting as we identify instruments that can be most useful. If your orientation is to be directive, for example, and you want to be able to tell clients what to do, you want to find instruments that best support that approach. If you are in a setting that encourages time-limited career counseling or one that expects clients to be fairly self-directed, then you will want to choose instruments that promote outcomes in a timely fashion and/or allow clients to work with assessments on their own. Because many of us will change orientation or setting over time, we should remain flexible and open to new instruments; we may suddenly have to find new instruments to better meet our needs and the needs of our clients.

It is not unusual for professionals to depend on a select group of assessments that work particularly well for them in their particular setting. These assessments complement a particular orientation and setting(s). We will describe the criteria we believe influence selections and that influenced our selections of the particular instruments described in this chapter. We expect that you will want to use a similar process in choosing ones that should be most helpful to you in your setting. We find it helpful first to be clear about the criteria; this makes it easy both to identify the appropriateness of what you choose and it helps one evaluate the need for new instruments as they move to new settings. As we take you through this process, think about your own orientation and setting and whether the criteria suggests similar or different instruments for you.

CRITERIA FOR CHOOSING ASSESSMENTS

Some of the criteria for choosing particular instruments would include (a) validity, (b) reliability, (c) cost, (d) time for administration, (e) client response to the instrument, (f) training needed for scoring, (g) scoring difficulty, (h) norms, (i) training needed for interpretations, and perhaps most important, (j) usefulness of the instrument to the client. How important each of these is may depend on a careful observation of the staff, the setting, and the clients to be served. For example, in some settings paraprofessionals might provide the initial contacts for clients. If so, we might need or choose instruments they can competently use. There are many good ones they can become competent with, such as card sorts, computerized assessments (SIGI, DISCOVER, CHOICES, etc.), the My Vocational Situation (MVS), the Occupational Dreams Inventory (ODI), the Self-Directed Search (SDS), and other self-directed instruments. The paraprofessionals can describe well the availability of other assessments, but not use them themselves. They can refer clients to others for individual assessments and career counseling. Those professionals will employ a different set of assessments that they are most comfortable with as well. The criteria for selecting the ones used depends on both the individual's background, training, place of employment, and personal preferences. It should also depend on some less obvious but equally important criteria that assumes we do some homework before making our decisions.

First Points to Consider: Validity and Reliability

There are two test properties that must be first considered in selecting instruments, independent of who will be using them. First, we must be concerned about their validity and reliability. We refer you to basic measurement books (Anastasi, 1988; Lyman, 1986) to appreciate the importance of these concepts. We also remind you that both of these are relative terms: You never find completely valid or reliable instruments, only some that are more valid or more reliable than others. Nevertheless, both validity and reliability need our careful and professional judgment, especially because many clients come to us expecting more than we can honestly provide. We need to be sure we are working with the very best of what is available and that we are always open to finding something better. This is one of our professional obligations.

Validity

Perhaps the most important test property to consider is validity. How well does the test really measure what it says it measures? In the career area this often means that if an instrument indicates a person has strong interests in certain occupations, how true is that? Validity information is gained in a variety of ways, such as looking at how well it predicts behavior and satisfaction of test takers (predictive validity), how close its relation is to constructs that seem theoretically similar (construct validity), and how unrelated it is to scores on measures that seem theoretically dissimilar.

It is also very important to examine the populations on which the instrument has been normed, and the similarity of these populations to the clients to whom you will be administering it. For example, if an instrument has been developed using college populations and you want to use it with adults, it would be very important to determine how valid the instrument is with your population.

This point is particularly true for members of racial–ethnic minority groups, disabled individuals, and other underrepresented groups. Often our assessment measures have not had significant numbers of these groups within the norming and psychometric development research. Thus, in many cases, we have little information regarding the validity of instruments for these populations. Although we have no reason to think there would be any race-based biological difference in scores, we do know that we should recognize the different social and cultural histories and experiences of these underrepresented groups. For an excellent review of validity issues of career assessment instruments as they apply to the four major racial and ethnic minority groups in the United States, see Leong's *Career Development and Vocational Behavior of Racial and Ethnic Minorities* (1995). For another excellent review of the current status of career assessments for women, see Walsh and Osipow's *Career Counseling for Women* (1994).

Reliability

Another critical property to examine is reliability. How stable is the instrument over time? If we give the instrument twice, spaced three weeks apart, and little has changed in our client's experience, will we get almost the same scores? This property is very important in career assessments. If a test has poor reliability and an individual is told one week that she has interests similar to a psychologist and the next week to a tax collector, this data is not very useful to her. Even more harmful is that clients usually don't retake tests, so if they were given unreliable information one week, they may act on it, never knowing it was the product of an unreliable instrument.

The developer of an assessment instrument is always concerned with how valid and reliable the instrument really is, and usually will be constantly refining it. New items can be added, or items that didn't contribute much to the reliability can be deleted or replaced with better items. Depending on the construct being assessed, however, we need certain levels of assurances that what has been measured is valid and reliable. Yes, we can qualify our reporting in appropriate ways, but if we can't speak with some certainty about the probability of success with the measurement of interests, aptitudes, skills, and other important traits, we lose credibility with our client.

If the available measures in this field were as valid and reliable as they are in some of the hard sciences, we could move quickly beyond discussion of the nuances of validity and reliability. In the hard sciences, it may be possible to predict a happening with some certainty and also be assured that it will always happen that way. That measure may be both perfectly valid and reliable. In dealing with people, and particularly where free choice will be part of the equation, there is no measure that is perfectly valid or reliable. The best of our instruments will always leave room for one to question the results. Even when the measure used is quite valid, the individual will take that information and process it with other information that is available. That is precisely why we need to spend time interpreting and integrating results from various standardized tests.

Several points should be made here. First, we must attend to the validity and reliability of our measures in the interest of selecting good tests and because we later depend on that information to support our professional interpretations or judgments. Additionally, however, we must recognize that we will always be choosing instruments that aren't as valid as we would like them to be in this area. Standardized tests are available to help us make better judgments; they do not make judgments for us or the client. Once we accept this point, we can properly view these measures the same way we do any other set of resources that are available to help us with the career counseling process. For further information regarding the validity and reliability of specific tests, see the references cited in Tables 12–1 through 12–6.

Other Points to Consider in Choosing Assessments

Let's continue our discussion of criteria for choosing a standardized instrument. Are we looking for an instrument to administer to one client or to a large group? When one wants assessments to be available for large numbers, then costs, time for administration, ease of scoring and reporting results, extent to which one needs training to interpret results, and usefulness of the results to the client all become issues. We sometimes choose a measure primarily because it is cost effective for large numbers, can be scored immediately, or the results do not require a professional interpretation.

An expanded criteria for consideration of what instruments to use in mass administrations would include not only the validity and reliability of the instrument, but the cost as well. Next would be how much time is involved in administration and the expected response of the client to taking it. Also, if you give it to one or a hundred students, how easy is it to score? Or even more important, can it be self-scored in some situations? Can one receive immediate feedback on the results or will it have to be sent away to be scored? Does scoring it require someone with training? Are there good norms for the group you are testing? Is there an interpretative guide that might let the client understand the results without seeing a counselor? In our career center, all these would be important considerations in deciding on an instrument to use in an administration to students. In Table 12–1, we have listed the criteria used, for example, in choosing the My Vocational Situation (MVS) over other standardized tests. One can see that it measures up well to the criteria suggested.

You may want to start with several low-cost screening tools like the MVS (Holland, Daiger, & Power, 1980). A critical review of the usefulness of the MVS is provided in an article by Holland et al. (Holland, Johnston, and Asama, 1993). There are many good short assessment instruments that are inexpensive, easily administered and scored, and useful in workshops or other situations where immediate scoring and feedback are important. Reviews of these appear in *A Counselor's Guide to Career Assessment Instru-*

TABLE 12–1   Criteria Used for Selecting the My Vocational Situation

Criteria	Comment
Validity	See References*
Reliability	See References*
Cost	Minimal
Time for administration	Very short
Client response to taking instrument	Usually positive
Training needed for scoring	Minimal
Scoring	Self-scoring, easy
Availability of norms for particular population	Excellent
Training needed for interpretation	Minimal
Usefulness to client	Considerable

*See *Mental Measurement Yearbook, 1985* (9th Ed., Vol. II, pp. 1,026–1,029) and/or Kapes and Whitfield's (2002) *A Counselor's Guide to Career Assessment Instruments* (4th Ed., pp. 30–32).

ments or any of the *Mental Measurement Yearbooks,* which are also where you will find extensive consideration of the issues of validity and reliability of most instruments. We also encourage you to read carefully the manuals for all instruments you choose. Authors are very concerned that you understand what is available to support their assessments. We should reinforce here, however, that typically one can and often does have to assess the usefulness of a measure as one part of a battery of assessment. That is, usually it is only one of a number of measures or indices that we have available or have administered, and it becomes important to consider how well it works in concert with those other instruments.

A BASIC BATTERY OF CAREER ASSESSMENT

In a general way, we look for methods of assessing the state of one's vocational situation (e.g., MVS-type measures), their interests, their personality, and perhaps their skills, aptitudes, values, and beliefs. We may need an assessment instrument that works well in each of these areas. When we are choosing a battery of instruments, we add to our criteria that the assessment instruments work well together or perhaps even complement one another. Sometimes you have to reassess the usefulness of an instrument when it is only one of many assessments you want to use. But let's look at a basic instrument for each of the areas we have identified and select one that might best meet the criteria we have suggested would be important. While we apply the criteria to the use of the instruments in a career center, you should think about how well each would apply where you work.

A BASIC INTEREST INVENTORY: THE SELF-DIRECTED SEARCH

The most widely used assessment of interests today is the Self-Directed Search (SDS) written by John Holland (Holland, 1985). It can be easily administered, self-scored, and self-interpreted, and it provides a vast array of information that a self-directed client can find particularly useful. It subtly helps teach a system or plan for further career exploration and, with the aid of several guides, it can direct one to further explore possible jobs or careers that would be appropriate for one with a particular pattern of scores. It has good validity and reliability, is easily administered, scored, and interpreted, is reasonable in cost, can be given to almost any client (reading level is minimal and Form E (Holland, Powell, & Fritzsche, 1994) is available for even lower reading levels), and fits well with other instruments routinely used in a career center. How it measures up to our criteria is illustrated in Table 12–2.

TABLE 12-2   Criteria Used in Selecting the SDS

Criteria	Comment
Validity	See References*
Reliability	See References*
Cost	Inexpensive
Time for administration	30–45 minutes
Client response to taking instrument	Usually good
Scoring	Self-scoring
Availability of norms	Extensive
Training needed for interpretation	Considerable
Usefulness to client	Varied

*See *Mental Measurement Yearbook, 1989* (10th Ed., pp. 738–740) and/or Kapes and Whitfield's (2002) *A Counselors Guide to Career Assessment Instruments* (4th Ed., pp. 276–287).

What helped most in determining our choice of this instrument was our decision to adopt Holland's six occupational themes as an organizing feature of our center (1985). Information is stored in the pattern suggested by the scores received on the instrument. Individuals look for additional information in line with their scores on the instrument, and this is the way it is organized in our career center. It also permits broad consideration of a variety of factors to be considered in career exploration, including occupational daydreams and interests and skills, and the client can easily ascertain how the scores were derived.

There are other good interest inventories that may be equally appropriate in other settings. One can argue for having more than one assessment of interests for some clients, but the basic day-to-day practical value of the SDS for us in our career center is convincing. Paraprofessional staff members can be helpful with the administration and interpretations, and it reinforces what we teach and what we want students to learn about the career exploration process. We want students to explore on their own, and we want the exploration process to organize and simplify a complex process. The SDS also allows for being able to provide immediate feedback, which is also quite important.

A Basic Measure of Personality

Personality measures may assume more importance in some settings than others, but it is fair to say everyone needs at least one measure that can assess the basic dimensions of the personality. Which dimensions we measure may depend on who our typical client is and the typical concerns of the client. In making career assessments in a school or college setting, you usually deal with high functioning individuals. You are looking for indices of fit with particular majors, careers, or job environments and you most often are sharing that information with the client. This makes some instruments more applicable than others. We opt for the NEO Personality Inventory (NEO-PI) by Costa and McCrae (McCrae, 1992) for some of the same reasons we provided for using the SDS. It has good psychometric properties (validity and reliability), can be self-directed and completed in a short period of time, has good interpretation guides or talk sheets to supplement an understanding of the results, and is inexpensive and unobtrusive for most clients. Not all measures of personality could meet that criteria.

After many years of personality assessment, there appears to have emerged some consensus about the essential indices to be considered. The NEO-PI is cited as measuring well all of "the big five" indices: neuroticism, extroversion, openness, conscientiousness, and agreeableness. All of these can be shown to be related to career decision making and all are dimensions that can easily be used by clients in understanding their particular approach to dealing with career issues and problems. The relationship of NEO-PI scores to SDS scores strongly supports the relatedness of personality and interests (Gottfredson, Jones, & Holland, 1993).

A quick review of how well it meets the criteria we have been establishing for choosing assessment measures appears in Table 12–3.

A Measure of Aptitudes and/or Skills

Career clients frequently ask for some test of their skills. They want to know what they really are good at, and yet, particularly with college students, they

TABLE 12–3   Criteria Used in Selecting the NEO

Criteria	Comment
Validity	See References*
Reliability	See References*
Cost	Moderate
Time for administration	40–45 minutes
Client response to taking instrument	Fair
Scoring	Hand scoring available
Availability of norms	Fair
Training needed for interpretation	Considerable
Usefulness to client	Somewhat

*See *Mental Measurement Yearbook, 1995* (12th Ed., pp. 861–868).

already know that based on their high school performance and often some work experience. What they more likely are asking is, What aptitudes or skills do I have that might better determine my choice of a major or eventually help me find employment? Even when the evidence is already there, they seek confirmation of it, or better ways to utilize the aptitude or skill they know they possess. One will hear something like, "I'm good at math, but I don't know what to do with it" or "I'm good at drawing, but who would hire me?" Sometimes the inquiry begins when a student is having difficulty with a course that is required in the major and that starts a reexamination of his or her strengths. It becomes a matter of believing that an alternative is needed. More times than not, they seek reassurance, and when you help them review their high school grades, their SAT or ACT scores, and the courses or life experiences they have enjoyed the most, they reconsider the need for any extensive reexamination of aptitudes or skills.

The SDS, for example, provides an inventory of skills and aptitudes as part of the assessment of an individual's identification with the six areas of interest. Most clients don't realize this or need to have it called to their attention. They complete the instrument with little hesitation and when confronted with the evidence for how well their estimates correlate with more objective measures of their aptitudes, they often elect not to take additional tests.

Laid-off workers or employees being asked to transfer to an entirely new job may be more insistent and in need of aptitude or skill measures. When appropriate, a good aptitude or skills measure or measures can be quite helpful.

The Campbell Interest and Skills Inventory (Campbell, 1995), a relatively new instrument, is an assessment tool that meets much of the criteria we have established for practical use in our center. It has good validity and reliability, is easy to administer, and is inexpensive. But at this time, it is not easily scored and requires considerable training before one can be comfortable presenting the results to a client.

Table 12–4 shows how it measures up on our criteria. In this case, some compromise with the criteria may be necessary to find a good measure. For example, choosing to measure aptitude in ways that will provide clients with evidence not already available to them may take some time. If they haven't accumulated enough evidence to be sure on their aptitudes and skills, they must expect to invest some time in finding more than reassurance.

At the high school level, the Differential Aptitude Test or something similar might make more sense. In many school districts, counselors are required to use particular aptitude measures and, of course, you should first learn and make use of as much as you can about those measures as opposed to introducing others.

TABLE 12–4   Criteria Used in Selecting the Campbell Interest & Skills Inventory

Criteria	Comment
Validity	See References*
Reliability	See References*
Cost	Inexpensive
Time for administration	Minutes
Client response to taking instrument	Good
Scoring	Machine scored
Availability of norms	Fair
Training needed for interpretation	Considerable
Usefulness to client	Useful

*See appropriate volume of the *Mental Measurement Yearbook*, and/ or Kapes and Whitfield's (2002) *A Counselor's guide to career assessment instruments*, (4th Ed., pp. 194–201).

Measures of Career Beliefs

The literature on self-efficacy suggests that often it is not what people have as aptitudes or skills, but what they *believe* they have that makes the difference in how they behave or will perform. A good part of career counseling is helping clients understand what they believe about themselves and their particular situation. Sometimes clients seek help when they most begin to doubt what they can do or believe they can do. Reassurance, or taking stock of where they are or what they have going for themselves, becomes very helpful. Our best inventory for this has been the Career Transitions Inventory (CTI) (Heppner, Multon, & Johnston, 1994). It promotes an examination of five of the most common beliefs that may affect one trying to negotiate a career transition. It was developed for adults who are going through voluntary or involuntary career transitions. It meets our criteria exceptionally well, as you can see in Table 12–5. A more complete discussion of the instrument appears in Chapter 13 in this book.

Other Supplementary Measures

The Hope Scale is a good example of a brief measure that has proven particularly helpful to us in working with groups of clients facing layoffs. Trying to establish in easy fashion whether there were participants in these groups with minimal goals (low self-efficacy) or confusion as to how to get there (low on pathways), we routinely use the Hope Scale, a 16-item inventory initially devised by C. R. Snyder (Snyder et al., 1991) to be used with children. We

TABLE 12–5   Criteria Used for Selecting the Career Transitions Inventory

Criteria	Comment
Validity	See References*
Reliability (for this group at this time)	See References*
Cost	Inexpensive
Time for administration	10–15 minutes
Client response to taking instrument	Usually positive
Training needed for scoring	Little
Scoring	Self-scoring
Availability of norms	Excellent for adults
Training needed for interpretation	Some
Usefulness to client	Considerable

*See Heppner, M. J. (1991) reference.

found that adults who indicated little sense of goals or pathways were ones who needed individual attention in workshops. We changed the name of the inventory to Intake Scale (with permission) and it screened a number of people who then were given more individual attention in workshops. It also holds up well on our criteria (see Table 12–6).

There are numerous such inventories available and they often serve a useful role when other more time-consuming assessments might not be practical. The Hope Scale (sometimes called the Intake Scale), like the MVS, can be used by the skilled practitioner with minimum training and can be scored in virtu-

TABLE 12–6   Criteria Used for Selecting the Hope Scale

Criteria	Comment
Validity	See References*
Reliability (for this group at this time)	See References*
Cost	Inexpensive
Time for administration	3–5 minutes
Client response to taking instrument	Positive
Training needed for scoring	Little
Scoring	Simple
Availability of norms	Limited
Training needed for interpretation	Little (usually not interpreted to client)
Usefulness to client	Helpful screening tool

*See Snyder et al. (1991) reference.

ally no time at all. The Occupational Dreams Inventory (ODI), a stand-alone adaptation from the SDS (see Fig. 12–1), is an easy way to begin a conversation with a client about career plans. We refer you again to either the *Mental Measurement Yearbook* or Kapes and Whitfield's (2002) reviews of some of these instruments.

BRINGING TEST DATA TOGETHER

We give tests to supplement other data we have on clients or that clients have on themselves. In many cases, we gather the assessment data to help establish a clearer picture of the client, and then, in an individual session, to convey that

Name _____   Date _____

- List five occupations you have considered in thinking about your future. List both ones you have dreamed about as well as those you have discussed with others.

- *Appeal*   *Occupations*

- ___ ___   _____

- ___ ___   _____

- ___ ___   _____

- ___ ___   _____

- ___ ___   _____

- Now arrange each in terms of their apeal to you today, i.e. place a 1 in front of the one which has the most appeal, a 2 in front of the one with the next most appeal, and so forth.

- Put a circle around the one(s) that others think you should do (parents, spouse, best friend, relative, teacher, etc.).

- Put an "I" in front of any that seem impossible because of requirements (educational, financial, personal, etc).

- Put an "F" in front of any that represent "fantasy" choices (fun but not realistic in your opinion).

- Put an "H" in front of any that might qualify more as what you would pursue as a hobby or avocation.

FIGURE 12–1   Occupational Dreams Inventory

information to our client. Both tasks require gathering enough of the right information so it can then be presented in a coherent and credible fashion to help us understand the client and eventually to help the client better understand him/herself. The process can be facilitated by putting all the test data on a single page or into a single report following a standard format. In Figure 12–2 we provide an example of how we typically record standardized test data with the SDS as the main instrument. This process helps the counselor see the relatedness of various scores. In putting all the scores on one page, we are forcing ourselves to be sure to use all the measures assessed in as integrated a way as possible. After all, we are looking at a single individual through multiple measures or lenses to support one composite picture.

The process just described—of being sure to properly use all the available data—is an equally appropriate approach to interpretation of a single set of scores from any one assessment. We should remember the test profiles are designed to be used primarily by professionals. The average client is not going to understand the results from a profile without your interpretation. As good as we are in interpreting data, clients don't always hear all we are trying to say or hear it as accurately as we hope. Our interpretations can be complemented with interpretative guides or "talk sheets," because they help make the results more easily understood and provide a written record for later reference by the client.

These guides or talk sheets should be available for all standardized assessment measures. If one is not available, we encourage you to develop your own. In Figures 12–3 and 12–4 we provide examples of particularly good ones, one for the MVS and the NEO-PI (Neuroticism, Extroversion, and Openness) Personality Inventory. In Chapter 13 the reader will also find one for the CTI (Career Transitions Inventory).

Integrating Test Data

We can best illustrate the integrated use of assessment data by showing our own use of a variety of measures with a single client. In this case, we present a client who was part of a two-day workshop where the assessments were administered and interpreted. This meant we needed to give careful consideration to several factors, including the time it would take to administer and score the measures, ease of scoring and interpretation, and because follow-up would be difficult, how easy would it be for the clients to understand the results later without our assistance. Because we typically work with each client as one member of a larger group and would need to do some of the interpretations in the group, we chose instruments that were easy to administer and complete; easy and quick to score and interpret; unobtrusive, because they would need to share results with others; and finally, instruments that as a battery of tests would not take too much of their time to complete.

Client's Name _____ Date _____

Interpretive Guide for Understanding Client's *SDS* Scores™

1. Background Data (age, employment status, sex, race, education, family history, etc.)

• Current Occupation/Major: _____ Code: _____

• Work History   Code

☐	_____	_____
☐	_____	_____
☐	_____	_____
☐	_____	_____
☐	_____	_____

Occupational Daydreams   Code

☐	_____	_____
☐	_____	_____
☐	_____	_____
☐	_____	_____
☐	_____	_____

Other Assessments (My Vocational Situation, Intake Scale, Career Transition Inventory, Myers-Briggs Type Indicator, etc.)

FIGURE 12–2 Interpretative Guide for Understanding Client's SDS Scores™

2. Codes to Explore—Full Exploration
(6–8 point rule)

3. Special Issues (flat profile—low or high; opposing interests; summary code very different from career goals; summary code skewed by work experience, societal roles, etc.)

4. Hypotheses:

Self-Directed Search™

Activities	R	I	A	S	E	C	
Competencies	R	I	A	S	E	C	
Occupations	R	I	A	S	E	C	
Self-Estimates	R	I	A	S	E	C	
	R	I	A	S	E	C	
Total Scores (Range: 2 to 50)	R	I	A	S	E	C	

Summary Code

Highest	2nd	3rd
☐	☐	☐

Counselor's Name _____

FIGURE 12–2 *Continued*

My Vocational Situation (MVS) is a questionnaire which measures how clear an understanding an individual has about his or her career plans. The first eighteen items make up the Vocational Identity Scale and will be used to determine the identity and stability of your career goals. Higher scores represent more clarity and certainty with the career decisions that you have made, whereas lower scores indicate that you have not made a definite decision about which career to pursue.

YOUR SCORE: 0   1   2   3   4   5   6   7   8   9   10   11   12   13   14   15   16   17   18

Interpretation of Your Score:

0-5   Scores within this range indicate that you may not have a clear idea about what college majors or careers would be best for you. You may need to learn more about your values, abilities, and interests and how they relate to career opportunities before you make any decisions about what career to pursue. Below are listed a few ideas about what you can do to help yourself get a clearer idea about what college major or career to pursue:

- Go through the Explore program
- Take a Career Exploration course
- Talk to a career counselor

- Ask about Faculty Mentoring at the Career Center
- Tell your advisor you want to learn more about majors
- Take the Missouri Occupational Card Sort

6-14   These scores indicate you have some understanding of careers and majors that you would like to pursue, and you are aware of many of your interests and abilities. You may not feel particularly pressured to make a decision now, but you have many of the resources needed to begin planning your future. You could benefit from some of the information that is available in the Career Center to help you find opportunities or experience in the fields you are considering, or to simply further your self understanding. Here are some things you could do to help clarify your goals:

- Take the Self-Directed Search
- Ask upperclassmen about choosing a major

- Read more about the careers you have interest in
- Take courses in the fields you are considering

15-18   These scores indicate that you feel confident with your major choice or have a good idea of your life's direction. You might still benefit from some of the resource information that the Career Center has to offer to help you further confirm your decisions. Also, the Career Center can help you to learn more about the career you have already chosen, in order for you to be better prepared for the challenges you must meet in order to succeed in that, or any other career. Here are a few ideas about what you can do:

- Talk to a faculty member or expert in the field
- Apply for a part-time job in your department

- Read more about your career interests
- Do research with faculty for course credit

FIGURE 12–3   Interpreting My Vocational Situation (MVS) Scores

The NEO inventory measures five broad domains, or dimensions, of personality. The responses that you gave to the statements about your thoughts, feelings, and goals can be compared with those of other adults to give a description of your personality.

For each of the five domains, descriptions are given below for different ranges of scores. The descriptions that are *checked* provide descriptions of *you*, based on your responses to the inventory items.

The NEO inventory measures differences among normal individuals. It is not a test of intelligence or ability, and it is not intended to diagnose problems of mental health or adjustment. It does, however, give you some idea about what makes you unique in your ways at thinking, feeling, and interacting with others.

This summary is intended to give you a general idea of how your personality might be described. It is not a detailed report. If you completed the inventory again, you might score somewhat differently. For most individuals, however, personality traits tend to be very stable in adulthood. Unless you experience major life changes or make deliberate efforts to change yourself, this summary should apply to you throughout your adult life.

Compared with the responses of other people, your responses suggest that you can be described as:

☐ Sensitive, emotional, and prone to experience feelings that are upsetting.

☐ Generally calm and able to deal with stress, but you sometimes experience feelings of guilt, anger, or sadness.

☐ Secure, hardy, and generally relaxed even under stressful conditions.

☐ Extroverted, outgoing, active, and high-spirited. You prefer to be around people most of the time.

☐ Moderate in activity and enthusiasm. You enjoy the company of others but you also value privacy.

☐ Introverted, reserved, and serious. You prefer to be alone or with a few close friends.

☐ Open to new experiences. You have broad interests and are very imaginative.

☐ Practical but willing to consider new ways of doing things. You seek a balance between the old and the new.

☐ Down-to-earth, practical, traditional, and pretty much set in your ways.

☐ Compassionate, good-natured, and eager to cooperate and avoid conflict.

☐ Generally warm, trusting, and agreeable, but you can sometimes be stubborn and competitive.

☐ Hardheaded, skeptical, proud, and competitive. You tend to express your anger directly.

☐ Conscientious and well-organized. You have high standards and always strive to achieve your goals.

☐ Dependable and moderately well-organized. You generally have clear goals but are able to set your work aside.

☐ Easygoing, not very well-organized, and sometimes careless. You prefer not to make plans.

FIGURE 12–4   Your NEO Summary
(Paul T. Costa, Jr., Ph.D., and Robert R. McCrae, Ph.D.)

We settled on the Hope Scale, the MVS, the SDS, the NEO, and the CTI (Career Transitions Inventory). We had breadth of assessments without taking too much of their time in completing them, and we found that each assessment contributed in some meaningful way to how we approached the participants and what they wanted to know about themselves. In broad brush, we used the Hope Scales and the MVS to quickly establish whether we had any participants who felt they were without goals or pathways or were without a reasonably clear sense of vocational identity to profit from the workshop format. When such was evident early, we could provide more individual time with these participants. We also used these two measures to help us make appropriate sense of the other assessment scores as will be evident from looking at the total array of scores presented on one interpretative guide that follows. We devised an "Interpretative Guide for Understanding Client's SDS Scores" and completed it on each workshop participant. You can follow our recording of the data as a series of steps that has us incorporate on a single page all the relevant observational and test data. In Step 1, Figure 12–5, we record the relevant background data, which usually includes age, employment status (previous and current), sex, race, education, family history, and other incidentals that might have bearing on understanding and interpreting the test data. Some clues, for example, may come from an intake form, from introductions made in the workshop, or from information offered in a phone conversation as one enrolled for the work-

Client's Name_____   Date_____

---

1. Background Data (age, employment status, sex, race, education, family history, etc.)

FIGURE 12–5   Step 1: Background Data

shop. Perhaps most important is identifying the expressed career choice(s) of the client. Surprisingly, this is sometimes overlooked, and yet it clearly will be a significant part of a client's eventual career decision.

In Step 2, Figure 12–6, we record the current occupation and work history of the client. If we are working with a student, occupation often may be more appropriately recorded as academic major. Using the *Dictionary of Holland Occupational Codes* (Gottfredson & Holland, 1996), we give that occupation a three-letter code. In Step 3, Figure 12–7, we record the occupational daydreams as taken from a personal data sheet.

We then code each occupational daydream again using *the Dictionary of Holland Occupational Codes*. We later will compare these with measured interests as established from the interest inventory and also from the occupational daydreams found on the first page of the Holland SDS interest inventory. The daydreams are recorded on the guide sheet because they too, like the

---

Current Occupation/Major: _____   Code: _____

Work History   Code

_____   _____

_____   _____

_____   _____

_____   _____

_____   _____

FIGURE 12–6   Step 2: Current Occupations and Work History

Occupational Daydreams   Code

_____   _____

_____   _____

_____   _____

_____   _____

FIGURE 12–7   Step 3: Occupational Daydreams and Other Assessments

expressed career choice(s), are often not given their due weight in the eventual discussion of choices based on the more objective test data. The daydreams too can be coded using the *Dictionary of Holland Occupational Codes*. It may appear as though we give too much attention to the daydreams, which are not as objective, but the evidence is that they predict eventual choice(s) about as well as any other measure we may employ. In fact, if one has already taken the SDS or some other interest inventory, we suggest you add the Occupational Dreams Inventory (ODI) mentioned earlier in this chapter. Dreams should always be considered in any discussion of career plans.

Next, we record other assessment data such as the MVS, the Hope Scores, or other Intake scores. We include here the relevant highs and/or low scores from the CTI. A rough classification of scores as high, moderate, or low makes it easy to record and interpret these scores. We include sample norms in Figure 12–8 for the My Vocational Situation (MVS), an Intake Scale, and the Career Transitions Inventory (CTI). You could devise a similar system for whatever inventories you use. We would add here any other measures that might influence the way we would interpret the eventual total array of test scores. A low MVS score or Hope scores, for example, would be important to note if we wanted to make appropriate use of one-on-one time with a client; that is, low scores suggesting individual time might be quite important or useful for the individual. All these scores are important overlays to interpreting the SDS scores that follow.

In Figure 12–9 one can see that the SDS scores can be recorded using actual raw scores from each of the five objective measures reported within the inventory: the activities scores, competencies scores, scores from the client's reactions to occupational titles, and the two self-estimates measures—one on abilities and the other on skills. In all, given that we have five measures and six scores on each measure, a total of 30 scores are recorded. When total scores are compiled for each of the six areas, and we have 36 scores from the interest inventory alone. All of these contribute to the summary code that is reported as the client's SDS code. One can by visual inspection see how each of the scores does or does not contribute to the final code. You also are recording self estimates or self-efficacy ratings for the client, and you can flag any inconsistencies for later discussion.

In Figure 12–10 there are three boxes for additional information about scores recorded so far.

Here we can make note of the author's suggested rules of interpretation for the SDS. In the box marked "Codes to Explore," we remind ourselves to list all three-letter codes that should be explored with the client based on the actual pattern of summary scores. Often referred to as the "rule of eight," it implies that summary scores really aren't different unless they total eight or more points (perhaps six or more points for older adults). Therefore, record all possible patterns here that should be explored. If the highest score, say R,

My Vocational Situation (MVS):   (Circle the appropriate level)

VI Score	11–18	7–10	0–6
Level of Vocational Identity	High	Moderate	Low

Intake Scale: (Circle the appropriate scores)

Scales	High	Moderate	Low
Agency/Goal	14–16	9–13	4–8
Pathways	15–16	10–14	4–9
Total	27–32	20–26	8–19

Career Transition Inventory (CTI) (Norms for revised 40-item version):
(Circle the appropriate scores)

Scales	High	Moderate	Low
Readiness	66–78	57–65	13–56
Confidence	48–66	39–47	11–38
Support	26–30	22–25	5–21
Personal Control	24–36	19–23	6–18
Independence	20–30	16–19	5–15

FIGURE 12–8

and the second highest score, say E, are only different by five points, you should explore RE occupations and ER occupations, because both are equally appropriate based on what has been measured. The client may be inclined to take the ordering literally and not explore fully unless one makes a point of it as part of the interpretation. (See manual for a more complete discussion of the rule of full exploration). A second box to the right of the SDS scores suggests that you make note of any special issues that need to be explained. For example, a low flat profile may need some explanation, or measured interests that seem to be the opposite of what were expressed, or a summary code that may seem to be overly influenced by previous work experience or a societal expectation, or a code that is rare and hence will not suggest many options when one looks for occupational alternatives. These are issues that may need to be pointed out and discussed as we try to make the best use of the test data.

Self-Directed Search™

Activities						
	R	I	A	S	E	C

Competencies						
	R	I	A	S	E	C

Occupations						
	R	I	A	S	E	C

Self-Estimates						
	R	I	A	S	E	C

	R	I	A	S	E	C

Total Scores (Range: 2 to 50)						
	R	I	A	S	E	C

Summary Code

☐ Highest   ☐ 2nd   ☐ 3rd

Counselor's Name _____

FIGURE 12–9

Finally, in the third box, we record hypotheses that we believe are worth exploring based on what we have observed and measured. These can be written in such a way that they can be shared, refined, or refuted with the client.

The Case of James

The use of the interpretative guide may be clearer if we apply the process to an actual case. In Table 12–7 we present scores for James (a participant in a workshop) who was laid off as a factory worker in rural Missouri. James was

Codes to Explore—Full Exploration
(6–8 point rule)

Special Issues (flat profile—low or high; opposing interests;
summary code very different from career goals; summary
code skewed by work experience, societal roles, etc.

Hypotheses:

FIGURE 12–10

56, white, male, working on his GED, and planning to attend a community
college now that he had time for it. The job he had was as a machine operator,
which is coded RIE. Previously, he had held jobs as shoe cutter (RSE), factory
inspector (RSE), and general factory worker (REC) all in the same plant. His
daydreams were to be a parole officer (SIE), an accountant (CRS), or a tax
preparation assistant (CES). Other assessments included a very low score on
the MVS (04); Hope Scores of 13 on Goals and 13 on Pathways; CTI scores
were high on readiness and independence, moderate on support and confidence, and low on control. SDS scores are reported in Table 12–7 and are generally low, although most recordings of the eventual code support the S code
to be highest and the C to be next, except that he didn't feel he had competencies in the C area (scored 3) or very high estimates of abilities or skills (4 and
3) in those areas. Codes to explore following the rule of full exploration
include SCI and SCE. Special issues to be noted include his minimal years of
education, his age, the relatively low profile of scores on the interest inventory, and the rather uncommon SDS code for an adult. At least two hypothe-

Interpretative Guide for Understanding Client's *SDS* Scores™

1. Background Data (age, employment status, sex, race, education, family history, etc.) Caucasion, male
age 56, working toward GED, laid off shoe factory worker

• Current Occupation/Major: _____ machine operator _____ Code: RIE

• Work History	Code	Occupational Daydreams	Code
☐ Shoe cutter	RSE	☐ Parole Officer	SIE
☐ Inspector	RSE	☐ Accountant	CRS
☐ Factory	REC	☐ Tax Preparer	CES
☐ Machine Operator	RIE	☐	
☐		☐	

Other Assessments (My Vocational Situation, Intake Scale, Career Transition Inventory, Myers-Briggs Type Indicator, etc.)
MVS = 04 Intake: Goal 13 Pathways 13 CTI – High on Readiness and
Independence but low on Personal Control

TABLE 12–7 Interpretative Guide for Understanding Client's SDS Scores™

Self-Directed Search™

	R	I	A	S	E	C
Activities	5	8	1	7	5	8
Competencies	4	1	2	8	5	3
Occupations	3	6	0	10	4	10
Self-Estimates	2	4	2	4	2	4
Self-Estimates	4	5	4	5	4	3
Total Scores (Range: 2 to 50)	18	24	9	34	20	28

Summary Code

S	C	I / E
Highest	2nd	3rd

2. Codes to Explore — Full Exploration
(6–8 point rule)

SCI
SCE

3. Special Issues (flat profile — low or high; opposing interests; summary code very different from career goals; summary code skewed by work experience, societal roles, etc.)

Age
Work experience
Uncommon SDS code

4. Hypotheses:

Would additional schooling be realistic?

Are daydreams realistic?

Counselor's Name _____

TABLE 12–7 *Continued*

ses present themselves: Is further schooling a realistic goal, and do the daydreams reflect appropriate next moves? Even before talking to him, you know you have at least two questions that need answers.

The talk sheet helps us focus on all the available data on the client. With practice, it helps one develop hypotheses about the client and it may help one see what is consistent and what still needs further exploration or explanation. The process is not unlike the one any professional—doctor, lawyer or accountant—might use in compiling information before an interview with their client. You might in time do as well without such forms, but initially they promote a discipline that can help make us all better counselors.

SUMMARY

Throughout this chapter, we have illustrated both the types of standardized instruments that are useful and the logic of utilizing a number of them in helping to construct a coherent picture of a client. We have emphasized how putting it all together on an interpretative guide helps with the process, and that it takes effort and skill to do this for a client. This chapter adds standardized tests to other approaches already discussed, such as the structured interview and the career geneogram. The next chapter will introduce some less standardized approaches to career assessments. While we probably will come to rely on a small group of assessments as we work with clients, we again stress that we need to always remain open to finding new measures and approaches to making information work for us and our clients.

REFERENCES

Anastasi, A. (1988). *Psychological Testing* (6th ed.). New York: Macmillan.

Campbell, D. P. (1995). The Campbell Interest and Skill Survey (CISS): A product of ninety years of psychometric evolution. *Journal of Career Assessment, 3,* 391–410.

Gottfredson, G. D., & Holland, J. L. (1996). *Dictionary of Holland Occupational Codes* (3rd ed.). Odessa, FL: Psychological Assessment Resources, Inc.

Gottfredson, G. D., Jones, E. M., & Holland, J. L. (1993). Personality and vocational interests: The relation of Holland's six interest dimensions to the five robust dimensions of personality. *Journal of Counseling Psychology, 40,* 518–524.

Heppner, M. J. (1991). The CTI is available from Mary J. Heppner, Ph.D., 201 Student Success Center, University of Missouri, Columbia, Missouri 65211.

Heppner, M. J., Multon, R. D., & Johnston, J. A. (1994). Assessing psychological resources during career change: Development of the Career Transitions Inventory. *Journal of Vocational Behavior, 44,* 55–74.

Holland, J. L. (1985). *Self-directed search* (1985 ed.). Odessa, FL: Psychological Assessment Resources, Inc.

Holland, J. L., Daiger, D. C., & Power, P. G. (1980). *My vocational situation.* Palo Alto, CA: Consulting Psychologists Press.

Holland, J. L., Johnston, J. A., & Asama, N. F. (1993). The Vocational Identity Scale: A diagnostic and treatment tool. *Journal of Career Assessment, 1,* 1–12.

Holland, J. L., Powell, A. B., & Fritzsche, B. A. (1994). *Professional user's guide.* Odessa, FL: Psychological Assessment Resources, Inc.

Johnston, J. A. (1999). *Occupational dreams inventory.* University of Missouri, Columbia, MO.

Kapes, J. T., & Whitfield E. A. (Eds.). (2002). *A counselor's guide to career assessment instruments* (4th ed.). Tulsa, OK: National Career Development Association.

Leong, F. T. L. (Ed.). (1995). *Career development and vocational behavior of racial and ethnic minorities.* Hillsdale, NJ: Erlbaum.

Lyman, H. B. (1986). *Test scores and what they mean* (4th ed.). Englewood Cliffs, NJ: Prentice-Hall.

McCrae, R. R. (1992). Ed. The five factor model: Issues and applications [special issue]. *Journal of Personality, 60* (2), pp. 175–532.

Mental Measurement Yearbooks. Lincoln, NE: Buros Institute of Mental Measurements of the University of Nebraska-Lincoln.

Snyder, C. R., Harris, C., Anderson, J. R., Holleran, S. A., Irving, L. M., Sigmon, S. T., Yoshinosu, L., Gibb, J., Langelle, C., & Harney, P. (1991). The will and the ways: Development and validation of an individual—difference measure of hope. *Journal of Personality and Social Psychology, 60,* 570–585.

Walsh, W. B., & Osipow, S. H. (1994). *Career counseling for women.* Hillsdale, NJ: Erlbaum.

▶ 13

The Career Transitions Inventory
A Tool for Uncovering Internal Resources and Barriers in Adulthood

Amanda was 43 when she came for career counseling. She had grown up in a working-class neighborhood in a northern U.S. industrial city. She and her husband had moved to the midwest to find work after the factory her husband worked in had massive job layoffs. Amanda had secured a job as a secretary in the Dean's office of a small college. She had done secretarial work ever since she graduated from high school, and presumed that is what she would continue doing. The Dean she worked for had other ideas for her. He wanted her to go to college and earn a degree. He indicated that he would pay for all her expenses through the college's staff tuition remission program. Although a generous offer, it terrified Amanda. She had no idea what she could be. The Dean had suggested she go for career counseling. The counselor used a battery of interest and skill assessment measures and provided extensive information about majors and careers that would be good matches for Amanda's personality and interests. The counselor encouraged Amanda to explore these career options more fully and make a decision among them. The Dean noted Amanda's lack of progress and again referred her to career counseling. This time the counselor didn't focus on Amanda's interests or skills, and didn't seem as concerned about finding the appropriate match. Instead, the counselor focused on Amanda's beliefs about herself and the world of work. The counselor assessed Amanda's psychological resources and barriers in this career transition. Amanda's counselor determined that Amanda had virtually no belief in her ability to be successful either in college, or in a profession following college. She had no role models from her own background and she had never been encouraged to pursue any higher educational goal. Amanda also worried about the impact this transition would have on her marriage and the self-esteem of her husband who had not completed high school.

Amanda is one of millions of Americans currently in some form of career transition. Although we know quite a lot about the initial transition that individuals make from school to work, much less is known about the transitions common in adult lives. Workers in their forties and fifties comprise the fastest growing segment of those in transition (Newman, 1995). Types of transitions vary greatly, but most can be categorized as either planned/proactive (Brown, 1995; Crace, 1993; Isaacson & Brown, 1993), where the individuals may feel dissatisfied in their chosen fields and actively seek change in order to better their situation. More common are transitions that can be categorized as unplanned or reactive (Brown, 1995; Crace, 1993; Isaacson & Brown, 1993), where the individual is forced by a dramatic life change, such as divorce, disability, or company layoffs, to change careers (Eby & Buch, 1995). Thus, career transitions can be planned or unplanned, voluntary or prescribed. With the differing contexts of transitions comes different counseling needs and strategies. Indeed, transitions in one's vocational life are now so common that our very definition of transition has changed. Arthur and Rousseau (1996) indicate that *transition* used to mean the movement between states. Now it refers to "prevailing cycles of change and adaptation including stages of preparation, encounter, adjustment, stabilization, and renewed preparation" (p. 378). Transitions are now a very normal and frequent part of most people's vocational lives.

Schlossberg (1984) has proposed a definition of transition that is broad and inclusive: "A transition can be said to occur if an event or non-event results in a change in assumptions about oneself and the world and thus requires a corresponding change in one's behavior and relationships" (p. 5).

Schlossberg proposes that how one adapts to life transitions will vary depending on:

1. how the individual perceives the transition, whether it is seen as on-time or off-time, gradual or sudden, permanent, temporary or uncertain
2. the characteristics of both the pre-transition and post-transition environments, which includes the various support systems of the individual
3. characteristics of the individual, such as their psychosocial competence or sex role identification (p. 5)

Of central importance to Schlossberg's model is the aspect of individual differences. It is evident to practitioners that there are individual differences in an adult's ability to move through the career re-evaluation and change process. Some do so with little difficulty, while others may continually try but never successfully make a change from where they are to where they want to be.

There are a number of external or environmental factors that influence an adult's progress, such as sexism, racism, heterosexism, classism, ageism, and a narrow structure of opportunity. These external variables have been written about extensively in both the popular and professional literature. Much less attention has been given to assessing internal, psychological barriers and resources adults bring to the career transition process (Heppner, 1991, 1998; Heppner, Multon, & Johnston, 1994). Researchers and practitioners have consistently called for studies that examine the influence of psychological factors and strategies for designing more targeted interventions (Jepsen, 1992).

Reasons for this lack of attention to the psychological resources and barriers in the career transition process have been well documented. The idea that career planning is a streamlined three-part process—identifying interests, matching interests with appropriate occupational information, and making a decision—goes back to Parsons and his 1909 book, *Choosing a Vocation.* This method still has many strengths today. In cases like Amanda's, however, the importance of also examining psychological issues that may be obstacles to this three-part progression is critical. Although we frequently read of the importance of not dichotomizing personal counseling and career counseling (Hackett, 1993), Amanda's story personifies the danger in doing so.

Regardless of how effective the counselor is in assessing skills, interests, and work-related values; how psychometrically sound the instruments used to make these assessment are; and how well equipped the resource library; the fact remains that if adults have psychological barriers or faulty belief systems, the progress of these adults will be slow to nonexistent. It is the role of the career counselor to help clients recognize their beliefs, barriers, and resources; to build on their strengths; and to find ways of countering their barriers. Only then will career dreams start becoming realities.

The purpose of this chapter is to present in depth an instrument designed to assess the psychological resources and barriers adults bring to a career transition. The chapter presents (a) an overview of the CTI, (b) a guide to interpreting scores on the CTI, (c) a guide to how to use the CTI as a tool for discovery, and (d) a revisit to the case of Amanda to describe how the CTI was used with her.

THE CAREER TRANSITIONS INVENTORY

Although the field of career development has developed numerous psychometrically sound measures to assess career interests, values, and skills, until recently no measures were designed to help clients assess and understand internal, dynamic psychological processes that may get in the way of the career transition process. Because having such instruments available to the career counselor is critical to effectively providing the holistic blend of the personal and career domains central to our model of life career development, we chose to provide an in-depth chapter on this one instrument to demonstrate how the use of an assessment instrument such as the CTI can help the client assess those resources and barriers that may be promoting or conversely serving as barriers to their career progress. In essence, the Career Transitions Inventory (Heppner, 1991; Heppner, Multon, & Johnston, 1994) is provided here as an example of an instrument designed to assess critical dynamic factors operating for the client and allow counselors to intervene in more targeted and specific ways. A detailed description of the instrument and its use follows.

The Career Transition Inventory (CTI: Heppner, 1991, 1998) is a 40-item Likert-type instrument designed to assess an individual's internal process variables that may serve as strengths or barriers when making a career transition. The responses of the items range between 1 (strongly agree) and 6 (strongly disagree). Factor analytic studies revealed five factors: (a) Career Motivation (Readiness), (b) Self-efficacy (Confidence), (c) Perceived Support (Support), (d) Internal/External (Control) and (e) Self versus Relational Focus (Independence–Interdependence). High scores are positive and indicate that individuals perceive themselves to be doing well in that area; low scores indicate barriers. Thus a high score on the Readiness factor would indicate that one is highly prepared and motivated to make a career transition (e.g., "I am feeling challenged by this career transition process and this knowledge keeps me motivated."). A high score on the Confidence factor means that clients are highly confident in their ability to make a successful career transition. Similarly, a high score on the Support factor indicates a greater amount of perceived social support associated with changing one's career situation. Finally, a high score on the Independence factor indicates that clients feel they can make decisions regarding their career as independent, autonomous individuals (e.g., "While family and relationship needs are important to me, when it comes to this career transition, I feel I must focus on my own needs."). Heppner, Multon, and Johnston (1994) calculated Cronbach's alpha coefficients for each of the factors and the total score for the CTI. These coefficients were as follows: .87 (Readiness), .83 (Confidence), .69 (Control), .66 (Perceived support), and .83 (Decision independence). The CTI has been found to correlate positively and significantly with age, marital status, length of time in the transition process, and five global ratings of coping (i.e., perceived level of stress in the career transition process). In addition, enduring personality traits such as those measured by the NEO personality inventory (Costa & McCrae, 1986) have been found to predict career resources as measured by the CTI. For example, openness to experience has been found to predict all five factors of the CTI, indicating that a willingness to try new things is an important personality variable predicting how one negotiates the career transition process. The CTI has been translated into both Chinese (Mandarin) and Japanese (Heppner, Fuller, & Multon, 1998).

Interpreting Career Transitions Inventory Scores: A Guide

In order to facilitate your ability to discuss the clients' scores, the following guide is provided. It is meant as an interpretative guide or talk sheet and can be used to provide the basic structure for exploration of the scales with your client.

The CTI begins with the following description, written in the first person, for your client to read: The Career Transition Inventory (CTI) is designed to help you understand the internal barriers that may be blocking you from moving ahead with your career transition, and conversely with your personal resources in dealing with your transition. There are five scales, each represents a different aspect of how you perceive yourself and your career transition process. By understanding more about the internal barriers and resources you are experiencing, you may be able to develop strategies to maximize strengths and overcome these barriers (Heppner, 1991, 1998).

The descriptions of the five scales give you an indication of what a high, medium, or low score may mean in your situation. Look first at your scores on each scale and be sure they accurately reflect what you believe to be true about yourself at this time. If they seem inaccurate, be sure to discuss it with your counselor. Remember, this is a guide to promote clarification and discussion of issues that surround making a transition; thus all scores can be seen as helping to clarify your situation.

High, medium, and low scores are indicated, which compare your scores with other men and women who were pursing a career transition. A high score means you score in the top 20 percent of adults in transition who provided norms for the CTI, medium indicates your scores are in the middle 60 percent, and low scores indicate you scored similar to the lower 20 percent of the normative sample. They are provided to give you some measure of comparison with other adults.

Readiness: Your score _____

This scale helps identify how willing you are at this time to actually do the things you need to do to achieve your career goals.

Sample items:

- I don't feel much internal "push" to work hard at this career transition.
- Each day I do something on this career transition process, I would say I'm motivated.

High scores indicate that you see few barriers in the area of motivation. You are, in effect, saying, "I am powerfully motivated to go through this career planning process." You are more likely to proceed quickly and put in extra effort to achieve your goals. For many of us, sometimes this motivation comes from something outside of our control: Divorce, a job layoff, the death of someone with whom you feel particularly close. For whatever the reason, your score indicated that you feel a strong sense of readiness to pursue your career transition.

Medium scores indicate that you are probably having mixed feelings about making a career transition. Part of you might be saying, "Yes, go ahead, make the change" while another part of you is saying, "No, it would be better to stay in your current situation." Sometimes you may feel unclear as to why you are not making more progress. Since the process of career transitions tends to take a strong level of motivation, it may be important for you to analyze what is serving to motivate you and what is serving to keep you from action.

Low scores indicate that you may be feeling that you have some barriers in the motivational area. This lack of motivation might relate to a number of factors in your life. Sometimes it is simply a matter of timing. You may feel that this is not the right time in your life to make a change. You may also feel that you lack good options or alternatives and thus lack the powerful, driving motivation that an attractive career goal can provide. Perhaps you feel that other issues in your life are a higher priority at this time. If you score low on this scale, try to analyze the issues in your life that are creating these feelings of ambivalence.

Confidence: Your score _____

This scale refers to your belief in your ability to successfully perform career planning activities necessary to make a career transition.

Sample items:

- In dealing with aspects of this career transition, I am unsure whether I can handle it.
- I feel confident in my ability to do well in this career transition process.

High scores indicate that you see few barriers related to your confidence. You are, in effect, saying, "I believe I have what it takes to make this career transition successfully." The stronger you are in your confidence rating the more likely you are to persevere with the career planning process when difficulties or obstacles occur.

Medium scores indicate that you have some confidence in your ability to make this career transition, but that confidence can waiver at times or be related to different aspects of the transition. It may be helpful for you to analyze the parts of this career transition that you feel confident about and those parts that really test your confidence. By becoming aware of these areas, you may be able to work specifically on the areas that seem most difficult to you.

Low scores indicate that you feel you have some barriers in the area of confidence. You may be feeling self doubt or a lack of belief in your ability to go through the career transition successfully. Perhaps you feel that you have done poorly in this process during past transitions and question your ability to perform well now. Perhaps important people in your life have questioned your ability to do well. Whatever the reason, you may be feeling low in self-confidence. We know that the most powerful way of changing these beliefs is by actually having successful experiences in the career transition process. In essence, you are proving to yourself that you can take small steps and succeed (e.g., taking this instrument, talking to a counselor, developing a resume).

Personal Control: Your score _____

This scale measures the extent to which you feel you have personal control over this career planning process rather than feeling that external forces will determine the outcome of your career transition.

Sample items:

- If you think you are really calling the shots in your career transition, you are only fooling yourself.
- The outcome of this career transition process is really up to those who control the "system."

High scores indicate that you see yourself as being in control of your career transition process. You see outside, environmental, luck, and chance factors as having little effect on your career planning process. You view factors such as effort, interest, and personal energy to be the most important factors.

Medium scores indicate that you may feel that some aspects of the career transition process may be in your control while others are out of your control. It may be important to analyze which parts you feel you can control and which you feel are not within your control. It may be helpful to check out if others view these assessments as realistic. Finally, put energy into the things over which you do have control.

Low scores indicate that you may be seeing barriers to your career planning process that come from external scores. A low score indicates you are likely to see something or someone outside of yourself as being in charge and controlling the outcome of your career transition process. You might be thinking that luck or chance control the outcome, or that the outcome will come from "those who control the system." You are less likely to feel that you can have a powerful effect on your own career transition process. While some parts of the career transition process may be out of your control, a much greater portion is in your control. In order to do an effective job of career planning, you may benefit from taking as much control as possible.

Support: Your score _____

This scale relates to how much support you are feeling from people in your life as you contemplate a career transition.

Sample items:

- People whom I respect have said they think I can make this career transition successfully.
- Significant people in my life are actively supporting me in this career transition.

High scores indicate that you are feeling a fair amount of support as you go through this career transition process. You may feel that people are providing you with various forms of support (emotional and tangible), which is making the process easier for you.

Medium scores indicate that you are feeling support, but perhaps not as much as you would like or feel you need as you think about going through the career transition process. It may be helpful to think about what support you are already receiving and what support you need and who can provide that support for you.

Low scores indicate that you are feeling barriers related to the level of social support from friends and family you are experiencing. Since career transitions can be difficult times for individuals, many people feel that having supportive people around them is very important. A low score on this scale is, in essence, saying that you don't feel a strong level of the support you need in this process. You may also feel that this lack of support affects your own ability to maintain the motivation and risk-taking you will need to be successful in this process. It may be helpful to think about what support you need and who can provide that support for you.

Independence: Your score _____

This scale indicates the level at which you view a career choice as being an independent decision as opposed to a choice that is made as a part of a larger relational context. This relational context may be family, friends, partners, or other significant others that may enter into your career planning process.

Sample items:

- Career choices affect others and I must take the needs of others into account when making a career transition.
- While family and relationship needs are important to me, when it comes to this career transition, I feel I must focus on my own needs.

High scores indicate that you are isolating your career decision as one that you are making independent from significant people in your life. This may be because you are presently living in an independent fashion or, even if you have significant people in your life, you are seeing this decision as one you will make independently. It may be important for you to examine this independence to determine if it may create negative consequences in the lives of people close to you.

Medium scores indicate that you probably see your career decision as dependent and interdependent. You may be feeling ambivalence about how much independence or interdependence you want to have in these decisions.

Low scores indicate that you see your career decisions as very intertwined with relationships you have in your life. You think of the career choices in terms of how they will effect other people you are close to, and you may have concerns as to whether the change you are contemplating will be uncomfortable for them. It may be important for you to analyze how much this focus is keeping you from moving ahead with your career choices. Perhaps you could have discussions with those significant people regarding your career needs to ask for their help in working them out. For clients who originate in more collectivist cultures greater interdependence of choice is to be expected.

This interpretative guide was meant to give you and your client a starting point for understanding the client's results. What follows are a series of tips on interpreting the CTI which may help improve the effectiveness of your interpretation.

Using the CTI for Exploration: A Tool for Discovery

The CTI was designed to help adults understand more about themselves at a time of transition in their lives. In the experience of the authors, many times adults will successfully go through the familiar career planning process of examining their interests, skills, and work-related values and understand how these matched with characteristics of the work world, but still be "stuck" or blocked from further movement. The CTI was developed as a tool for understanding some of the internal dynamics that may stop people from getting to new places in their careers and also for understanding what unique psychological resources they bring to the career transition. Having explored scores on the CTI with numerous adults in transition, ten helpful procedures have become apparent:

1. Use the CTI with a Healthy Tentativeness.

The CTI is best used as a tool of discovery and exploration. The instrument was designed to help establish a dialog between the client and counselor. The scales provide a common language for the discourse. The client's scores provide data to compare with the norms of other adults in a similar situation. Thus, in using the CTI with a client, it is most useful to look to it for clues in order to more accurately conceptualize the career planning process for the individual. Thus it should be interpreted tentatively and interactively, as in the following interchange:

Counselor: *It looks like your score on the Confidence scale is kind of low compared to other adults in career transition who have taken this instrument. How does that fit with your perceptions of yourself?*

Client: *I've never been a very self-confident person and this is no different. With something as big as this career change, I just don't know if I've got what it takes to do it.*

Counselor: *So this score seems pretty accurate on how you are seeing yourself right now.*

Client: *Yes.*

Counselor: *We know that one's belief in one's ability to make the transition is a very important part of making it successful. Perhaps we can explore the reasons for your low level of confidence and ways to promote a stronger sense of self.*

Client: *I think that would be really helpful.*

2. Normalize scores and Avoid Blame.

It is important for interpretive purposes for clients to receive normative information about where their scores fit with other adults in career transition. Thus, providing the normative range of high, medium, and low scores can be informative. It is critically important that clients do not blame themselves for having perceived barriers. The counselor has a crucial role in normalizing clients' perceptions and helping clients integrate their scores into their larger environmental and personal context. There are many reasons, for example, why adults may score low in motivation (Readiness) for the career change. If an interpretation is being done with an adult who has a low score on the Readiness factor, it may be helpful to say something like:

Counselor: *Adults score low on Readiness for a number of reasons. Sometimes it is just not a very good time in their lives to have to go through the intensive process of change. Sometimes they feel unclear about where they are going and thus don't feel very motivated to get there. I wonder how this score fits for you and what some of the reasons might be in your own life.*

Client: *I think I just feel so depressed about my prospects that it's hard to get very motivated.*

Counselor: *So you feel this score might be an accurate indication of your motivation at this time.*

Client: *Yes, I feel it's a tough job market for anyone, but being my age and black sure doesn't help my prospects in this community.*

Counselor: *Sounds like you are having a pretty normal reaction to your situation. I think you're right that it is a difficult job market right now and unfortunately racism and bias in hiring is still a fact. Both of these factors make it even more critical that we strategize ways we can enhance your motivation in this difficult situation.*

3. Scales Represent States Not Traits.

It is important that clients recognize that the individual CTI scales represent psychological states that are highly susceptible to alteration, not life-long, unchangeable personality traits. It may be also important to emphasize that becoming aware that one experiences this psychological barrier is a first step toward changing oneself. The confidence factor is a good example of the changeable nature of these constructs. Confidence is a feeling of self-efficacy about one's ability to make a career transition successfully. We know from the self-efficacy literature (Bandura, 1977; Hackett & Betz, 1981) that self-efficacy beliefs can be altered in four primary ways: (1) performance attainment, (2) vicarious learning (modeling), (3) verbal reinforcement, and (4) physiological state. Thus, in discussing the CTI confidence scale it may be helpful to present some of this information to the client.

Counselor: *A lot of adults lack confidence in their ability to go through a career transition successfully. Even if they feel confident about other things in their lives, they may lack confidence with regard to a career change.*

Client: *Yes, this has really thrown me for a loop. I feel afraid to even request the application for graduate school much less fill it out.*

Counselor: *You are not alone. Many adults I work with feel that way. One way people go about changing their confidence level is to break down the transition into small steps in which they can be successful and thus feel greater confidence in their ability (performance attainment).*

Client: *Yes, I think I need to do that. I think because I'm a first generation college student, I just haven't had much exposure to people who went to grad school and it makes it seem really scary.*

Counselor: *Sometimes adults really benefit from being in a group with other adults who are going through a similar process. Sometimes just seeing others similar to yourself going through a career change can really inspire confidence in you (vicarious learning). Adults also find it important to have people in their lives who believe in them and their ability, and communicate that to them (verbal reinforcement).*

Client: *Yes, I think I need to surround myself more with people who will support me for going for what I want, rather than making me feel like it's a pipe dream. Talking with you has also been helpful. You have made me feel more calm about the whole process (physiological state).*

4. Separate Out What Aspects of the Transition Are Controllable and Which Are Not.

It is important when interpreting the control dimension to help the client discern what is in their control and what is not. It is not helpful for the client to feel that "everything about their situation is in the hands of 'the system'," but it is true for many individuals that they do lack control of certain parts of the process. The CTI was constructed and much of its validation was completed with adults who had been involuntarily thrust into career change. Their need for change was based on the agricultural crisis in the midwest and on factory closings resulting from the broader changes of our society moving from an agricultural manufacturing base to an information and service base. Because of this involuntary and in many cases sudden change, they did experience an accurate loss of control. It may be helpful to facilitate clients' ability to sort out what is in their control and what is not. For example, it might be helpful to say something like:

Counselor: *There are parts of this career change process that you have a lot of control over, such as how prepared you are, how much you know about yourself and your skills, and how effective your resume is. There are other parts that are less in your control, such as economic changes and whether or not the plant will re-open. It is generally most effective to focus on those parts we can control and do as much as we can in those areas.*

Client: *Yes, when something like this happens you really feel thrown to the wind.*

Counselor: *It may be helpful for us to really sort out what things you do have control over more specifically.*

Client: *Yes, that might help me feel less hopeless.*

It is also important to be sure that we as counselors do not limit the growth in control our clients perceive themselves as having by using techniques that may reduce their feelings of control. For example, a recent study indicated that the greater the confidence the career counselor had in his or her skills, the less growth in control clients felt over their own career transition. (Heppner, Multon, Gysbers, Ellis-Kalton, & Zook, 1998).

5. Understand That High Scores May Not Always Be Best—The Independence/interdependence Dimension.

Most of the other CTI factors have a pretty clear directionality; that is, it is generally more helpful to be ready, confident, feel a lot of control, and perceive a lot of support. The independence/interdependence factor is a little more complicated. Although it may be true that being totally independent makes career choices easier, sometimes this can also have damaging effects. For example, men who have traditionally viewed themselves as making independent career choices have expressed shock and surprise at how much those choices have upset the family unit. At the other extreme has been research that has demonstrated that women tend to be very interdependent in their career decision making, often foregoing their own needs in consideration of the needs of husbands, children, employers, and so forth. It is important that both men and women explore the advantages and disadvantages of both independent and dependent decision making. This factor is further complicated by cultural and worldview differences. For clients who come from more collectivist cultures, rather than individualistic ones, greater interdependence would be expected. Thus it might be that in interpreting a particularly high independence score a counselor might say something like:

Counselor: *I wonder how your decision to make this change right now might effect others in your life?*

Conversely, if the client has a particularly low score, indicating a great deal of interdependence, perhaps a statement like this would be appropriate:

Counselor: *It seems like you feel very committed to making sure your career change doesn't disrupt the lives of others. Can you tell me more about how you see your career needs fitting in with people you are close to?*

The client can then explore the impact of an independent versus interdependent stance and what alteration, if any, he or she wants to make.

6. Explore the Importance of the Scale to the Individual.

It is important to examine each dimension as it relates to the unique personality and environmental context of the individual. In general, we know that social support is important in the lives of individuals. We know that it may play an important role in buffering stressful life events. But even with this dimension we need to incorporate the concept of individual differences. Some people need less social support than others; more does not always mean better. Helping a person assess both the level of support *needed* and the current level of support may be an important role for the counselor in exploring this scale:

Counselor: *Your score on social support was in the low range. Does that seem accurate?*

Client: *Well, I've always been an independent person—kind of doing things for myself. I've never thought of it as much of a deficit.*

Counselor: *Yes, I agree it could indeed be a strength. I'm wondering, however, if you feel like you need more support than you are getting at this time of transition.*

Client: *No, sometimes I feel like people at my church try to be too helpful and I kind of feel pushed to accept their support when I really don't want or need it.*

Counselor: *So you feel you are getting as much social support as you need, and in some cases wish people might back off a little and give you more space.*

7. Build on Strengths.

As people trained in test interpretation, many times we focus heavily on the barriers and barely mention a client's strengths. The CTI can be an important tool for building on the psychological resources that clients perceive they have as reflected in high scores. Clients need to recognize their unique strengths and understand how these strengths can really facilitate career transitions.

Here is an example of emphasizing strengths:

Counselor: *"Your confidence score is high. In fact, your score is in the upper 20 percent of all adults who were currently going through a major career transition. Your confidence score is a really important strength—we know that the degree to which you feel confident not only is related to the amount of effort you will expend, but also your persistence with the tasks needed to make this transition successful.*

8. Use the Career Transitions Inventory As a Vehicle for Integrating Personal and Career Issues.

Researchers and practitioners have emphasized the need to stop the dichotomization of career issues and personal issues (Hackett, 1993). Unfortunately, we have not provided practitioners with many tools to assist in that goal. Our traditional instruments assess a client's career-related interests, but often do not provide an entree into exploring the critical psychological components of the transition. Thus, the CTI is meant to aid in the integration of personal and career issues. It is meant to provide a vehicle for dialog about some of the harder issues that can stop adults from achieving their dreams.

Counselor: *Seems like you are having some ambivalence about this process. The homework that we decided on might help in your job search process has not been completed.*

Client: *Yes, I know I should be doing more, but it feels scary.*

Counselor: *I was looking at the CTI you took when you first came and again noted the very high interdependence score. I wonder if it would be helpful to revisit how this career transition is affecting your partner.*

Client: *Well, yes, it's affecting her a lot. Every time I come here it makes her anxious, anxious that I'm not happy, that I might find something better. Maybe, in another city, we won't be able to stay together.*

Counselor: *Yes, it seems like there are a lot of ways our society makes it difficult for lesbian relationships to survive anyway, and it sounds like your partner feels that your potential career change heightens that instability.*

Client: *Yes, I try to reassure her but it feels scary to her, and to me for that matter.*

9. Use Creativity in Exploring Meanings of the CTI Scales.

As a tool of discovery, the CTI can be used in many creative ways. As counselors it is important to explore alternative modes of helping clients see their situation. Some counselors are quite creative in getting their clients to explore their beliefs and needs:

Counselor: *Even though you scored low on the confidence scale, I want you to picture yourself as scoring very high on it—topping it out. Explore a typical day of feeling totally confident in your abilities to make this change successfully. How does it feel? How are you behaving differently? What messages are you giving yourself about your ability?*

Another favorite technique is using writing to help clients explore their scales more fully. Sometimes this is done in a session where the counselor asks the client to do a two to three minute "free write" on how they perceive the meaning of their scales. The following are some examples from a client:

Readiness (High): Ready? Yes, I feel ready! I feel for the first time in my life that I can really do my own thing! The kids are gone. I don't have to be their constant caregiver. I can do or be whatever I want. I just need to figure out what journey I want to take and then do it.

Support (Low): I don't feel very much support. My friends think I'm nuts for quitting my academic position when I don't have a clue where I'm headed. Occasionally someone will say, "Gosh, I admire your courage. I could never do it." But somehow that just leaves me feeling worse.

A longer writing technique is using a journal. Ask clients to explore their reactions to each scale in journal form. Ask them to bring it to the next session and read whatever portions they are willing to share with you.

10. *Always Ask Clients to Summarize What They Learned From Exploring Their Results.*
Any test result interpretation is subject to distortion and misunderstanding. The best way to ensure that clients are clear about what the results mean and don't mean is to ask for their summary of what they heard.

Counselor: *By way of closing our session today, I'd like you to take a few minutes and tell me the main things that came out of taking and discussing your CTI results.*

Revisiting Amanda

Now that we have a picture of how the CTI is scored and some guidelines for interpretation, let's revisit Amanda as she and her counselor use the CTI to help map a strategy for the counseling process.

Amanda's scores were converted to percentiles and displayed in Figure 13–1.

When first glancing over Amanda's scores, we can get a composite picture of her barriers and resources. We see, for example, that Amanda had extremely low scores in confidence, support, and independence and moderate scores in readiness and control. Our general strategy was to discuss each of these factors and develop a plan for changing barriers into resources. We started by reinforcing Amanda's strengths. Although within the moderate range, Amanda had a fair degree of readiness and felt a fair degree of internal control. We talked specifically about how these characteristics could help make the career transition easier. Next we discussed the reasons for the low confidence score.

Amanda said that her employer was really the first person in her life who had ever expressed any belief in Amanda's ability to get a college degree. She felt it would take some time for her to really believe it herself. She felt fear about jumping into college and was giving herself a lot of messages like "people like me don't go to college." Amanda and her counselor set three initial goals that were designed to foster her self confidence:

- To examine how her past environment had fostered low self confidence, especially around educational and career aspirations
- To break down the career transition process into small doable steps where she could feel efficacy and reinforcement
- To join a support group of first-generation college students who were enrolled at the college where Amanda was working

Additionally, Amanda's low feelings of support were also addressed. Amanda felt some fear that her relationship with her husband would change

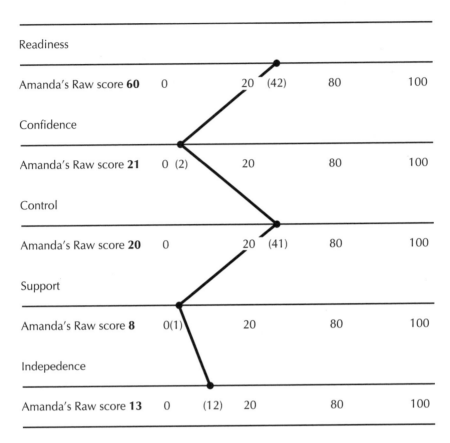

FIGURE 13–1　Amanda's CTI Profile

as she explored new roles for herself. She felt he was insecure and feared that Amanda would pursue a college education and then leave him. Amanda also expressed the need to have more people in her life who could offer support and encouragement. Thus, she set two specific goals she related to increasing her level of social support:

1. To explore how Amanda and her husband could work through his anxiety and insecurity related to her career choices.
2. To develop a plan for Amanda to increase her level of social support and find people who would reinforce her progress toward her goals.

Amanda's independence score also reflected her strong need to make sure her career plans didn't upset anyone in her environment. This led to a number of sessions that focused on how Amanda felt about herself and what she felt she deserved from her relationships. We discussed the importance and validity of both independent and interdependent decision making and agreed that a healthy balance should be the goal. Amanda talked about how she had always been the one who had compromised for the needs of others. It was new for her to think about prioritizing and affirming her own needs.

Amanda worked with her counselor for twelve sessions. The goals set through use of the CTI formed the framework for the counseling process. Thus, Amanda's scores facilitated a more targeted counseling intervention. The scores helped Amanda explore the psychological barriers that had been keeping her from progressing on her career development. The scales gave Amanda and her counselor a common language with which to explore her process of development.

Amanda's story as an example of one adult in career transition is illustrative of the need to help clients as whole people, complete with the full range of psychological strengths and barriers, faulty beliefs, and intertwined personal and professional lives. We must move beyond the sole use of matching people and occupations to a more complex understanding of the unique dynamics that both promote and limit adults' self-actualization. The Career Transitions Inventory was included as an example of an instrument that may be a helpful vehicle for exploring these complex dynamics.

REFERENCES

Arthur, M. B., & Rousseau, D. M. (1996). Conclusion: A lexicon for a new organizational era. In M. B. Arthur and D. M. Rousseau (Eds.) *The boundaryless career* (pp. 370–382). New York: Oxford Press.

Bandura, A. (1977). Self-efficacy: Toward a unifying theory of behavior change. *Psychological Review, 84,* 191–215.

Brown, D. (1995). A values-based approach to facilitating career transitions. *The Career Development Quarterly, 44,* 4–11.

Costa, P. T., Jr., & McCrae, R. R. (1986). Personality stability and its implications for clinical psychology. *Clinical Psychology Review, 6,* 407–423.

Crace, R. K. (1993). Athletes in transition: A general workshop outline. Montreal, Canada: AAASP Convention. *Career Development Quarterly, 44,* 64–66.

Eby, L. T., & Buch, K. (1995). Job loss as career growth: Responses to involuntary career transition. *The Career Development Quarterly, 44,* 26–42.

Hackett, G. (1993). Career counseling and psychotherapy: False dichotomies and recommended remedies. *Journal of Career Assessment, 1,* 105–117.

Hackett, G., & Betz, N. E. (1981). A self-efficacy approach to the career development of women. *Journal of Vocational Behavior, 18,* 326–339.

Heppner, M. J. (1991). The CTI is available from Mary J. Heppner, Ph.D., 201 Student Success Center, University of Missouri, Columbia, Missouri 65211. E-mail HeppnerM@Missouri.edu

Heppner, M. J. (1998). The Career Transitions Inventory: Measuring internal resources in adulthood. *Journal of Career Assessment, 6,* 135–145.

Heppner, M. J., Fuller B. E., & Multon, K. D. (1998). Adults in involuntary career transition: An analysis of the relationship between the psychological and career domains. *Journal of Career Assessment, 6* 329–346.

Heppner, M. J., Multon, K. D., Gysbers, N. C., Ellis-Kalton, C., & Zook, C. E. (1998). Examining the relationship of counselor self-efficacy and selected client process and outcome measures in career counseling. *Journal of Counseling Psychology, 45,* 393–402.

Heppner, M. J., Multon, K. D., & Johnston, J. A. (1994). Assessing psychological resources during career change: Development of the career transitions inventory. *Journal of Vocational Behavior, 44,* 55–74.

Isaacson, L. E., & Brown, D. (1993). *Career information, career counseling and career development* (5th ed.). Boston: Allyn and Bacon.

Jepsen, D. A. (1992). Annual review: Practice and research in career counseling and development, 1991. *The Career Development Quarterly, 41,* 98–129.

Newman, B. K. (1995). Career change for those over 40: Critical issues and insights. *Career Development Quarterly, 44,* 64–66.

Parsons, F. (1909). *Choosing a vocation.* Boston: Houghton Mifflin.

Schlossberg, N. K. (1984). A model for analyzing human adaptation to transition. *The Counseling Psychologist, 9,* 2–18.

▶ 14

Identifying and Analyzing
Life Career Themes

In the first phase of career counseling presented in Chapter 1, emphasis is placed on gathering and understanding client self and environmental information and the behavior clients exhibit using qualitative and quantitative procedures and instruments such as those described in Chapters 9 through 13. Why is this emphasis important? It is important because we believe that what clients say about themselves, others, and the worlds in which they live, what they say about their environmental barriers, racial identity statuses, and levels of acculturation, and the language they choose to represent these statements may be the crucial mediating processes in their lives. Understanding these statements may provide you and your clients with insights into clients' dynamics (internal thoughts and feelings) concerning presenting problems, hopes, dreams, and other possible problems and issues that may emerge as career counseling unfolds. Bingham (2001) underlined this point when he stated

> *Clients could be encouraged to "tell the story" of their lives, and through that narrative, identify the recurrent themes. Then the manner in which they organize those themes and make sense of them becomes the basis for extrapolating about the future (p 26).*

Many years ago Kelly (1955) described this phenomenon as individuals looking at their worlds through self-created transparent patterns or templates in order to make sense out of them. He used the term "personal constructs" to describe these patterns and stated that personal constructs are ways individuals construe their worlds. Gerber (1983) suggested that the language people use represents their underlying conceptual schemata, and, in turn, their conceptual schemata determines their behavior.

One way to understand client information and behavior is to focus attention on these constructs or *life career themes*, as we call them, that clients use to
understand themselves, others, and their worlds. What language do they use?
What is the nature and extent of their vocabulary? Is their vocabulary fully
developed? Is it limited? Is it based on stereotypes? Does it contain distortions? What language do they use to describe possible environmental barriers, their racial identity statuses, and their levels of acculturation?

How important are life career themes in persons' lives? Mangione (1993)
suggested that they are very important because they guide our daily lives.

*We do, in fact, live themes out in our daily lives. Themes are not merely
abstractions; they are the foundations of everyday experience and infuse the
manner in which a person gives meaning to or construes his or her existence,
relationships, work situations, choices, and encounters. These themes exist
even if the person is not aware of them. Becoming aware of them changes one's
relationship to the themes and certainly elaborates them in the process, but
talking about the person's life is not what creates the themes. They are there,
not articulated, but affecting the person nevertheless. A person's relationship
to his or her life themes can evolve and develop over a lifetime (p. 112).*

Understanding client information and behavior begins to emerge in the
first session as you interpret what you hear and see and then form tentative
hypotheses about the meaning of the information and behavior. We believe
that the understanding process that unfolds through the use of interpretation
and the forming of tentative hypotheses can be enhanced by using the concept
of life career themes. To use the concept effectively requires in-depth knowledge of as many models as possible that explain human behavior from sociological, psychological, and economic perspectives. Such knowledge provides
the clues, concepts, and vocabulary to help you see, understand, and interpret
client information and behavior in terms of life career themes from many perspectives. What is seemingly unexplainable client information and behavior
often becomes explainable because a particular model of human behavior
gives you a way to see, understand, and explain them.

To assist you to enhance your skills to hear, see, interpret, and form
hypotheses about client information and behavior in terms of life career
themes, this chapter first describes the concept of life career themes. This is
followed by brief discussions of the counseling techniques of interpretation
and forming hypotheses. Then the largest part of this chapter is devoted to a
presentation of a selected number of models of human behavior that can provide you and your clients with a variety of useful ways to see, express, and
describe life career themes. These example models are introduced primarily
to show you how to interpret client information and behavior in terms of tentative hypotheses in the form of life career themes and then to select and use

intervention strategies to help your clients reach their goals and resolve their problems. The focus is on the cues and language these models can supply to help you identify and analyze clients' life career themes.

WHAT ARE LIFE CAREER THEMES? HOW DO WE IDENTIFY AND ANALYZE THEM?

Life career themes are words that people use to express their ideas, values, attitudes, and beliefs about themselves (*I am* statements), about others (*others are* statements), and about their world views (*life is* statements). An understanding of life career themes is important because they provide us with ways to understand the thought processes of our clients. They help us picture our clients' representational systems, and they help us gain insights into client information and behavior. Much like world views, life career themes act as filters "through which phenomena are perceived and comprehended. As a set of conceptual rules representing one's core beliefs, (they guide) one's significant actions" (Miller & West, 1993, pp. 3–4).

Life career theme identification and analysis requires a structure to organize and guide the process. The structure we recommend is life roles. While there are a number of life roles that could be used, we suggest beginning with two—worker and personal roles. Once you begin identifying themes based on these two roles you can apply the theme identification process to other life roles. Life roles are used because they can provide a direct and realistic way to organize life career themes that directly relate to clients, where they are, and the worlds in which they live and work.

Life Roles	Models
Worker role identity	Data, ideas, people, things Vocational personalities and work environments Transferable skills identification
Personal role identity	Feminist identity development Racial/cultural identity development

Models of aspects of human behavior from sociological, psychological, and economic perspectives offer ways to describe human and environmental characteristics in many different ways. They supply the language with which to phrase client life career themes. We suggest the above models as examples because they can be easily linked to the life role identity structure. Each model presents a particular way of looking at, interpreting, and expressing client information and behavior.

To carry out theme identification and analysis, your task is to take the images formed about your clients from the samples of their information and behavior obtained during the gathering information phase of career counseling and translate these images into the language of the models. The language of the models then becomes the language used to express possible life career themes that may be present.

Remember, this process is a shared one in which you and your clients think about themes together. It is a teaching–learning process where you and your clients are both teacher and learner. Your task as counselor is to supply the language of models. Your client's task is to share experiences and information. Then together, the process of theme analysis unfolds, often tentatively at first, as ideas are exchanged and themes are discussed.

Steps Involved in Theme Analysis

The first step in life career themes identification and analysis begins in the first session and continues into other sessions as you and your clients are gathering client self and environmental information. As you have seen, this can involve the use of qualitative procedures such as the life career assessment interview, career genograms, and an occupational card sort. It can also involve the use of quantitative instruments such as the Self-Directed Search, the NEO Personality Inventory, and the Career Transitions Inventory. As the information these and similar sources provide is gathered, images are formed about what clients are like.

The next step involves translating the images you and your clients have formed into the language of one or more of the models you may be using. In effect, you and your clients look at the images formed through the eyes of the model or models and interpret together what is seen in their language. For example, if you are using Holland's classification system (1997) as your model, you could use one or more of the personality types he describes as possible descriptors of the client images you and your clients have formed. The developers of the Strong Interest Inventory (Harmon, Hansen, Borgen, & Hammer, 1994) did this when they cast part of the interpretation of the Strong Interest Inventory into Holland personality–environment type language.

The last step in theme analysis is developing an in-your-mind profile of the themes that you and your clients have derived from the client images you and your clients have formed. One way to do this is to visualize the client themes that have been identified as brief newspaper articles complete with headlines. In your minds you and your client write the article describing your client in terms of themes and then summarize the key themes as boldface news headlines. This is an excellent exercise to bring you and your client together, to correct any misperceptions, and to add details where needed. It is a way to bring themes into focus.

Some Points to Remember in Theme Analysis

Some career counseling approaches emphasize the gathering of all the data about clients before attempting to explain—hypothesize about—client behavior. We believe that these approaches are not very effective or efficient because when you are working with clients you will be dealing with their unique streams of behavior and their private logic (Nikelly, 1971). We recommend that instead of waiting to interpret client information and behavior into life career themes until all the information about them is gathered, you and your clients begin immediately in the first session to interpret client information and behavior into life career themes. As this unfolds, tentative hypotheses are formed by you and your clients about their unique combinations of themes and their resulting behavior. As the counseling process unfolds, you and your clients will accept or reject hypotheses in part or totally on a continuing basis. Rather than trying to impose psychological certainties after all the information is in, the use of interpretation and the forming of hypotheses invites you and your clients to continue with the task of understanding the life career themes they may be using, to test out your understanding of them with your clients, and to profit from mistaken or divergent views.

Sometimes in the career counseling process you will note life career theme inconsistencies in clients. These often are difficult to understand. A possible way to resolve inconsistent and contradictory themes is to use a technique called two points of a line (Dreikurs, 1966). This technique suggests that inconsistencies and contradictions in themes are simply a matter of our inability to grasp the logic that binds them into a coherent whole. If you are able to connect two divergent themes, it may be possible to understand your clients' behavior in a wide range of situations. As in geometry, the location of a line can be determined by two points. The key to resolving apparent inconsistencies and contradictions is to find the string that links the points together. Some clients who are aware of their weaknesses counter those weaknesses through compensation. Thus you may observe their more primitive behavior sometimes and their compensating behavior at other times. For example, a client may exhibit primitive behavior in a stressful situation. The fact that clients are using compensation is, in itself, a useful piece of information that will help you understand them better.

It is important to keep in mind that you need to avoid premature and absolute categorization of clients based on the themes you identify. Life career theme analysis is not a technique to help you gather perceptions about clients and then label them for all time on the basis of these perceptions. Instead, life career theme analysis is a technique that serves as a point of departure for you and your clients to explore, hypothesize, and plan together. As themes are identified, they serve as discussion points to aid both you and your clients to better understand who they are, their concerns, and where they may be going.

Finally, as you are using life career theme analysis as a part of the information gathering phase of career counseling, keep in mind that you need to look at each bit of information about your clients in a number of ways. What does it mean as a sample? Is this a common or unusual occurrence? With what does the information correlate? Does it often follow or precede certain events? Is it a sign of an underlying condition? What does it symbolize?

INTERPRETATION: A NEEDED
SKILL IN THEME ANALYSIS

The counseling technique of interpretation is a necessary skill if you are going to be effective in theme analysis. Although there are many definitions of what interpretation is in counseling, Clark (1995) observed that there is a common element in all of the definitions he reviewed, and that element was that "the client is introduced to a new frame of reference" (p. 483). It is important to note that this new frame of reference goes beyond where your clients are; something new is presented to them.

As information gathering in career counseling continues to unfold, the use of the technique of interpretation helps make explicit the life career themes present in your clients' responses while these themes may still be meaningless to them. A major goal of career counseling "is to elicit inside information [from clients] so that it can be taught back to them or learned directly by them" (Field, 1966, p. 24). As career counseling progresses, such a framework makes it possible for you and your clients to make the connections between these themes on the one hand and client problem resolution or goal attainment on the other hand. Carlsen (1988) made this point in describing a type of therapy titled *developmental meaning-making*. She stated:

> *Clients who may never have explored themselves—and thus, never really known themselves—begin to understand the patterning and programs which have shaped their lives. Ordering and synthesizing this new information, they open their eyes to new possibilities and are often able to stand back with a new perspective on themselves. And, parallel to their cognitive understandings come new awareness and recognition of the influence and meaning of their affective experience—not one without the other, but intertwining and developing in a dialectical synergy of life development (p. 4).*

Kottler and Brown (1992) defined interpretation as an "attempt to impart meaning to the client by introducing new concepts and frames of reference" (p. 62). The selected models of human behavior organized around life roles that appear later in this chapter offer new concepts and frames of reference. They supply possible new language to express your clients' life career themes.

Interpretations usually start with your statements such as "could it be that...," "you believe that...," and "it sounds like...." How and when you interpret client information and behavior and what you focus on specifically will depend in part on your orientation to counseling. Your experiences may also play a part in interpreting client information (Clark, 1995). Remember, too, that this is a shared experience between you and your client.

FORMING TENTATIVE HYPOTHESES: ANOTHER NEEDED SKILL IN THEME ANALYSIS

Another needed skill in life career theme analysis is the ability to form tentative hypotheses about the meaning of client information and behavior. What is a hypothesis? According to Walborn (1996), "In counseling and psychotherapy, a hypothesis is an educated hunch that is grounded in theory" (p. 224). What do hypotheses do in the counseling process? Walborn (1996) suggested that they keep sessions focused, they help "to keep the therapist's [counselor's] expectations in line with reality" (p. 227), they can challenge clients' interpretations of their problems, and they can foster the development of a collaborative relationship—the working alliance. Walborn (1996) put it this way:

> The client's pain is exchanged for the therapist's [counselor's] understanding, as expressed in the hypothesis. Even an incorrect hypothesis is a gift (p. 229).

As we pointed out earlier, gathering information about your clients begins with the presenting problem or issue during the first session. As gathering information using qualitative and quantitative procedures is underway, so is interpretation, theme analysis, and the forming of tentative hypotheses. One flows into the other. The dynamic and complex nature of these interacting processes requires you to be an active, involved counselor, well grounded in various theoretical models of human behavior. The dynamic and complex nature of these interacting processes also requires that you are willing to take some risks in your interpretations and tentative hypotheses. You know that if your clients disagree with your hypotheses as the shared process of theme analysis continues to unfold, they will feel comfortable confiding their thoughts with you because of the strong working alliance you have formed together.

The major purposes of gathering information about your clients is to shed light on their presenting problems and issues, provide opportunities for them to go beyond their presenting problems if they wish, and to begin to focus on problem solutions. This is accomplished through interpretation, providing your clients with a language system to describe problems and issues through forming tentative hypotheses about life career themes toward the goal of selecting interventions to assist them to reach their goals and resolve their problems. How do we know if we are on the correct path in forming hypotheses? "The emphasis is not on the content of the hypothesis, but rather on the impact that the hypothesis has on the therapeutic relationship [working alliance] and, ultimately, on positive change" (Walborn, 1996, p. 242).

SELECTED MODEL EXPLANATIONS

What follows in the next section are selected models of aspects of human behavior organized around the structure of life roles described earlier. For our purposes, we use the life roles of worker and personal identity to supply the perspective and the language to identify and express your clients' life career themes. Brief explanations of these models are provided along with some examples of how to apply them to life career theme analyses.

Worker Role Identity

Data, Ideas, Things, People
The most widely used and influential occupational classification system is the *Dictionary of Occupational Titles* (1991), published by the U.S. Government Printing Office. Prediger (1976) extended the data, people, and worker function ratings described in the *Dictionary of Occupational Titles* to include ideas. Revisions of Prediger's original formulation appeared in several sources including Prediger, Swaney, and Mau (1993), Prediger and Swaney (1995), and Swaney (1995). The most recent definitions of data, ideas, people, things appeared in the *Technical Manual: Revised Unisex Edition of the ACT Interest Inventory* (Swaney, 1995) as follows:

> *Data (facts, records, files, numbers, systematic procedures). Data tasks are* impersonal *tasks that expedite goods/services consumption by people (for example, by organizing or conveying facts, instructions, products, etc.). Purchasing agents, accountants, and air traffic controllers work* mainly *with data.*
>
> *Ideas (abstractions, theories, knowledge, insights, new ways of expressing something—for example, with words, equations, or music). Ideas tasks are* intrapersonal *tasks such as creating, discovering, interpreting, and synthesizing abstractions or implementing applications of abstractions. Scientists, musicians, and philosophers work* mainly *with ideas.*

Things (machines, tools, living things, materials such as food, wood, or metal). Things tasks are non-personal *tasks such as producing, transporting, servicing, and repairing. Bricklayers, farmers, and machinists work mainly with things.*

People. People tasks are interpersonal *tasks such as caring for, educating, serving, entertaining, persuading, or leading others—in general, producing a change in human behavior. Teachers, salespersons, and speech pathologists work mainly with people (pp. 2-3).*

Swaney, K. B. (1995). *Technical Manual: Revised Unisex Edition of the ACT Interest Inventory (UNIACT)*. Iowa City, Iowa: The American College Testing Program, pp. 2–3. Used with permission,

Our purpose in presenting this model is to focus on its application to the process of life career theme analysis. Of particular interest is the language it can supply to help describe the images you form with your clients during the career counseling process. Some sample applications of theme analysis using the language of data, ideas, things, and people are shown in Table 14–1.

Vocational Personalities and Work Environments

Holland's (1997) theory of vocational personalities and work environments categorizes personalities and environments into six types as follows:

Realistic Personality and Environment

Persons with a predominantly realistic personality tend to be more oriented to the present and to dealing with the concrete rather than the abstract. They are people who believe they have athletic or mechanical ability and prefer to work in the outdoors with their hands, tools, machines, plants, or animals rather than with people. They prefer the straightforward, measurable, and tried-and-true rather than the unknown and unpredictable. They often exhibit a straightforward stick-to-itiveness and sense of maturity.

The environment is one that encourages and rewards success in the use of one's hands and in the manipulation of things. It is a world of the tangible and predictable, which rewards with and values money, possessions, and power.

Investigative Personality and Environment

Persons with a predominantly investigative personality tend to be more oriented to the abstract and problem solving. They like to solve problems that require thinking, especially involving the scientific, technical, and mathematical. They tend not to be particularly socially oriented and prefer academic and scientific areas. They value the intellect and believe it is the tool with which to deal with the world.

TABLE 14–1   Sample Applications of Theme Analysis

Typical Client Dialogue	Component Descriptors	Theme Statements
"I like to make copies of original artwork." "Monogramming clothing is fun."	*Data:* Creative—design reproduction, craft skills, composition, applied arts	Can duplicate originals. Products show attention to detail. Can be counted on to complete tasks.
"It is important to have everything organized and in order." "They say I'm good with numbers."	*Data:* Abstract—numerical skills, symbols and ideas, information/data collection, data entry technology skills	Likes to manipulate financial data. Intrigued by computer technology. Prefers to organize information for budgets.
"I love to write. "I lose track of time when I am putting ideas on paper."	*Ideas:* Artistic—Entertainment interests, performing art (music, acting, etc.), literary creative design	Is a sensitive performer and artist. Has the ability to express feelings in writing. Has an original way of doing things.
"I would like to devote my life to the study of the adrenal gland." "Each answer leads to another question."	*Ideas:* Investigative—social science, medical science, natural science, applied technology	Likes to construct theories to explain world conditions. Constantly comparing and contrasting ideas. Has the capacity to research and publish.
"It feels good to be active and perspire." "Being outdoors makes me high."	*Things:* Physical—recreational skills, agriculture/outdoor stamina/strengths for jobs, performance oriented	Can show you how to do things. Possesses physical skills for heavy work. Contact with nature spurs activity.
"People always seem to come to me for advice." "I like being around young people… they are so stimulating."	*People:* Instruct—persuade, help to perform, ability to communicate, serve others	Enjoys selling others. Wants to teach others. Likes counseling and caring for others.
"Being an office manager would be challenging." "I feel I have some expertise that would be of value to others."	*People:* Manage—supervise, consult, act as mentor, leadership	Aspires to be a consultant. Wants others to follow one's lead. Finds directing others to accomplish tasks rewarding.

The environment is one that encourages and rewards success in the use of the intellect and in the manipulation of the abstract. It is a world of observing, investigating, and theorizing, and it values and rewards with status and recognition.

Artistic Personality and Environment

Persons with a predominantly artistic personality tend to be more oriented to the imaginative and creative, using feelings as a guide to whether something is right. They have, or believe they have, artistic, innovative, or intuitive abilities and prefer to avoid structured work settings and conformity. They value the aesthetic and often prefer to relate to the world through the products of their work such as paintings, plays, and music.

The environment is one that encourages and rewards the displays of the above-mentioned values. It is a world of the abstract, aesthetic, and original. It rewards with recognition, status, and increasing freedom to create in one's own way.

Social Personality and Environment

Persons with a predominantly social personality tend to be more oriented to the problems and growth of people and interpersonal relationships. They like to work with people directly, and are good with words. They like to inform, teach, help, and train others. They often are academically oriented. However, they tend toward the impulsive and intuitive rather than the methodical and scientific.

The environment is one that encourages and rewards success in the above-mentioned values and tends to promote social activities. It is a world of people and relationships that is often changing, and it values social skills and the ability to promote change in others. It tends to reward with recognition and approval from peers and those being taught and helped.

Enterprising Personality and Environment

Persons with a predominantly enterprising personality tend to be more oriented to the overcoming of political and economic challenges. They are, or believe they are, good at talking and using words to persuade, influence, and manage for organizational or economic goals. They tend to be more assertive and dominating than other types. They often value and seek out new challenges and tend to be self-confident as well as social, although this is often at a surface level.

The environment is one that encourages and rewards success in the above. It is a world of continual new challenges to be overcome, valuing and rewarding power, status, and money.

Conventional Personality and Environment

Persons with a predominantly conventional personality tend to be more conforming and conventional, preferring the structured and predictable. They like to work with data, and have, or believe they have, clerical or numerical ability. They prefer to follow others' directions and carry out activities in detail. They tend to value the neat and orderly and prefer not to be responsible for the intangible and unpredictable.

The environment is one that encourages and rewards exacting management of data and details. It is a world of facts that is practical and organized, where dependability and attention to detail are rewarded. Rewards tend to be in the area of economic success and status involving material possessions and recognition of superiors and peers.

Holland's theory states that by comparing a person's attributes to each model type, we can determine which type the individual resembles most. Because individuals resemble more than one type, we also determine to what extent they resemble the other types. The three types that the individual most resembles describes that person's code. For example, a person who is a counselor might have the code SAE, which indicates that this person resembles the social type most and the artistic and enterprising types to a lesser degree.

The codes are most easily understood using Holland's hexagonal model. The hexagon with the first letter of each type looks like that shown in Figure 14–1.

Types that are adjacent to each other on the hexagon are most similar than types directly across from each other. S is more similar to A and E than it is to R. Codes consisting of closely related types occur more frequently than those that do not. For example, codes such as ESC and RIC occur more frequently than codes such as CSI and IES.

The language used by Holland to describe personality types and environments is very useful in translating the images of clients into theme statements.

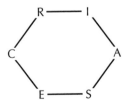

FIGURE 14–1   Holland's Hexagonal Model

It can be easily related to how clients think and talk about themselves. You also will find that Holland's descriptions are used in a number of interest inventories as a means of interpreting the results to clients.

Transferable Skill Identification

In his book What Color is Your Parachute?, Bolles (2001, p .72) described transferable skills as "the most basic unit—the atoms" of occupations. He pointed out that many skills are transferable and that they can be grouped into three families: data (information), people, or things. In another publication, *The Three Boxes of Life* (1981), he proposed the following way to categorize transferable skills:

- Using my hands
- Using my body
- Using words
- Using my senses
- Using numbers
- Using intuition
- Using analytical thinking or logic
- Using originality or creativity
- Using helpfulness
- Using artistic abilities
- Using leadership, being up front
- Using follow-through

In each of these subcategories from *The Three Boxes of Life* a number of specific skills are identified, and examples of where these skills may be used are provided. The language used to describe the skills and the examples provided can be used by you and your clients to help identify and describe skills. The language used provides the nucleus around which life career themes can be grouped. If you are not familiar with skill identification as described by Bolles, you may wish to read *What Color is Your Parachute?* (Bolles, 2001).

COMBINING WORKER ROLE IDENTITY MODELS

The selected models that we have suggested to help you identify and describe client life career themes related to the worker role can be used separately or in various combinations. For purposes of this chapter we have combined all three models in this next section (see Boxes 14–1 to 14–6) to show how they can be used in combination for theme analysis. All of the examples that follow use the same format. First, a personality type is described. Then examples of transferable skills associated with that type are listed. Finally, possible life career themes are presented that may emerge from your interactions with cli-

---

BOX 14–1   Realistic

The realistic personality uses physical skills to work on or make products. This interest can be satisfied in a variety of work ranging from routine to complex jobs. It may involve using physical skills to work on or make products. It also may involve dealing directly with things. Often tools, machines, or measuring devices are used to make or change a product or build, repair, alter, or restore products. Complex tasks are involved such as adjusting and controlling things or using knowledge and reasoning skills to make judgments and decisions. Examples and prior experiences might include repairing a bicycle, mowing lawns, typing, highly skilled crafts, using a printing press.

Transferable Skills

Skills	*Specific Operations*
1. Using hands	1. Assembling, constructing, building; operating tools, machinery, or equipememt; showing finger dexterity, precision handling, and repairing
2. Using body	2. Physical activity, muscular coordination, outdoor activities

Possible Life Career Themes

Likes detail; likes to complete tasks; systematic structured; efficient; confident; handles objects; works with tools; work with machines; conforming; precision work; practical; methodical; materialistic; frank; honest; humble; natural; persistent; modest; shy; stable; thrifty

---

ents during the gathering information phase of the career counseling process. Possible life career themes are presented in the form of tentative hypotheses, such as "As I have listened to you describe some of your experiences at work, it sounds as if you dislike routine and close supervision."

Personal Role Identity

As with worker and learner roles, there are many ways to describe your clients' personal roles. We have chosen two examples of personal roles that can provide a descriptive vocabulary for life career themes analyses. The first personal role identity is the role that evolves from being a woman. The model of human behavior that we have chosen to represent this role is titled the *Feminist Identity Development Model* (Downing & Roush, 1985). It appeared earlier in Chapter 4 and is reprinted here because it provides women clients with

---

BOX 14–2   Investigative

The investigative personality has an interest in researching and collecting data about the natural world and applying them to problems in medical, life, or physical sciences. This interest may be satisfied by working with the knowledge and processes involved in the sciences. Conducting research and analyzing, evaluating, explaining, and recording scientific information as well as using scientific or technical methods, instruments, and equipment in work are involved. Planning, scheduling, processing, controlling, directing, and evaluating data and things also are involved. There may be contact with people, but dealing with people is not important to the work. Examples and prior experiences might include computer work, operating complex machines, assisting in a laboratory, finding the location of an unfamiliar street, tracing down a short in electrical wiring, finding the ingredients to a special recipe, comparative shopping, examining a cut or bruise.

Transferable Skills

Skills	*Specific Operations*
1. Using analytical thinking or logic	1. Researching, information gathering, analyzing; organizing, diagnosing, putting things in order comparing, testing, evaluation
2. Using senses	2. Observing, inspecting, examining; diagnosing, showing attention to detail

Possible Life Career Themes

Analytical; efficient; cautious; likes to investigate; curious; methodical; seeks to understand; thinks to solve problems; precision work; independent; modest; seeks to organize; reserved

---

vocabulary to identify and reflect on life career themes that can emerge from their developing identity as women. The second personal role identity that we present is the role that evolves from being a person of color. The model we have chosen to represent this role is titled the *Racial/Cultural Identity Development Model* (Sue & Sue, 1999). As the authors for this model pointed out, it is "a conceptual framework to aid therapists in understanding their culturally different client's attitudes and behaviors" (p. 128). We label these attitudes and behaviors as life career themes.

The two models of human behavior used for the personal role identity are rich in life careeer theme possibilities. They provide the descriptive vocabulary that surrounds identity development as a woman and as a person of

---

BOX 14–3   Artistic

The artistic personality has an interest in creative expression of feelings or ideas. Complex mental skills are used to create new knowledge or new ways of applying what is already known. This includes different problems or designing projects and methods; using new ways to express ideas, feelings, and moods; and using imagination to create ideas and moods. Examples and prior experiences might include handicrafts, photography, art, painting decorating, playing in a band, or singing in a choir.

Transferable Skills

Skills

1. Using originality/creativity

2. Using artistic ability

3. Using intuition

Specific Operations

1. Imagining, inventing, designing; improvising, adapting, experimenting

2. Composing, playing music, singing; shaping materials, creating shapes or faces, using colors; showing feelings and thoughts through body, face or voice; using words expressively

3. Showing foresight, acting on gut reactions, quickly sizing up a situation

Possible Life Career Themes

Dislikes routine; dislikes supervision; expressive; intuitive, original; adventurous, likes novelty, change, variety; attention-getting; impulsive; independent, nonconforming; spontaneous; abstract thinking

---

color. Using such vocabulary enables you and your clients to consider themes that may have emerged from environmental barriers, socialization, and levels of acculturation.

Feminist Identity Development

Passive Acceptance.   In this first stage clients have passively accepted the inherent sexism and discrimination of society and may believe it to be justified. There is an acceptance of traditionally held gender roles that support the superiority of males.

BOX 14–4   Social

The social personality has an interest in helping individuals with their mental, spiritual, social, physical, or occupational concerns. This interest can be satisfied through jobs in which maintaining or improving the physical, mental, emotional, or spiritual well-being of others is important. Speaking and listening well, communicating simple ideas, and having direct contact with the people being helped are also important. Examples and prior experiences might include being a disc jockey, public speaking, writing for the school paper, and organizing a basketball game.

Transferable Skills

Skills	*Specific Operations*
1. Using words	1. Reading, copying, editing, writing, teaching, training, memorizing
2. Using helpfulness	2. Drawing out people, motivating, counseling; appreciating, sharing credit, raising others' self-esteem

Possible Life Career Themes

Social contact; adaptable; interested; cooperative; kind; likes friends to approach; insightful; generous; sociable; guiding; understanding; popular; idealistic; convincing; friendly; expressive; committed

---

Revelation.   The second stage may be triggered by a life event that jars clients into a realization that the systematic oppression of women is not valid or right. Clients may start feeling guilty about their own past actions and lack of awareness.

Embeddedness–Emancipation.   This stage is often characterized by a dichotomization of the sexes with all men being perceived negatively and all women positively. In this stage women may seek more communion with other women to the exclusion of men. Women may look for other women in the workplace who share their perceptions regarding gender inequity and bond with them for support and encouragement.

Synthesis.   At this stage women are evaluating men as individuals as opposed to an oppressive group. They are valuing the uniqueness of other

---

BOX 14–5   Enterprising

The enterprising personality has an interest in influencing others and enjoys the challenge and responsibility of leadership. Activities involved may include setting up business contracts to buy, sell, talk, listen, promote, and bargain; gathering, exchanging, or presenting ideas and facts about products or services; leading, planning, controlling, or managing the work or others and as a result gaining prestige, recognition, or appreciation from others. Examples and prior experiences might include managing a paper route, selling candy or tickets, Jr. Achievement, being a Candy Striper, babysitting, or starting a money-making project.

Transferable Skills

Skills	*Specific Operations*
1. Using leadership	1. Starting new tasks, ideas, taking the first move; organizing, leading, making decisions; taking risks, performing, selling, promoting, persuading

Possible Life Career Themes

Dislikes routine; adaptable; adventurous; dislikes supervision; seeks reward and recognition; ambitious; energetic; independent; sociable; persuasive; manipulating; aggressive; competitive; impulsive; assertive; optimistic; self-confident

---

women and recognizing the impact of internal and external factors that influence women's lives.

Active Commitment.   When clients reach this stage they are ready to take a much more active role in shaping their own destiny and changing harmful environmental factors. These clients are seeing the need to take on the role of making the world a more just place for themselves and other women. Although Downing and Roush (1985) believe that few women reach this stage, those that do can be especially exciting to work with in career counseling.

Racial/Cultural Identity Development

Conformity Stage.   Like individuals in the passive-acceptance stage (Jackson, 1975) and the pre-encounter stage (Cross, 1971), minority persons are distinguished by their unequivocal preference for dominant cultural values over

---

This section from Sue, D. W. & Sue, D. (1999). *Counseling the Culturally Different* (3nd Ed). New York: John Wiley & Sons, pp. 129, 132–133, 133–134, 135, 136. Used with permission.

BOX 14–6   Conventional

The conventional personality is organized to get the most work done in the least amount of time. Setting up assignments and methods in advance and repeating the same task many times may be involved. These tasks can usually be done in a short time. Activities involved may be those requiring accuracy and attention to details. Examples might include record keeping, billing, filing, or recording, keeping a checkbook, developing a budget, and savings.

Transferable Skills

Skills	*Specific Operations*
1. Using numbers	1. Taking inventory, counting, calculating; keeping financial records, managing money; number memory
2. Using follow-through	2. Following through on plans, instructions, attending to detail; classifying, recording, filing

Possible Life Career Themes

Likes details; likes to complete tasks; careful; persistent; systematic-structured; efficient; conforming; practical; conservative; orderly; inhibited; conscientious

---

their own. White Americans in the United States represent their reference group and the identification set is quite strong. Lifestyles, value systems, and cultural/physical characteristics most like White society are highly valued while those most like their own minority group are viewed with disdain or are repressed (Sue & Sue, 1999, p. 129).

Dissonance Stage. No matter how much an individual attempts to deny his/her own racial/cultural heritage, he or she will encounter information or experiences inconsistent with beliefs, attitudes, and values held by the dominant culture. An Asian American who believes that Asians are inhibited, passive, inarticulate, and poor in people relationships may encounter an Asian leader who seems to break all these stereotypes. A Latino individual who may feel ashamed of his cultural upbringing may encounter another Latino who seems proud of his/her cultural heritage. An African American who may have deceived himself or herself into believing that race problems are due to laziness, untrustworthiness, or personal inadequacies of his/her own group, may suddenly encounter racism on a personal level. Denial begins to break down, which leads to a questioning and challenging of the attitudes/beliefs of the conformity stage.

In all probability, movement into the dissonance stage is a gradual process. Its very name indicates that the individual is in conflict between disparate pieces of information or experiences that challenge his or her current self-concept. People generally move into this stage slowly, but a traumatic event may propel some individuals to move into dissonance at a much more rapid pace. Cross (1971) states that a monumental event such as the assassination of a major leader like Martin Luther King can oftentimes push people quickly from the conformity stage into the ensuing dissonance stage (Sue & Sue, 1999, pp. 132–133).

Resistance and Immersion Stage.   The culturally different individual tends to completely endorse minority-held views and to reject the dominant values of society and culture. The person seems dedicated to reacting against White society and rejects White social, cultural, and institutional standards as having no validity for him or her. Desire to eliminate oppression of the individual's minority group becomes an important motivation of the individual's behavior. During the resistance and immersion state, the three most active types of affective feelings are *guilt, shame,* and *anger.* There are considerable feelings of guilt and shame that in the past the minority individual has sold out his/her own racial and cultural group. The feelings of guilt and shame extend to the perception that during this past sellout, the minority person has been a contributor and participant in the oppression of his/her own group and other minority groups. This is coupled with a strong sense of anger at the oppression and feelings of having been brainwashed by the forces in White society. Anger toward oppression and racism is directed outwardly in a very strong way. Movement into this state seems to occur for two reasons. First, a resolution of the conflicts and confusions of the previous stage allows greater understanding of social forces (racism, oppression, and discrimination) and his/her role as a victim. Second, there is a personal questioning of why people should feel ashamed of themselves. The answer to this question evokes feelings of guilt, shame, and anger (Sue & Sue, 1999, p. 133–134).

Introspection Stage.   Several factors seem to work in unison to move the individual from the resistance and immersion state into the introspection stage. First, the individual begins to discover that this level of intensity of feelings (anger directed toward White society) is psychologically draining and does not permit one to really devote more crucial energies to understanding themselves or to their own racial–cultural group. The resistance and immersion stage tends to be a reaction against the dominant culture and is not proactive in allowing the individual to use all energies to discover who or what he or she is. Self definition in the previous stage tends to be reactive (against White racism) and a need for positive self definition in a proactive sense emerges.

Second, the minority individual experiences feelings of discontent and discomfort with group views that may be quite rigid in the resistance and immersion stage. Often, in order to please the group, the culturally different individual is asked to submerge individual autonomy and individual thought in favor of the group good. Many group views may now be seen as conflicting with individual ones. A Latino individual who forms a deep relationship with a White person may experience considerable pressure from his or her culturally similar peers to break off the relationship because that person is the "enemy." However, the personal experiences of the individual may, indeed, not support this group view.

It is important to note that some clinicians often erroneously confuse certain characteristics of the introspective stage with the conformity stage. A minority person from the former stage who speaks against the decisions of his/her groups may often appear similar to the conformity person. The dynamics are quite different, however. While the conformity person is motivated by global racial self-hatred, the introspective person has no such global negativism directed at his/her own group (Sue & Sue, 1999, p. 135).

Integrative Awareness Stage.   Minority persons in this stage have developed an inner sense of security and now can own and appreciate unique aspects of their culture as well as those in U.S. culture. Minority culture is not necessarily in conflict with White dominant cultural ways. Conflicts and discomforts experienced in the previous stage become resolved, allowing greater individual control and flexibility. There is now the belief that there are acceptable and unacceptable aspects in all cultures, and that it is very important for the person to be able to examine and accept or reject those aspects of a culture that are not seen as desirable. At the integrative awareness stage, the minority person has a strong commitment and desire to eliminate all forms of oppression (Sue & Sue, 1999, p. 136).

PRACTICE IN IDENTIFYING THEMES

Because the concept of themes is abstract, it is more difficult to explain than it is to demonstrate by example. Although some examples were provided throughout the chapter, more follow. As explained previously, themes are ideas, beliefs, attitudes, and values that people hold about themselves, others, and the world at large. These *I am*, *others are*, and *life is* statements have a lot to do with peoples' behavior. By looking at behavior—both words and actions—life career themes can be inferred or directly observed (Mosak, 1971).

Worker Role Identity

Client Statements	Possible Themes/Identity
To have a job that provides many extra fringe benefits.	*To receive direct benefits*
To receive a large yearly pay increase or bonus.	
To have a job which provides personal comfort and good working conditions.	
To have ample work breaks or get time off.	
To be able to manage money or resources.	
To be my own boss. To be independent	
To be free to make my own decisions.	
To be directly responsible to no one at work.	
To work with little supervision.	
To be free to vary my working hours.	
To be able to question the customary way of doing things.	*To achieve ideals*
To be able to explore various aspects of a job.	
To discuss which of a number of alternatives better explains a situation.	
To believe the work I do is important or significant to others.	
To be able to consider myself a creative person.	
To know exactly how my supervisors expect a job to be done.	*To be responsible*
To be able to see the results of my work at the end of each day.	
To be able to measure how much work I have done.	
To know the problem on which I am working has a correct solution.	*To be responsible*
To know that when I have finished a task, it is done once and for all.	

Client Statements	*Possible Themes/Identity*
To size up a person or situation for decision making.	*To provide leadership*
To be responsible for making major decisions that affect the work of other people.	
To be responsible for hiring and firing people.	
To coordinate the work of others.	
To be able to verbally influence a group of people.	
To know a large number of the people with whom I work.	*To have social contact*
To be around workers of the same age and interests.	
To be spoken well of by supervisors.	
To know and associate with fellow workers.	
To have other workers ask for my personal advice.	
To make a deal with someone.	*To negotiate*
To find ways to settle an argument.	
To act on gut reactions.	
To confer with people about solving problems.	
To listen and bring understanding to both sides of an argument.	
To keep records, inventory, or charts and make appointments.	*To organize*
To collect information, gather materials or samples.	
To calculate, compute, or manipulate numbers.	
To classify information or organize it into categories.	
To move something into place; to move or repair.	*To handle*
To examine, inspect, and handle with precision.	
To groom, make up, or work with precision.	
To work, smooth out, grind, stress, press materials and products.	
To do my best work the room must be free of distractions.	*To establish routine*
To have an established daily routine.	
To have chores done on a regular schedule.	
To arrange my time so that each task is done at the same time every day.	
To allow me to work on one task at a time.	

Client Statements	Possible Themes/Identity
To be physically active	To be active
To participate in outdoor sports.	
To have hobbies and interests involving muscular coordination.	
To be involved in doing something active.	

Feminist Identity

Client Statements	Possible Themes/Identity
I don't think women should be put in charge at the office. They really don't make very good leaders. I get along much better with men.	Passive acceptance identity theme
Yes it does seem like our math teacher spends more time with the boys, but that is because boys are more likely to go into math.	
I could kick myself for the many times I have doubted or discounted other women when they were courageous enough to expose the harassment that was going on. I never considered myself a feminist. I just went in, did my job and that was that. But when I was passed over again for that job, I started realizing they weren't really making promotions based on competence or previous job performance.	Revelation identity phase theme
Men I have known are not trustworthy. I have given up on them. At least with women, they may not have as much power, but at least I know they have my best interest at heart. I am looking for a more woman-centered place to work. Perhaps it is a man's world, but I don't have to work for or with them.	Embeddedness–emancipation phase theme
Seems like I really underestimated my abilities. Some of what happened to me was a result of my own internal conflicts, other things were overt discrimination. I've had good male bosses and some real abusive ones. I am a lot wiser now about identifying the losers earlier.	Synthesis identity phase theme

Client Statements	*Possible Themes/Identity*
I have come to the conclusion that a part of this change is really up to me. During a lot of my life I blamed others or waited for others to fix things. I now understand that I really need a job that promotes change for women and men at both the individual and societal levels.	*Active commitment identity phase theme*

Racial/Cultural Identity

Client Statements	*Possible Themes/Identity*
I don't want a job because of affirmative action. I just want to be viewed as me. I never thought of myself as Black. I just think of myself as a person.	*Conformity identity theme*
My high school math teacher actually told me that people like me couldn't succeed in the field of business. I realized he meant because I was from Puerto Rico. Before that I had never experienced racism personally. His comment really stopped me cold.	*Dissonance identity theme*
They say that they want to hire minorities, but only minorities that look and act White. I refuse to sell out that way. I believe it is my mission in life to work for and with other Native Americans—Whites are certainly not going to help us because they represent the system.	*Resistance and immersion identity theme*
I think I used to feel so much anger about racism, that I couldn't see past it. I still realize how discrimination effects me and other Latinos. But now I'm also spending time looking at the positive aspects of my heritage and how I can further develop my skills needed to advance in my career.	*Introspection identity theme*
It took a while for me to understand that celebrating diversity didn't have to mean putting anybody else down. I feel very comfortable now in working with all like-minded persons for the betterment of humanity.	*Integrative awareness identity theme*

SOME FINAL POINTS ON LIFE CAREER THEME ANALYSIS

The goal of this chapter was to share with you the process of life career theme analysis. To do this we selected several models of human behavior from a variety of perspectives. We organized them by the life roles of worker and person, and applied the theme analysis process to them. Now that you have seen how the process works using these models, you can use other models of human behavior and apply them to additional life roles. Remember, for the purpose of life career theme analysis, we use the language (vocabulary) of the models to provide clients with ways to express and make explicit the themes that drive their behavior. The goal is for you and your clients to come together to explore theme possibilities.

REFERENCES

Bingham, W. C. (2001) Donald Super: A personal view of the man and his work. *International Journal for Educational and Vocational Guidance, 1*, 21–29.

Bolles, R. N. (2001). *What color is your parachute?* Berkeley, CA: Ten Speed Press.

Clark, A. J. (1995). An examination of the technique of interpretation in counseling. *Journal of Counseling and Development, 73*, 483–490.

Carlsen, M. B. (1988). *Meaning-making: Therapeutic processes in adult development.* New York: W.W. Norton.

Cross, W. E., Jr. (1971). The Negro-to-Black conversion experience: Towards a psychology of Black liberation. *Black World, 20*, pp. 13–27.

Cross, W. E., Jr. (1995). The psychology of Nigresscence: Revising the Cross Model. In J. G. Ponterotto, J. M. Casas, L A. Suzuki, & C. M. Alexander (Eds.), *Handbook of multicultural counseling* (pp. 93–122). Thousand Oaks, CA: Sage Publications Inc.

Downing, N. E., & Roush, K. L. (1985). From passive acceptance to active commitment: A model of feminist identity development for women. *The Counseling Psychologist, 13*, pp. 695–709.

Dreikurs, R. (1966). The holistic approach: Two points of a line. In *Education, guidance, psychodynamics.* Proceedings of the Conference of the Individual Psychology Association of Chicago. Chicago: Alfred Adler Institute.

Field, F. L. (1966). *A taxonomy of educational processes, the nature of vocational guidance, and some implications for professional preparation.* National Vocational Guidance Association. Unpublished manuscript.

Gerber, A. (1983). Finding the car in career. *Journal of Career Education, 9*, 181–183.

Harmon, L. W., Hansen, J. C., Borgen, F. H., & Hammer, A. L. (1994). *Strong Interest Inventory applications and technical guide.* Stanford, CA: Stanford University Press.

Holland, J. L. (1997). *Making vocational choices* (3rd ed.). Odessa, FL: Psychological Assessment Resources, Inc.

Jackson, B. (1975). Black identity development. *Journal of Educational Diversity, 2*, 19–25.

Kelly, G. A. (1955). *The psychology of personal constructs, Volume 1. A theory of personality.* New York: W.W. Norton.

Kottler, J. A., & Brown, R. W. (1992). *Introduction to therapeutic counseling* (2nd ed.). Monterey, CA: Brooks/Cole.

Mangione, L. (1993). Life themes manifest through artistic creativity. In J. Demisk & P. M. Miller (Eds.), *Development in the work place.* Hillsdale, NJ: Erlbaum.

Miller, M. E., & West, A. N. (1993). Influences of world view on personality, epistemology, and choice of a profession. In J. Demick & P. M. Miller (Eds.), *Development in the workplace.* Hillsdale, NJ: Erlbaum.

Mosak, H. H. (1971). Lifestyle. In A. G. Nikelly (Ed.), *Techniques for behavior change.* Springfield, IL: Charles C. Thomas.

Nikelly, A. G. (Ed.). (1971). *Techniques for behavior change.* Springfield, IL: Charles Thomas.

Prediger, D. J. (1976). A world-of-work map for career exploration. *The Vocational Guidance Quarterly, 24,* pp. 198–208.

Prediger, D. J., & Swaney, K. B. (1995). Using UNIACT in a comprehensive approach to assessment for career planning. *Journal of Career Assessment, 3* (4), 429–451.

Prediger, D. J., Swaney, K. B., & Mau, W. (1993). Extending Holland's hexagon: Procedure, counseling applications, and research. *Journal of Counseling and Development, 71,* 422–428.

Sue, D. W., & Sue, D. (1999). *Counseling the culturally different* (3rd ed.). New York: Wiley.

Swaney, K. B. (1995). *Technical manual: Revised unisex edition of the ACT Interest Inventory* (UNIACT). Iowa City, IA: American College Testing.

U.S. Department of Labor. (1991). *Dictionary of occupational titles* (4th ed., Rev.). Indianapolis, IN: JIST Works.

Walborn, F. S. (1996). *Process variables: Four common elements of counseling and psychotherapy.* Pacific Grove, CA: Brooks/Cole.

► 15

Understanding and Working
with Resistant Clients

Little has been written about client resistance in career counseling. Much more has been written about client resistance in counseling and psychotherapy literature (Cavanagh, 1982; Hill & Williams, 2000; King, 1992; Walborn, 1996). Why is this so? One reason may be that some counselors have conceptualized and practiced career counseling as being devoid of process and relationship; career counseling for them focuses mainly on outcomes and methods within a relatively short period of time, from one to three sessions (Osipow, 1982). The perspectives and structures they use to guide their work in career counseling do not provide for the concept of client resistance.

Blustein and Spengler (1995) pointed out that client resistance, seen or unseen, can occur whenever counseling takes place, however the counseling is labeled. It doesn't matter whether counseling is labeled psychotherapy or career counseling.

In psychotherapy, counselors give much attention to helping people make changes they can imagine but have not yet been able to invoke due to internal conflicts, anxiety, cognitive distortions, family restrictions, and the like. In actuality, career counseling may be no different (Blustein & Spengler, 1995, p. 304).

Why do clients resist? In helping individuals make changes in their lives through counseling, whether labeled career counseling or personal counseling, we will evoke resistance in clients. In fact, Walborn (1996) defined resistance as the fear of change.

This is my working definition of resistance. It reflects a major paradox of therapy: clients come to therapy asking for help in changing their lives, but

*they simultaneously behave in ways that are not conducive to change. People
do not want to give up their habits. They fear change. To change is to face the
unknown. Clients prefer the security of their maladaptive thoughts and
behaviors to the risks of change (p. 238).*

Cavanagh (1982) suggested three reasons why clients may resist change.
First, he pointed out that growth is painful. It is painful for some clients to stop
old behaviors and start new behaviors because starting new behaviors often
requires becoming self-reliant, admitting self-deceit, and reexamining basic
beliefs and values. It is hard work! Second, maladaptive behaviors that may
need to be changed do provide a service to clients. They often provide a
distraction, help to vent anger, and atone for guilt. Third, some clients may
have counter-therapeutic motives. They want permission not to change, they
want to prove that somebody else is to blame, and they want to defeat the
counselor.

It is important to remember that for some clients, career counseling is
straightforward. For them, change is minimal, so little or no client resistance
is present. But for many clients, whether by conscious choice or unconscious
action, resistance in some form at some level is part of career counseling
because change is involved. Personality dynamics, irrational beliefs, motivational issues, environmental concerns, and distorted thinking may permeate
clients' views of themselves, others, and their worlds and can often short-cir-
cuit the best use of tools and techniques in career counseling. Yost and Corbishley (1987) pointed out that resistance in career counseling is often seen
most clearly in "the client's failure to complete the tasks of the stage—that is,
to provide information, to set goals, or to do assigned homework" (p. 52).

Amundson (1998) highlighted this same point in his focus on clients who
do not perform up to expectations—clients he labeled reluctant clients.
"Learning to work with reluctance can be a challenging task, but it also can be a
source of great satisfaction. It is often the difficult clients that push the buttons
of the 'counsellor' and test the limits of counselling abilities. As counsellors
successfully work within challenging situations, new counselling skills are developed and refined and self-confidence grows" (Amundson, 1998, p. 47).

To be effective in working with clients who may be resistant, for whatever
their reasons, it is important to acknowledge that resistance can and does
occur in career counseling. If you do not acknowledge this, then you will not
look for resistance in your work with clients. And, if you do not look for resistance, you will not see it. As a result, you may misread and misunderstand
some client behavior as career counseling unfolds.

What does client resistance look like? For the purposes of this chapter we
present selected examples of different types of resistance that may be exhibited by clients in career counseling. These examples include fear of counseling,
fear of taking responsibility, making excuses, irrational beliefs, faulty informa-

tion processing, and overt physical behavior. Then we turn our attention to presenting selected specific techniques that can be used in responding to client resistance in career counseling. The techniques presented include forming a client–counselor working alliance, joining, metaphors, confrontation, and labeling and reframing. While this chapter focuses on client resistance, it would not be complete without a brief examination of how and why counselors may resist too. The chapter closes with a brief discussion of counselor resistance.

RECOGNIZING RESISTANCE: SOME EXAMPLES

Fear of Counseling

Client resistance due to fear of counseling is a type of resistance described by Meara and Patton (1994). It can take three forms. One form is fear of the counselor. A second form is fear of the counseling process, while a third form is fear of discovery. Fear of the counselor focuses on clients' fears that counselors will not meet their expectations. Fear of the process revolves around such concerns as a lack of faith on the part of clients in the counseling process, clients' feelings that they lack competence to be involved in the work of counseling, and the fear of working with authority figures. Finally, fear of discovery describes feelings of clients learning unwanted knowledge about themselves.

Fear of Taking Responsibility

Another type of client resistance can be labeled the fear of taking responsibility (King, 1992). Accepting responsibility for decisions is one of the most difficult things clients face in their lives. Counselors' awareness and appreciation of the potential burden and threat that taking responsibility represents to clients are prerequisite to dealing with resistance in a positive manner. In his treatment of clients, Low (1966) discovered that anything sounds more hopeful and more comforting than the bleak prospect of having to undergo training in self-discipline. "Even brain tumors, mental ailments and hereditary 'taints' are preferable to that dreadful indictment as being a weak character and needing training in self-control" (p. 279). Some pain is only temporary; however, the fear of being unable to perform hits directly at clients' self-worth and the inability to adequately determine their existence. This presents the ominous prospect of continual, everlasting pain. Insulation and manipulation become necessary defense mechanisms for client survival.

Defense mechanisms and sabotaged communication serve as safeguards of self-esteem. This allows for an evasion of life tasks. It is always possible to collect more or less plausible reasons to justify escape from facing the challenges of life. We often do not realize what we are doing. Some strategies are intended to ensure against failure, exposure, or other catastrophes. The strategy used may have the effect of making it impossible for clients to meet onerous responsibilities—or at least it may delay the "moment of truth." Clients may try to disqualify themselves from a race they do not wish to run. If the race must be run, can failure be justified?

Defense Mechanisms

Basic defense mechanisms are familiar. However, we are just beginning to appreciate the subtle and complex ways clients use various strategies in adjusting to threatening conditions. For example, a subtle strategy we all use is called buying double insurance. No matter what the outcome, one can afford to take a partial chance because the safety of the individual is secured. Perhaps you can remember a report that you kept putting off and then just before the deadline, you worked feverishly, completed it, and turned it in at the last minute. By doing so you ensured your self-worth. If your supervisor did not like the report, it was because you did not have enough time to do an adequate job. If your supervisor did like it, you proved your unusual superiority.

This strategy is even more complex in an academic environment that places value on superior performance. The problem presented is described often as an inability to concentrate on school studies. The real problem occurs with some students who may not dare to attempt a true test of their intellectual capacity. The strategy used is buying insurance against the failure of being of ordinary intellect. According to Shulman and Mosak (1967):

Such students are overly ambitious and demand that they be on top. They cannot afford to take the chance that their best efforts may leave them in the average range of their class. At first they make resolutions to study and indeed fantasize that they will study exceedingly well and do much outside reading on the subject. But they rarely do the necessary work. In a few weeks they are behind, and the chances for doing well are diminishing. Now they feel disappointed in themselves and even less inclined to study. People who want to be on top have no interest in studying hard to achieve only an average passing grade. This is shown in their procrastination, inability to concentrate. and restlessness when they begin to study. Throughout this unproductive activity they maintain a feeling of intellectual superiority. Trouble with studying and poor grades are blamed on bad habits, nervousness, lack of discipline, dull teachers, or uninteresting courses. Such students console themselves with the thought that they are really bright but are just unproductive for the moment. If only they were able to study properly, they would be at the top of the class. If they should happen to get high grades in spite of not studying, that is all to the good. They may even boast, "I never opened a book." If a poor grade is received, it is not because they are stupid, but because they are lazy. In our society most people would prefer to be regarded as lazy rather than stupid (p. 82).

As a last resort such students may recall their earlier IQ scores and tell themselves that they are bright. They tell themselves that they could make good grades if they really wanted to. A high IQ score allows them to maintain their superiority without having to take academic risks.

Sabotaged Communication

We are educated at an early age not to venture or risk statements that might eventually be proved wrong or described as foolish. We learn how to avoid "owning" statements. Very often during a discussion, statements of obvious belief are prefaced by, "Don't you think … ?" We frequently use the words *you* and *it* to direct ownership away from ourselves in conversations. Owning is threatening.

There is an advantage to mystifying situations so that there is always room for doubt and, therefore, justified inactivity. If the situation gets too threatening, one can always justify gracious withdrawal. Keeping communication incomplete allows for the freedom to do what one pleases.

Some communication tactics that allow the individual to maintain freedom from commitment and responsibility follow (Low, 1966):

Literalness
Rejecting of a statement made by another without opposing it openly is a device that can be used to block efforts, combat views, or reject suggestions by means of misinterpretation of the words the other person uses. The following is a situation that represents this sabotage approach:

Client: *I have been working on the behavior contract for several weeks and I don't see any results.*

Counselor: *You must not be discouraged.*

Client: *I am not discouraged. But, of course, if no one sees progress….*

Discrediting
Acceptance of the validity of another person's statement may imply one's own intellectual and moral inadequacy. Should the counselor's statement be fully accepted, the client's simplicity or stupidity is thereby implied. The tactic of discrediting ensures that the process of change does not proceed too fast

or too far. A position of no obligation is maintained by using a verbal pattern of "but-knocking." But-knockers acknowledge the premise and then proceed to attack or deny its applicability to their situation.

Counselor: *Here is an outline of a conflict resolution procedure that has been used successfully in a number of companies.*
Client: *Very interesting. I can see how it would work with those large West Coast companies, but our company is quite different.*

Disparaging the Competence or Method
The client must prove that the counselor is qualified and unqualified, expert and inept, proficient and unskilled, all at the same time. The dilemma is solved by a simple trick: the counselor's competence is asserted explicitly but solidly denied by implication. The client's conscience is saved. For example, a client who consults a counselor on improving his or her ability to handle stress may demonstrate trust by continuing visits but use phrases with disparaging implications, thus denying the client's ability to be helped.

Client: *My uncle was telling me about a new stress reduction technique . . . it seems to work for him . . . there must be something . . .*

Tactics of this kind permit the client to maintain the illusion of cooperation while at the same time disrupting or opposing the process. If the counseling process does not work, the method used or the counselor's incompetence was at fault, neither of which was the client's responsibility.

Challenging Accountability
A common rejection of pursuing further exploration is the recourse to heredity. No one on any account can be held responsible for a difficulty inherited from one's ancestors ("No one in our family does well in math."). Accountability also can be directed toward other sources such as unique temperaments and moods, past traumatic experiences, and metaphysical or religious experiences. By presenting a "hopeless" situation, the client takes no responsibility. Labeling is one way to support this type of thinking. After all, what can be expected from a "dyslexic" child or a "mental" patient?

Making Excuses

Another way of understanding, interpreting, and working with resistance is to consider the concept of excuses. Snyder, Higgins, and Stucky (1983) defined excuses as "explanations or actions that lessen the negative implications of an actor's [client's] performance, thereby maintaining a positive image for oneself and others" (p. 4). Making excuses for their actions or inactions may be a way for clients to resist taking responsibility for their behavior, for not responding to the demands of the career counseling process and the tasks which may be involved.

What are some common excuses that clients may use? Snyder et al. (1983, pp. 4–7) described the following categories of excuses and some sample excuses within each category:

Lessening Apparent Responsibility

This category of excuses can be described as the "I didn't do it" category. The excuses included are designed to tell people that the excuse maker had nothing to do with something bad. This category contains denial, alibis, and blaming excuses.

Denial.   A denial excuse occurs when a person states they had nothing to do with what happened.

Alibi.   When individuals use this excuse they feign ignorance of something. They imply that they couldn't have done something because they didn't know about it or they weren't there.

Blaming.   As one client put it: "It's like this. If it's not my fault, it's her fault, and if it's not her fault, it's still not my fault" (p. 5).

Reframing Performances

In this category, individuals attempt to change the direction or to lessen the intensity of what happened or didn't happen. This is the "It's really not so bad" category.

Minimization.   This excuse attempts to manipulate the size, shape, and intensity of an event or behavior. Something did occur, but it wasn't too bad.

Justification.   Here the excuse maker supplies reasons for the excuse. There is after all a rationale for why I am saying what I am saying.

Derogation.   One way to handle a difficult situation is to put it down, to downgrade the person or situation. "The professor doesn't know as much about [counseling] as I do" (p. 6).

Lessening Transformed Responsibility
This is the famous "yes, but" category of excuses. An admission is made of something in the first word "yes." Then it is taken away and explained in the word "but."

"I couldn't help it." The most popular form of "yes, but" is "Yes, but I couldn't help it" (p. 7). There are outside forces at work that made me do it.

"I didn't mean to." This kind of excuse diverts attention away from the act a person did. After all the person is really a good person. It wasn't really me. I wouldn't do such a thing. Blame is placed on internal or external conditions.

Adapted from Snyder, C. R., Higgins, R. L., & Stucky, R. J. (1983). *Excuses: Masquerades in Search of Grace*. New York: John Wiley & Sons, pp. 4–7. Copyright 1994. Used with permission.

Irrational Beliefs

In your work with clients during career counseling, you may hear statements that Lewis and Gilhousen (1981) referred to as career myths. According to these authors, career myths are statements that reflect clients' thoughts about the career development process that are based on underlying irrational beliefs. Here are some typical client statements.

- "I am not sure if I want to do this the rest of my life."
- "I want to be sure that I don't have to change majors at midyear and lose my credits."
- "I think I had better be sure since I am deciding for the rest of my life." (Lewis and Gilhousen, 1981, p. 297).

The irrational belief underlying such statements is, "I must be absolutely certain before I can act (make a decision, gather information, do anything that requires risk)" (Lewis and Gilhousen, 1981, p. 297). Such thinking creates a paradox. The client must be sure before action can take place, but there is no way the client can be sure unless the client acts first.

Faulty Information Processing

Another way to listen to and understand clients during career counseling is to focus on how they think, on how they process information. Dowd (1995, pp. 13–14) identified seven examples of what he calls faulty information processing:

Arbitrary Inference

Especially prevalent in depression, this refers to the process of drawing a conclusion without data to support that conclusion or even with data contrary to that conclusion. For example, a client may see himself or herself as an occupational loser despite any evidence for that belief, or despite even having had success in past jobs.

Selective Abstraction

This is implicated in both depression and anxiety and, indeed, in several personality disorders as well. In selective abstraction, the individual selects one or more details of a situation and conceptualizes the whole from those few details. These fragments are generally consistent with the cognitive set characteristic of that problem, so that an anxious person will focus on elements of danger and a depressed person, on elements of loss. For example, a client may see clearly occupational deficiencies but not occupational successes.

Overgeneralization

This refers to the tendency to draw conclusions about another person or situation, which may be true, and then generalizing these conclusions to situations where they may not be true. This is especially true of individuals suffering from panic disorders and post-traumatic stress disorders. For example, because a client has been laid off from one job due to a lack of job skills, he may assume that he lacks skills for all future positions.

Magnification and Minimization

This refers to a tendency to either overestimate or underestimate the significance of an event. For example, a client may believe that a lack of ability in mathematics may be of little importance to a desire to become an engineer (a minimization), or conversely, that a grade of "D" in one chemistry course dooms the chances for ultimate success as an engineer (a magnification).

Personalization

This refers to a tendency to infer a relationship of external events to oneself in the lack of any apparent connection, and is highly implicated in depression and in the paranoid personality disorder or style. For example, a client my assume that a work rule is directed at him or her personally, when, in fact, it is aimed at solving a company problem.

Dichotomous Thinking

This is characteristic of anxiety, depression, and a host of personality disorders or styles and is commonly referred to as "all-or-nothing" thinking. The individual assumes, for example, that if events are not all good or safe, they are all bad or unsafe. Thus, a client may believe that if he or she does not perform work tasks flawlessly, he or she has failed the employer and himself or herself.

Catastrophizing

Especially implicated in anxiety disorders, this refers to a tendency to construct the worst possible situation from an undesirable event. For example, a client may assume that lack of success in landing a specific contract for the company may mean that he or she will be fired and eventually end up as a "bag person" on the streets.

Reproduced by special permission of the publisher, from "Cognitive Career Assessment: Concepts and Applications," by T.E. Dowd, 1995, *Journal of Career Assessment, 3* (1), pp. 1–20. Copyright 1994 by PAR, Inc. Further reproduction is prohibited without permission of PAR, Inc. Odessa, FL, 33556.

Overt Physical Behavior

Client resistance can be manifested not only in what clients say during career counseling but also in their overt physical behavior as career counseling unfolds (Meara & Patton, 1994). Some clients are silent and passive. Some clients show up late for career counseling sessions; some clients do not show up for career counseling at all. Other clients terminate career counseling prematurely because they can't (won't) deal with important issues, with change.

Such overt physical behavior on the part of clients creates a real challenge for counselors. How do we interpret such client behavior? Some counselors personalize this behavior and end up blaming themselves. "My client did not show up for our second interview; it must be my fault." "My client is always late for our appointments; it must be something I am doing as a counselor that causes this."

While issues of counselor competence may be involved in causing such client behavior, a more likely reason most of the time is client resistance. Being silent or passive, showing up late, or not showing up at all are ways clients can escape from the pain of change, or from anxious situations. If the client is not there or is only there for a short time, then the pain of change can be postponed or at least lessened. Various defense mechanisms, including excuses, are used to explain why they didn't show up or why they were late. Remember Low's (1966) admonition: "Even brain tumors, mental ailments and hereditary 'taints' are preferable to that dreadful indictment as being a weak character and needing training in self-control" (p. 279). Clients may go to extreme measures—being late, not showing up—to avoid dealing with changes that may require taking responsibility.

DEALING WITH RESISTANCE

As we stated previously, Yost and Corbishley (1987) defined resistance as clients' "failure to complete the tasks of the stage ...." (p. 52). In our terminology this means that clients may display resistant (defensive/evasive) behavior during any of the various phases of the career counseling process in order to protect themselves from change. They may express fear of counseling. They may be afraid to take responsibility. They may make excuses. They may hold irrational beliefs or may use faulty information processing. Finally, as one more example of resistance, they may physically remove themselves from career counseling so that they are not in harm's way.

The question at this point is why? Why do many clients put energy into resistance? As suggested previously, resistance protects clients from having to change, from having to face troublesome issues in their lives directly.

When people come to the therapist's office, they are emotionally hurting. The last thing they want is to hurt more. It is no wonder that one of the client's major tasks is to not change, to avoid the risks of greater anxiety and emotional pain. (Walborn, 1996, p. 244).

Resistive clients have their own unique, idiosyncratic patterns for survival. Understanding that resistance can and does take place in career counseling, recognizing the patterns resistive clients use, and knowing how to work with resistance within the career counseling process are crucial. Although no strategies are guaranteed to clear away resistance, the following examples of counseling strategies, including the client–counselor working alliance, joining, metaphors, confrontation, and labeling and reframing, may be helpful.

Working Alliance

In Chapter 8 the role of the working alliance in career counseling was discussed. However you come to understand and work with client resistance in career counseling, it is important to remember that a strong client–counselor working alliance is the foundation. As Walborn (1996) suggested, "Resistance melts with time and understanding, as the therapeutic relationship matures" (p. 244).

A strong client–counselor working alliance may also open the door to provide new insights about ways to interpret client behavior. Meara and Patton (1994) made this point when they suggested that where a strong working alliance exists, counselors

… can conceptualize behavior in career counseling the same way they do in personal counseling (e.g., resistance). A client who terminated early or seems reluctant to participate in building the working alliance might be labeled as resistant rather than uninterested or undecided. Client resistance can be worked with effectively if the counselor is able to recognize it and can then help the client overcome it. (Meara & Patton, 1994, pp. 174–175).

Joining

Joining is more than empathy, the reflection of feeling, or other relationship concepts associated with client-centered counseling. To join with clients you must be able to appreciate their life struggles, not just the feelings of the moment. The feelings in the immediate setting may or may not be part of the joining process. When you join with clients, you let them know that you are aware of their total life struggles. To do this you can draw on your own experiences and wisdom that relate to roles, stages, and events that structure the tasks of life. Clients are faced with different responsibilities as they move through life. Each brings a unique response to common life-role and task responsibilities. You may need to relate clients' career change dilemmas to other aspects of their lives, such as parenting an adolescent, an unexpected illness, or a financial crisis. What is it like to be 8 years old, 26 years old, or 45 years old? Can you respect the power of such responses as depression, alcoholism, and delusions? This must be done in the context of daily living problems and career decision making. Ultimately, you will need to identify clients' areas of pain, difficulty, or stress and acknowledge that, although they cannot be avoided, you will respond to them sensitively. Joining is letting your clients know that you understand them. It is letting them know that you are working with and for them. Only under this protection can clients have the security to explore alternatives, try the unusual, and change. You need to cross over the line to join with your clients to help them accept the responsibilities of their daily struggles. Your position is that of an active but neutral listener. You help your clients tell their story.

As soon as possible you should start working with your clients' strengths. Focusing on weaknesses and negative barriers is not very fruitful. By confirming what is positive about your clients, you become a source of self-esteem. Look for and emphasize positive functioning while pursuing goals of change. It is important that you be nonjudgmental about previous attempts to cope. Even when an obviously negative situation is discussed, your clients should not feel that they are being criticized or being made to feel guilty. Acknowledge that you have received the message: "You seem to be engaged in continuous struggle …." Stress that you are willing to work with them on the problem. When there is a feeling of partnership, joining has been accomplished.

Metaphors

Metaphoric language has been an important therapeutic tool since the first counselor attempted to understand fully a client's experience of the world. Traditionally, counselors have developed metaphors to demonstrate empathy and to suggest alternative interpretations of presenting problems. This use of metaphor, created by the counselor, does not change a client's problems; rather, it changes perception of the problem and allows for solutions as yet unconsidered. In this manner, metaphor has provided both a linguistic tool to facilitate empathy and an intervention technique with a history of therapeutic value (Wickman, Daniels, White, & Fesmire, 1999, p. 389).

The use of metaphor techniques in career counseling has become very involved in some circles, almost requiring the user to be a combination poet, linguist, choreographer, and biofeedback specialist. Our intent, however, is to accent the simple and straightforward aspects of the use of metaphors. In doing so we focus on storytelling and retorts that stimulate reframing. We want to bring attention to stories, anecdotes, and idioms as communication devices to use with resistive clients.

As clients tell their stories, they will often use metaphoric images in their descriptions. Listening for these images is an important counselling skill. Embedded within the images is information about how they see problems and how they see their abilities to overcome the barriers they are facing (Amundson, 1998, p. 72).

Fundamentally, through metaphoric techniques we can confront someone with a problem that can be solved in some way. The solution arrived at may not be the only solution, but it can be one possible solution. The way the problem is solved can provide a solution for others in a similar circumstance. The characters and the story experience must be directly related to clients' problems. Examples of the sources of such stories include poems, novels, poetry, fairy tales, fables, parables, songs, and movies.

Gordon (1978) stated that metaphors are a way of talking about experience. Clients will take what is heard and relate it in terms of their own experience. As this is occurring, they may gain insight into their concerns. Experiences of the past become infused with their present models of the world. In addition, these new representations may provide counselors and clients with a mutually understandable way of discussing present problems. "Metaphors are thoughts to help clients express themselves more fully so that they can communicate better and become more aware of their feelings" (Hill & Williams, 2000, p. 677).

The purpose underlying storytelling is that others' experiences in overcoming similar problems will suggest to clients, either directly or indirectly, ways to deal with their situations. Counselors can present stories about previous clients who had similar problems. These other clients' problems should have resolutions similar to the kind needed with present clients. Even if the resolution does not quite fit, clients will see that a resolution may be possible and perhaps may begin searching for one. As long as the metaphor and problem are structurally similar, clients will consciously or unconsciously relate to them. Once clients' problems are identified with the story line, clients are free to incorporate, use, or reject the resolution offered.

It may seem paradoxical, but the most effective use of metaphors results from a combination of spontaneity and planfulness. Spontaneity allows for a natural integration of material. The quality of presentation usually is better because the flow is less inhibited. However, the content of a metaphor must be short and to the point, and this requires a degree of planfulness that provides structure and a degree of simplicity that helps avoid doubt and confusion.

The more formal sources already have a built-in structure. In many cases it becomes a matter of casting the characters and then punctuating the storyline for effect. The less formal material is often derived from personal sources. It is not unusual to refer to one's own experiences. Reference to successful methods used by other clients also works. Personalizing material often is a great motivator.

Another major source for metaphor material is the universal experiences that are common to almost all people. For example, a child's struggle and ultimate success in learning to tie her shoestrings are parts of a universal challenge–success experience. The first day of school, the first date, and other common first-time experiences can provide both structure and personalization. You may wish to have a set of "universals" that you can use with common problems.

What follows are some sample metaphors. The first metaphor was used with a client who was afraid to leave home for a job offer in another community. The second metaphor was used with a client who was always excusing himself from taking responsibility because of a previous illness. The third metaphor was used with a client who often let play interfere with work.

Metaphor 1

Because you grow plants in your house, you will understand my concern. I had this cluster of plants in a large pot. They seemed to be getting along all right. I watered them and took care of them, but they didn't seem to have a healthy look. They were crowded together. So in spite of their apparent satisfactory survival, they didn't seem to be able to grow. I decided to separate them into several pots. I repotted them. At first they looked kind of lonely and puny. But after proper care, they began to grow. They did not have to share the water and nutrients in the common pot. Now they had their own pots. Even the plant I left in the original pot prospered. Everything grew better. Eventually, they were all equally strong and prospering. It may be difficult to imagine how a cluster of plants can be divided and then each one become a strong separate potting, but it happened to me.

Metaphor 2

There was this excellent baseball player. He was an outfielder and his specialty was hitting and stealing bases. One day an unfortunate accident occurred. He was running from first base to third base and had to slide into third base. His cleats caught on the turf and he broke his leg. He went through a long rehabilitation process. During part of the process, he developed a limp, but gradually all traces of the broken leg disappeared. He seemed to be able to run almost as fast, but in the back of his head he wondered if he had lost speed. He went back to playing baseball. There were no apparent signs of the injury—except on those occasions when he would ground the ball to the infield and be thrown out at first base. He would limp after he crossed first base and returned to the dugout. Ironically, he did not limp when he got a hit and roared into second base with a double.

Metaphor 3

Life is a business. Granted, there ought to be time in everybody's routine to play, to amuse oneself with games, and to divert attention from the serious aspects of the business of living. Nevertheless, life is not a game; it is a business that must be toiled at and attended to. Its business is to create and maintain values (family, community, education, religion, sociability). To play with the business of life means to gamble.

   If you start a game, you are not obligated to continue it. You may drop it because you don't like it or because it bores you or because luck is against you or because you have a headache. Conversely, if you engage in business (job, marriage, the rearing of children, helping a friend, civic activities) you are under obligations to continue it, to see it through, to finish what you have started. Headaches, boredom, dislike, and strain are no justification for shirking the duty you have assumed or the commission you have accepted. Games are personal inclinations; business is group obligation. Games are pleasures; business is a task. A task may be pleasing, which means that pleasure and task can be combined. But if a game, no matter how pleasurable it is, interferes with the serious task of business, the thing to do is to stop the game and to continue the business. Tasks must have unquestioned priority over games. In life, even a plain conversation with a neighbor acquires the character of a task. It imposes the obligation to be courteous, to be friendly, to show humility, to create good will, and to avoid criticism and intellectual snobbishness.

Confrontation

Although you may experience a certain degree of discomfort in using confrontation, it can be a most useful approach in dealing with client resistance. To use it effectively it may be helpful to link it to other strategies. For example, the Adlerians often employ the "stroke-and-spit" strategy. Cultivating a common social interest and tracking the focus of attention will build a joining-type process—positive stroking. In "spitting," the counselor discloses the skillful maneuvers of clients by pointing to the specific behavior they use to achieve their purposes. Here-and-now behavior is the usual focus, with the disclosure being unpleasant enough that the clients no longer desire to continue the behavior (Nikelly and O'Connell, 1971). If you "spit in someone's soup" they tend not to want to repeat the behavior. Humor and exaggeration can be used to soften a confronting focus. Such a disarming approach will reduce the likelihood of guarded or defensive behavior: "Let's see if we can make it worse" or "You are very clever; by pretending to be weak, you have become powerful."

If your clients are using irrational beliefs to guide their daily living at home, in school, or on the job, it is recommended that you help them become aware of this and deal with it in terms of a chain of events, A–B–C–D–E. To illustrate the use of this procedure, the following case is presented. The case used was adapted by Weinrach (1980) from a case originally presented by Ellis (1977).

Jose: An Overview

Jose is trying to enter the labor force for the first time. He is an 18-year-old high school graduate with a background in automobile mechanics. His native language is Spanish. His oral English is adequate, but his written expression is poor. His other basic skills are also weak. He reported being depressed because he would never be able to get a job and told of having been rejected after his last job interview. This case is presented to demonstrate the applicability of Ellis's (1977, p. 44) Irrational Idea No. 1: I must do well and win the approval of others for my performance or else I will rate as a rotten person.

Activating Experience (A): Performed poorly during job interview and was subsequently not offered the job.

Beliefs (B)
Rational Beliefs (r^B) (wants and desires): I would have liked that job. I don't like getting rejected. Being rejected is a big inconvenience. It was unfortunate that I did so poorly in the interview. Getting a job may be harder than I expected.

(continued)

Irrational Beliefs (i^B) (demands and commands): It is awful that I got rejected. I can't stand being rejected. Being rejected means that I am a rotten person. I'll never get a job that I want. I will always do poorly on job interviews.

Consequence (Emotional) of beliefs about activating experience (C): Depressed, worthless, rejected, helpless, hopeless.

Disputing or debating irrational beliefs **(D) (stated in the form of questions):** What is so awful about having not been offered a job? What evidence do I have that I can't stand having been rejected? How does having been rejected from one job interview make me a rotten person? How do I know that I will never get a job that I want? Why must I always do poorly on job interview?

Effects of disputing or debating irrational beliefs (E)

Cognitive Effects (c^E): Nothing makes it awful to have been rejected, especially as a lot of people apply for the same job and it is impossible for everybody to get that job; I can stand rejection. This isn't the first time I was turned down, but I don't like the feeling. Being rejected only means that I wasn't offered this particular job and in no way does that make me a rotten person. It is too soon to tell whether or not I'll ever get a job that I like, but being 18 would suggest that I have time on my side. I'll just have to wait and try some more. I don't have to do poorly on job interviews for the rest of my life. Maybe a little practice will help. I do have some bad traits that seem to come out when I am under stress. But all humans have some bad characteristics. If they didn't, they'd be perfect and no human is perfect.

Emotional Effects (e^E): I am disappointed but not depressed.

Behavioral Effects (b^E): I will go for more job interviews; I will get some lessons from my counselor on how to act during interview and then practice with my peers and parents. I will register with State Employment and local CETA program for kids my age.

Summary: As a result of RET, Jose ceased making self-deprecatory statements. He also began to see that the situation was not, as he had previously defined it, hopeless. Nor was he helpless. There were things he could do to improve his chances for a job. Once he felt disappointed and not depressed, he regained the emotional energy to try to find a job again.

From "A Rational–Emotive Approach to Occupational Mental Health," by S. G. Weinrach, 1980, *The Vocational Guidance Quarterly, 28* (3), pp. 213–214. Copyright 1980 by the American Counseling Association. Adapted with permission. No further reproduction authorized without written permission of the American Counseling Association.

Labeling and Reframing

Labeling and reframing (Bandler & Grinder, 1979; Harman & O'Neill, 1981; King 1992) clients' expressions provide a way to help them see themselves and their world differently. By providing new words and ways of organizing those words, you can help your clients by providing them with new patterns for organizing and viewing their worlds. Motivation and attitudinal changes often are associated with the labeling and reframing processes.

A change of frame is a primary event. A change of label is a secondary consequence. Reframing is a change in the frame of reference we use to look at some particular behavior, such as a moral perspective versus a medical perspective or an individual–personal view versus a family systems view. Relabeling should be reserved for those instances in which there is a change in label with no change in frame of reference, for example, neurotic versus psychotic. Both labels remain in the medical framework.

An excellent example of reframing occurred in Mark Twain's *Tom Sawyer*. Tom was able to reframe the painting of a white fence from something that was work and undesirable to something that was fun and desirable. His friends accepted his reframing of the task and proceeded to join in painting the fence enthusiastically. This does not mean that all reframing is controlling, but it does provide a different perception that suggests new behavioral responses to an old stimulus.

Labeling and relabeling skills are aimed at extracting your clients' experiences and bringing them to their attention with new verbal descriptions that punctuate their importance. Bolles (2001) does this when he helps people identify their functional job skills. He asks individuals to describe something that they do well. He then relabels these descriptions as functional job skills. For example, being a good mother and taking care of children is labeled as the functional skill of caring for people and helping others. The homemaker role is divided into various functional skills that can be relabeled as functional skills transferable to other jobs or roles. Labels provide a focus. When clients are considering career decisions, their experiences may need to be relabeled in terms of functional job skills. Academic skills often are relabeled, but social skills, leisure skills, and survival skills are sometimes overlooked.

Relabeling and reframing focus on the positive aspects of the individual. The emphasis is on what persons can do and the competencies they possess. For individuals who typically are described as having a low self-concept, relabeling and reframing techniques can be crucial and may need to be accented continually.

Reframing consists of a change of perception that implies a behavioral response that will be different or accented. This also may involve a change of values. For instance, a con artist and a salesperson have many of the same skills. Negatively described behavior often contains skills needed for survival. For example, reframing the ability to read nonverbal cues may allow the con artist to be successful. These skills also are valuable for a salesperson. Negatives can sometimes be reframed as positives.

Reframing also can be used to confront clients. A paradoxical situation can be created with resistant and unmotivated clients. Inappropriate classroom behavior may be reframed as a means of getting revenge and showing one's power so that the person will feel worthwhile. It is advantageous to reframe descriptions that are not behavioral into behavioral statements. This allows for specifying and interpretation.

COUNSELOR RESISTANCE

Counselor resistance—a strange topic of discussion for a chapter on client resistance? Not really, because resistance, wherever it originates, must be addressed in career counseling, and sometimes it originates in counselors.

Why would resistance originate in counselors? Cavanagh (1982) suggested that need gratification on the part of counselors may be involved. Counselors may have a need to punish, control, or convert clients. He also suggested that counselor dislike for some clients may be part of counselor resistance.

Cavanagh (1982) lists ten possible signs of counselor resistance. He suggested that a counselor may do any of the following:

1. Cancel appointments or arrive late. (Counselors always have "good reasons" for being late; people in counseling seldom do.)
2. Talk *at* the person instead of listening *to* and talking *with* the person.
3. Daydream and doze off.
4. Talk about himself or herself instead of about the person in counseling.
5. Forget pertinent information about the person.
6. Set up impossible requirements.
7. Suddenly discover that the person has "a special problem" and try to refer the person to another counselor who specializes in the problem.
8. Refuse to consider as important the areas that the person perceives as important.
9. Be sarcastic or "buddy-buddy" with the person.
10. Introduce areas of discussion that are of interest to him or her but are not necessarily helpful to the person (p. 261).

SOME CLOSING THOUGHTS

In this chapter we have identified and described examples of ways clients or counselors may exhibit resistance during career counseling. Our purpose was to highlight the point that whenever clients are involved in change, client resistance is probably not far behind. In fact, client resistance is to be expected. The topic of change does not actually have to be discussed. Just the thought of possible change stimulated by the presence of a counselor may initiate client resistance. Another purpose was to provide you with a language system to identify and describe client resistance so that when it is exhibited you will recognize it. Finally, we brought to your attention that sometimes counselors are the problem.

But being able to only recognize client resistance is not enough, so we also presented sample counseling techniques that can be used to respond to client resistance. Our purpose was to underscore the active role you need to take in dealing with client resistance directly. If you know what the behavior (client resistance) is and you have hypotheses about why it is being exhibited, then you can respond to it directly and naturally within the context of the working alliance. Remember, "Whatever the cause, client resistance impedes progress and cannot be ignored" (Yost & Corbishley, 1987, p. 53). At the same time, we underscored that resistance may not reside only in clients. As counselors, we must examine our motives and understand that while we believe we are part of the solution, at times we may actually be a part of the problem.

REFERENCES

Amundson, N. E. (1998). *Active engagement: Enhancing the career counselling process.* Richmond, B.C: Ergon Communication.

Bandler, R., & Grinder, J. (1979). *Frogs into princes.* Moab, VT: Real People Press.

Blustein, D. L., & Spengler, P. M. (1995). Personal adjustment: Career counseling and psychotherapy. In W. B. Walsh & S. H. Osipow (Eds.), *Handbook of vocational psychology: Theory, research, and practice* (pp. 295–329). Mahwah, NJ: Erlbaum.

Bolles, R. N. (2001). *What color is your parachute?* Berkeley, CA: Ten Speed Press.

Cavanagh, M. E. (1982). *The counseling experience: A theoretical and practical approach.* Belmont, CA: Brooks/Cole.

Dowd, T. E. (1995). Cognitive career assessment: Concepts and applications. *Journal of Career Assessment, 3 (1),* 1–20.

Ellis, A. (1977). *How to live with and without anger.* Pleasantville, NY: Readers Digest Press.

Gordon, D. (1978). *Therapeutic metaphors.* Cupertino, CA: Meta Publications.

Harman, R. L., & O'Neill, C. (1981). Neuro-linguistic programming for counselors. *The Personnel and Guidance Journal, 59 (7),* 449–453.

Hill, C. E., & Williams, E. N. (2000). The process of individual therapy. In S. D. Brown & R. W. Lent (Eds). *Handbook of counseling psychology* (pp. 370–710). New York: John Wiley & Sons, Inc.

King, S. M. (1992). Therapeutic utilization of client resistance. *Individual Psychology, 48,* (2), 165–174.

Lewis, R. A., & Gilhousen, M. R. (1981). Myths of career development: A cognitive approach to vocational counseling. *The Personnel and Guidance Journal, 59 (5),* 296–299.

Low, A. (1966). *Mental health through will training* (14th ed.). Boston: Christopher Publishing.

Meara, N. M., & Patton, M. J. (1994). Contributions of the working alliance in the practice of career counseling. *The Career Development Quarterly, 43,* 161–177.

Nikelly, A. G., & O'Connell, W. E. (1971). Action-oriented methods. In A. G. Nikelly (Ed.), *Techniques for behavior change.* Springfield, IL: Charles C. Thomas.

Osipow, S. H. (1982). Research in career counseling: An analysis of issues and problems. *The Counseling Psychologist,10 (4),* 27–34.

Shulman, B. H., & Mosak, H. H. (1967). Various purposes of symptoms. *Journal of Individual Psychology, 23,* pp. 79–87.

Snyder, C. R., Higgins, R. L., & Stucky, R. J. (1983). *Excuses: Masquerades in search of grace.* New York: Wiley.

Walborn, F. S. (1996). *Process variables: Four common elements of counseling and psychotherapy.* Pacific Grove, CA: Brooks/Cole.

Weinrach, S. G. (1980). A rational–emotional approach to occupational mental health. *The Vocational Guidance Quarterly 28, (3),* 208–213.

Wickman, S. A., Daniels, M. H., White, L. J., & Fesmire, S. A. (1999). A "primer" in conceptual metaphor for counselors. *Journal of Counseling and Development, 77,* 389–394.

Yost, E. B., & Corbishley, M. A. (1987). *Career counseling: A psychological approach.* San Francisco: Jossey-Bass.

▶ 16

Using Information in Career Counseling

We find ourselves in the midst of revolution and the implications are far-reaching. It is a revolution not of the sword but of the word. Career counselors, like most people, now have phenomenal access to the printed word or information. This revolution brings power to everyone, particularly the educated. We may find ourselves with an additional responsibility to bring the benefits of the revolution to the less educated and the many clients who due to poverty or other forms of marginalization do not have the same access to technology.

Not long ago this chapter would have focused primarily on how and where you could find career information, and then would have stressed the importance of making it available to clients. We now are at a point where the information is often too readily available and, in fact, sometimes there will be too much of it to be useful. Whereas clients once may have been forced to make decisions with too little information, today they are more apt to be confronted with how to make decisions with too much information. Counselors need to be able to recognize symptoms or complaints of information overload—not necessarily good information, but too much of it. The key issue for career counselors today is identifying accurately the real needs clients have for career information. Once needs are established, other issues, such as why and when to provide career information, how to provide it, how much to provide, what good sources are, and how we help sort out the quality of the information, become important concerns.

In this chapter then, we discuss how to identify clients' needs for information, problems with objectifying these needs, our own needs for gathering information, why and when we must provide information, assessments that help us with the process, and some good sources of information. This chapter will demonstrate that the appropriate and effective use of career information is an important task, but not a simple one.

IDENTIFYING CLIENT NEEDS FOR INFORMATION

We should not assume that all of our clients need career information. While they may present themselves as needing information, this could mask other concerns. They may come to us believing they only need information, but in the first few minutes of the initial interview they may suggest that other issues are more pressing and that information may instead be useful later. Or, you may see that responding to a simple request for information only further confuses rather than solves a problem. Information is powerful, but it can be confusing, overwhelming, or seemingly irrelevant if not offered at the right time. Knowing whether, when, and how to provide it is part of the essence of good career counseling. Information must be harnessed and offered in appropriate ways to be beneficial. Career counselors develop skills at doing this that can make them particularly helpful at times when those without such skills may not be so helpful.

Review here some typical client requests that have been expressed in early career counseling sessions. Try to ascertain whether the need is for information, and if or when providing it would be helpful.

A 55-year-old woman recently divorced:

Cl: *I don't know what to do next. I never thought I would have to work outside the home, but now without a husband to support me, I need to find a career for myself.*

An 18-year-old college freshman:

Cl: *Everyone in the family is in medicine and I always thought I would be too. But now I'm not so sure. I'm good in science and I like it, but what else can I do with it? I'm not sure I want to be in school for ten years and besides, I don't see myself working with sick people or in a hospital.*

A 50-year-old navy officer about to retire:

Cl: *I've enjoyed 20 years overseas doing maintenance and supply work, but where can I apply those skills in civilian life?*

A seemingly disappointed college graduate:

Cl: *I'm not doing the kind of work I thought I would, and I don't see any way out of the job I have. I don't know what else I can do with only a major in journalism.*

These four clients represent quite different life situations, although not necessarily different needs. The recently divorced woman who never thought she would have to work outside the home may be much like the college freshman just discovering the need to think about something other than medicine. Neither felt much need to think about alternatives until recently. But how each will deal with this recent need for information may make our response to their requests quite different. Seemingly both need information, but we don't immediately know what other needs may be confounding their situations. Is the recently divorced woman, for example, still dealing with the ending of a long-term marriage so that she cannot look objectively at alternatives? Is the college freshman looking for an alternative to medicine only because she is disappointed at not being in what she thought would be some exciting classes the first year in college? Clearly, we need more clarity about their situation before we can assess the needs for information in either case.

The naval officer, 20 years overseas, may seem like a classic example of someone in need of information, assuming he wants to move into another career. But we must be careful not to assume he is not coming to us with a fairly clear agenda and much information, only asking us to confirm his choice. Again, we will need more clarity about his situation before deciding if and when more information would be appropriate. Finally, the disappointed college graduate working at an entry-level job that does not meet her needs may really be more concerned with remedying the present situation than looking for an attractive alternative. We clearly do not have enough information to be helpful yet in any of the cases presented.

A common theme in all these cases is that it is difficult to judge the needs for career information before we have sufficient information about a client's total situation. A request taken at face value in an opening session too often leads to either the provision of career information not needed or not valued at that time. Our diagnostic skills are important here: We are trying to appropriately assess our clients situations first, and only then can we decide whether, when, how, and what kind of career information is needed.

A further nuance of a decision to respond to the need for career information is the professional judgment you must make regarding how the client will make use of it. You can build a case for a client who has a simple need for information and you will provide it. You can observe that it is helpful and is being incorporated appropriately in the client's thought processes. Other times, however, you may have provided information but observe that little use is being made of it, or, worse yet, that it is being used inappropriately. A client is seemingly moving toward some new option but ignores the new information provided. These examples further argue the need to adequately assess the needs for information before we provide it.

CAREER INFORMATION NEEDS
FROM A PERCEPTUAL POINT OF VIEW

In career counseling we are acutely aware of the importance of a perceptual frame of reference. So often the issue is not what reality is, but what one perceives it to be. Our perceptions may tell us one thing, the client's perceptions another. When we engage in deciding on whether, when, and how to provide career information, we may err in favor of seeing it as an objective process. We may perceive a need for particular information and then try to find and provide it, considering ourselves experts at it. But let us look at why that approach, from a perceptual point of view, may not serve our client's needs.

When a client comes to us with a perceived need for information, we accept this as an accurate perception. We provide the information and then perceptions of career opportunities, as an example, become more accurate. Encouraged by this, we provide more information, but then begin to see that the additional information is not being used appropriately. For example, the client may ignore some of it or distort other bits of it. In our objectivity, we see the need to reinforce some ideas or correct others. The process becomes more complicated because the client filters what was said; only some parts are heard and other parts heard are distorted. We begin to wonder if we are miscommunicating. The reality we see is not the reality seen by the client. We can begin to understand that, like the emphasis placed on understanding the initial problem in counseling, we have a similar difficulty perceiving the need for the most appropriate time to provide career information and how it should or will be used.

It may appear that the simple process of the counselor providing career information is very complicated. We intend to present it that way. The process involves not simply drawing on resources from the library, computerized systems, or the internet. It is a complicated process that demands the same care and attention we give all other parts of the counseling process. Because we need to be sensitive to the pervasive role of information at all phases of counseling, we must acquire an in-depth appreciation of not only what is available but how, when, and in what form to provide it.

LOOKING AT OUR OWN
NEEDS FOR INFORMATION

Although we must examine carefully our clients' needs for information, we should also consider our own needs for acquiring and making use of these expanding sources of information. This information explosion and changing notions about work, leisure, employment, and life roles means we must constantly search for new resources if we are to keep ourselves current. To be creative in helping one prepare for an ever-changing world, we must become comfortable and conversant with materials from a variety of sources. It would appear as though one media may become particularly good at providing some kinds of information while another form of media may become the key source for other kinds of information. Although we may prefer one source more than another, we eventually will have to draw on all sources. We must become masters of information and current technology to remain informed and effective. This means maintaining subscriptions to printed materials, using resources on video, accessing company home pages and chat rooms, communicating via teleconferencing, and a whole lot more. In-service programs and continuing education for ourselves in new media forms is essential for us, because professional expectations are changing for us as well as for our clients.

At the same time we are encouraged to learn more about information available through technology, we need to keep a perspective on the more traditional ways many of our clients will continue to access career information. We can, for example, speculate on the influence of computerized information in much the same way that we can look back on the influence of television. While the potential was enormous, it took time before television became the pervasive influence it is today. Over time it became a dominant influence in most homes but, more important, today there are still significant numbers of people who do not have access to television. Similarly, there are still large numbers of people who do not have access to computers or technology in general. While career information may come to us in technologically sophisticated ways, there will continue to be significant numbers of people—many of them our clients—who will access information in other ways. In fact, for some, important resources for information will continue to be limited to more personal, informal sources that will not receive much coverage in this book. These important sources include family, relatives, community members, elders, ministers, peers, teachers, and other people with whom we may never interact. Nonetheless, these people may exert more influence on our clients through word of mouth communication than any information we may find electronically.

Whatever the sources, the importance of being able to know, retrieve, and assess up-to-date information will become even more of a challenge. It is a task far beyond the reasonable efforts of any one individual. The journals of some of our professional organizations regularly provide reviews of career-related materials. The National Career Development Association's (NCDA) *Career Development Quarterly* and the National Association of Colleges and Employer's *Journal of Career Planning & Employment* are two good examples. NCDA started this service years ago. Initially it was almost exclusively a review of print materials, but increasingly it reviews audio tapes, videos, films, CD-ROMS, and similar new sources of information.

WHY WE PROVIDE INFORMATION

Beyond the fact that clients believe they have needs for information, providing information within the career counseling process serves numerous purposes. These purposes are either educational or motivational (see Table 16–1).

In the educational realm, we can hypothesize that information will inform thought, expand and extend it, or correct it. These are distinctly different purposes, and the way we approach providing information in each of these categories would be quite different. Informing the thought process is a far simpler task than correcting it.

To inform might be a straightforward process, while correcting may involve helping someone give up information that has served a seemingly useful purpose for some time. For example, a client may hold onto the distorted impression that she cannot go back to school because she did not complete high school or a college degree program years ago. By holding on to that information, she may not consider many attractive career alternatives believing that she does not think she would have access to them.

We may find it helpful to think of these differences as one would in advertising. Are we telling someone about the product, informing them of additional benefits of the product, or correcting their impressions of the product? If, for example, a person has a distorted impression of a product, we have a far different task than simply providing information.

In the motivational realm, we use information to stimulate, challenge, and confirm. Perhaps the biggest challenge in career counseling is learning to use information in a motivational way.

Some information by itself would not be motivating, but provided at the proper moment it may make all the difference in a career-planning process. Some kinds of information can prove motivating before one makes a decision, and other kinds of information are more important after one makes a decision. Before making a decision clients may only hear the global or general information about a career possibility, but later, having made a decision to enter a particular field, they may be open to hearing more of the specifics about their choice.

TABLE 16–1   Purposes of Career Information

Educational	Motivational
To inform	To stimulate
To expand and extend	To challenge
To correct	To confirm

When you consider the millions of dollars advertisers spend to motivate us to use their products, you have a perspective on our task. Counselors must stimulate or challenge clients with career information—a formidable task even for those with unlimited budgets. We must learn to do it with appreciation of what we refer to as "teachable moments." These moments come when you have information to give your client that your client feels can be used at a particular time. This is another way we claim our professional identity—we are experts at knowing when to provide information.

WHEN TO USE CAREER INFORMATION IN COUNSELING

Timing is everything. This adage is especially true in deciding when to use career information. Considering that a career decision is an ongoing process, it is appropriate to find ways to provide information at all three phases of the process. In the first phase (Exploration), we may need to be assessing the clients' needs for information as they begin a process of exploring a variety of concerns. The process may have us hypothesizing about the clients' needs for information as well as their other needs. The client, for example, might lack information and know it, or lack it and not know it; a client may have adequate information and be using it appropriately, or have adequate information and not be using it appropriately or be distorting it; or a client may have more than enough information and be coping with it, or he may be overwhelmed by it.

We can offer a two-by-three table as a way of conceptualizing where clients are initially: They come with too little information, about the right amount, or too much information, and, on the other dimension, they either know it or do not know it (see Figure 16–1).

Seemingly, we could provide examples of clients who fit into each of these categories, and we could suggest hypotheses about when to provide

Information

Client Status	Too little	About right	Too much
Knows it			
Doesn't know it			

FIGURE 16–1   **Client Status versus Available Career Information**

information for each of them. The art and science of these hypotheses would not be that exact, but clearly clients with too little information should initially be treated in a manner different from ones who have too much information. And clients who know what they need are different from those who lack insight into what they need. Our diagnostic skills, as always, are taxed and honed in identifying just where our clients are as they begin the career counseling process. What makes it even more complicated but fascinating is that the initial categorization can change quickly; we may find one who begins with too little information and knows it, suddenly become confused by too much information. Or, vice versa, a client with too much information may sort it out quickly and need more information.

Phase One in a career decision-making model (Exploration) leads to Phase Two (Understanding). In this second phase, we can confirm any hypotheses we made in Phase One about our clients' needs for information. If we thought they needed information and we provided it, we can observe in subsequent counseling sessions whether it has been incorporated and whether it has influenced their understanding. If not, we may need to try a different tactic. We know that sometimes clients do not understand the first time through and this requires that we explore other ways. Because it is an ongoing process, we can review and process again and again. We only hope to improve on our clients' understanding before they reach Phase Three (the Action phase), when they act on information. This three-phase model is portrayed graphically in Figure 16-2. It emphasizes the ongoing nature of the process, the way in which we constantly depend on feedback from our clients to refine the process, and the clear need to make ongoing assessments about the timing of the provision of information. It is a far more complex and interesting process than first meets the eye. It is one more place where we can practice and refine our skills as counselors.

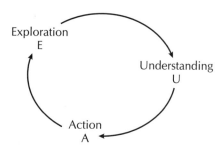

FIGURE 16–2   A Decision-Making Model Applied to Career Counseling

HELP IN ASSESSING THE
NEED FOR INFORMATION

If clients find it difficult to assess their needs for career information, we might want to enhance their judgments or our own by looking for clues in some of the assessment tools frequently employed in career counseling. The My Vocational Situation (MVS) presented in Chapter 12, for example, provides a quick indication of what clients might need at the time they present themselves for counseling. It provides a vocational identity score (1 to 18), with a low score suggesting that clients have an unclear picture of their career situation. This may be one indicator of a need for career information. In addition, question 19 specifically asks clients about their needs for information in various areas. The Career Transitions Inventory (CTI), discussed in detail in Chapter 13, also helps both clients and counselors see particular needs. Clients with low or flat profiles on interest inventories may be clients who need more information. Finally, however, clients may be all too clear about their needs for information, or their initial presentation of a concern makes obvious their needs. We do not want to suggest that you not take their judgments seriously, but we do want to caution you to continually assess the need. It can be deceiving, because some clients believe the more information the better, and it can change quickly, leaving either the client or the counselor confused about the importance of providing it.

ESTABLISHING HOW MUCH
INFORMATION IS HELPFUL

Nothing is more helpful in refining a process than feedback. We can ask clients for feedback, but sometimes it is not easy for them to provide it. We can suggest they look up something as homework, or we can ask that they try a computerized career information system like SIGI or DISCOVER, or suggest they look at some information available on the internet and then inquire in the next session as to how helpful it was. We can ask them to bring career information into the session for further discussion. If we make use of it within the counseling process, we can observe immediately how it is being used or incorporated into our clients' thinking. We then have one more clue as to the need and the effectiveness of the information being provided.

Feedback is important both during and after the counseling process. Too often we can be left wondering if the information provided was actually used and, if so, whether it was as good as we thought. Without some kind of feedback from former clients, we miss the opportunity to improve our own use of career information. Encourage clients to stay in touch or drop a note after a reasonable time to let you know what was helpful. Some counselors or agencies routinely send form letters to clients six weeks after termination and request feedback. This practice encourages both reflection and evaluation that can be useful to both you and your clients.

SOURCES OF CAREER INFORMATION

There are many good sources of career information. Some texts are particularly good at describing and defining the information available (Isaacson & Brown, 1997; McDaniels & Gysbers, 1992; and Zunker, 2002). But there has been an explosion of new information and sources as well. More information is available on video, in computerized systems, and, most recently, on the World Wide Web. Clients are not apt to have equal access to all these sources, and yet, because "information is power," one of our roles is to help our clients grasp that power. To do so, we need to be comfortable with all of these sources ourselves.

We cannot overstate the impact of technology in making information available to people, including our clients. As we write this, we see many of our standard career informational references available on the World Wide Web. The *Occupational Outlook Handbook*, for example, is easily accessed complete with pictures on the Web. This is one of many resources promoted through National Association of Colleges and Employers (NACE). Employment opportunities and job resources on the Internet, commonly known as the Riley Guide, provide users with immediate access to resources previously available only to a select few. Most companies maintain sites on the Web where users can access extensive, up-to-date information about them that may be of help in job searches. Home pages allow users to send information about themselves to prospective employers. Resumes can be constructed and sent via the internet. CD-ROM technology and Web technology have merged to make it possible to have unlimited information—encyclopedia size—not only easily available but with a link to a Web site that can provide constant updates. Peterson's Guides to both undergraduate and graduate schools are available on the Web. Virtual career centers are on the Web, as are career assessments. In short, whatever was available in print is now available electronically at competitive prices. We are probably at a place where various media—print, computer, video, and other sources—will merge in creative ways. In the meantime, we can expect a continued explosion of ever-changing career information to be forthcoming.

Using the Internet to complement your sources of career information and other resources in career planning is essential. However, it is not yet a science—more an art. New sites appear almost daily. Sites you start to rely on one day are gone the next. It may, however, be useful to bookmark particularly good sites for your personal use. Find ones in those areas where you most need information on a routine basis. We expect you may need favorites in at least each of the following areas. We list ones our staff members in a college career center have found particularly useful. As these invariably change, log on to our homepage for new or additional ones (career.missouri.edu). We provide a representative list in each area, not an exhaustive one. The following is a sampling of current sites on the Web that may be helpful to both career counselors and clients:

General Career Guidance and Information
http://stats.bls.gov/ocohome.htm (Occupational Outlook Handbook)
http:www.rileyguide.com (Riley Guide, General guide for job seekers)
http://career.missouri.edu (University of Missouri's Career Center)

Resumes, Cover Letters and Interviewing
http://career.missouri.edu (University of Missouri's Career Center)
http://campus.monster.com (Monster.Com)

Networking
http://www.industryinsite.com (General Reference)

On Line Career Assessments
http://www.self-directed-search.com (Self-Directed Search Interest Inventory)
http://www.keirsey.com (Keirsey Personality Inventory)
http://www.rileyguide.com (Riley Guide)

Internships
http://campus.monster.com (Monster.Com)

Job Searches
http://jobs.pj.org (Philanthropy Journal)
http://www.cool2serve.org (National Service)
http://www.nationaservice.org (National Service)
http://www.nonprofits.org (National Service)
http://www.EscapeArtist.com (International Jobs)

Company Profiles
http://www.vault.com (Vault Reports)
http://www.wetfeet.com (Independent directory for jobs and company profiles)
http://company.monster.com (Monster.Com)
http://www.IMDiversity.com (Diversity perspective on jobs)

Graduate Schools
http://www.gradschools.com (General Information)
http://www.petersons.com (Petersons Guide to Graduate Programs)

Some of these will have changed by the time you read this, but by accessing these you will learn of links to other career-related sites. Bookmark those you find to be most useful for you in working with clients. Whether we find information on the Web or in print form, on CD-ROM or on audiotapes, once found, our basic skills as counselors are further challenged—helping clients find career information and use it to their advantage.

Some Less Obvious Sources of Career Information

Increasingly we are counseling clients who either do not have access to the many sources of career information just described, or equally important, who have and will continue to rely on other sources. For many clients of different ethnic, religious, or cultural backgrounds, the family, elders in the church or tribe, or a prophet, sage, or some other authority may be the ultimate source of information. We do not shape or influence these sources in the same way that we shape and describe the use of computerized systems, but we must learn to appreciate and understand the importance of these influences. This is another important reason why we need to listen for feedback from our clients. We cannot assume they will find our sources as useful as the ones they already are using. We need to listen for subtle clues about what the really meaningful sources of information are to our clients. Too often these are not brought into the conversation, significantly diminishing the impact of our time together with clients. The importance of understanding another's background in an increasingly global world is a fascinating and essential perspective for career counselors. We must try to weave together a variety of sources and recognize that the ultimate decisions made in career counseling are not ones we necessarily need to explain in any objective fashion. This may be one way to view the process, but clearly it is not the preferred way for many of our clients. The more you work with clients from different backgrounds, the more you learn that your way is only one of many ways.

Methods of gathering, sorting, evaluating, deciding whether or not to use information and whether or not to act on it may be dependent on ethnicity, race, gender, sexual orientation, cultural or socioeconomic background, and a host of other variables. We can only learn so much about these differences from our textbooks. Much will always be dependent on listening well to our clients. In preparation for that, when assigned a client from a different racial or ethnic background, we might want first to inventory our own experience with such differences. Ward and Bingham (1993) created a Multicultural Career Counseling Checklist (MCCC) (see Table 16–2) that is "... designed to help you think more thoroughly about the racially or ethnically different client to whom you are … providing career counseling." You simply read and check the statements that apply. You learn what you know and what you need to find out for your client.

Ward and Tate (1990) created a Career Counseling Checklist (CCC) (see Table 16–3), later modified by Ward and Bingham (1993), which serves as a checklist for the client to tell you what he/she knows about the world of work, and the influences of age, gender, disability, and socioeconomic background. It also includes questions regarding the role of the family in career decision making. When administered early or before counseling, it not only provides you with useful information from your client on important issues, but it communicates that you are interested in making these issues part of career counseling. You may find you want to establish still other ways of assuring that you remain open to learning about these differences.

To make effective use of career information, now available in a wide variety of forms, is a daunting challenge for career counselors. We now have all the information out there that we need; the challenge is to help your clients sort out what is needed, when it is needed, how and when it can best be used, and what the important sources are. Helping clients to put it all together for themselves can be a complicated but fascinating process that draws on many of our professional skills.

TABLE 16–2   Multicultural Career Counseling Checklist

If you have a client of a different ethnicity/race than yours, you may wish to use this checklist as you begin to do the career assessment with your client.

The following statements are designed to help you think more thoroughly about the racially or ethnically different client to whom you are about to provide career counseling. Check all the statements that apply.

My racial/ethnic identity _____

My client's racial/ethnic identity_____

I. Counselor Preparation

❑   1. I am familiar with minimum cross-cultural counseling competencies.
❑   2. I am aware of my client's cultural identification.
❑   3. I understand and respect my client's culture.
❑   4. I am aware of my own world view and how it was shaped.
❑   5. I am aware of how my SES influences my ability to empathize with this client.
❑   6. I am aware of how my political views influence my counseling with a client from this ethnic group.
❑   7. I have had counseling or other life experiences with different racial/ethnic groups.

(continued)

TABLE 16–2 *Continued*

- ❏ 8. I have information about this client's ethnic group's history, local sociopolitical issues, and her attitudes toward seeking help.
- ❏ 9. I know many of the strengths of this client's ethnic group.
- ❏ 10. I know where I am in my racial identity development.
- ❏ 11. I know the general stereotypes held about my client's ethnic group.
- ❏ 12. I am comfortable confronting ethnic minority clients.
- ❏ 13. I am aware of the importance that the interaction of gender and race/ethnicity has in my client's life.

II. Exploration and Assessment

- ❏ 1. I understand this client's career questions.
- ❏ 2. I understand how the client's career questions may be complicated with issues of finance, family, and academics.
- ❏ 3. The client is presenting racial and/or cultural information with the career questions.
- ❏ 4. I am aware of the career limitations or obstacles the client associates with her race or culture.
- ❏ 5. I understand what the client's perceived limitations are.
- ❏ 6. I know the client's perception of her family's ethnocultural identification.
- ❏ 7. I am aware of the client's perception of her family's support for her career.
- ❏ 8. I know which career the client believes her family wants her to pursue.
- ❏ 9. I know whether the client's family's support is important to her.
- ❏ 10. I believe that familial obligations are dictating the client's career choices.
- ❏ 11. I know the extent of exposure to career information and role models the client had in high school and beyond.
- ❏ 12. I understand the impact that high school experiences (positive or negative) have had on the client's confidence.
- ❏ 13. I am aware of the client's perception of her competence, ability, and self-efficacy.
- ❏ 14. I believe the client avoids certain work environments because of fears of sexism or racism.
- ❏ 15. I know the client's stage of racial identity development.

III. Negotiation and Working Consensus

- ❏ 1. I understand the type of career counseling help the client is seeking (career choice, supplement of family income, professional career, etc.).
- ❏ 2. The client and I have agreed on the goals for career counseling.
- ❏ 3. I know how this client's role as a woman in her family influences her career choices.
- ❏ 4. I am aware of the client's perception of the woman's work role in her family and in her culture.
- ❏ 5. I am aware of the client's understanding of the role of children in her career plans.
- ❏ 6. I am aware of the extent of exposure to a variety of career role models the client has had.
- ❏ 7. I understand the culturally based career conflicts that are generated by exposure to more careers and role models.
- ❏ 8. I know the client's career aspirations.

TABLE 16–2   *Continued*

❏   9. I am aware of the level of confidence the client has in her ability to obtain her aspirations.
❏ 10. I know the client understands the relationship between type of work and educational level.
❏ 11. I am aware of the negative and/or self-defeating thoughts that are obstacles to the client's aspirations and expectations.
❏· 12. I know if the client and I need to renegotiate her goals as appropriate after exploring cultural and family issues.
❏ 13. I know the client understands the career exploration process.
❏ 14. I am aware of the client's expectations about the career counseling process.
❏ 15. I know when it is appropriate to use a traditional career assessment instrument with a client from this ethnic group.
❏ 16. I know which instrument to use with this client.
❏ 17. I am aware of the research support for using the selected instrument with clients of this ethincity.
❏ 18. I am aware of nontraditional instruments that might be more appropriate for use with clients from this ethnic group.
❏ 19. I am aware of nontraditional approaches to using traditional instruments with clients from this ethnic group.
❏ 20. I am aware of the career strengths the client associates with her race or culture.

Reproduced by special permission of the publisher, *Psychological Assessment Resources,* Inc., Odessa FL. From the *Journal of Career Assessment,* Volume 1. Number 3. copyright 1993 by PAR, Inc. Further reproduction is prohibited without permission from PAR, Inc..

TABLE 16–3   Career Counseling Checklist

The following statements are designed to help you think more thoroughly about your career concerns and to help your assessment counselor understand you better. Please try to answer them as honestly as possible. Check all of the items that are true for you.

❏   1. I feel obligated to do what others want me to do, and these expectations conflict with my own desires.
❏   2. I have lots of interests, but I do not know how to narrow them down.
❏   3. I am afraid of making a serious mistake with my career choice.
❏   4. I do not feel confident that I know in which areas my true interests lie.
❏   5. I feel uneasy with the responsibility for making a good career choice.
❏   6. I lack information about my skills, interests, needs, and values with regard to my career choice.
❏   7. My physical ability may greatly influence my career choice.
❏   8. I lack knowledge about the world of work and what it has to offer me.
❏   9. I know what I want my career to be, but it doesn't feel like a realistic goal.
❏ 10. I feel I am the only one who does not have a career plan.
❏ 11. I lack knowledge about myself and what I have to offer the world of work.
❏ 12. I do not really know what is required from a career for me to feel satisfied.
❏ 13. I feel that problems in my personal life are hindering me from making a good career decision.

(continued)

TABLE 16–3   *Continued*

❏   14.   My ethnicity may influence my career choice.
❏   15.   No matter how much information I have about a career, I keep going back and forth and cannot make up my mind.
❏   16.   I tend to be a person who gives up easily.
❏   17.   I believe that I am largely to blame for the lack of success I feel in making a career decision.
❏   18.   I have great difficulty making most decisions about my life.
❏   19.   My age may influence my career choice.
❏   20.   I expect my career decision to take care of most of the boredom and emptiness that I feel.
❏   21.   I have difficulty making commitments.
❏   22.   I don't have any idea of what I want in life, who I am, or what's important to me.
❏   23.   I have difficulty completing things.
❏   24.   I am afraid of making mistakes.
❏   25.   Religious values may greatly influence my career choice.
❏   26.   At this point, I am thinking more about finding a job than about choosing a career.
❏   27.   Family responsibilities will probably limit my career ambitions.
❏   28.   My orientation to career is very different from that of the members of my family.
❏   29.   I have worked on a job that taught me some things about what I want or do not want in a career, but I still feet lost.
❏   30.   Some classes in school are much easier for me than others, but I don't know how to use this information.
❏   31.   My race may greatly influence my career choice.
❏   32.   My long-term goals are more firm than my short-term goals.
❏   33.   I have some career-related daydreams that I do not share with many people.
❏   34.   I have been unable to see a connection between my college work and a possible career.
❏   35.   I have made a career choice with which I am comfortable, but I need specific assistance in finding a job.
❏   37.   My gender may influence my career choice.
❏   38.   I have undergone a change in my life, which necessitates a change in my career plans.
❏   39.   My fantasy is that there is one perfect job for me, if I can find it.
❏   40.   I have been out of the world of work for a period of time and I need to redefine my career choice.
❏   41.   Making a great deal of money is an important career goal for me, but I am unsure as to how I might reach it.
❏   42.   My immigration status may influence my career choice.

REFERENCES

Holland, J. L., Daiger, D. C., & Power, P. G. (1980). *My vocational situation.* Palo Alto, CA: Consulting Psychologists Press.

Isaacson, L. E., & Brown, D. (1997). *Career information, career counseling, and career development* (6th ed.). Boston: Allyn and Bacon.

McDaniels, C., & Gysbers, N. C. (1992). *Counseling for career development.* San Francisco: Jossey Bass.

Ward, C. M., & Bingham, R. P. (1993). Career assessment of ethnic minority women. *Journal of Career Assessment, 1,* 246–257.

Ward, C. M., & Tate, G. (1990). *Career Counseling Checklist.* Atlanta: Georgia State University, Counseling Center.

Zunker, V. G. (2002). *Career counseling, applied concepts of life planning (6th ed.).* Pacific Grove, CA: Brooks/Cole.

▶ 17

Developing Plans
of Action

Seeing our clients take proactive steps with their career plans is one of the truly rewarding parts of the career counseling process. Helping them turn a dream into reality is validating and affirming for both the counselor and the client. How this happens is sometimes the result of a well-developed set of goals and a plan of action, and other times it happens in seemingly unsystematic and unexplainable ways. That is, career goals and a plan of action are best understood or explained when they follow a rational set of steps. We know other times the process seems quite intuitive, and particularly for members of racial and ethnic minority groups and for women, the process of getting to where one wants to be can be nonlinear and perhaps even circular, with the process recycling through various layers of the decision. Either way, helping a client become clear about their career goals and establishing plans of action is another important step that deserves our attention as part of the career counseling process.

In this chapter, we begin by looking first at the outcomes we can expect to emerge from career counseling. This leads us naturally to a closer examination of the process by which such outcomes or goals or plans come to be formulated. Finally, we conclude with a section on some techniques that will increase the chances that clients leave career counseling with the career plans and goals they envision for themselves.

WHAT CLIENTS TAKE FROM CAREER COUNSELING

When one looks carefully at the research evidence on outcomes from career counseling, it is easy to conclude that it is a valued and helpful process (Phillips, 1992; Heppner & Hendricks, 1995). In fact, the effects reported in a summative manner from a variety of studies of career interventions (Brown & Ryan Krane, 2000; Spokane & Oliver, 1983; Spokane, 1991) suggest that the outcomes may be even more impressive than what is reported as outcomes for psychotherapy. This should make us inquisitive as to what clients say happens for them in career counseling. What is it that they report as so helpful?

First, we often hear clients express a new or renewed sense of hope or determination about doing something they said they wanted to do. In terms we introduced earlier in the book, they may have a better sense of agency or hope (Snyder et al., 1991) and talk in clearer terms about the pathways to follow in pursuit of their goals. Their "goals" are not to be confused with our "goal" of creating a strong working alliance. In the working alliance, we reference goals to be achieved in the counseling relationship—goals important to our working together as counselor and client, while here, we reference goals as some specifics to be worked on in creating a plan of action for the client.

Clients will attribute much to counseling and to the support, understanding, and encouragement they feel from their counselor and from the relationship they experienced (Fuller & Hill, 1985; Heppner & Hendricks, 1995). We should not overlook the importance of this relationship, and perhaps the process of career counseling will eventually prove to be far more important than has been reported. It may, however, be more difficult to collect the evidence for its importance than for the more objective changes one can observe.

We will often hear about new discoveries or insights from career counseling; these can be learnings or insights about themselves or about opportunities for themselves. Reports of changes in the way clients see themselves or their opportunities are common in the research on outcomes of career counseling (Holland, Magoon, & Spokane, 1981).

We should be encouraged by the evidence for all that can be attributed to career counseling, but we do not want to overlook what happens within the process. Clients come to new understandings and insights and see new opportunities for themselves, but how does this happen? How do they put things together for themselves? How do their goals and a career plan of action emerge and what do we do to encourage such planning?

In a comprehensive review of 62 recent studies of career counseling (Brown & Ryan Krane, 2000), there emerged considerable support for the idea that positive outcomes are related to the inclusion of five critical ingredients. While any one of them is important, the combination of the five seems most powerful. The five, in no particular order, are written exercises, individualized interpretations and feedback, information on the world of work, vicarious learning experiences like exposure to models who have attained success in the career exploration process, and attention to building support for one's career choices. We suggest a few ways of incorporating each of these in career counseling and encourage the career counselor to think of other creative ways of doing so. If each is important, and a combination of all is more important, we need to attend to creatively incorporating all of them in our interventions. We also refer you to the chapter by Brown and Ryan Krane for a more thorough description of their important findings.

A first ingredient is the incorporation of written exercises. We might include a simple intake form that requires the clients to write about themselves in a brief manner. We might ask them to complete a series of "incomplete sentences" about their career plans. Completing the Occupational Dreams Inventory (ODI) may make one focus on past, present, and future career plans.

A second ingredient to include is individualized interpretations and feedback. These may be comments on written papers or exercises, comments made about career plans in counseling sessions, interpretations of tests, or inventories. Such feedback depends on providing it in the context of a strong working alliance. Only in that context will it be seen as important and meaningful to the client.

Third, we provide information on the world of work. We may assume our clients know and can use information and do not need help finding it. We devoted an entire chapter, however, to being sure we are not too quick to assume what our clients needs and understandings are regarding career information (See Chapter 16).

The authors add an interesting observation of their own a year later after further reviewing these findings (Brown & Ryan Krane, 2001): "Studies that have asked clients to rate how helpful different aspects of the interventions were to them consistently [report] the most helpful activities [were] those designed to help clients search for and use occupational information" (p. 6). Specifically, the use of career information *within* counseling sessions was highlighted, as opposed to the more common practice of giving a client homework to locate and examine career information.

Fourth, we provide vicarious learning experiences. We can expose our clients to role models who have attained success in their chosen fields of study. On the college campus, that may mean finding them peers, faculty and staff members, community members, and alumni who are open to being interviewed about their work.

Fifth, we build support for their career choices. That may mean emotional or social support. It may mean helping them make connections with people in your network or in other ways of helping them expand on their own network of professional contacts. We may promote rehearsals and immediate reinforcement of career plans that are brought up in counseling sessions.

In Chapter 16, we presented career decision making as a three-step process. The first step referred to exploration, the second to understanding, and the third referred to action-taking steps. It is a continuous process, one step leading to the next, and so forth. As you learn more about yourself, you may see need for more information about the work world before taking action. This may be a good representation of a process followed by some clients and it probably is close to the way we believe a systematic person would proceed. It is a crude representation at best, but it does accurately represent three parts that continually are changing in an equation. It may be more difficult to represent the way other less systematic clients proceed. We know, for example, there is an intuitive and nonlinear process that may be equally effective for some clients (Gelatt, 1991). We also explored in Chapter 2 how a theory of "planned happenstance" and a personal career theory (PCT) (Holland, 1997) might be equally effective processes. In short, we must be careful not to impose one process when another would better serve a client. Using one model or a combination of models, however, we try to help clients move toward some plan of action.

Whichever model proves most helpful to your thinking about the process, be clear that you should place an emphasis on eventually taking some action. It may be short-term or long-term action, within the time frame of counseling or well after it, but career counseling should provide a framework for good planning. And while clients may talk about other outcomes of counseling, some of those don't require you to do anything in particular. A good goal or plan of action usually requires discussion, refinement, rehearsal, modifications, and a whole lot more before being successfully implemented. Clients need help with these steps and there are a variety of things we can do to improve the chances they will eventually act on them.

DEFINING CAREER GOALS AND PLANS OF ACTION

To be logical, we want to have a plan before we take action. This may not always be true, but that's the order we give it—plan, then act. We often speak of our goals, for example, and then, with help from others, set about trying to devise a plan of action for achieving them. This plan can be simple or complex, short or long term, individual or group, specific or general, but it always involves some goal(s) that should be understandable and achievable. In career counseling, we help the client put together an understandable scheme for achieving particular goals that becomes the plan of action. It is true that most of us do not set goals or make plans on a regular basis, but we admire the few who do. Career plans usually emerge from a process of setting goals. Once goals are identified, we look for ways to achieve them.

THE BASICS OF PLANNING

Like career counseling, a career plan needs to be seen as an ever-evolving process. While we can characterize the planning part or action phase as the last part of a three-part process, it is more accurately a continuous process or loop where one may be working simultaneously on all three parts—exploration and understanding about self, exploration and understanding about one's environment, and equally important, exploration and understanding as to how to act on these insights or learnings.

Out of career counseling then should come plans of action, concrete objective steps for doing something different from the way one did them before. What do we know about making plans that would be helpful to clients who may have had little experience with the process? There are a number of things to impart to clients during the process of counseling. Most important, recognize that counselors can set the stage for developing goals and making plans as early as the first session. In fact, it should be communicated early that goals and plans of action are expected outcomes of career counseling. Clients may need to be instructed on this early and often. We can easily become comfortable with simply talking about a plan and never actually making one. That is why sometimes you hear clients with high praise for counseling and no mention of actions taken as a result of such efforts. It may be necessary to illustrate in concrete terms what you mean by an action plan. For example, early on in counseling a counselor might make a statement like this:

Counselor: *You may learn a lot about yourself and some new career options you hadn't thought of before, but equally important, I hope you'll be able to be clear as to a course of action that you could follow. Could you see yourself, for example, with a goal of taking a new job in another field by the end of this year? I'd like you to be thinking about that and what specific plan of action that might require. I'd like to think I could be of some help to you as you develop that or a similar plan of action for yourself.*

This statement emphasizes both the need for a plan and the need for a timeline. These are two concrete ideas to suggest early in the process. They may need to be reemphasized throughout career counseling as clients often resist efforts to move toward action. In fact, often that is what brought them to career counseling— not being able to set a goal or establish a plan of action for themselves.

Keep in mind that a client's early attempt at stating a plan of action may only be a statement of an immediate need. It may come before Exploration or Clarification that will eventually change the Action that seems appropriate. It may not represent a long-term plan for action. Some clients come to counseling not knowing they need more information about themselves or their options before being able to state a plan of action. They come to counseling only expressing their immediate need. Let's look at some examples of statements made in opening interviews that should illustrate our point.

Client: *I must chose a major by tomorrow so I can preregister for next semester.*

Client: *I want to quit my job and go into something where there are fewer hassles.*

Client: *I've been fired again and I need help finding a new job.*

These statements may be good clues as to why a client came for counseling, but they don't provide all the information necessary for establishing an eventual plan of action. Choosing a major may be a long-term goal, but chances are that a client will need more time and probably some specific information about self or careers before setting it as the immediate goal of counseling. Quitting a job because one wants something with fewer hassles may or may not make sense, but clearly more information is needed before agreeing to work with that as a goal or endorsing it as a plan of action. Likewise, in the third example, we see that helping a client find another job is an appropriate long-term plan of action, but we want the client to give serious consideration to what has gone wrong in previous jobs before seeking another job.

Two points can be made from these examples. First, it is important to make a distinction between what is offered as an immediate goal or plan and the eventual goal or plan. Second, we need to view the creation of goals and action plans as an ongoing process. This last point should not negate the initial statement of a goal and a plan of action, because it is that statement that brought the client to career counseling. It may well be a good indication of what may need to be clarified and refined in counseling. It is usually an accurate indication of where we must begin as we help clients establish a goal and develop a plan of action.

We need to be be sure that clients give equal time to both short- and long-range plans of action. Some clients only see immediate goals, others see only the long-term ones and need help focusing on the necessary short-term goals. Whatever the case, we can help them make plans according to a criteria that better assures them of success in meeting their goals.

CRITERIA FOR CAREER GOALS AND ACTION PLANS

Goals and eventual plans of action should be formulated to meet an objective criteria. This takes practice, but it makes it easier to later observe progress toward meeting the goals or recognizing the steps still to be taken. Krumboltz and others (Blocher, Heppner, & Johnston, 2001; Gysbers & Moore, 1987; Krumboltz, 1966) present particularly helpful criteria to use in establishing a goal and eventually a plan of action. In brief, goals should be specific, observable, time specific, and achievable. To help our clients with plans that meet these criteria, we need to provide some help. It is not simply doing what comes naturally.

Goals Should Be Specific

Attention to specificity is necessary to keep a client from simply making vague statements like, "What I need is a new job,...more money,...a new major," when it will be more helpful to have the client state the kind of job, the amount of money, or the specific major to pursue. Again, clients tend to initially be vague about goals, but with practice they can become quite specific. That is one of our roles: to see how goals or plans can be made more specific. It is hard to lay out a plan of action without first being specific about goals.

Goals Should Be Observable

A second part of the criteria argues for goals to be observable. It helps when a client can see the goal: "I will enter graduate school," "take a new job," or "earn my diploma." These are all specific and observable goals. You can see that the client either did or did not do what he or she intended to do. Both the client and the counselor can observe this. Again, a client may not be inclined to state goals in such a manner. The counselor may need to help frame goals this way.

Goals Should Be Time Specific

Mentioning the time needed to meet a goal is also important. Those observable goals just mentioned might better be stated with some mention of a reasonable time line. The previous examples might become "I will enter graduate school by September of this year," "I will take a new job before the end of the year," or "I will earn my diploma by June of next year." These would all be specific, observable, and time specific.

Goals Should Be Achievable

Finally, goals should be achievable. In the optimism of new learnings or the discovery of new possibilities, one can to be overly optimistic or ambitious about goals. "I will enter graduate school by September and have my master's degree in a year" is unrealistic when serious inquiry reveals that the program is a two-year program. Again, the counselor's role is to help the client set reasonable and attainable goals without dampening one's enthusiasm for undertaking something new.

The goal-setting stage may be an important place to help minority clients or men and women who are taking nontraditional life paths plan and strategize for the probable environmental barriers that may stand in the way of reaching their desired goal. Racism, sexism, homophobia, and ageism all may influence societal and institutional willingness to support the goals of your client. This may also be a time when counselor advocacy is important in helping clients actively overcome barriers that are standing in the way of attaining their dreams.

Goals May Need To Be in Writing

It sometimes helps to have goals in writing. Some people relate positively to written reminders of what they intend to do; others find it unnecessary to put what they see as the obvious in writing. Here we believe a counselor needs to attend to whatever is reinforcing for a particular client. After all, the intent is primarily to help clients find reinforcement for doing what they say they want to do. The career counselor should do whatever is helpful in documenting changes in counseling.

Goals Should Be Articulated

Another point to emphasize is the importance of articulating the plan. Although we may think a plan of action should be obvious, the client may not see it that way. We should encourage the client to work at verbalizing a plan throughout counseling. This promotes planning as an ongoing process and allows you to contribute to the refinement of the plan. It also gives you feedback on what is being heard in counseling. Often a client will verbalize a global or overly ambitious plan, much to your surprise. Because a good plan may take input from both of you, you need to hear it as it is being put together. Only a well thought out and articulated plan will ever be put into action.

Techniques that May Help to Establish Career Plans

There is no one way to establish a goal or goals for oneself. A plan of action may also be quite individualistic, but we should work to establish a repertoire of techniques and interventions that aid the process. Some of these are listed below, but be vigilant in adding to the list as you learn from your own experience.

   1. Establish early and often the expectation and need for goals and a plan of action. Let clients know what they can realistically expect as outcomes.
   2. Make goals and plans of action reasonable. Clients may need help seeing what is reasonable. Too often their prior experience has not helped them with either goal setting or organizing a plan of action, or they are seeking

counseling because they haven't been able to establish goals or make plans. Teach the process if necessary. Provide time in counseling for them to learn and practice the process, review goals and plans, critique them, rehearse them, and help them refine them. Provide support and nurturing for these new skills.

3. See that goals and plans are built and can be evaluated according to a meaningful and objective criteria. The client, as well as the counselor, should be able to observe and document progress.

4. Reinforce in as many ways as possible the means to effective goals and plans of action. It is far easier to create a goal or a plan than to act on it. Provide opportunities for clients to talk through their goals and plans, to write them out, rehearse them, and to visualize themselves achieving them. Push them to openly share these ideas with significant others. Consider establishing a routine during career counseling for formulating and reviewing progress toward setting their goals and developing plans of action. Help them adjust their goals and plans as appropriate and help them recognize and celebrate any progress toward achieving their goals or implementing any part of the plan of action. These reinforcements are essential to a client's ultimate success. And because reinforcements are often hard to provide to a client who is unclear about goals or plans, this may be another reason clients value so much their time in career counseling.

5. Individualize the process according to the needs and preferred style of each client. What seems helpful for one client may be counterproductive for another. Structure, for example, may enhance one's ability to act, or it may be a hindrance. Teaching a client to focus may be helpful or it may be unnecessary. Visualizing a plan, writing out a plan, rehearsing the plan may be a help for one and only a meaningless exercise for another.

6. Don't be hard on a client or yourself when things don't go according to plan. There are a myriad of very good reasons why goals are not achieved and plans are not followed. Expect successful approximations from some, failure from others, delaying tactics, excuses, and unexplained inactivity from others. Complex and often demanding actions are being considered. Sometimes we may only know a fraction of the reasons why a client does or doesn't act. We often find that we can learn from one client how to better help another client.

Making goals and plans work is the final and perhaps most difficult of the steps involved in career counseling. We need an equally varied repertoire of skills to make it a productive part of the entire process. To become good at it requires practice, follow-up, and feedback from our clients. With that kind of help, we become better at meeting the real needs of our clients.

REFERENCES

Blocher, D. H., Heppner, M. J., & Johnston, J. A., (2001) *Career planning for the 21st century*. Denver, CO: Jove Publishing Company.

Brown, S. D., & Ryan Krane, N. E. (2000). Four (or five) sessions and a cloud of dust: Old assumptions and new observations about career counseling. In S. D. Brown & R. W. Lent (Eds.), *Handbook of counseling psychology* (3rd ed., pp. 740–766). New York: Wiley.

Brown, S. D., & Ryan Krane, N. E. *Critical Ingredients in Career Counseling: Some new data*. In S. Whiston (Chair), *Do career interventions make a difference? An overview of research*. Paper presented at the annual convention of the American Psychological Association, San Francisco, CA, August 2001.

Fuller, R., & Hill, C. E. (1985). Career development status as a predictor of career intervention outcomes. *Journal of Counseling Psychology, 29,* 388–393.

Gelatt, H. B. (1991). *Creative decision making*. Los Altos, CA: Crisp Publications.

Gysbers, N. G., & Moore, E. J. (1987). *Career counseling: Skills and techniques for practitioners*. Englewood Cliffs, NJ: Prentice Hall.

Heppner, M. J., & Hendricks, F. H. (1995). A process and outcome study examining career indecision and indecisiveness. *Journal of Counseling and Development, 73,* 428–437.

Holland, J. L. (1997). *Making vocational choices: A theory of vocational personalities and work environments* (pp. 205-210). Odessa, FL: Psychological Resources, Inc..

Holland, J. L., Magoon, T. M., & Spokane, A. R. (1981). Counseling psychology: Career interventions, research, and theory. *Annual Review of Psychology, 32,* 279–305.

Krumboltz, J. D. (1966). Behavioral goals for counseling. *Journal of Counseling Psychology, 13 (2),* 153–159.

Mitchell, K. E., Levin, A. S., & Krumboltz, J. D. (1999). Planned happenstance: Constructing unexpected career opportunities. *Journal of Counseling and Development, 77,* 115-124.

Phillips, S. D. (1992). Career counseling: Choice and implementation. In Brown & R. W. Lent (Eds.), *Handbook of counseling psychology* (2nd ed.), pp. 513–547. New York: Wiley.

Snyder, C. R., Harris, C., Anderson, J. R., Holleran, S. A., Irving, L. M., Sigmon, S. T., Yoshinobu, L., Gibb, J., Langelle, C., & Harney, P. (1991). The will and the ways: Development and validation of an individual differences measure of hope. *Journal of Personality and Social Psychology, 60,* 570–585.

Spokane, A. R. (1991). *Career Intervention*. Boston: Allyn and Bacon.

Spokane, A. R., & Oliver, L. (1983). The outcomes of vocational intervention. In W. B. Walsh & S. H. Osipow (Eds.), *Handbook of vocational psychology* (pp. 99-136). Hillsdale, NJ: Erlbaum.

▶ 18

Bringing Closure to Career Counseling

"In career counselling, we need to include some ceremonial elements to honour what has been accomplished and to signify the coming changes through action planning"
—*(AMUNDSON, 1998, P. 203)*.

Bringing meaningful closure to a counseling relationship is often a most difficult task for counselors. There are a number of reasons for this difficulty, perhaps foremost is American's general uneasiness with endings of all kinds. Examples of this uncomfortableness are visible in everyday endings, such as our leave-taking behaviors after a visit with friends or relatives. These endings are many times prolonged and include numerous references to when the parties will get together again. These behaviors seem to serve the purpose of denying the fact that this visit is in fact ending. Some of the most important, most honest, communication we have with others is spurted out in the last few moments of a long visit. Endings make us uncomfortable. Thus, in counseling, both counselors and clients may resist closure. They may continue in the counseling relationship after it has ceased to be useful in order to avoid the feelings associated with the end of the relationship.

An important training issue for counselors is to examine their own attitudes toward endings. If endings are of particular difficulty for counselors, they may profit from reading books or articles related to dealing with loss. Time should be set aside during supervision to discuss counselor concerns with closing relationships. In some cases, the counselors may need to seek counseling themselves if their personal issue with closure is limiting their effectiveness as counselors. For most counselors, however, the discomfort that accompanies endings can be alleviated through receiving information about what elements contribute to effective closure in career counseling.

Very little has been written about the importance of closure in career counseling. This lack of focus on closure in part may be due to the view that career counseling is perceived as short-term and structured with few of the emotional loose ends common in social–emotional counseling sessions. As this book has pointed out, this description of career counseling does not fit a large majority of career counseling cases. The role of work in people's lives cannot be neatly compartmentalized from their social–emotional lives. Thus, effective career counseling includes a broad approach to the person and one that encompasses all aspects of the person's context and emotion. Research indicates that contrary to popular belief, clients value and recognize the importance of the working alliance in career counseling (Bikos, O'Brien, & Heppner, 1995; Heppner & Hendricks, 1995). With this more holistic view of career counseling comes the need to attend to all aspects of the relationship including the integral issue of bringing closure to the relationship, saying good-bye. This "closing ceremony" (Amundson, 1998, p. 203) is important to plan for from the very beginning days of the counseling relationship.

This chapter addresses four related topics. First, the context of closure is discussed, including the various reasons for closure. Next, a special kind of closure is covered, the premature termination that occurs when the client ends counseling before the counselor believes he or she is ready. Following this is a discussion of the feelings associated with closure, and finally information on what constitutes effective closure is provided.

THE CONTEXT OF CLOSURE

Closure happens at a number of different times for varied reasons. The context of the closure is an important element in determining the form it will take. There are three primary reasons for closure.

Initial Goals Have Been Met

The client and counselor feel the initial goals for counseling have been met and there is no longer a need to meet. In the best of scenarios, closure occurs when the needs that originally brought the client to counseling are satisfied. This may mean that the client has become clear about his or her major or career choice, or has worked through the difficulties felt on the job, as examples. Although these clients may need reassurance about the counselor's availability should additional needs arise, these closure sessions are usually the clearest and most rewarding for both the counselor and the client.

No Action at This Time

The client knows what needs to happen next in the career planning process, but has decided not to take action at this time. In this situation the client has "gone to the edge of the lake" but is not quite ready to jump in. This is descriptive of clients who have clarified their interests, skills, and values, and know exactly what path they need to take, but for a number of reasons are unable or unwilling to take that path at the current time. One way to assess specific reasons for this inability to take action is through use of the Career Transitions Inventory that is described in depth in Chapter 11. The client may lack motivation, confidence, support, independence, or feelings of control. By helping clients understand the reasons for their inaction, they can choose if they want to work on the psychological barriers and try to overcome them. Many times situational variables prevent forward movement: small children needing care, lack of financial resources to support the training necessary to change careers, or too little emotional energy following a divorce. It is important that clients do not feel blamed for their lack of activity. The counselor can normalize the situation and reassure the clients that when they are ready to take the next steps, the counselor will be there to provide assistance.

A Lack of Depth or Meaning

The counseling session itself lacks depth or meaning. The pain that originally brought the client to counseling has lessened and the motivation to work in counseling has eroded as well. A certain amount of discomfort, confusion, or pain is usually necessary to give clients the motivation to initiate counseling. This pain can be caused by the stress of job loss, difficult relationships with coworkers, or the anxiety caused by indecision in choosing a major or career field. It may also result from the pain and uncertainty many adults feel when approaching particularly important trigger points in their lives, such as turning 40, or coming to the age themselves when a same-sex parent died. Sometimes this pain is eased by the cathartic effects of talking to a counselor for a few sessions. Even though the problem is not resolved, the client no longer feels the powerful affective reaction that initially motivated them to work on these issues in counseling. Thus they choose to end the counseling relationship.

How the counselor chooses to handle this type of closure depends to a great extent on the consequences of the closure on the individual client. For many clients this type of closure is normal and will result in few dire consequences. They have received some immediate help to get them through the current issues, and they will opt to use services again should they have recurring problems. In the current health care arena that places a value on time-effective counseling, this type of short-term problem resolution is becoming the norm. In some situations, however, the counselor may need to encourage the client to continue even though the initial pain has subsided, for example, in situations where there is physical or psychological danger to the client should he or she choose to stay in an unhealthy work situation. In this case, the counselor's role may be to help the client recognize these inevitable consequences: (a) The counselor feels he or she cannot work with the client. These reasons have been discussed with the client. Or conversely, (b) the client feels he or she cannot work with the counselor. These reasons have been discussed with the counselor. Sometimes in the course of counseling a mismatch occurs between the counselor and client, for a variety of reasons. The client, for example, may be at a stage of identity development that makes it difficult to work with a particular counselor. As we have discussed in Chapters 3, 4, and 5 on gender and diversity issues in counseling, if a client is at a stage of identity development characterized by a dichotomization of the sexes or races, it may be difficult for this client to constructively work with a counselor of the opposite sex or different race. Another potential reason for a mismatch is when the counselor feels ill equipped to handle particular client issues due to lack of appropriate training or biases that the counselor holds about specific groups of people. In any case, it is vital that the counselor and client work through their differences before making a referral to a more appropriate counselor. Thus, these different contexts of the closure session in many ways prescribe the form the closure session will take. For example, if a client is being referred due to inability to work with a particular counselor, the closure session will focus on different issues than if it were an ending based on goal accomplishment.

THE SPECIAL CASE OF PREMATURE CLOSURE

Perhaps one of the most difficult contexts of closure is that which has been referred to in the literature as premature termination (Ward, 1984) or closure. This occurs when the client decides to end counseling before the counselor believes the client is ready. Premature closures often occur when the client simply does not show up for the next scheduled appointment. Brown and Brooks (1991) mention four possible reasons for premature closures: (1) clients believe they have achieved their goal, (2) clients fear what may be uncovered in the counseling process, (3) failure of counseling to meet the client's expectations, and (4) lack of client's commitment to counseling in the first place.

Although premature closures occur in most settings, it is imperative that the counselor examine the reasons behind the termination. Sometimes this examination results in information concerning aspects of the career counseling setting or procedures that actually promote premature closures. In a study examining critical negative and positive incidents in career counseling (Heppner, O'Brien, Hinkelman, & Flores, 1996), the following comments were made that illuminate some possible reasons for premature termination:

I got the feeling the counselor had little interest in me as a person. She had her little routine of giving me these tests and telling me what I should be. I felt she treated every client exactly alike—with the same mechanized roteness. Why would I go back for more of that?

This quote exemplifies the importance of building a working alliance, viewing career counseling as a process rather than procedure, and valuing the uniqueness each client brings to the process.

As a Black person, I just didn't feel like my counselor understood me or the issues I was addressing. She looked like she had always been one of the privileged. The counseling agency had a White feel to it—I didn't feel comfortable there.

Although premature closures occur with all client populations, there is strong evidence that they are especially prevalent with clients from underrepresented groups (Sue & Sue, 1999). This client's quote emphasizes the need to examine ways in which the counseling setting is discouraging to members of underrepresented groups.

We worked together for a couple of sessions, then he referred me to the career resource library to "collect information." He said I should call him when I was done looking. I felt dumped—like he had no interest in helping me any further.

The art of integrating information into the career counseling process is critical. As discussed in Chapter 16, clients and counselors need to develop a specific plan for identifying and interpreting career information. Turning a client loose to "explore on your own" may be one of the quickest routes to a premature closure. Clients need to feel assured that their counselor will work with them throughout the process and not abandon them in a sea of unfamiliar occupational information.

Having never been to career counseling before I guess I just didn't know what to expect, but clearly I wasn't ready to pursue counseling right now.

As we highlighted in Chapter 8, talking about client and counselor expectations is of critical importance in the opening sessions of career counseling.

Being sure that the client understands what career counseling is, and perhaps more importantly, is not, can avoid premature closures that are precipitated by unclear expectations.

HANDLING PREMATURE CLOSURES

A point of decision occurs for the counselor when a client does not show up for an appointment. How much responsibility the counselor should take in encouraging the client's return is a matter of professional judgment. Generally, calling the client has the following advantages:

- It allows for the expression of caring and concern for the client.
- It gives the counselor a chance to collect information about the reasons for the client's premature closure and to learn there were ways the counselor or counseling agency may have unknowingly contributed to the client's decision not to return.
- It allows for referral to another counselor or agency when appropriate.
- It gives the counselor the opportunity to "leave the door open" to future visits when the client feels ready to begin again.

FEELINGS ASSOCIATED WITH CLOSURE

Understanding the range and complexity of emotions related to closure will help the counselor normalize diverse feelings and facilitate the client's processing of their emotions. A wide diversity of feelings are associated with endings in counseling.

I'd rather talk the talk than walk the walk.
Although most effective career counseling is a blend of talk and action, the client may feel that ending counseling puts more pressure on them to take major steps in their own behalf. The client may have become quite comfortable with the talk about the career planning process; the action may elicit much greater fear and discomfort.

I feel nurtured in this nest—don't kick me out.
For some clients the nurturing and intimacy that is part of counseling is a unique experience. The relationships in their own lives do not provide the kind of support and caring they feel in counseling. This nurturing feels good and they do not want to give it up. These feelings provide a rich environment for encouraging the client to develop more meaningful and nurturing relationships. One might emphasize that they have clearly been able to develop this relationship with you as the counselor and that these same skills may be used to foster other nurturing relationships.

I don't have to say good-bye if I don't come back.
Sometimes clients will simply avoid the whole process of closure by repeatedly canceling or not showing up for appointments. Through this form of avoidance the client does not have to go through the discomfort of endings, but also misses out on the satisfaction that comes with closure.

It wasn't all that good anyway, so why process it?
Many times people are less uncomfortable with anger than with sadness or loss. Thus when they feel an ending approaching they may distance themselves from it through a process of disenchantment (Bridges, 1980). This disenchantment may take the form of discounting the counselor and the counseling process. The client may start believing that the counselor is withholding information or not being as helpful as originally thought. This disenchantment serves the purpose of making the ending easier because the relationship was "not that important anyway."

Thank goodness I've accomplished my goals and have my Thursday evenings free again.
Being in counseling is work. It's not uncommon for a client to feel relief at not having to come to counseling any more. The counseling may have been very helpful in accomplishing needed goals, but the client may nonetheless feel freedom when it is over. Being able to talk about this relief in an authentic manner is an important goal of the closure session.

WHAT CONSTITUTES AN EFFECTIVE CLOSURE?

Closure sessions vary greatly depending on the level of working alliance that has developed and how effectively the goals or tasks of counseling have been achieved. But even within this individual variation there are at least seven commonalties in what makes for effective closure.

1. Typically there will be a review of the content of what has transpired during counseling. Effective closure sessions are a time for reflection on the journey of career counseling, where the client was when first coming to counseling, and the path that has brought them to this ending. This reflection may focus on the initial confusion and uncertainty the client felt and how through the process of counseling the client gained new clarity about self and the world. Especially important in this review of content is emphasizing the role the client had in shaping the journey, and the transferability of skills learned in the process to new situations. This discussion provides an opportunity for the counselor to describe the dynamic and reoccurring nature of career choice and change and to emphasize that the client may very well be using the skills learned in these sessions for future career planning. Reviewing the content

helps the client understand more about how the individual parts of the process came to make up the whole. As Amundson (1998) describes: "I have found it important to highlight 'Moments of Movement' ... points in the process where there seem to be clear indicators of a change in perspective. (p. 191)." An example of how this processing of context might sound like this:

Counselor: *We have been on quite a journey together for the last six weeks.*

Client: *Yes, I feel pretty different than when I stumbled in here, not knowing what you do, or what I could even ask for.*

Counselor: *Yes, you were pretty confused then. Your divorce had only been final for a little over a week and you didn't know what direction your life should take.*

Client: *Yes, and I hadn't realized how dependent I'd become on Mike and how I had lost a great amount of self-esteem in the ending of my marriage.*

Counselor: *You really demonstrated strength and resiliency in reaching out for help and coming to this place you knew nothing about.*

2. Equally important to a review of the content of the sessions (what happened) is the process of the sessions (how it happened). Examining the process includes talking directly about the working alliance that developed between the counselor and client and how that relationship unfolded over time. Focusing on the process is especially important if there has been conflict in the counseling relationship. A careful examination of how both the counselor and client dealt with the conflict can be a powerful learning experience.

An example of how this review of the process of the session might go like this:

Counselor: *I remember when you first came to counseling I felt your anger and despair at being overlooked for so many positions.*

Client: *I felt really bad and when I saw you; I wondered if a White person would really understand what I'd been going through.*

Counselor: *I really wanted to help, but I wasn't sure you would let me.*

Client: *Well, not until you passed my tests.*

Counselor: *Tests?*

Client: *I was checking you out. Were you racist? Did you really mean what you said? Would you follow through, or were you just saying what you thought I wanted to hear?*

3. Closure sessions are also a time to reemphasize the strengths of the client in dealing with these important life issues. It is often difficult for clients to own their part in what was effective in counseling, so it is important to reflect on those strengths at this time of closure.

Here is an example of restating the strengths of the client:

Client: *You have really helped me understand how much I've let being a female stop me.*

Counselor: *You have shown a lot of sophisticated understanding about the role of all kinds of environmental factors in limiting your perceived options.*

Client: *Yes, thanks to you I feel like I can explore many more areas now and that I might actually have some skills to succeed in them.*

Counselor: *I appreciate your reinforcement of my role in your new enlightenment about options. I also want to hear you own the part you had to play in reclaiming your dreams.*

Client: *Yes, I have gone after it with a vigor.*

Counselor: *Indeed!*

4. The closure session is also a time for evaluation. What went well? What went poorly? What was the most helpful event in counseling? What was the most hindering event? Reflecting on these questions together can provide extremely helpful information to both the client and counselor. It is often difficult for the client to express negative feelings to the counselor. The client may need help in doing so. We can normalize the fact that all counseling has highs and lows. Understanding more about individual client's experiences helps the counselor and the client understand the change process in counseling.

This is an example of how the evaluation might sound:

Counselor: *In every counseling relationship there are peaks and there are valleys; there are interventions that go well and others that fall flat. I wonder if you feel you can share with me the most helpful and least helpful parts of this process for you.*

Client: *Sure. The most helpful part was you believing in me and affirming my choice to get out of law and pursue my dream of becoming a potter.*

Counselor: *And on the flip side, what was least helpful or perhaps even what hindered your progress?*

Client: *Well, I know you wanted to check me out, but those interest inventories were kind of a waste of time. I didn't need them and I could have spent the time in more productive ways.*

5. Often in interactions there are things that go unexpressed. Sometimes it feels like it isn't the right time to say something, or we wonder how the comment might be received. Sometimes we are driving home from a session or reviewing a tape and we think, "I wish I would have told my client … " Providing a time and place for "things unsaid" (Wheeler & Kivlighan, 1995) can be another important aspect of the closure session.

The following is an example of a way to raise the issue of things unsaid:

Sometimes in relationships, things are left unsaid. You (or I) may think or feel something but not express it. Then later, we may have wished we would have been more assertive. Take a moment and reflect on anything unsaid or unfinished between us.

6. The closure session provides a place for discussing the varied emotions related to a relationship ending. Here it is important to normalize a range of feelings and reinforce honesty and candidness of expression. It may be important to discuss how some clients feel fear and abandonment while others feel relief. Understanding more about the client's own feelings provides helpful closure to the relationship. As counselors we also need to be in touch with and authentically communicate our own feelings during this time.

An example of what introducing the topic of feelings related to termination might sound like:

Counselor: *As we talked about for the last couple of weeks, this is our last session. People have a range of feelings about endings like this—some feel relief, others feel fear or lack of self-confidence, others want to avoid any discussion of endings. I wonder how you are feeling about this being our last session together?*

7. The closure session is also a time of next steps. This discussion may take several forms depending on the individual context. The counselor and client may review next steps in the career planning process. Sometimes these next steps are taken individually, sometimes through the help of a referral source, and sometimes there is a need to return to the counselor for additional assistance. The important point here is that the client should have a clear picture of next steps, and feel confident in performing them. The client should also feel welcome and encouraged to return to the counselor as the need arises. What we know from psychotherapy research is that there is often a rebound effect after counseling has ended, where the client may feel lost and in need of further assistance from the counselor. Developing an atmosphere that makes it as easy as possible for the client to reconnect with the counselor is important. Some counselors use the term "booster shot" or "tune up" to describe these sessions. Because clients are familiar with these terms the normalcy of getting a "tune up" makes it easier for them to call.

An example of leaving the door open might sound like this:

Counselor: *Even though this is our last formally scheduled time, I always tell my clients I'm available in case they feel the need for a tune-up.*

Client: *A tune-up?*

Counselor: *Yes. Sometimes clients feel like they come to a point where they are stuck, or struggling, or just need to check in and talk about how things are going for them. Sometimes they feel like they need a little reaffirmation of their choices, or reinforcement of their efforts. Whatever the reason, I want you to know my door is open for you.*

Closure sessions take time and planning to be effective. Thinking about our own feelings about the client and the termination prior to the session is critical. Preparing our clients for the last session so that they feel comfortable and confident is also critical. One technique for this preparation is asking the client to think about these five questions prior to coming to the last session. This serves to prepare the client and deepen their level of sharing.

Questions to Ponder Before the Closure Session:

1. What feelings are you aware you are having related to this termination?
2. Please take some time to reflect about what aspects of counseling were the most and least helpful to you.
3. What are the most important things you learned about yourself?
4. Are there things left unsaid between us that you could share with me now?
5. What are your next steps? What does the next part of the journey look like for you?

In addition, it may be helpful for counselors to look over this seven-point checklist and determine if their closure session was complete and thorough.

Closure Session Checklist

Did I:

1. Review the content of what happened in counseling?
2. Review the process of what happened in counseling?
3. Reemphasize the client's strengths that were evident in counseling?
4. Evaluate what went well and what went poorly?
5. Explore things unsaid in counseling?
6. Discuss feelings related to the ending of the counseling relationship?
7. Provide clear and direct structure for the client's next steps?

In many ways the closure session is one of the most difficult, but also the most important, sessions of counseling. It is in this session that the counselor and client summarize the journey of counseling—both what happened and how it happened. The effectiveness of the process can be assessed, things left unsaid can be said, strengths of the client and counselor can be reinforced, and the client can be left with a clear plan for the future. When these issues are avoided, rushed, poorly timed, or delivered in a unthoughtful manner, the whole impact of counseling is lessened. When the closure session is well thought out and planned, it can be one of the most satisfying and meaningful sessions for both the counselor and the client.

REFERENCES

Amundson, N. E. (1998). *Active engagement: Enhancing the career counselling process.* Richmond B.C. Canada: Ergon Communications.

Bikos, L., O'Brien, K. M., & Heppner, M. J. (1995). *Therapeutic alliance as a component of career counseling: A comparison and outcome study.* Unpublished manuscript, University of Kansas-Lawrence.

Bridges, W. (1980). *Transitions: Making sense out of life's changes.* Reading, MA: Addison-Wesley.

Brown, D., & Brooks, L. (1991). *Career choice and development.* San Francisco: Jossey-Bass.

Heppner, M. J., & Hendricks, F. (1995). A process and outcome study examining career indecision and indecisiveness. *Journal of Counseling and Development, 73,* 426–437.

Heppner, M. J., O'Brien, K. M., Hinkelman, J. M., & Flores, L. Y. (1996). Training counseling psychologists in career development: Are we our own worst enemies? *The Counseling Psychologist, 24,* 105–125.

Sue D. W., & Sue, D. (1999). *Counseling the culturally different: Theory and practice* (3rd Ed.). New York: Wiley.

Ward, D. E. (1984). Termination of individual counseling: Concepts and strategies. *Journal of Counseling and Development, 63,* 21–25.

Wheeler, J. L., & Kivlighan, D. M., Jr. (1995). Things unsaid in group counselling: An empirical taxonomy. *Journal of Counseling and Development 73,* 586–591.

Index